Otherness in Question

Labyrinths of the Self

a volume in
Advances in Cultural Psychology

Series Editors:
Jaan Valsiner, *Clark University*

Advances in Cultural Psychology

Jaan Valsiner, Series Editors

Otherness in Question

Labyrinths of the Self

edited by

Lívia Mathias Simão
University of São Paulo

and

Jaan Valsiner
Clark University

INFORMATION AGE
PUBLISHING

Charlotte, North Carolina • www.infoagepub.com

Library of Congress Cataloging-in-Publication Data

Otherness in questions : labyrinths of the self / edited by Lívia
Mathias Simão and Jaan Valsiner.
    p. cm. -- (Advances in cultural psychology)
  Includes bibliographical references.
  ISBN 1-59311-232-7 (pbk.) -- ISBN 1-59311-233-5 (hardcover) 1. Other
minds (Theory of knowledge) 2. Other (Philosophy) 3. Self (Philosophy)
I. Simão, Lívia Mathias. II. Valsiner, Jaan.
  BD213.O83 2006
  302.5--dc22

                                     2006026591

ISBN 13: 978-1-59311-232-5 (pbk.)
         978-1-59311-233-2 (hardcover)
ISBN 10: 1-59311-232-7 (pbk.)
         1-59311-233-5 (hardcover)

Printed in the United States of America

CONTENTS

PREFACE

Otherness in Question
Labyrinths of the Self
or
348

It was June 2002. We were dining in one of the many restaurants of São Paulo, Brazil—*348, Parilla Porteña.* Located at the number *348* of a small street of one of the "uncountable" neighborhoods of São Paulo, the restaurant celebrates one of the tangos immortalized by the Argentine singer Carlos Gardel, who was born in Tolouse, France, and has immigrated to Argentina when he was about 3 years old. We could listen the Castellan of a tango in the background, while the animated people of the tables chat in Portuguese.

Perhaps inspired by that multicultural ambience, perhaps by the willing of listening from some colleagues about human diversity, perhaps celebrating the end of one more nice stay of Jaan Valsiner in São Paulo, we became to draft—in one napkin of *348*—the schedule of a possible book on the *question of otherness*.

From then to now, we were working on *348*, counting to the collaborative and instigating contributions of our invited colleagues, who had joined us from Brazil, China, Germany, Korea, India, Portugal, Scotland, Spain, Switzerland, Russia, the Netherlands, and United States of America.

At this moment, we are glad in inviting the reader to also join us in trying to understand the *labyrinths of the self.*

Lívia Mathias Simão and Jaan Valsiner
São Paulo and Cambridge, June 2006.

PART I

CONCEPTUAL ROOTS OF "OTHERNESS"

CHAPTER 1

THE ENIGMATIC OTHER

Ernest E. Boesch

I am invited to write about "The Other," yet, I hesitate. Why? I have dealt with others all my life, privately, of course, but also professionally. I have tested them, analyzed them, diagnosed them, advised them—why then do I not feel competent to deal reasonably, in rational scientific terms with the problem of "The Other?"

The reason may be that I more and more tend to conclude that "The Other," ultimately, remains a tightly sealed secret. After all, this is why we design various subterfuges for gaining insight into this enigmatic companion of ours. We observe his and her gestures, facial expressions, tone of voice, the reactions toward pleasing or frustrating events, we ask them to complete stories, interpret inkblots, tell dreams, we put electrodes on their heads and skin, push them into electronic scanners—all to break open the seal. But still, the secret remains.

One of my teachers, Edouard Claparède, invented the method of *"reflection parlée,"* of "spoken thinking." His subjects had, while solving a problem, continuously to tell what went on in their minds, thereby—so was the expectation—revealing the trace of their reflections. Yet, what the experimenter collected was not a private, but a communicative, somehow socialized thinking. Comparably, the dream a patient tells his analyst is different from the nightly dream—even the dreamer himself will be dis-

Otherness in Question: Labyrinths of the Self, 3–9

mayed by his inability to reproduce faithfully his inner experience. Telling a thought or a dream requires structuring what in one's mind was present only as fleeting images and vague bits of sentences, giving it rational cohesion and translating it into language, which implies all the limitations and transformations of that medium. The secret remains.

Does it matter? Of course, it does! How often do we not feel irritated by what we said ourselves, having the impression that it did not really express "what we meant," but still feel at a loss to correct it. And a listener may believe to have understood the meaning of our words and then be baffled by a contradiction between our action and our statement. We may be certain to "know" intimately our spouse, children, friends, and suddenly be surprised by some apparently "out of the way" saying or doing. And so I have to confess that when, as a psychologist, I formulated careful conclusions based on tests and analyses, I all my life often felt somehow guilty of pretending expert knowledge in spite of still remaining ignorance.

Society is, of course, conscious of the continuous uncertainty relating to "The Other," and has devised its ways for dealing with it. We hand a person a lovingly chosen gift, yet always somehow doubting whether she or he would like it. But there is no need to worry—liking it or not, the receiver will express delight. Displeasing news—unless too serious—will not provoke open despair or anger, but will be received with an appearance of objective rationality. We have learned to present socially adequate responses to all kinds of situations. Even the open expression of violent emotions—in grief or joy—may in some cultures be socially modeled and may hide the inside reactions as much as does the emotional restraint elsewhere. Society wants us to standardize how we express emotions and speak about ourselves, and it does so in an all encompassing way. We learn to speak like others, up to the minute intonations of dialect, we seem (and even believe) to share their tastes in food, fashion, art, music, and politics. This cultural modeling makes us oblivious of the basically enigmatic nature of "The Other." We are convinced to know him or her, can anticipate how he or she will react, even imagine how they feel and think. In this respect, psychoanalysis is an eye-opener. It may have its snags and drawbacks, but it leads to penetrating the social standardizations, to take words not for what they seem to mean, but as carriers of often complex private connotations—which to unravel may even take a very long time. Yet, cultural modeling has its undoubted use in social interaction. The standardization of behavior and expression which it generates has even led some thinkers to state that our "I" is but an introjection of "The Other."

Let us, then, raise a second problem. Indeed, what would we introject? In fact, "The Other" is a fiction. There exist only others, but no Other.

And these others are a multiple variety. The shouting politician, the glib banker, the dreaming poet, the harsh policeman, the cruel torturer, the compassionate healer, the Mother Theresa, Hitler and Stalin, the Eskimo in his snow igloo, the bushman in his cave, the insane in the asylum, the beggar in the slum—those and many more are "others." A pet animal may be an other to its master, while, at the opposite end of the scale, God is "The Other" to whom we address our prayers—God, although possessing no human qualities, is even the prototype of "otherness." In fact, "other" simply means "not like I." What of all this should I introject? Even looking only at the ones close to us, the members of one's family and friends, even those are often such different that introjection would threaten to be rather chaotic. And remaining ignorant of much of their inner being, we could in fact at most imitate their speech and action, but certainly not their dreams, feelings or private thoughts. Of course, in the process of constructing our self all we experience around us has its impact, but the process implies selections, evaluations, transformations—in short, what Piaget called a dynamic interplay between assimilations and accommodations. Terms which are certainly more appropriate to the psychological nature of development than "introjection."

This leads to the probably central problem concerning "The Other." Otherness is a relating term. There is no other without an "I." Therefore, "The Other" is seen in the perspective of an individual, and this perspective changes, of course, with the individual's action situation—and accordingly, then, the image of "The Other" changes, too. I have read that in World War I German and English soldiers, dug in their opposite trenches, at Christmas climbed out of their hideouts and congregated in the no-man's-land, fraternized by eating together, exchanging presents, playing soccer against each other, and promised to shoot not at each other but over the heads. But in the days to come, of course, friendship turned into hostility again, first on command, then by accidental hits, then by a change of perception. That sums up the problem of "The Other." Lovers who craved for one another, may change to indifference and even to hatred, and will in the course progressively alter their mutual perception. In other words, our image of "The Other" is not constant. Of course, social role stereotypes may reduce this inconstancy, but they do so only in appearance. A student's view of her professor may vary considerably, although her manifest behavior might not show it.

Let us look at it more systematically. I do never see "The Other" as he sees himself, and he never sees me as I see myself. Our proprioception and heteroception differ in essence. Bringing the two visions together may appear to be quite natural in self-perception. I feel my movements and gestures to be in exact synchrony with my intentions and feelings, and I have no choice than to assume the same for "The Other." This leads me to construct a kind of relationship between external appearance and the hidden inside. Somebody looking like that, I might then feel, is kind or brutal, warm-hearted, or egoistic—a sort of personal, "intuitive" taxonomy born out of a mixture of projections and experiences. But then it may happen that we feel dismayed by our own mirror image—our image may somehow appear different from how we imagine ourselves to be, and we may ask with some feeling of unease or astonishment, "Is this really me !?" Suddenly, our taxonomy of appearances clashes with our inside experience. We see ourselves like an Other, but it does not fit with our inside-perception. In our mirror-rich cultures such may occur only exceptionally, having become accustomed to our daily mirror image. Yet, in situations of fatigue or depression, the discrepancy between inside experience and outside appearance can become felt, even painfully. In seminars on day-dreaming therapies I often asked students to imagine themselves in front of a mirror, and they not rarely produced embarrassed, anxious, or even destructive fantasies.

In fact, in front of the mirror we evoke the discrepancy between a private and a social self. This is why many persons, women probably more than men, spend much time in front of the mirror in order to create an image of themselves they believe to be socially pleasant. And in doing so they may even be quite conscious of the fact that the appearance they create is not how they "are really." Thus, we become aware, too, of the fact that "The Other" may also try to hide his inner reality. However, whether he tries or not, his appearance remains intransparent. And yet, it may be vitally important to know what it conceals. Because the attitude and intentions of "The Other," his or her appreciation of ourselves, may seriously affect our own action and being.

Of course, we can talk with her or him, trying to understand their attitude, but words, we know it, can deceive, even unintentionally. Therefore, our perception of others is always fraught with speculation, guessing—in short, it is projective. While, in the I-other relationship, introjection is a questionable term, projection remains of central importance. In fact, to be more exact, I should say "projection and transference." Because our evaluations of "The Other" draw from two sources: The own inner experience, the proprioception, and the previous experience with other "others." As we have to assume—and do so intuitively—that "The Other" feels and thinks as we do, we inevitably encounter experiences which contradict our projections. Thus, our perception of "The Other" is influenced by projections modified by previous other-experiences, or transferences. To these two basic sources are added, of course, the influences by the actual interaction, our present action tendencies, and the particular reactions of "The Other."

This rather complex process operates throughout the course of development, and the increasing amount of self-and-other-experience will refine "The Other"-perception. It results in continuously differentiating, with age, the capacity for empathy. There are psychologists who believe empathy being present already at a very early age of about 3 years. This confounds empathy with a kind of spontaneous mimic induction, as can be observed in a child that starts being sad when it sees another weeping. I call this the manifestation of a "functional disposition," similar, for instance, to the capacity for various vocalizations which initiate the development of language but is certainly not yet language, as little as the mimic induction can already be considered to be empathy. Thus, empathy implies a complex construction of "The Other," integrating, as its essential basic elements, our proprioceptive experiences, modified and enriched by the various experiences made in social contacts, and, finally, strongly influenced by the personality myths of the cultural group—which tend to define how individuals should act, think, feel, behave, according to their kind and status. Of course, this other images are somehow flexible, in as far as they adapt to individual persons and situations.

Considering all this, empathy appears to be a functional potential which is limited, action related and therefore unstable. It is limited, of course, by the extent of our self- and other experiences as well as the cultural myths. Therefore it may function adequately with regard to known persons in familiar situations, but may fail us with strangers, especially in foreign cultures. It is, second, action related because "The Other" can be of varying relevance for our actions. Remember that he or she can be a source of gratification as well as threat, may frustrate or reward, help or obstruct. Whether he or she will be a friend or an adversary is often uncertain, and thus we look out for signs helping our empathy to see through the outer appearance. Which, of course, will depend upon our familiarity with the cultural context. This causes some instability of the empathic process, since situations change, action motivations vary. Frequent are the vacillations in the self-other relationship to be observed in the interaction between a child and his or her mother or father, but, more extreme are the radical transformations of empathy in the course of conflicts between previously loving partners, or when friends suddenly turn to enemies in a situation of war.

There exists no Other, I said, only others. Their multitude makes empathy selective. Not only does it, as I just pointed out, function more or less adequately according to different individuals, but there are others with whom we refuse to empathize. In other words, we can activate or de-activate empathy. Soldiers are systematically trained to de-empathize, but to a minor extent this is even true for certain professions, such as surgeons, dentists, policemen, debt collectors. For those, de-activating empathy is needed for the efficient exercise of their activities and for protecting their own personal stability. Yet, more generally, we can observe that we all tend to refuse empathy to persons we despise, dislike, fear, or hate. Our empathic openness diminishes, too, with anonymity or distance of "The Other"—as demonstrates the bomber pilot who coolly drops his lethal charge, or the daily examples of exploitation, profiteering, cheating, mistreatment in commerce, industry, politics, or crime. Empathy, it thus appears, is no general, quasi automatic reaction; it can be activated to different degrees, can be refused to some, directed particularly toward others.

This, then, seems to point at a final funtion of empathy. Of course, it serves to stabilize interactions, to increase the—apparent—transparency of our social environment. Yet, we appear to use it, too, for stabilizing or even optimizing our self-image. On the one hand, empathizing with persons we value positively creates a feeling of identification as well as—quite unconsciously—a feeling of superiority: Understanding "The Other's" inner thoughts and emotions provides an impression of power. To derive self-enhancement from one's belief to understand the secret longings and fears of others is not limited to psychologists or psychoanalysts, but also nonprofessionals may profit in their self-esteem by sympathyzing with others. On the other hand, refusing to empathize is self-rewarding, too, although in quite a different way. Empathy is a costly behavior. It may facilitate social intercourse, but for a price: it limits one's freedom to pursue personal goals. It forces us to take into account the intentions, wishes, tastes or aversions of "The Other" and constrain our action accordingly. Being unconcerned by such considerations, one may of course gain a feeling of unhampered action potential.

Thus, who is "The Other?" We may feel safe in the warmth of our family and friendships, we may trust each other, be confident to know their opinions, their attitude toward ourselves, but it may all too often appear to be a fragile confidence, betrayed by many smaller or more serious conflicts. Thus, "The Other" remains an enigma, and we feel inclined to distrust him or her the farther we venture out of our familiar world. *Homo homini lupus*—"The Other" as a prey, openly or concealed, is more common than we like to admit. The distrust may be hidden under politeness and smiles, but is made obvious in the many laws trying to regulate human relationships, in the law insurances to which a great number of people subscribe. History shows even that to be insufficient. We have—only a lifetime ago—experienced the breakdown of empathy in a considerable part of the German population, where families, friendships, marriages split into hostile sections; we have witnessed similar splits among before friendly parts of the Serbian population; we look with dismay at the hatred between North-Irish Protestants and Catholics, and register impotently the wanton killings between religious, ideological, economical, or racial factions in many parts of the world. Psychology has apparently found ways to desensitize soldiers for the pains they would have to inflict. It would be a better use of our science to find methods for sharpening empathic sensibility. This is by far not yet done enough, mostly, I surmise, because we think empathy to be a natural endowment of mankind. It is not, as I tried to show in these sketchy pages. Our image of "The Other" is culturally molded, and so are our attitudes toward him or her. But, as I tried to show, too, it is also related to our self-image. Thus, empathy education would have to intimately relate the image of "The Other" and the ways of dealing with ourselves. An enormous task which, I fear, psychology is still far from mastering.

CHAPTER 2

WHY "OTHERNESS" IN THE RESEARCH DOMAIN OF SEMIOTIC-CULTURAL CONSTRUCTIVISM?

Lívia Mathias Simão

My concern in this text is to set a discussion about the pertinence of the philosophical notion of otherness for deepening the understanding of I-Other relationships in the frame of the semiotic-cultural constructivism. By semiotic-cultural constructivism, I refer to the contemporary perspective in psychology that has emerged from an ever-changing amalgam of ideas of classical theoreticians, mainly Lev Vygotsky, Mikhail Bakhtin, William James, George Herbert Mead, Pierre Janet, Jean Piaget, Henri Bergson, and Kurt Lewin. Among its contemporary representative approaches are those of Ernst Boesch and Jaan Valsiner.[1] I use the label "semiotic-cultural constructivism" for referring to a dynamic set of contemporary perspectives in psychology that focus especially on the process of individual development in which I–other interactions are unfolding from—as well as simultaneously forming—the cultural space (Simão, 2005).[2]

From this amalgam of ideas, the semiotic-cultural constructivism has emerged as a theoretical-methodological, epistemological, and ethical perspective in psychology that focuses on the inter and intrasubjective construction of human individual subjectivity. This process is considered bidirectional (Valsiner, 1989)—each actor actively transforming the communicative messages received from the other, trying to integrate them in his or her affective-cognitive basis, the latter being also subject to transformations during that process.

Setting a discussion about the pertinence of the philosophical notion of otherness for deepening the understanding of I-Other relationships necessarily implies to focus on *the availability of someone for the involvement with the different* of himself (*somebody else*), which characterizes the relationship with the otherness. However, this involvement is always a process filled with tensions, not only because of the usual differences the I and the Other realize one another, but mainly because of the impossibility for them of fully conceiving and accessing "the other different" in that relationship.

The Portuguese poet and thinker Fernando Pessoa (1888-1935), in his *Livro do Desassossego* (the Book of Disquieting), can perhaps help us in the quest for understanding this last point:

> One of my constant concerns is to understand how other people exist, how there are souls but mine, consciousnesses which are strange to my consciousness which, being conscious, seems to be the single one. I fully understand that the man who is in front of me and talk to me with similar words to mine's, and makes gestures that are as those I make or could make, is in some extent my fellow. The same, however, happens to me respect to the pictures I dream with, to the characters I see in the novels, to the dramatic people that pass in a stage through the actors who perform them.
>
> Nobody, I suppose, truly admit the real existence of another person. He can concede that the person is alive, feel and thinks like him; but it will always be some anonymous element of difference, some materialized disadvantage....
>
> I am not shamed of feeling like that because I have already realized that everybody feel likely. What seems to happen with the disdain between man and man, with the unconcern which allows oneself to kill people without feeling that one is killing, as amongst the soldiers, is that nobody pay the due attention to the apparently nonsense fact that the others are souls too. (Pessoa, 2000, my translation[3])

Departing from the feelings of "strangeness" and from the "gap" the I experiences facing the possible existence of the other, as brought out by Fernando Pessoa, we can get to a preliminary understanding of the main characteristics of the I-other relationship in view of the notion of otherness. This comprehension will always be preliminary in its character of being ever provisional, always demanding our straining for understanding it. Perhaps its heuristic value lies exactly in its nebulosity, as in our effort for grasping its meaning in the context of our concerns some new and more generalized meaning can appear. In other words, the notion of otherness should itself be an alterity to us in our quest for understanding our nature as human beings.

This search will be done through the axis of two joined notions that are nuclear for both frameworks here put in dialogue: the notions of *temporality* and *I-other relationship*. These notions are, in some sense, forcefully in connection, as if we are talking about *relationship* we will be necessarily touching to the temporal dimension. However, many different features of this connection can be in principle taking into account, according to different traditions in philosophy and psychology. For the present discussion, I have chosen to establish a dialogue between some philosophical ideas of Lévinas and some central ideas in the scenario of the semiotic-cultural constructivism.

The I-Other Relationship as Noncoincidence

The first aspect to be approached here is the Levinasian discussion of the phenomenon of noncoincidence. According to Lévinas (1993), time always guarantees noncoincidence, a noncoincidence between I and Other that happens in the *diachronic* nature of time. For the I there will always be the feeling of impossibility of coincidence to the other, of nonadjustment to the other. In this respect the I-Other relationship would embrace a primordial rupture, which precedes any tentative and possibility of relation. In other words, the construction of the I-Other relationship is settled in the character of noncoincidence between I and Other, in a primordial character of rupture, instead of continuity and sameness.

However, almost paradoxically, besides the just mentioned feeling of impossibility of coincidence, temporality also brings up to the I the feeling of being ever in relationship with the world, here included the Other. As far as the I experiences simultaneously both feelings—while being tuned in to the relationship there is the noncoincidence with the other-there will always be the longing for coincidence, as well as the expectation that it becomes realized.

In this sense, the time carries dialogically a dual phenomenon: the impossibility of I-Other coincidence shifting in an ever quest for it, so keeping the I and the Other in relationship, where there is no possibility of coincidence and so on. We are here very close to Boesch's notion of *ist-wert* and *soll-wert* (Boesch, 1991),[4] where one's try, as much as possible, to approximate both values (Boesch, 1991). *In the present discussion, the I and the Other trying to approximate the noncoincidence to the coincidence between them.*

The Solitude of the I

Talking about the solitude of the existence, Lévinas points to the fact that the statement that we never exist alone is a trivial statement. I am indeed surrounded by things and beings to which I keep on transitive relations; through the senses of sight, taste, empathy I am along with them. However my existence is absolutely *intransitive.*[5] People can share everything but their existence. "Being is, in this sense, to isolate myself by my existence" (Lévinas, 1993, p. 81, my translation).

Lévinas argues that the interpretation of the "primitive mentality" by Lévy-Bruhl, breaks his idea of the solitude of the existence because it implies that we can break that solitude by participation; as if by participating we could not only see the other, but also being the other. However, he argues, the idea of fusion does not fit to the modern consciousness because that idea would lead to a kind of ecstatic fusion, where no duality could be preserved in the I-Other relationship (Lévinas, 1993, p. 81).

In his concern about the solitude of the existence, Lévinas throws into relief that it is not a matter of factual isolation, as in Robinson's Crusoe novel. Nor it is a matter of incommunicability of consciousness contents. The solitude of the existence unavoidably happens because of the indissolubility between the existent and its action of existing. According to him, if the relationship between the existent and his action was broken off, the *hypostasis*, the vital event thanks to what the existent links itself to its existing, would also be ruptured (Lévinas, 1993, pp. 81-82).

Lévinas points that the existence can be conceivable without the existent, that who is still existing, the *extant.*[6] However, the existence cannot be conceived without the existing, the ongoing process of being in existence. The existence without existent configures the anonymous *"il y a"*[7]: there are books on the table, it is raining. Although behind this anonymity there is always an existent entity, Lévinas is trying to emphasize here the action of *being*, something that must be expressed by a *verb*, instead of by a substantive (Lévinas, 1993, p. 85).

Ortega y Gasset (1957/2003) touches in similar points when he emphasizes that the *radical solitude* does not mean that the I is the only thing that exists for the subject. It means that his decisions, willing, and feelings are not transferable. In terms of Ortega y Gasset, it is the life that is nontransferable, as only each one of us can live our own life (pp. 52-53). The I is the only instance that does not exist, but *lives* or *is living*. (p. 48, my translation)

On the other hand, the remained reality—but not the I—is what exists, as it

appears, springs up, jumps, resists me, affirming itself inside the field of my life. (p. 48, my translation)

Living is, therefore, not only to exist inside my own mind; on the contrary, it is to be outside of myself, constantly facing the world circumstances (Ortega y Gasset, 1957/2003, p. 54). The I and the Other live in radical solitude, as none of them can live the life of other. But each one living his own life means also to experience the longing for mutual coincidence, the quest for it, and the ever experience of non-complete coincidence. This aspect addresses us to that of the Other as a Mystery for the I.

The Other as a Mystery

The following interrelated dimensions are among those mainly implied in the relationship with the otherness, as synthesized by Laupies (1999):

1. the subject legitimates the other as a subjectivity comparable, and at the same time different, of that of his own;
2. there is an impossibility for the subject's clear and neat apprehension of the other as subjectivity, as well as of the experiences lived by the other, although there is the possibility for the subject to interact with the other about his reported experiences; this insuperable *opacity* and *nebulosity* imposes the permanent *tension between the implicit and explicit* in the relationship with the otherness.

As emphasized by Delamarre (1996), the impossibility of full access by the I to the other is neither an issue of some linguistic inaptitude, nor of some insincerity in their relationship. The matter is that the other's thoughts and desires are never immediately given to the I, nor can they be deduced through a reduction to the similarities between the I and the other. There is in the other an infinite power of fleeing from the I, of constituting itself in a secret for the I, of being unpredictable for the I.

Still according to Delamarre (1996), the I grasps in the Other both the signs of his inaccessibility and the signs of the thoughts he wants to keep concealed from the I, as in a kind of cryptogram offered by the Other to the sight of the I. However, the Other's striving for sheltering his secret would not happen if he was not conscious that he could betray himself both by his discourse and his body.[8]

If it is so, it could be added that we, psychologists, in our quest for other's narratives and nonverbal expressions are, in fact, in the quest for another who—we know—at some moment could "betray his secrets." Here we are entering, once more, in the ethical terrain, as the Other could call us in order we try together to betray his secrets, or not.... However, this not means that we should embark in a kind of naïve omnipotence of the psychologist over the Other, whether be it in research or in professional practice, as the easy and full knowledge of the Other by the I is a matter out of question.

As Lévinas (1993) himself stated, the power of the Other over the I's existence is a mystery for the I in itself. The point here is not the unknown, but the nonknowledgeable. This latter aspect points to the fact that the Other is not an "other I," he is not an other self of the I, participating of an ever shared existence with the I. In short, he cannot be reduced to the existence of the I. This point is also relevant to our reflections about some constructivist ideas:

> The relationship with the other is neither an idyllic and harmonious relationship of communion, nor an empathy through which we can put ourselves in his place: we recognize him as similar to us and at the same time exterior [to us]; the relationship with the other is a relationship with a Mystery. (Levinas, 1993, p. 116, my translation)

Boesch (2006) is very close to the Levinasian mystery encompassed by the I-Other relationship, when he talks about the meaning of messages caught by someone from some—apparently—trivial event, like the present sound of the rain dropping in some empty pail I am now listening. Boesch says:

> Message without a content one could spell out. Nothing else than a feeling of meaningfulness, somehow the opposite of what depressive patients complain about: That nothing makes sense, that all is meaningless. A real puzzle to a psychologist who wants to define meaning in terms of structure or information (Boesch, p. 59)

Keeping here the I-Other relationship in focus, the Other would be a messenger inspiring feelings of meaningfulness to the I, bringing him messages to be deciphered. The I-Other relationship is indeed a hermeneutic relation (Simão, 2005). The hermeneutic task of the subject in his never accomplished quest for penetrating the Mystery of Otherness, by its turn, addresses us to the symbolic action of the I toward the unknown future.

Present Time, Time to Come, and Time to be

For Lévinas (1998), to act is to assume the present time, is to be in relationship with one's self-existence. On the one hand, it is to be servile to the existence; on the other hand, there is the authentic manifestation of being in the present time (p. 35). In this sense, the instant is the accomplishment of the existence by excellence. Each instant is a beginning, a birth of the I (pp. 92-93).

The *hypostasis*, as the event thanks to what the existent links itself to its existence, creates a situation where the subject as existent becomes the owner of his existence, that existence so becoming momentarily a present attribute of the subject, the subject henceforth having his identity in the present.

Lévinas emphasizes:

> The event of *hypostasis* is the present. The present departs from itself or, in other words, it *is* the exit from itself. It implies a veer from the course of itself in the infinite weave—with no beginning or end—of existing. The present strays and renews: begins; it is the beginning itself. It has a past, but only as memories. It has an history, but it is not history. (Lévinas, 1993, p. 89, my translation)

The present is, therefore, the existing of the subject in his fleeting identity, departing in action from the instant of "here and now" to the next instant, the unknown future, which will be then momentarily experienced, and so on.

Lévinas (1993) emphasizes that *alterity* and *time to come* are both inapprehensible. According to him, it should be taken into account that the exteriority involved in the *time to come* and the exteriority in its spatial dimension are different kinds of exteriorities. This is so because the *time to come* has a character of being completely surprising. In such an extent, the anticipation of the future is not more than "the present of the time to come." It is not the real or authentic time to come, because the latter is not possible to be captured. The time to come astounds us and takes possession of us (p. 117).

We can say, therefore, that the Levinasian approach to *time to come* poses in relief the aspect of unpredictability, weather specifically in I-Other relationships, weather in other general processes involving the emergence of novelty. In all cases, the key point is that the subject needs to be open to the relationship with the unknown, being the Other emblematic of that Mystery in the relationship of alterity.[9] He even points that the time to come is Otherness. Our relationship with the time to come is the same relation with the alterity of the Other. In such an extent, it would be impossible to talk about the time from the perspective of the isolated subject, in terms of an exclusively personal and predictable duration (Lévinas, 1993, pp. 117-118).

This is otherwise a fundamental in the Levinasian notion of alterity. As the relationship with the other is future, it is unpredictable:

> The anticipation of the future, the projection to the future ... is not more than the present of the future, it is not the authentic time to come; the time to come is what one's cannot grasp, it is what falls on us and takes possession of us. The time to come is the other. The relationship with the time to come is the relationship with the other itself. (Levinas, 1993, p. 117, my translation)

> The relationship with the time to come, the presence of the time to come in the present also seems to be accomplished in the face to face relationship with the other. The face to face relationship would represent the time accomplishment itself: the invasion of the time to come by the present not happens to the solitary subject; on the contrary, it is the intersubjective relationship. The condition of the time is the relation amongst the human beings, the history. (Levinas, 1993, p. 121)

Here Lévinas (1979/1993) shifts the idea of a "subject being in the present time"—as if the subject was embarking in a timeline outside of him—to the idea of the "present time and the subject coming into the existence at once," at each coming instant. The idea of the time to come independently of the subject is shifted into the idea of time to be in relationship with the Otherness. As I already have pointed out, the relationship with the Otherness implies the desire to be open to the unknown, the availability for the involvement with the different (p. 1).

Desire and Future

The peculiar feature of a relationship of alterity rests in the tacit assumption by the I that—concerning the Other's affairs—he cannot anticipate the future in terms of "as ... if," that is, in terms of as "if I were you." To such an extent, in the relationship of alterity, the subject experiences intersubjectivity as a coconstructed illusion, as discussed by the semiotic-cultural constructivism (see, for instance, Valsiner, 1998, pp. 34-35; Valsiner, 2000).

On the other hand, to assume the constructed illusion of intersubjectivity does not mean necessarily to give up of relating to the Mystery of the Other. On the contrary, from this perspective, it means to try to be nearer to that Mystery trough the dialogue, as a tentative—never completely accomplished—for clarifying the opacity and nebulosity of the Other's messages. It is the core of the intersubjective striving and quest for the future.

From Lévinas' perspective, the Other is not "as if it were an other I," as an other self that shares its existence with the I. It is not a kind of idyllic and harmonious relationship, schedule by communion and empathy, in which the I can put him in the place of the Other and vice-versa. On the contrary, it demands the availability from the subject to relate to someone who is not only different from him, but who surpasses him. As pointed out by Laupies (1999), this availability is possible only from the *desire*, as a tendency of the subjective consciousness for going beyond itself through the relationship with somebody else (the *alter*); that one who is felt as different, supplementary, beyond the subject's oneself.

Nevertheless, Lévinas (1993) warns that, besides that kind of relationship, the relationship with the Other also encompasses the current relationship with the Other in the course of the everyday life. In this latter kind of relationship, the manifestations of the radical solitude and alterity of both are usually concealed by social-cultural rules and norms. In this relational field, the I then try to know the Other through the empathy, as an other self, as an alter ego (p. 126).

However, even in this everyday relationship there is no way for full reciprocity between them, what breaks the contemporaneous existing of one related to the other, preventing them of being successful in their enterprise of communicative empathy as they would like to be (their *soll-wert* in the relationship, in Boesch's terms). This is so because neither the intersubjective space is symmetrical, nor the Other's exteriority is due to some lack of conceptual or spatial identity compared to the I. In such an extent, the Other not only is an *alter ego* of the I, but he is also and mainly what the I realizes he *is not*. (Lévinas, 1993, pp. 126-127).

The prototypic relationship Lévinas (1993) takes into consideration is the erotic one, in which the feminine is the term that, according to him, completely retains the alterity.[10] He points out that the most important in the notion of *feminine* is not its opposition to *masculine*, but its character of occultation, of pudency:

> The Other is not someone against who we brave to, someone who menaces us and wants to dominate us. The fact of being refractory to our power does

not represent a power superior to ours. His whole power consists in his alterity. His mystery constitutes his alterity. (Lévinas, 1993, p. 130, my translation)

Lévinas (1993) follows stating that the existent comes true through the subjectivity and consciousness, while alterity comes true through the movement of departing to the place of the nonknowledgeable (cf. p. 131).

In some sense, we can say that the dialogue between the semiotic-cultural constructivism and the philosophy of alterity is the dialogue between two places: the knowledgeable (as supposed by the subject who is constantly reconstructing his relationship with the other) and the unknowledgeable (the impossibility of full knowledge as lived and experienced by the subject in his relationship with the other).

As the relationship with the otherness requires that the I surpasses himself in the tension among *what each of them are*, *what each of them are not* and *what each of them can be* in that relationship, we are here touching on the dimension of the responsibility for himself in the future.

Futurity and Responsibility

Lévinas (1993) calls our attention to the ethical issue concerning to afford oneself in the here and now of our life, that is, to the ethical issue concerning to oneself present.[11] For Lévinas, the subject is a duplicated being because he is always busy with the responsibility for himself, for his corporeality, for his own identity. This is another source of his solitude, what Lévinas call the captivity of identity (pp. 94-95). The dialectical relationship between the existing and the existent in the present time brings about the subject's mastery over its existing, the sovereignty of the existent. Nevertheless, that sovereignty has for the subject the price of the impossibility of separating him from himself, the price of his present identity. According to Lévinas's words, the identity "is not an inoffensive relationship with oneself, but is to be enchained into oneself" (Lévinas, 1993, pp. 92-93, my translation). The subject is not free for everything; as it is impossible for him to be alienating of himself, he is unavoidably responsible for himself.[12]

To be enchained to oneself is neither due to the burden of past times nor to the disquieting unknown future. For Lévinas, the responsibility brought about by the present is, in last resort, linked to the fact that as it happens from now, ignoring the history, it becomes the only possible reference for any compromise (Lévinas, 1979/1993, p. 93).

To assume responsibility implies to anticipate the future, that is inherent to life (Ortega y Gasset, 2003). Because of the aforementioned linkage among present, future, and otherness, it also implies responsibility of the I for the Other. This means to stress the focus on the subjectivity of the I, and not only upon the anteriority or precedence of the Other, as it has been overemphasized in discussions on the notion of alterity in Lévinas. By investing the I with responsibility for the Other, Lévinas implicitly points up to the relevance of the former: the importance of the Other lies in the fact the I should be responsible for him.

Bernet (2002) suggests that what Lévinas has substituted was not the I by the Other, but the egological subject by the ethical subject. Besides, and also important to our discussion, he highlights the activeness of the Levinasian subject, who is responsible for and affected by the Other. The ethical subject

> is characterized not by its spontaneous, free power, but by a responsibility for the *other* which comes from the *other*. This responsibility accrues to a subject that is marked, at the deepest level of its experience, by its sensibility, which brings it into the other's proximity, or by its vulnerability with respect to the other. This vulnerable sensibility is thus an affectivity that is always already inhabited by the other, and delivered up to the other. As a consequence, ethical sensibility is an affectivity that comes to me entirely from the other; it is the result of being affected by the other's imperative, traumatizing demand. Instead of being open to the other in the mode of intentionality or ecstatic transcendence, I am, in the very intimacy of my affectivity, always already the other's "hostage." (p. 90)

Departing from the Levinasian issue of the *impossibility of coincidence between I and Other*, we discussed the interrelated points concerning to the *solitude of the I* and the *Other as a Mystery for the I*. Up to that, some other focal points of the Levinasian discussion about the time and the other have emerged: *present time, future time, desire,* and *responsibility* in the relationship with the other as alterity.

Henceforth we can explore some possibilities opened by that discussion for the approaching of I-Other relationships by the semiotic-cultural constructivism.

ON THE SEMIOTIC-CULTURAL CONSTRUCTIVIST PATHS IN THE DIRECTION OF ALTERITY

On Desire and Futurity

Perhaps the first point of contact between the semiotic-cultural constructivist ideas and the notion of alterity happens—emblematically—through the issues of *desire* and *futurity*. As already pointed out, the relationship of alterity demands from the subject to surpass himself, in the tension among *what is, what it is not,* and *what could come to be* in the relationship with the other. We can recognize here the dimensions of futurity and desire, which are strongly present, for instance, in Boesch's *oeuvre* (Boesch, 1977, 1991, 1993).

Another frontier between the two fields of ideas here in focus could be made by the notion of intersubjectivity. Again in an emblematic way, that notion seems to function as a mediator of some approaching between both focused fields.

Wertsch (1998) calls our attention to the fact that intersubjectivity and alterity are not mutually exclusive aspects in social interactions, but "part of an integrated, dynamic picture" (p. 111). Borrowing from Rommetveit (1992), he points to the fact that the pure intersubjectivity is a kind of rationalist dream, which presupposes that literal and fix meanings would be possible to be shared. However, still according to him, intersubjectivity should be viewed as a tendency of the human communication for operating in a dynamic tension with the other (cf. Wertsch, 1998, p. 112-113).

This way of focusing on intersubjectivity is possible thanks to the dialogical perspective in the process of socialization. As highlighted by Wertsch (1988) in the frame of reader-text interaction, the dialogical perspective shows the nonplausibility of the idea of fixed meanings received by the subject, consequently focusing on "how an interlocutor might use texts as thinking devices and respond to them in such a way that new meanings are generated" (p. 115).

Rommetveit (1992) asked the question of how the notion of communicative shared codes, that is, intersubjectivity, could fit to the asymmetrical relationships among the participants in the communicative process. Rommetveit's question leads us to think that what the participants coconstruct is the *belief* in the possibility of sharing something: the interactors treat their environment *as if* they would be sharable. Intersubjectivity would be, then, a coconstructed illusion by the participants of an interaction. A very relevant illusion for dealing with the reality, indeed. It would allow both, involving oneself in the interaction and clarifying some of its meanings, while hiding other.

Bringing Rommetveit's (1992) notion of intersubjectivity to take part of his own elaborations about the human development, as for instance in Valsiner (1998, pp. 34-35; 2000) can contribute for the dialogue between semiotic cultural-constructivism and philosophy of alterity. The idea of I-Other reality as a coconstructed *belief* constraining the subject's development instead of the idea that interaction is settled in some reality outside and independent of the subject—shifts the I position facing the Other. The question is no more to grasp the reality in which the other is also included, but to constantly negotiate with the Other what that reality *was (as present memories), what it is (as present experiences),* and *what it could be (as present expectations).*

Intersubjectivity as a coconstructed illusion necessarily brings to this process the above-discussed features of *noncoincidence, solitude,* and *Mystery* present in I-Otherness relationships. However, one of the main peculiar features of a relationship of alterity rests in the tacit assumption by the I that—concerning the Other's affairs—he cannot anticipate the future in terms of "as ... if," that is, in terms of as "if I were you." To such an extent, we should add that concerning intersubjectivity there would be more than a coconstructed illusion, meaning a tacit awareness of its character of illusionary construction. The subject works subjectively in a field marked by uncertainty as both the necessary and the only possible way for symbolic action. In this vein, it is also remarkable that the semiotic-constructivist approaching to intersubjectivity and its vicissitudes in the course of I-Otherness relationships still appear much more related to the content of the interaction than to how the participants feel and realize themselves one in relation to the other (cf. for instance, Simão, 2003, 2004a).

Finally, perhaps the moment in which the semiotic-cultural constructivism seems to be nearest of the issue of alterity respect to futurity is through the notion of constraint, as developed by Valsiner (1998):

> Constraints ... are temporary organizational devices, constructed in action and ideation, in dialogue between persons, between persons and contextual expectations, or between personal sense and collective-cultural meanings. (pp. 3-4)

As discussed elsewhere (Simão, 2005), the concept of constraint accounts for dialoguing situations in which the I and the Other allow one another some symbolic actions, while mutually discouraging other. The potential power of the concept of *constraint* to understand I-Otherness relationships seems to me not fully explored yet. This seems true specially respect the post-Hegelian dialogism the concept of *constraint* embraces, moreover present in Valsiner's oeuvre as a whole: every movement allowing some clarity will have—unavoidably—its shades. In this sense, the interlocutor's symbolic actions would be "temporary devices" guiding the interpersonal relation, possibly thanks to the diversity of the I-world views in construction by each of them.

On Futurity and Responsibility

In the Jamesian (1920) tradition inherited by the semiotic-cultural constructivism (see for instance, Simão, 1999; Valsiner & Van der Veer, 2000), the future cannot be rationally grasped because, as something that was not accomplished yet, the information about it is too scarce. The only possibility to design conceptions about the future is founded on projections from the present time. These projections are conceived via emotional—not rational—apprehension, as a way for the subject to try to decrease the discomfort produced by the ambiguity of his future. Based on his projections, the subject then acts in some direction, unavoidably making options (Barbalet, 1997, pp. 118-119).

According to the semiotic-cultural constructivism, facing the impossibility of a clear and neat aprehension of the future, the subject acts in terms of "as ... if." Otherwise he would be paralyzed. In doing so, the subject is and should be always in movement (see Valsiner, 2006, in this volume).

In such an extent, the semiotic-cultural constructivism accounts for the ways by which the human subject transforms the uncertainty of the "time to come" in a representation in the present time, calling it "future," which enables him to keep on acting.

One of the main implications of the human relationship with time is that, although without the possibility of clearly foreseeing the future, the subject meets himself in the situation of being, in principle, responsible for his options, that is, for his projections from the present. Here we are again in the scenario of the possibilities for tuning between *is-wert* and *soll-wert,* in the field of individual and socio-cultural limits of tolerance in each situated case (Boesch, 1991).[13] This sets the ethic issue concerning to oneself future, as pointed to by Lévinas.

Taking into account the relationship of alterity in Levinasian terms allows us to deep our reflections about the "as ... if" process, stressing not only the term "if" of that relation (the constructivist concern about futurity), but also the term "as" (the Levinasian concern about the present). As should be clear up to now, I am not proposing to substitute emphasis, but to emphasize more the *inclusive separation* of the terms in "as ... if," in the direction already took by the semiotic-cultural constructivism (Valsiner, 1989; Valsiner & Cairns, 1992).

Inclusive separation is a kind of relationship in which the members are temporarily and contextually linked, but never fused, preserving their individual subjectivity, which guarantees their same possibility of being in relation. It is a systemic relationship, meaning that the members are related one another in such a way they form a temporarily organized whole. This whole, for its turn, can only be realized in the experiential perspective of the actors (the members in relationship), only by themselves as privileged positioned in their experiential living places (see, for instance, Diriwächter, in press). In this holistic structure, the members "are distinguished from each other (i.e., they are separated), the separation [being] the background upon which their relationship can be investigated" (Valsiner, 1998, p. 15). The key point of this comprehension is that the relationship between I and Other encompasses three elements: the I, the Other, and the relation between them.

We adopt here the theoretical frame of Herbst's (1995) cogenetic logic. Being the relation itself the third element for understanding I-Other relationships, the pitfalls of linear causality and fixity in its comprehension can be avoided; the third element—the relation—will force us to take into account the dimension of temporality in its nonrepeatability and changing. The dialogical relationships themselves form a triadic unit (Herbst, 1995) constituted by the I, the Other, and the relational meaning of the dyad they form in that situation. This meaning—which is situational, changeable and pertinent to the relation, and not to each separated element—accounts for the maintenance of the I and the Other as inclusively separated instances (Simão, 2003, 2004b).

The dialogue itself is an experience that gives opportunity for a meta-construction of meanings (not necessarily contemporary to the ongoing relationship, or conscious) by the I and the Other, meanings that concern to the experience of being in relation to this or that person about this or that matter. The meaning of any event, for the I would emerge from the triadic organization formed by the experienced Other (the "*as*"), by what was expected or desired from him (the "*if*"), and by the meaning in the relational margin between them (the " ... " between them). In other words, the meaning of an I-Other relationship poses from the onset of its emergence, although not necessarily consciously for the subjects, the issue of choosing and fitting different possible versions touching to the present and the future of their relation, according to the different possible constructions of their "as ... if."

Noncoincidence and Emergence Of Novelty

In the semiotic-cultural constructivism we have some other bridge ideas that are fruitfully leading us to the direction of deeply approaching the issue of alterity. Among them is the notion of irreversibility of time brought in from Bergson, next to Baldwin's idea about the impossibility of complete coincidence among models or events. They are the sustenance for proposals about the bi-directionality in I-Other interactions accounted for instance by Valsiner (1989) and Wertsch (1993).

The perspective of bi-directionality in the socialization processes presupposes that the messages of one interlocutor, which is directed to the other, will never be a kind of "mirrored input" processed by the receiver. On the contrary, the messages will always be understood in this or that manner, implying a transformative action on the former message by the receiver. This transformative action occurs thanks to the embeddedness of multiple kinds of constraints, ranging from the contextual interpretation each actor does of the "here and now" in the dialogue to the actor's longings, desires, fears, and hopes (see for instance, Boesch, 1992; Valsiner, 1998).

Persons who talk with one another will always talk from their different phenomenological locations and they address different phenomenological places. Asymmetry is inherent to the dialogue, as it has been pointed out for instance by Foppa, Linell, Marková, Valsiner, and Wertsch. Asymmetrical relationships have also been part and parcel of the ethical discussions in the frame of semiotic-cultural constructivism. As discussed by Linell (1995), Foppa (1995), Marková and Foppa (1991) and Marková (1997), disagreements and misunderstandings are inherent to the real and good dialogue; they are not a 'noise' that should or even can be avoided or controlled on behalf of the best dialogue. They are part and parcel of the best dialogue, ethically understood.

Bi-directional and asymmetrical processes, in turn, are responsible for the emergence of novel configurations in I-Other relationships, as the I and the Other are constantly questioning for approximating the *is-wert* (Boesch, 1991) of noncoincidence to the *soll-wert* (Boesch, 1991) of coincidence between them at some moment.

From a Levinasian perspective, the most relevant aspect of that emergence of novelty would be a more acute sense of the I about itself, discovered in the proximity with somebody else. Nevertheless, as that proximity is asymmetrically structured, my relationship to my fellow is never reciprocal to that from him to me. It is an irreversible relationship where I am never even with him (Lévinas, 1998, p. 12).[14]

Asymmetrical relationships, address to the permanent tension in I-Other relationships.

On Anonymity

The anonymity encompassed by the Lévinasian "*il y a*" can also provoke some reflections in the frame of the semiotic-cultural constructivism. "*Il y a*" seems to be near to "zero signifier" and "zero meaning," a notion brought from semiotics (cf. Ohnuki-Tierney, 1994) to cultural constructivism by Valsiner (1998). According to Ohnuki-Tierney (1994), "zero signifiers" are signifiers without materiality, that is, without any representation through linguistic labels or objects. Notwithstanding, they are of critical importance for semiotic systems. The meaning of "zero signifiers" can range from very specific to wide types of "nothingness." Culturally, the objectification of a "zero signifier" is often a serious transgression that, exactly by its transgression value, can be part of symbolic practices by the social agents.

Among the main features of the "zero signifier," three are of interest here:

(a) the absence signalized by the "zero signifier" is meaningful;
(b) this meaningfulness is contextual;
(c) there is a dialogic relationship between the "zero meaning" and its context:

> the floating signifier represents empty but full meaning, while the unmarked is assigned the absence of a specific property that characterizes the marked counterpart. (Ohnuki-Tierney, 1994, p. 61)

As pointed out by Valsiner (1998), zero signifiers are constructed semiotic devices that utilize the *absence of* something *as if this is* something in itself" (pp. 67-68). Valsiner gives the example of conversations in which taboo words are not mentioned. Not mentioning those words is a "contextually meaningful nothingness," it is "somethingness."

As meanings are constructed and reconstructed by dialogical opposition, the meaning of A is always understood in its—usually nonexplicit—relationship with something that is non-A. In such an extent, as each sign addresses simultaneously the presence and the absence of something, it will simultaneously address to that something denied or hidden. These aspects are also present in Marková's, as well as in Herbst's theoretical elaborations about dialogical relationships (cf. also Valsiner, 1998, pp. 46-47, 67-68, 120-121).

In the frame of the philosophy of alterity, Lévinas draws an analogy between Bergson's positive meaning of negation and his own elaborations about that. For both of them, thinking about *nothing* implies a movement of the spirit rejecting *something*. However, Lévinas criticizes Bergson's ideas: in Bergson's scenario of negation there is still a hidden content that is the protagonist; the *nothing* still keeps a substantive character. Lévinas will state that for him, instead, the presence of absence is not relevant because of a kind of residual content, but because of the very and only atmosphere of some presence, the presence of the absence. Indeed, this atmosphere could become latter a content, but it is formerly impersonal, a field of forces, the *il y a* (cf. Lévinas, 1986/1998, pp. 73-74).

Similarly, having the character of "nothingness meaning somethingness" (see *a*, above), "zero signifiers" carry with them this implicit existential atmosphere. If it were so, "zero signifiers" are not substantives, but essentially verbs, action, because they are the presence in action of something that is absent in substantive.

Indeed, taboos are more than not mention a meaningful word; not mentioning that word means to avoid the *actual action* of some undesirable, dangerous entity, exactly because that entity is there, in its hidden presence, *unable to actually act, but simultaneously being able to be about to act.* In the popular belief of Catholic religiosity, for instance, do not mention the word "devil" or referring to it by metaphorical names, avoids that the evil entity comes from darkness and acts in the real world of living people. The meaning of presence and nonpresence, acting and not acting are then inherent to the relationship (Herbst's triadic unit).

This is also close to Boesch's actional notion of "taboo zones." To act is always to be in a symbolic relation—consciously or not—to the object of the action. In this relationship, objects are not "neutral or external" to the subject. Objects are meaningful ideational or material cultural objects. They are born from the process of symbolic action in the subject-world relationship and have the potential of dialogically regulate the subject's further actions.

Taboos belong to this sort of ideational objects. They are context dependent in allowing a particular kind of action or in preventing it. In such an extent, they are formed in the history of culture-individual relations, and will form "taboo zones" for further individual actions. Because of their *actional value* (Boesch, 1980), they do not have an "objective value in themselves." On the contrary, what counts is the functional-subjective value of honoring or transgressing the taboos via acting on some ideational or material objects in the cultural context of the grouping everyday life. Still according to Boesch (1991), usually positive and negative meanings are blended in "taboo zones," therefore their ambivalence (pp. 35, 149). From this perspective, like "zero signifiers," material or mental contents signalizing taboos have their importance not in its substantiation, but in their *potential actional value of being honored or transgressed* (see *b* and *c*, above).

Similarly, taking into account the afore discussed impossibility of coincidence between I and Other, there will be dimensions of the Other which are inapprehensible to the I, dimensions which are hidden and the I tries to grasp, to *decipher from the presence* of the Other in action. Indeed, the only way I can try to grasp the Other is symbolically acting on his symbolic actions: on what he says, when and how, on his regard, his glance, his smile, his laugh, his nodding, his bending, his silence. The key point here is, of course, not the other's action as viewed by some uninterested observer outside of the I-Other relationship. On the contrary, it is exactly the meaning of the Other's action as symbolically constructed by the I in their relationship that counts, weather they are constructed in the history of relationship with some specific Other, weather in the history with multiple Others, usually both cases simultaneously. Likewise, the constructed histories of past symbolic interactions as well as those of expected ones, weather they are and were "rea" or "imaginary." The matter is, in sum, meaningfulness and context (see *a* and *b*, above).

Another aspect that deserves consideration here is the indeterminate character of the Other as *somebody else*.[15] Similarly to "zero signifier," *somebody else* can have only a contextual meaning; its connotation depends upon a dialogic relation with the context. This connotation happens on the basis of something supposed, not explicit, as well as based on the desire of penetrating in the Mystery of the Other. For deciphering that Mystery, the I interprets Other's actions. Doing so, he objectifies the unknown Other as a "known other," transgressing the frontiers of the Mystery encompassed by the Other. However, doing that, he looses the Other in its Otherness, remaining in relationship with the "knowable other," showing himself surprising and unknowable, as Otherness, so transgressing the I.

In sum, there is (*il y a*) always something in the Other that is fleeing to the I. In this sense, the Other is for the I like a "zero signifier." The I cares more about for what is inapprehensible in the Other, for what is hidden in its silence or behind its open actions, than for what can be easily grasped.

In such an extent, the relevance of the I-Otherness dialogical relationship lies in what is hidden, in its nebulosity, because both of them offer themselves one another as opportunities for interpretation, each opportunity representing different I-Other relationships.

ON SOME POSSIBLE FUTURE CONSTRUCTIVIST PATH IN THE DIRECTION OF ALTERITY

Based on the discussion stated in this chapter, I would like to briefly suggest two intermingled directions concerning the issue of alterity for future theoretical-methodological research in the domain of semiotic-cultural constructivism.

The fist direction is related to the hermeneutic task of the I facing the Otherness.

Understanding the I-Other relationships demands to take into account the projected and desired future by the subjects, that is always changing as the relationship itself develops. Changes, by its turn, are related to possible and not-possible movements of the I trying to approximate the *ist-wert* to the *soll-wert* (Boesch, 1980) in relating to the Otherness. Both, possible and not-possible movements of approximation are conveyed by various by constraints (Valsiner, 1998) in a tensional and also ever-changing field of alterity (Lévinas) that demands

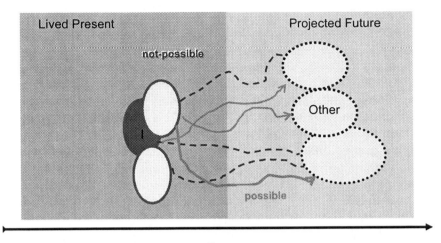

Figure 2.1.   Subject's self-moving to alterity related to Other's self (some movements are possible, others not).

the I symbolic actions of deciphering, although never full accomplished (see Figure 2.1).

The second direction concerns to the future as the uncertainty phenomenologically present to be dealing with. As illustrated in Figure 2.1, futurity is in the present, as a projection of the desired. In such an extent, de-contextualization (Valsiner, 2001) based on and from the present is necessary for dealing with the projected and desired future.

However, because of constraints enabling some interactions and disabling others, such a de-contextualization will require that the I surpasses himself in the tension among *what each of them are, what each of them are not,* and *what each of them can be in the relationship.*

Nevertheless, the future is not phenomenologically empty, as a recipient that is filled with experiences as the times goes by, so shifting into present. As already stated, the future is a representation in the present time, made by the I to transform the uncertainty of the "time to come" that enables him to keep on acting. In such an extent, the I himself is also projected inside that future, as well as the I-Other relationship (Herbst's triadic unit). At this point, comes again the tension conveyed by striving toward the desire for grasping the other, which is never completely attained.

Figure 2.2 is a transformation of Figure 2.1, trying to show this aspect.

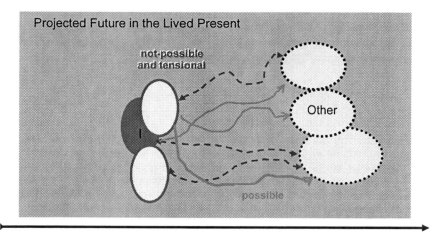

time

Figure 2.2.   Subject's self-moving to alterity related to Other's self (some movements are possible, others not. Double arrows shows tensions experienced in the present, related to the projected future and to the impossibility of completely grasping the Other).

Completely grasping the Other would mean fusion, the disappearance of the relationship, the disappearance of the difference. If we assume the impossibility of I-Other full-coincidence as inherent of human existence, we should also assume that this same human existence not only allows sharing—one of the cornerstone process of semiotic-cultural constructivist understanding of human life—but also states limits and even prevents some forms of sharing as a condition for its proper existing, a condition for the existence of the human existence.

ACKNOWLEDGMENTS

The ideas presented in this chapter were developed as part of my research activities on "History and Philosophy of Psychology: Semiotic-Cultural Constructivism" at the Department of Experimental Psychology of the Institute of Psychology, University of São Paulo, Brazil. This research program is granted by the *National Council for the Scientific and Technological Development*, Brazil. Although the ideas here approached are of my entire responsibility, I would like to thank to Ernst E. Boesch (Saarbrücken, Germany), Jaan Valsiner (Clark University, USA.) and Nelson Ernesto Coelho Junior (University of São Paulo, Brazil) for keeping on critically discussing my ideas for the last 10 years. I would also like to thank to people of *Kitchens Seminars* and *Social and Cultural Psychology of Genocides Seminars* (Clark University, USA., Fall 2005) for the opportunity of discussing some of my ideas with them.

NOTES

1. I am using the term "semiotic" in a sense near of that discussed by Eco (1990/2004). According to him, in the *semantic* or *semiosic* process of interpretation the subject fills the linearity of a text with meaning. In the *semiotic* or *critic* process of interpretation, on the other hand, the subject tries to explain the structural reasons of possible semantic interpretations (p. 12).

2. I am using this label only as an instrument for temporarily, guiding and flexible purposes for qualitative research in the frame of philosophy of psychology. From my point of view, labels and categories should be transitory clippings.

3. The original text in Portuguese is:

   Uma das minhas preocupações costantes é o compreender como é que outra gente existe, como é que há almas que não sejam a minha, consciências estranhas à minha consciência que, por ser consciência, me parece ser a única. Compreendo bem que o homem que está diante de mim, e me fala com palavras iguais às minhas, e me faz gestos que são como eu faço ou poderia fazer, seja de algum modo meu semelhante. O mesmo, porém, me sucede com as gravuras que sonho das ilustrações, com as personagens que vejo dos romances, com as pessoas dramáticas que no palco passam através dos actores que as figuram. Ninguém, suponho, admite verdadeiramente a existência real de outra pessoa. Pode conceder que essa pessoa seja viva, que sinta e pense como ele; mas haverá sempre um elemento anónimo de diferença, uma desvantagem materializada.... Não me envergonho de sentir assim porque já vi que todos sentem assim. O que parece haver de desprezo entre homem e homem, de indiferente que permite que se mate gente sem que se sinta que se mata, como entre os assassinos, ou sem que se pense que se está matando, como entre os soldados, é que ninguém presta a devida atenção ao facto, parece que abstruso, de que os outros são almas também. (Pessoa, 2002, pp. 296-297)

4. The correspondent terms in other languages are: *is-value* and *should-value* (English; cf. Boesch, 1991); *valeur réelle* and valeur visée (French; cf. Boesch, 1995); *valor real* and *valor visado* (Portuguese; cf. Simão, 2002).

5. From the Latin word *intransitivu*, addressing to the nontransmissible in the context of Levinasian philosophy.

6. cf. The Fontana English Dictionary, London: Collins, 1967, p. 174.

7. The correspondent term in English is *there is*. The correspondent terms in some Romance languages are: *há* (Portuguese); *hay* (Spanish); *c'è/ci sono* (Italian). I will keep, henceforth, the original French term minted by Lévinas, *il y a*.

8. For an introductory discussion about the interrelated subject of dissimulation and betray in I-Other relationship see also Laupies (1999, pp. 108-112).

9. Lévinas (1979/1993) takes the event of the death as the prototypical meeting with the Other as alterity (see pp. 119-121).

10. Ortega y Gasset (1957/2003) also develops a similar discussion about the matter (pp. 119-143). In both discussions there would be reflections to state on some of their statements. These reflections, however, could not be done without consideration of their historical-cultural ambience, as well as of ours, what would digress from my purposes in this chapter.

11. Lévinas' emphasis on this aspect is related to the precedent discussion about time and instant.

12. From here would unfold important questions touching to cultural constraints as laws, taboos and norms, related to human rights and to the frontiers between mental sanity and madness, and so forth.

13. Many strands of reflection and discussion concerning the so-called areas of psychology of personality and psychopathology unfold from this point. They are, however, outside of the scope of this chapter.

14. For a deeper approach to Lévinas' reflections on interpersonal asymmetry, responsibility and ethics, see Lévinas (2000, pp. 192-197).

15. *Autrui* (French), *altrui* (Italian), *outrem* (Portuguese).

REFERENCES

Barbalet, J. M. (1997). The Jamesian theory of action. *The Sociological Review, 45*(1), 102-121.

Bernet, R. (2002). Levinas's critique of Husserl. In S. Critchley & R. Bernasconi (Eds.), *The Cambridge Companion to Levinas* (pp. 82-89). Cambridge, MA: Cambridge University Press.

Boesch, E. E. (1977). The medical interaction: A study in Thailand. *The German Journal of Psychology, 1*(1), 13-27.

Boesch, E. E. (1980). Action et objet: Deux sources de l'identité du moi [Action and object: Two sources of the Me identity]. In P. Tap (Ed.), *Identité individuelle et personalization* (Vol. 2, pp. 23–37). Toulouse, France: Privat.

Boesch, E. E. (1991). *Symbolic action theory and cultural psychology.* Berlin, Germany: Springer-Verlag.

Boesch, E. E. (1992). Culture-individual-culture: The cycle of knowledge. In M. von Cranach, W. Doise, & P. Mugny (Eds.), *Social representations and the social bases of knowledge: Swiss monographs in psychology* (Vol. 1, pp. 89-95). Lewiston, NY: Hogrefe & Huber.

Boesch, E. E. (1993). The sound of the violin. *Schweizerische Zeitschrift für Psychologie, 52*(2), 70-81.

Boesch, E. E. (1995). *L'Action Symbolique—Fondements de psychologie culturelle* [French revised edition of Symbolic Action Theory and Cultural Psychology]. Paris: L'Harmattan.

Boesch, E. E. (2006). A meditation on message and meaning. In J. Straub, D. Weidemann, C. Kölbl, & B. Zielke (Eds.), *Pursuit of meaning* (pp. 59-82). Bielefeld, Germany: Transcript.

Delamarre, B. (1996). *Autrui* [Somebody else; approximated possible translation to English]. Paris: Ellipses.

Diriwächter, R. (in press). Genetic Ganzheitpsychologie. In R. Diriwächter & J. Valsiner (Eds.), *Striving for the whole: Creating theoretical syntheses* (p. 25) Somerset, NJ: Transaction.

Eco, H. (2004). *Os limites da interpretação* [The limits of interpretation]. São Paulo, Brazil: Perspectiva. [Translation of *I Limiti dell'Interpretazione*]. (Original work published 1990)

Foppa, K. (1995). On mutual understanding and agreement in dialogues. In I. Marková, C. Graumann, & K. Foppa (Eds.), *Mutualities in dialogue* (pp. 149-175) Cambridge, MA: Cambridge University Press.

Herbst, D. P. (1995). What happens when we made a distinction: An elementary introduction to co-genetic logic. In T. A. Kindermann & J. Valsiner (Eds.), *Development of person-context relations* (pp. 67-79). Hillsdale, NJ: Erlbaum.

James, W. (1920). Remarks on Spencer's definition of mind as correspondence. In *Collected Essays and reviews*. New York: Longmans, Green. (Reprinted from the *Journal of Speculative Philosophy*, 1878, *12*, 1-18).

Laupies, F. (1999). *Leçon philosophique sur Autrui* [Philosophic Lessons on *Autrui*]. Paris: Presses Universitaires de France.

Lévinas, E. (1993). *El tiempo y el otro* [The time and the other]. Barcelona, Spain: Paidós. [Translated from *Le Temps et l'Autre*]. (Original work published 1979)

Lévinas, E. (1998). *Da existência ao existente* [From the existence to the existent]. Campinas, Brazil: Papirus. [Translated from *De l'existence à l'existent*]. (Original Work published 1986)

Lévinas, E. (2000). *Totalidade e infinito* [Wholiness and infinite]. Lisboa, Portugal: Edições. (Original work published 1980)

Linell, P. (1995). Troubles with mutualities: Towards a dialogical theory of misunderstanding and miscommunication. In I. Marková, C. Graumann, & K. Foppa (Eds.), *Mutualities in dialogue* (pp. 176-213). Cambridge, MA: University Press.

Marková, I., & Foppa, K. (Eds.). (1991). *Asymmetries in dialogue*. Hemel Hempstead, England: Harvester Wheatsheaf.

Marková, I. (1997). On two concepts of interaction. In M. Grossen & B. Py (Eds.), *Pratiques sociales et mediations symboliques* (pp. 23-44). Berlin, Germany: Peter Lang.

Ohnuki-Tierney, E. (1994) The power of absence: Zero signifiers and their transgressions. *L'Homme, 34*(2), 59-76.

Ortega y Gasset, J. (2003). *El hombre y la gente* [Man and the populace]. Madrid, Spain: Alianza. (Original work published 1957)

Pessoa, F. (2002). *Livro do desassossego* [Book of disquieting]. São Paulo, Brazil: Companhia das Letras. (Original work published 1997)

Rommetveit, R. (1992). Outlines of a dialogically based socio-cognitive approach to human cognition and communication. In A. H. Wold (Ed.), *The dialogical alternative: Towards a theory of language and mind* (pp. 19-44). Oslo: Scandinavian University Press.

Simão, L. M. (1999, May). *Ação, interação, objeto e cultura: a contribuição de Ernst Boesch* [Action, interaction, object and culture: The contribution of Ernst Boesch]. Conference presented at the I North-Northeast Congress of Psychology. Salvador, Bahia, Brazil.

Simão, L. M. (2002). A noção de objeto e a concepção de sujeito em Boesch [The notion of object and the conception of subject in Boesch]. In L. M. Simão, M. T. C. C. de Sousa, & N. E. Coelho, Jr. (Eds.), *Noção de objeto, concepção de sujeito: Freud, Piaget e Boesch* [Object notion, subject conception: Freud, Piaget and Boesch] (pp. 87-120). São Paulo, Brazil: Casa do Psicólogo.

Simão, L. M. (2003). Beside rupture—disquiet; Beyond the Other—alterity. *Culture & Psychology, 9(*4), 449-459.

Simão, L. M. (2004a). Alteridade no diálogo e construção de conhecimento [Alterity in the dialogue and knowledge construction]. In L. M. Simão & A. Mitjáns Martinez (Eds.), *O outro no desenvolvimento humano: Diálogos para a pesquisa e a prática profissional em psicologia* [The Other in the human development: Dialogues for researching and profissional practicing in psychology] (pp. 29-39). São Paulo, Brazil: Pioneira Thomson Learning.

Simão, L. M. (2004b). Semiose e diálogo: Para onde aponta o construtivismo semiótico-cultural? [Semiosis and dialogue: To where the semiotic-cultural constructivism points to?]. In M. T. C. C. de Souza, (Ed.), *Os sentidos de construção: O si mesmo e o mundo* [The meanings of construction: The self and the world] (pp. 13-24). São Paulo, Brazil. Casa do Psicólogo.

Simão, L. M. (2005). *Bildung*, culture and self: A possible dialogue with Gadamer, Boesch and Valsiner? *Theory & Psychology, 15(*4), 549-574.

Valsiner, J. (1989). *Human development and culture: The social nature of personality and its study.* Lexington, MA: D. Heath.

Valsiner, J. (1998). *The guided mind: A sociogenetic approach to personality.* Cambridge, MA: Harvard University Press.

Valsiner, J. (2000, July). *Interaction as hypergame: Development under uncertainty.* Paper presented at the third conference for Sociocultural Research, Campinas, Brazil.

Valsiner, J. (2001). *Comparative study of human cultural development.* Madrid, Spain: Fundación Infancia y Aprendizaje.

Valsiner, J. (2006). Human development as migration: Striving towards the unknown. In L. M. Simão & J. Valsiner (Eds.), *Otherness in question: Labyrinths of the self* (pp. 349-379). Greenwich, CT: Information Age.

Valsiner, J., & Cairns, R. B. (1992). Theoretical perspectives in conflict and development. In C. U. Shantz & W. W. Hartup (Eds.), *Conflict in child and adolescent development* (pp. 15-35). Cambridge, MA: Cambridge University Press.

Valsiner, J., & Van der Veer, R. (2000). *The social mind: Construction of the idea.* Cambridge, MA: Cambridge University Press.

Wertsch, J. V. (1993). *Voices of the mind: A sociocultural approach to mediated action.* Cambridge, MA: Harvard University Press.

Wertsch, J. V. (1998). *Mind as action.* Oxford, England: Oxford University Press.

TRANSPARENCY IN THE MEANING MAKING

Lívia Mathias Simão and Álvaro Pacheco Duran in Interview With Ernst E. Boesch

This interview was held during the sunny morning of September 4th 2004, at Ernst E. Boesch's home, in Saarbruecken, with a break for a "cafezinho," kindly in behalf of the Brazilian guests.

Otherness in Question: Labyrinths of the Self, 37–50
Copyright © 2007 by Information Age Publishing

Legend:

B: = Ernst E. Boesch (Saarbruecken, Germany)
L: = Lívia Mathias Simão (University of São Paulo, Brazil)
A: = Álvaro Pacheco Duran (Private Psychotherapist, São Paulo, Brazil)
----- = unintelligible
(?) not sure about the previous word
(...) = long pauses in conversation

B: So, shoot!
L: As Textor and Lonner said in the introduction of your book *Symbolic Action Theory and Cultural Psychology*, you are a very good football player!
B: Me?... I've never kicked a ball! I don't know what they meant with that...
L: OK..., so let's do it seriously.... I read your article "A Meditation on Message and Meaning" and I tried to talk to you while I was reading, as if you was there, making some questions during my reading. And I think that could be a nice beginning for our interview...
B: Yes, you are the interviewer, you start it as you like it...
L: Well, I think that one of the most intriguing pieces was when you said, in page 8, "Namely, that evil, like terror, undoubtedly has many roots, some in defects of the social system, others in human nature, but, unsuspected, some also in positive domains of culture; I tried to substantiate this concerning art and religion, leaving aside philosophy and science, where similar demonstrations might have been possible. In addition, I held that enemies are not always unwelcome threats, but that we often seem to need and even seek them for our self-confirmation. Of course, this is too short a summary of my theses, but it may suffice here for our problem." Then, I would like to know if you could tell us something more about this idea ... of construction through alterity or otherness. Because you are telling that sometimes we are looking for the enemies ... we are searching for the enemies, and that in some sense this is good to us. I would like to understand more this relationship with the enemies. Additionally, I would ask you if it is a theme that you have approached in *From Art to Terror*. Because, as the book was written in German, it could be nice to know, and to allow for the public...
B: For the English speaking audience...
L: Yes, if this idea of searching for the enemy is an idea that you have approached in *From Art to Terror*, and how we can make relations...

B: Well, it is one chapter in this book, the chapter is entitled "Welcome Enemies, Lost We." We have to go back to the idea exposed in the first chapter of this book ("Art, Faith, Terror") that, unsuspected, some evil is also existing in positive domains of culture. I tried to show especially with regard to religion that a positive aspect of culture may imply to some extent also negative ones. Because we live in a world which I called the non-I world. This non-I world is rewarding, it gives, protects; *but* it also threatens, restrains, limits. In order to establish a balance between I and world, the I cannot only seek pleasure, positive rewards, but it also has to prove capable of withstanding the negative sides of the non-I-world, of fighting adversities. This is a main aspect of what I called the action potential. Well, in order to attain something which I like, I may have to encounter somebody who opposes me, who may threaten my pleasure. It is my action potential which gives me the power or at least the hope to be able to resist. And each success in overcoming an adversity increases my confidence of being able to face also others—the experience of a specific action potential gives raise to a feeling of general action potential. Therefore, I always strive at proving my ability to oppose resistance, proving my action potential strengthens my self-image and improves the I-non-I relationship.

L: Each time is a new time....

B: Yes, each time is a new time, and may also tend towards improvement. If I am able to jump a fence this high, I'd like next to try a higher one. If I can overcome an adversary of this strength, the next one might be stronger, and so I train myself to withstand also those. There exists a yearning for perfection in the area of competence, of beauty, and there may also be a similar yearning for perfecting one's ability to resist adversities.

L: It is like an extension of that idea expressed in the *Sound of the Violin?*

B: Yes.

L: Because it is the fighting for The Perfection in terms of Art.

B: It is the continuous striving for perfection, a striving without end, because the perfection I reach is always imperfect. Whatever form I give to an idea or an action is unavoidably non-I, with all its limitations and imperfections. By its very existence, it suggests a more perfect realization. So there is no end to the striving for perfection. The perfection we realize remains provisional. That is why the artist always starts a new work after having finished one, the scientists never stops searching for better solutions.

L: Yes, and this is in parallel with the idea....

B: The same may also apply to enemies. I need an enemy for proving or enhancing the value of myself and my group. The more evil an enemy, and the more my opposing him or her is valiant, the stronger the self-reinforcement I can gain from it. In medieval times knights had their noble adversaries, in modern conflicts there is often no limit to vilifying and darkening the opponents. Thus the enemy becomes a means for enhancing one's self-value. In that sense, enemies can be welcome.

L: Welcome, yes.

B: But they can also welcome in other respects. Take the nonbelievers, the enemies of religions. We fight them for the glory of God. The glory of God has a meaning because it guarantees our redemption. It is another way of striving for perfection.

L: It is because God is good for me?...

B: In a sense, I would say that there are two kinds of believing people: The ones are the "inside believers"—the introverts who don't care about the outside world—, while we might call the others the "outside believers," those who try to spread the Gospel. And these tend to feel that the more they fight enemies of the faith, the more they are loved by God. I think this is important if we want to understand what is going now in the Near East and in the war of Muslims against Christians. It was one of the reasons I wrote this book. I felt puzzled by the suicide practices in this whole fight, which in spite of its political and economic reasons is basically a religious war. So, trying to understand, I wrote these two articles. On the enemies, and on Art, Faith and Terror.

L: I have also another question.

B: Which one?

L: In the case of the welcome enemies, should we think on this theme in relation to the idea of barriers and frontiers? Can I say that welcome enemies are people that I see as frontiers, in terms of what you wrote in 1991?[1]

B: I am not sure about that.... You could say that the enemy or the adversary is a barrier, rather than a frontier. And it could even be a welcome barrier, like a barrier I can climb or jump. Because enemies give me the possibility of proving my action potential, my possibility of overcoming obstacles and thereby reaching perfection.

L: But not a frontier....

B: A frontier is a place where normally I have to stop. While a barrier is an obstacle which I try to overcome.

L: But you can cross a frontier: You may say, well, if I cross it, I can go into the new, but also the strange.

B: If I cross the frontier I have to change my usual behavior.

L: Yes, yes.

B: OK, I can cross it if I feel able to change my behavior. But usually a frontier is rather a place where I stop. For instance, a frontier between two people is determined by the social laws of interaction. And if I transgress it, that destroys or transforms the whole relationship.

L: Yes, I see.... I was thinking by analogy to what you told about Picasso on "A Meditation on Message and Meaning": in trying to understand Picasso, he was in a sense a welcome enemy. Because in the process you have enlarged your potential, and then he was not so important as a welcome enemy anymore...

B: Well...

L: I thought that in this specific and rough sense you changed your behavior because you approached the picture and you changed yourself while trying to understand and feel more sensitive about the picture...

B: I see.... Ok.... We can always try to apply notions like frontier and barrier to anything about which we are talking. But I didn't intend to use the term in this way. What you say about Picasso, my relationship to Picasso, I would rather see it in the context of other concept, which I use, which is *increasing the transparency of the world*. Because Picasso at the beginning was a intransparent piece of my reality, which became a challenge. I have formulated a Symbolic Action Theory, and here was Picasso with his enigmatic kind of art. Can the Symbolic Action Theory help to understand this intransparent piece of reality? Picasso, like other phenomena, forced me somehow to check the validity of my theory, to see whether it allowed to expand the transparency of my world. Something, of course, which the I is continuously striving at. Now, is it useful to try to apply the term frontier to this? If I try to understand you, if you try to understand a patient in your office, we can of course call this overcoming a barrier, even establishing a frontier. I really did not bother to apply these terms in such situations. Yet, they may prove useful where you strive at increasing the transparency of your world.

L: Yes, perhaps we can, or I can, in my studies, abandon a little the idea of frontiers and barriers and try to go, with you, to move to the idea of transparency and coordination. It might perhaps be more realistic.

A: I would say that the search is a search.

B: Yes. To want to make the world transparent means, of course, transparent for me, to make it appear understandable.

A: Yes.

B: I wrote some sentences about the difference between explaining and understanding. Saying "I understand that" doesn't mean that I can explain it. "I understand" means that I can sympathize, I can empathize, I can deal with it; to understand why this person acts in this way, does not necessarily mean that I can explain it rationally. So transparency is always for me.

A: The objective of that explanation is only a kind of understanding, isn't it?

B: "Explanation" is that kind of understanding which relates cause and effect to each other in a controllable way.

A: Yes.

B: But if I say "I understand why Picasso did that," I do not mean that I can explain it in any scientific way. It is some kind of intuitive feeling "Oh, I see! In this situation I would probably do the same." It is empathy. So, "transparency" belongs to a kind of terms that are frequent in my work, which relate to subject reactions and are difficult to objectify. Remember the article "Why does Sally never call Bobby 'I'?"

B: But you wanted to know about the relationship between Art and Terror?

L: Yes, what is mainly their relationship?

B: I started with a very simple example. Think of the house. What is that? It is an area where you transform reality according to your wishes. In other words, you create an outside which is conforming to your inside. That is what I called an inside-outside-balance. Now, the house is surrounded by walls. What for? To keep out the non-I world. The garden is surrounded by fences or walls to keep out pests and intruders. In other words, this inside-outside balance has continuously to be guarded against intrusions of the non-I world. Then, however, I asked a question: We fill our surrounding with beautiful things, somehow expressing by it our inside. But now it may happen that somebody puts an ugly picture on his wall —what can that mean? To study this question, I took the example of Picasso's *Demoiselles D"Avignon*. Do you know it?

L: Yes, yes.

B: Why did Picasso paint this ugly picture? My attempt to answer this question fills a whole ninety pages. The key to this answer comes from Picasso himself. He said—telling to one of his friends— "That time, I went to the *Musée Etnographic*," the Ethnological Museum in Paris. The Ethnographic Museum was not like nowadays, beautifully arranged, but it was full of dust, dirt, and disorder. He looked at the Negro masks and, he said, "I suddenly understood what the Negroes made these masks for. They were fetishs, intercessors, to defend against all the evil spirits in the world. And I, I suddenly understood that I did the same thing with my painting. That my painting was conjuring against evil forces in the world—evil forces all around." Now, this refers in fact to an anthropologically basic trait of human beings, who in all cultures tend to relate themselves to some kind of universe.

L: Yes.

B: The basic human question is always "in what kind of universe am I living?" And that appeared to be Picasso's question as well. Don't take it as a scientific question. People who sit at the beer table in the pub and heatedly discuss globalization or politics in far-away countries, why are they interested in it? Because of this kind of global intuition. Of course, their's is not a scientific idea of the universe, and yet they express a kind of total belongingness. It is this question, too, which also induces the human experience of the *numinous*. "Numinous" means the intuition of an all pervading mysterious force in the universe.

L: It is the phenomenological universe....

B: No, it is not phenomenological.

L: No?...

B: No, phenomenological means that you can give it a shape, that you can somehow describe it. But you can't describe it, it is, as I said, an intuition, rather more like a feeling.

L: I mean that it is prereflexive...

B: Yes, yes. And this, as I said, may lead to the intuition of the numinous, although I do not yet call it religious. You can have an idea, an intuition of numinous forces in the world without it being religious in the usual sense of the word. For instance, in a Thai community a vulture resting on the roof of your house will bring misfortune and create anxiety. This is not yet religion, but implies a feeling of the numinous, relating to a force beyond our rational understanding. Such anxieties are frequent—think of the fear of ghosts. So, what do we do with these disquieting feelings? We try to rationalize them. We try to relate them to reasons which may make them understandable. Now, you are a psychologist, you might try to understand them psychologically. But people who do not reason rationally might relate the numinous to some kind of superior power. And they would try to understand the nature of this superior power, relate it to some religious revelation, which then gives raise to further elaboration of religious ideas. Which includes ideas about what this superior power requires from you. If you don't fulfil these requirements, then this power may turn against you. Here seems to lie the origin of the ominuous side of religion, because, should you not respond to the demands of the superior power, you would loose all Grace, risk punishment in all enternity. And therefore you are called to fight those others, the disbelievers who live contrary to God's wishes, in order to prove your faith and loyalty.

L: Hum, hum.

B: For example, if God commands that an adulterous woman be stoned, she has to be thus executed—otherwise one would risk the wrath of God.

L: Yes. I have to do what must be done, in some sense

B: Well, to summarize in a few words this first chapter,[2] it starts from the attempts to establish an inside-outside balance, to protect one's own against the non-I world. It then points at the general human intuition of being related somehow to a global world, which gives rise to the idea of a numinous, all-encompassing power. This induces ideas concerning the nature of this power and its relationship to humanity, i.e. religious conceptions. The religious promises combined with threats finally result in aggression against nonbelievers. So much in a nut-shell.

L: And the Art? Should the production of art be another way of dealing with this inside-outside balance?

B: Well, the Art.... Do you know Mondrian?

L: Yes.

B: He strove at finding the ultimately perfect picture – imagining that it would magically deliver the world of its evils. It was striving for perfection in a formal, but ultimately also in a religious sense. Which suggested to me that the artist somehow aims at the same kind of total perfection as the religious believer. The analogy was true and wrong at the same time. The resurrection by religion is transcendent, the one by art remains mostly immanent. So I stuck to the more structural problem by which the volume starts: Picasso's *Demoiselles D''Avignon.* Which were, in fact, a revolution not only structural, but human: Picasso had, in this picture, introduced a new freedom in painting: The deformation of the human form.

L: OK, about Picasso....

B: This structural revolution introduced in Art has a more general meaning. It opened the possibility of arbitrariness (I called it *Beliebigkeit* in German) also beyond visual Art, in music, fashion, ultimately even in religion. Which was accompanied by an increased emphasis on originality. Which, in a sense, replaced the striving for perfection. This makes it rather difficult nowadays to distinguish Art from mere virtuosity. One may consider this also to be a sort of destructive development, yet, I do not, in the last chapter, carry the analogy between art and faith too far, but only try to point at some similarities in their development.

L: I have a question about this arbitrariness.... Can we say, in few words, that arbitrariness ... means or can promote variation, and that this is in some sense a frontier or an opposite way for perfection? Perfection is more linked to the idea of ... something congruent and ... with not too much variation? Can we think on this idea?

B: I would agree with what you say. Arbitrariness implies freedom. So you can allow anything, even aggression, as in Picasso's deformation of the human form. Perfection is both similar and different. It forces you to act towards an imaginary goal, and to withstand anything which opposes it. So in the striving for perfection, aggression is only defensive.

L: Hum, hum, that's important....

B: So ... the relationship has rather to be seen in connection with perfection. The believer strives for perfection in his belief, which leaves him no option. While the nonbeliever leaves you free to believe differently. And may thus transform hostility into competition.

L: The idea that I grasp from him, from Gadamer, was that when he talks about the hermeneutic circle, he is in fact talking about a frightening relationship with the meaning. So, the I is always frightening for the meaning. As, for instance, when I talk to Álvaro, I am trying to be understood by him. But I know that I would not be exactly understood. Anyway, I would talk to him... On the other hand, as he will answer me, he will give me a kind of feed-back and new ideas, and here the idea of divergence... So, anyway, I keep on talking with him. I think that this is like that idea you are developing in *Welcome Enemies*, in the sense he could be a welcome enemy. Because we will try to dialogue, always knowing that, even with a high grade of empathy, we will not share... and the good thing is that we will not match completely.[3] But the only way I can fight to this frightening problem is talking with him.... And this is, to me, the main idea of the hermeneutical circle. It is a circle that is a kind of ... I don't know how to say in English ... *redemoinho* ... [whirl], you know, when wins and you have that thing in the ... that [gestures]

B: feed-back circle?...

L: Yes, feed-back circle ... And I am always inside of this feed-back circle, because I am always inside of culture...

B: Yes. But that is not the idea inside this article.[4]

L: No?

B: No. The article was written as a response to a deterministic theory. I said: "Look, by doing something I continuously act on, transform or create culture. Once created, it is an objective fact, which acts back on me. Thus, the individual creates and perpetuates culture, but at the same time assimilates culture. By explaining it, the individual in a sense recreates culture in the medium of language. There is a theory saying that language conserves and transmits culture and thus the individual only has to assimilate it. But in the process of assimilation, it is at the same time transformed and in some ways, even if only minimally, recreated. A circle which is never completed."

L: This is good because ... to keep the circle in order to continue in a kind of spiral. A last question about that subject, culture: here you use the notion of culture as an immense pool of messages, etc. But what about the concept of action field?[5] It was so better than the idea of pool of meanings.... Here you have an idea of pool of meanings, messages. And former you told us about the idea of culture as a field for action.

B: As a field?

L: Yes, that concept you have brought from Kluckhohn and Kroeber.... That idea of field seems to me more dynamic than the idea of pool of messages...

B: Well, in fact I took the field concept from Lewin. But anyway, you may use both terms. An action field is not empty, it contains many possible meanings among which we select, and which we interprete, choose among the various possible ones those meanings which we consider to be relevant for our actions.

L: But at the same time it is a field for action...

B: Yes, of course, of course....

L: I will think about.... Let me try to understand: when you act in the field, you select meanings...

B: You select meanings.

L: Yes, I agree, I agree.

B: You would be overwhelmed by the multitude of meanings, if you did not select according to your intentions and interests.

L: Yes, we will be crazy with no selection....

B: Culture is your field of action, in which you operate your selections.

L: Yes, it is probably a prejudice of mine with the idea of "pool"...

B: Yes, pool, in the way I use the term, implies a possibility of choice.

L: OK...

B: In other words, pool means a range for choosing.

L: Which means not static, not the same, because you create culture...
You "put things in the pool and take them out".....
[laughs]

B: Saarbruecken, when you come here, is a static field. But where you
go there, which places you select to go and what you do there,

L: is not static

B: that is all dynamic!

L: OK, ok, now I am pacified! [laughs]

L: Well. And what about music? If you could tell us something about
listening...

B: Yes, I thought that you should ask a question about music, because
it is one of the most difficult topics I wrote about in the last three
books. What kind of action is it to listen music? Now, you tell me.

L: Me?

B: Yes. [laughs]

L: But you are the interviewee!... You are interviewing me!... Well, I
think that could be something like ... when I listen music, it seems
that with me—I have now the limit of the language in English, but
anyway.... I can remember some situation, when I listen to a piece
of a music, because of the music.... This is the basic thing and the
less interesting to me.... I can also be inspired to by music and
think on other things I have never realized that I though.... But I
can also go through the music, as when.... For instance, last week
we were in Cracovia, Poland. We were going around with our
friends and we have only one day to spend there. So, we select
some things to do and one of them was a concert, a *cameratta*. And
we went there, it was in a very interesting place for a concert,
because it was in a museum, a small museum, with all the walls covered by their canvas. However, I was with a big, big headache! My
headaches are completely uncontrollable.... And I thought: "I am
here, to listen a good music, and now this headache... Well, what
can I do?..." I set there and I though: "Well, I am here and I will
try to profit the best I can." And I put myself just listening and listening and listening.... And then, it was not suddenly, but seemed
suddenly to me, the headache has disappeared. And I talked to
Álvaro that I "dave" in the music ... and I was just there.... That's
the idea of prereflexiveness I was telling about. The only thing I
remember is that in the break [interval] I thought: "Well, these figures!..." Because the canvas, many of them, specially on the right
side, was of formal men, old men, *chevalliers*, with their hats and
dark clothes.... And it seems they were looking at us, the audience.
I thought: "It is crazy, these men seem to be looking at us and saying: 'oh, you are there, in 2004 listening a concert!' "This kind of

fantasy, you know.... But this was the only reflexive thinking I can remember. Almost all the time, I was just listening. And I think that's all about that experience.... Did I win the examination?... [laughs]

B: That's is very interesting and you could write an article about it. The question is what kind of action were you doing in listening to music.

L: It is an action with the goal of letting myself stay there.... That's the main goal. I thought: "Well, I am here, I am with headache, let me take advantage of this moment." I had my headache, but on the other hand, I tried to strive against it...

B: As for my question: Listening to music, of course, is an action. But what is its goal? You wanted to spend an agreeable evening, and that, for any reason whatsoever, included music. You could have chosen something else, but, again for whatever reason, you did not (the goal of an action always has to be defined positively—by what we aim at—, and negatively—by what we exclude). What then made music agreeable, so much even that it cured your headache? There may be many reasons, some of them hidden in your earlier music experiences. But there seems to be a general quality which makes music pleasant for so many people: It transforms reality in a way which can be directly felt and experienced. Take an example: Our voice, when we speak or shout or cry has a sound spectrum close to noise. In singing, this spectrum changes, the sound becomes pure, and the more so when the singer is somebody like Maria Callas. Similarly, our breath when blown into a flute is transformed into beauty. Music turns the plain, the unobtrusive into striking perfection. This not alone by its sound, but also by the balance of its rhythm. And perhaps not least by the solemn enclosure within which it is performed. Of course, this does not apply to rap music or techno sound (which probably would not have cured your headache), their appeal is different, due to the excitement by noise and action which, by disregarding usual frontiers, suggest a feeling of freedom. This is indeed a general statement—for understanding YOUR listening to music, it would have to be scrutinized for individual conditions.

L: I guess that this is a summary of your chapter on music?

B: Yes, although on its eighty pages it says much more.

L: But the book also contains a chapter on the "Homo narrator"— could you in a few words sketch its message?

B: Well, basically it says that man is a storyteller in continuity. He or she tells short stories on simple incidents, long stories on periods of her or his life. We tell stories to others in order to position our-

selves with regard to our social partners, or we tell stories to ourselves in order to structure our self-view, for self-justification, even
self-accusations, for differentiating our perception of the world
and of our experience. This can be observed in the daily narra-
tions of people, but becomes, of course, particularly evident if we
look at the sequence of stories produced by writers over the years.

Boesch himself is a continuous storyteller. Perhaps as Pablo Neruda,
Boesch is continuously telling his story as well, like good storytellers do.
He can keep us fascinated by the music of his words while we are listening
or reading them.

NOTES

1. Boesch (1991):

    Resistances can take the form of barriers, such as a river to cross, or a
    wall to climb. Yet, I would suggest a distinction between the terms
    "barrier" and "frontier!" A *barrier* is an area that is difficult to over-
    come, and may need particular interposed actions for the passage;
    once the barrier is crossed, however, the action can proceed more or
    less as before. A *frontier*, in contrast, marks the separation between two
    areas of behavior which requires an area-specific adaptation in the
    form and direction of action taken by the individual. The experience
    of resistance gives rise to the basic idea of an antagonistic potential of
    the external world, while a frontier creates a binary opposition
    between the "here" and the "beyond." The "here-area" is mostly
    transparent and well known; it thus provides security, but also often
    uneventfulness and boredom. The "beyond-area" is less transparent
    and less well-known; it thus easily creates uncertainty and anxiety, but
    also curiosity and excitement—it partakes of the ambivalence of the
    "otherness-symbolism" (...) Crossing a frontier is generally not under-
    taken without precautions. Already on approaching a frontier, we tend
    to change our behavior. Our action becomes more conscious, more
    deliberate, less carefree. (p. 113)

2. Boesch is referring here to the first chapter of his book "Von Kunst bis Ter-
    ror: Über den Zwiespalt in der Kultur," 2005. Göttingen: Vandenhoeck &
    Ruprecht.

3. This is an implicit reference to the idea stated in by Linell (1995), Foppa
    (1995), Marková and Foppa (1991) and Marková (1997) that disagree-
    ments and misunderstandings are inherent to the real and good dialogue
    and should not be understood as a "noise" to be avoided or controlled in
    the dialogue. For some other implications of this statement, see Simão
    (this volume).

4. Boesch is referring here to his chapter titled "Culture-Individual-Culture:
    The cycle of knowledge," 1992. In M. von Cranach, W. Doise, & P. Mugny

(Eds.), *Social representations and the social bases of knowledge*: *Swiss monographs in psychology* (Vol. 1, pp. 89-95). Lewiston, NY: Hogrefe & Huber.

5.   Referring to Boesch's concept of culture as an action field (see Boesch, 1991).

REFERENCE

Boesch, E. E. (1991). *Symbolic action theory and cultural psychology.* Berlin, Germany: Springer-Verlag.

Part II

OTHERNESS AND DIALOGICALITY: FEELING INTO PHENOMENA

CHAPTER 3

THE FEELING OF A DIALOGICAL SELF

Affectivity, Agency, and Otherness

João Salgado

Here I am. And just before I begin writing these first lines—there you are. I am addressing you, the reader of this text, in this present moment of yours—a moment that will probably remain imaginary to me. Unknowingly you are already answering and questioning me. Not from your present moment, but from my anticipation of you. Every word and every pause, every utterance, and every hesitation, all have your accent—and your absent, yet overwhelming, presence.

I try to understand your future mind in order to get your agreement, at least your reaction. In order to create some possibility of meaning. You are in me. Yes, we are together. But, right now, I am alone and using Bakhtin's (1979/1986) expression, the only "judge and witness" of these lines—that I might wipe out in the end—is me. And no: you will never understand me the way I am, because there is always a radical difference between me and you. You are my potential *Other*. And since there is always a radical difference between us, there is also a radical difference

Otherness in Question: Labyrinths of the Self, 53–71

within myself. For now, the actual *Other* is me. Paradoxically, while writing these lines, the actual *Other* was exactly you. Thus, for me, at this moment, you are me.

How separate are we? How close? How different, and yet how similar? We are united by this dialogue, but your active understanding of this same dialogue will be different from my understanding of this dialogue with you.

At the moment, this is the most vivid image I can get of the otherness features of our lives. I am addressing you, the I is always in the act of addressing Other(s). As such, a human existence is a dialogical existence and this communicational existence lies in the "heart of the subject" (Jacques, 1991). Following Bakhtin, Marková (2003a) stated that "To be is to communicate, and to communicate means to be for another, and through the other, for oneself" (p. 257). When I was engaging in the previous dialogue with you, the reader, I was actually using my communicational abilities to dialogue with myself. It is through *Others* that my-self comes to being and gains sense and meaning.

However, this dialogicality of life should not blind us to the irreducible difference between two different communicational agencies. I am different from you and it is exactly by this constant and ever-changing act of addressing others that I become and remain different. Intersubjectivity, the possibility of creating a field of common understanding, is an essential step. However, this intersubjectivity is only the necessary attunement for the negotiation of differences.

In my point of view, one of the greatest challenges of a dialogical approach is precisely the self. Otherness permeates the constitution of a sense of self and agency, but, within a dialogical framework, the self must remain as a necessary element. *I* and Other are bounded together, but they linger on as asymmetrical, different but in constant dialogue. Paradoxically enough, my contribution to this volume about otherness will focus precisely on the dialogical constitution of subjectivity, especially in the affective and motivational dimensions of that process. Dialogism (Holquist, 1990; Linell, in preparation; Marková, 2003b; Salgado & Gonçalves, in press) and the dialogical self-theory (DST), created by Hermans and his colleagues (Hermans, 2004; Hermans & Kempen, 1993; Hermans, Kempen, & Van Loon, 1992) will be the departing point of this journey. However, I will try to create some sort of "surplus of seeing" on this framework by incorporating related but different perspectives.

The Dialogical Strategy and the Recovering of Subjectivity

This distinction between I and Other and the possibility of bridging this gap has been a topic of discussion for centuries. More recently, the refusal of the Cartesian isolated mind has created the need to reconsider the role of others in the constitution of the human subject (Salgado & Ferreira, 2005).

In a rather interesting discussion launched by Coelho and Figueiredo (2003), Marková (2003a) clearly distinguishes two kinds of ontological orientations underlying different notions of intersubjectivity. A first one claims that *I* and *Other* remain as two separated existences, while the second one considers *I* and *Other* as an irreducible dyad, that is, *I* and *Other* are bounded, but still distinct and asymmetrical elements. Even if this classification does not exhaust all the possible readings on this matter, this distinction is useful as a device to clarify possible global orientations about otherness.

The first ontological orientation implies an exclusive separation (Valsiner, 1998) between *I* and *Other*. Then, the individual mind remains, in a sense, isolated, enclosed in a solipsistic world. This strategy implies that individuals exist as separate entities that may or may not interact. We will obviously fall into one of the possible kinds of dualism generated since Descartes (Marková, 2003b; Salgado & Ferreira, 2005).

Valsiner (1998) points out that there is an alternative to deal with these ever-lasting problems of dualism, it being, to consider the duality of human life in its several features. That implies the choice of a different strategy, namely, the inclusive separation. Following this alternative thesis, self and other (but also person and society, mind and body, and so on) will appear as two distinct but necessarily united elements. The second ontological orientation presented by Marková (2003a), considering *I* and *Other* as an irreducible dyad shows to be closer to this alternative.

Indeed, the inclusive separation is, in my point of view, a dialogical strategy (Ferreira, Salgado, & Cunha, 2006; Salgado & Ferreira, 2005). My understanding of a dialogical approach, clearly inspired by Bakhtin (1981, 1929/1984, 1979/1986, 1993), is a framework that assumes four main axiomatic principles (see Salgado & Gonçalves, in press):

1. The principle of relational primacy: A human life is always a relational life;
2. The principle of dialogicality: Human relations are dialogical relations, that is, relations with other human beings are relations where the two bounded elements are responsive and creating a communicational interchange;
3. The principle of alterity: Therefore, a dialogical relation implies a relation with an Other (person, group, community, society) with whom a person relates with;

4. The principle of contextuality: All dialogical relations occur within a specific sociocultural context that creates a specific intelligibility for the exchange.

Within this framework, *I* and *Other* will be conceived as an asymmetrical dyad involved in a dialogical relation of addressivity and response-ability (Rommetveit, 1998). As Marková (2003b, 2003a) defends, Ego and Alter are bounded *and* distinct elements, involved in a simultaneous relation. However, what is this Ego? Marková's (2003a) words state that: "*Ego-Alter* exist only in the realm of communication. They can stand for the self, groups, sub-groups, communities, societies and cultures" (p. 257). Since Marková is a social psychologist, this can be valuable, but yet, there is still something to be done: to describe how personal subjectivity can be achieved following a dialogical and communicational strategy. Indeed, we need to return to subjectivity and reanalyze it from this perspective (Salgado & Hermans, 2005). Each one of us is always in a process of anticipating and responding to events of the world and consequently creating our own subjectivity:

> This is the kind of adaptation—to the demands that *might emerge* in the immediate future – that makes all psychological functions necessary for the organism's survival and life success. The highest level of organization of such pre-adaptation tools is human subjectivity.... Restoration of the focus of subjectivity in psychology is not a change of perspectives (or yet another "revolution" after behaviourist, cognitivist, ecological, or other of such kind). It is the restoration of the appropriate subject matter of the discipline —the subjective phenomena of *psyche*. (Valsiner, 2005, pp. 682-683)

I am not forgetting that this world is populated and made meaningful by other human beings. For us, even the world of monological objects is not an objective world: that world would be better conceived as a world of interobjectivity (Moghaddam, 2003), in which some kind of psychology of the second person (person-person-object) must be taken for granted (Rommetveit, 2003). However, in our constant dialogical adaptation to this world, subjectivity is there, under construction and waiting for us, psychologists.

Searching for a Dialogical Self

The DST has been evolving in the last decade as a tool to incorporate the Bakhtinian legacy into the analysis of the self (Hermans, 2004; Hermans & Kempen, 1993; Hermans, Kempen, & Van Loon, 1992). The starting point is the notion that human existence, as language, gains meaning through addressivity and responsiveness (Holquist, 1990). Meaning making is always the result of the coordination of, at least, two human beings.

Thus, each human being is launched in a world of otherness. It is through others that we enter a given sociocultural world, itself a world permeated by different languages, praxis, and routines that live in a constant dialogical struggle. This diversity of social discourses and praxis—the Bakhtinian world of *heteroglossia* (Bakhtin, 1981)—enables polyphony, that is, enables the possibility of an active appropriation of different "voices.".

Strongly influenced by this notion of polyphony, Hermans, Kempen, and Van Loon (1992) offered us a new conception of self:

> we conceptualize the self in terms of a dynamic multiplicity of relatively autonomous *I* positions in an imaginal landscape.... The *I* as the possibility to move, as in a space, from one position to the other in accordance with changes in situation and time. The *I* fluctuates among different and even opposed positions. The *I* has the capacity to imaginatively endow each position with a voice so that dialogical relations between positions can be established. The voices function like interacting characters in a story.... Each character has a story to tell about experiences from its own stance. As different voices these characters exchange information about their respective *Mes* and their worlds, resulting in a complex, narratively structured self. (Hermans, Kempen, & Van Loon, 1992, pp. 28-29)

The polyphony of the dialogical self, albeit an important dimension, is not its main feature (Salgado & Hermans, 2005). As Valsiner (2004) clearly stated: "the crucial question of the DST is not reiteration of the multivoicedness of the Self, but its dynamic structure" (p. 4). The obtained picture is one that depicts the person as an agency that is constantly addressing others and, as such, constantly in a process of positioning and repositioning toward those audiences (physically present or not).

More than a final-end, I take this perspective as a starting point for generative questions. For instance, what does *I* mean in this context? How is this process of moving from one position to the other (the relational dynamics)? How specific meanings are created? And what is the role of the *Other*?

The reflection about all these topics is beyond the scope of this article, but I will stick to some of those that seem to deserve a careful examination. The first has to do with the notion of *I*. A dialogical approach to the self must be committed with the clarification of a subjectivity constituted through otherness. Otherwise, the global approach will seem quite similar

to the multiple modern disengaged self or the social constructionist annihilation of selfhood. In fact, Richardson, Rogers, and McCarroll (1998),
reflecting about the DST, stated that:

> they never address the question concerning on what basis or by what stan-
> dards moral deliberation proceeds, or how, in general, discrepancies among
> contending voices and values are resolved or harmonized.... Thus, in the
> end, it seems that this version of the dialogical self might amount to an
> assemblage of essentially unrelated fragments almost entirely lacking in
> agency or responsibility. Or, this view may actually presuppose an attenu-
> ated version of the modern, punctual self that relates to the world and itself
> in a disengaged, instrumental manner. (p. 513)

This is not, at all, the presupposed orientation of the DST (see Salgado
& Hermans, 2005). In fact, subjectivity, agency and responsibility are at
the core of a dialogical approach. Nevertheless, if a "self acts because of
some motives, goals and reasons" and if "Acts are intentional, and for
them to be effective, they require personal commitment and responsibility" (Marková, 2003a, p. 257), we must ask how to take agency into
account. Those motives and goals must be searched and their regulation
explained. What I will suggest, inspired by Valsiner's (2005; see also in
this volume) theory of affects, is to look at affectivity and its semiotic regulation as a main dimension of a dialogical self.

This first topic relates to a second one. In a dialogical point of view,
agency is a communicational agency. As Bakhtin (1993) persuasively
claimed, we have no alibi in life. The very idea of an *I* position implies
relatedness and orientation toward others and the immediate future.
This constant responsibility, this eternal repositioning from moment to
moment, implies the appropriation of the *Other's* eyes. Therefore, we
must not only recognize the existence of a flow of different I positions,
but the subjective appropriation of the *Other*. This has been a frequently forgotten topic within the DST (Ferreira, Salgado, Cunha,
Meira, & Konopka, 2005). Indeed, there is a global tendency to
describe the self as a sort of an independent set of I-positions without
an acknowledgement of the Others with whom the person is relating.
This explains why there are so many articles devoted to the discussion
of the dialogical relations between different I-positions and so few works
focused on the relationships with other persons within particular contexts. Therefore, the global picture given by this kind of description
becomes dangerously similar to a kind of solipsistic and disengaged
self—something incoherent with the axiomatic principles of a dialogical approach.

Appropriating Otherness: A Triad

Who is the *Other*? This is not an easy question and it may so be that we will never end up with a concrete answer. There is always an interlocutor, the person who is actually there in the moment, questioning and answering. However, as Bakhtin (1981) recognized, long ago, there are multiple addressees (Leiman, 2002, 2004). Each human action is addressed to someone, physically present or not—and I would add, consciously present or not (Salgado & Gonçalves, in press).

Therefore, it is possible that, in order to describe a dialogical subjectivity, we may need to take a triad into account (Ferreira, Salgado, & Cunha, 2006; Salgado & Ferreira, 2005; see also Marková, 2003b for a related perspective). As such, in a single moment we will have three bounded elements. First, there is an *I*, defined as the center of the here-and-now experience, necessarily involved in the process of addressing an *Other* (an *Other*-in-the-self). In a dyadic interpersonal experience of turn taking, this raises no doubts: we have two persons, one talking, the other listening, and their roles may be reversed. However, there are always differences between the "real" *Other* and the *Other*-in-the-self. This *Other*-in-the-self is an appropriated and felt Other. However, when we engage in some sort of self-reflection in the form of autodialogue, who is this Other-in-the-self? It may be an imagined other (as when I started to address the imagined reader in the beginning of this chapter) or it may be the same person, but constituted as a virtual other. As Bakhtin (1979/1986) wrote in his notes: "A person at the mirror. Not-I in me, that is, existence in me; something larger than me in me" (p. 146). However, in a self-reflective autodialogue, while the *I* is addressing *Other*, there is also a "witness and a judge" of this whole process, listening, evaluating, participating in the process of questioning and answering. In order to emphasize the communicational and dialogical ontology of subjectivity, we have been calling this third party "potential audiences" or "inner audiences" (Salgado & Ferreira, 2005). Thus, even in the solitary moment in which the I turns to itself (an inward *you*) negotiating the meaning of himself or herself, three poles are involved: "the self constitutes itself as an *it* which can stand before the inward *you*" (Jacques, 1991, p. 191). When engaged in an intersubjective communication with another person (with a "real other"), subjectively we will find the *I* addressing the *Other-in-the-self*, a process permeated by an internal dialogue with inward audiences.

This is the global stage for the scene of the lived moment. However, a lived and meaningful moment is not an empty one. I and those audiences negotiate and coconstruct meanings. The communicational experience is filled with content in the form of meaningful voices.

A Note About Bakhtin's Notes

Bakhtin (1986) wrote about something similar to this triadic solution, but in a way that indicates his idealist and phenomenological roots. Reflecting about the inward selfhood, he recognizes alterity. However, that derivation of alterity seems quite dependent on self-consciousness:

> This is analogous to the problem of man's self-awareness. Does the cognizer coincide with the cognized? In other words, does man remain only with himself, that is, remain solitary? Do not all events of human existence here change radically? Such is indeed the case. Something absolutely new appears here: the supra-person, the *supra-I*, that is, the witness and judge *of the whole* human being, of the whole *I*, and consequently someone who is no longer the person, no longer the *I*, but the *other*. (Bakhtin, 1979/1986, p. 137)

I appreciate the metaphor of the witness and judge and the necessary call for otherness in the process of self-creation. However, this dyadic solution does not explain the difference between the experiencing person and the reflected image of that person. This seems to be a major problem for dyadic solutions of dialogicality—they create the risk of being trapped in self-consciousness as the main matter for the institution of subjectivity, instead of communication. It must be said that this passage is taken from his unpublished notes and we will never completely know if he would later subscribe such words. Nevertheless, it is interesting to notice that in his last years Bakhtin himself showed signs of some remaining idealism, still attributing to consciousness some fundamental value. Francis Jacques (1991) probably completed the task of replacing consciousness for communication as the ground of subjectivity and knowledge.

Voices and the Lived Experience

Since we have no alibi, we must always position ourselves toward others. To refuse to have a position is, in itself, a positioning. We have no choice, except to choose. Our choices, our acts, our utterances can be seen as "voices," an almost phenomenological element (Valsiner, 2004) of the theoretical stage composed by a triadic subjectivity.

In my view, the concept of voice is closely related to the lived experience. At least, this is implicit whenever Hermans defends that each different voice tells—I would say, more broadly, enacts and experiences—a different narrative.

But, what exactly is referred to as "voice" in this context? On one hand, we may follow Josephs' (2002) suggestion that, instead of conceiving voice as a static entity (e.g., a social role or a trait), we should see this notion as the global and meaningful orientation created in each lived moment: "A voice is rather an emotionally grounded and personally constructed—in short: a meaningful—focus on one's life in the here and now" (Josephs, 2002, p. 162). As such, we may assume the concept of voice as something referring to the meaningful and felt Gestalt of a moment, oriented to multiple audiences or addressees. An utterance, a deed, a gesture—all these are examples of the many forms that a voice can have, at least when we look for its objectified qualities. However, for the *I* who addresses *Others*, voice is the lived and motivated act of addressivity. As such, the personal experience of voice is strictly related to the actual experience of establishing a relationship with multiple addressees, physically present or not. In terms of lived experience, this is the way by which the *I* comes to being. This is quite similar to the notion included in Holquist's (1981) glossary of Bakhtinian terms: according to him, Bakhtin considered voice as the speaking consciousness, filled with wills and intentions (e.g., see Bakhtin, 1929/1984).

On the other hand, the Bakhtinian notion of voice is also clearly referring to the cultural and social side of this process. While voicing something we are using words that come from others, anticipating their own voices. Thus, voice implies a personal appropriation of a given culture and context and, therefore, a single voice is a personal composition of several ones. The present may be a moment of monologization, in the sense of integration of the several voices involved in a triadic relationship.

Therefore, it must be stated that we must not delude the person on those symbolic resources that may be shaping our moment. As Josephs' stated, it could be said that we use labels from communities we feel connected with in order to specify our positioning of the moment, but the resulting voice is always personally experienced in a specific way:

> Notice here that the label of a voice is not the voice itself: my "I as a psychologist voice" is probably different from your "I as a psychologist voice." Thus, naming the voice by *social role label* (psychologist) does not say anything about its *personal meaning*. (Josephs, 2002, p. 162)

Finally, in order to incorporate the temporal dynamics in this description (see Valsiner, 2004), this addressivity may be conceived as a movement toward a personally constituted and anticipated future—the projected minds of the multiple audiences. This means that each human experience is always enacted toward others and also toward a future, close or distant.

Self/Other and Affectivity

To assume a position means to assume a direction toward others. As Richards et al. (1998) noticed a dialogical conception of self must take into account agency and agency implies an evaluative stance in front of the world: "Understanding is impossible without evaluation. Understanding cannot be separated from evaluation: they are simultaneous and constitute a unified integral act" (Bakhtin, 1979/1986, p. 142).

Therefore, it makes more sense to claim with Valsiner (2004) that all our mental life is an affective life and, in order to create a broader picture of a dialogical self, we need to analyze the realm of feelings. We are moved by and through feelings. In a way, they are embodied elements of human experience that guide our conduct. At the same moment, they are vital relational elements. Feeling is relating and human relating creates mindfulness.

Emotions, Feelings, and Affects

Mainstream psychology has been increasingly focusing on emotions, especially on the so-called primary emotions (e.g., Ekman, 1992). The growing focus on these embodied elements of human experience is certainly welcomed, since it represents a search for a more integral account of human experience. In order to get a holistic approach of human subjectivity, it seems more or less obvious that we need to unite that which has been separated, such as body and mind or feelings and rationality.

However, this focus on those primary emotions may blind us to the centrality of affects in human life. Indeed, one of the most discussed matters is whether or not do we have those primary emotions and what are the universal categories of such reactions (see Izard, 1992; Ortony & Turner, 1990; Turner & Ortony, 1992). Such a line of inquiry presupposes an Aristotelian pursuit of natural kinds (Danziger, 1997; Salgado, 2003): emotions exist as natural objects that must be accounted for in a universal language.

This excludes the fact that, whenever we are making an observation of psychological data, we are using cultural mediating tools that come from our own cultural background. There is no reason to doubt that our emotions have biological predetermined roots. In turn, those roots constrict our possibilities—as all sides of our body. We are unable to fly, to see in the dark, and we are unable to stop our immediate pain whenever we cut ourselves—and all this is a constriction of our given body. However, interesting as it may be, this search for a classification of "primary" emotions may block a deeper understanding of the centrality of affectivity in human lives and the cultural side of all this process.

First, the primary emotions, such as fear, surprise, anger, sadness, interest, disgust, or joy, may have different labels in different cultures and, consequently, different meanings and leading to different types of activity (Valsiner, in this volume). Second, if primary emotions are an interesting topic of analysis, feelings seem a more promising matter of study. We know that we have emotions because we feel our bodily reactions in our being in the world and we reflexively appropriate them. Thus, as Valsiner (in this volume) reminds us, our subjectivity may be properly conceived of as a relational and affective state in constant development, in which different emotions are distinguished through our semiotic and reflective activity. The human body is not only the body in itself, but a felt and appropriated body: "the body that I am is not the body that I have" (Jacques, 1991, p. 17). Finally, emotions refer to quick and drastic body changes (Damásio, 1994). They remain as powerful reactions throughout life, but this does not capture all our affectivity. We are always permeated by a felt experience of the constantly changing body in its being in the world, something related with the Damásio's (1994) notion of "background feelings."

These feelings appear to be a central topic in the creation of a sense of agency and self and continue throughout life (Stern, 1998). They contrast with the Darwinian perspective of categorical and discrete emotions and our language has a tremendous difficulty in capturing their dynamics (Valsiner, 2005, and in this volume). This explains why Stern's (1998, 2004) notion of "vitality affects" may be so interesting at this point. To Stern, from the very beginning of life, human experience is permeated and guided by those background feelings, elicited by changes in motivational states. They may occur in the presence of categorical affects, but this is not necessarily the case. Thus, the vocabulary that Stern found more appropriate for this continuous experience of affectivity is dynamic and kinetic: "crescendo," "decrescendo," "fading," "exploding," "bursting," "elongated," "fleeting," "pulsing," "wavering," "effortful." Furthermore, they guide actions and relations with the world, especially the world of others. Feelings imply an orientation, in the sense that they guide the immediate future actions of the person (Valsiner, 2005, and in this volume). Operative since birth, they remain throughout life as the immediate side of each lived moment, a fundamental level for the constitution of an agent of addressivity. Throughout development, they will become regulated by the semiotic devices appropriated by the child, something that enables us to surpass the apparently unavoidable constraints of a body. Indeed, those cultural devices, after all, enable us to fly, to see in the dark and to stop a pain with analgesics—and to shape our affective experience of being in the world. However, the implicit level of affectivity is never wiped off of the map of our existence: there is always a task to fulfill, the subjective appropriation of our experience.

Affects and Intersubjectivity

This focus on feelings may seem like one is stepping back into an isolated and solipsistic mind. In contrast with that possible view, I propose a view a vision of feelings as s way of communication with others and with ourselves. In other words, the communicational field is a field of feelings: "Human sympathy and shared consciousness is governed by powerful emotions of pride and shame, of generosity and guilt, of moral goodness or evil" (Trevarthen, 2001, p. 105). On one hand, they relate (and simultaneously differentiate) the agent and the other; on the other hand, during development they become highly structured by those intersubjective relations.

To fully understand this reasoning, it is useful to review studies relating to the development of intersubjectivity during infancy (Aitken & Trevarthen, 1997; Bräten, 1998, 2003; Stern, 1998; Trevarthen & Aitken, 2001). The global picture is well stated by Trevarthen and Aitken (2001), highlighting the communicational abilities of infants, clearly grounded in affective exchanges:

> there is good evidence that even newborn infants, with their immature though elaborate brains, limited cognitions, and weak bodies, are specifically motivated, beyond instinctive behaviours that attract parental care for immediate biological needs, to communicate intricately with the expressive forms and rhythms of interest and feeling displayed by other humans. (p. 3)

Contrasting with traditional view that the infant start their lives in an enclosed autistic world, developmental psychology has been arguing that the most striking feature of the new born is the capacity to engage in communication with other human beings. For example, Bräten (1998) establishes that we are born with an orientation to others—we have, since the very beginning, a "virtual other." In turn, affects enable this communication with adults, since the infant mind "reveals" itself as a manifestation of affectivity. Thus, even the most basic affects, such as fear or sadness, have a communicational potential enabling the adult's understanding of the infant. This reading may be, in fact, a misreading or an illusory reading, but it is a fundamental step for the creation of an intersubjective field (Rommetveit, 1992). Given the lack of autonomy in the earliest period of life, the infant needs this reading of his or her state, colored as a state of affect. In that movement, the infant is regulated by another by routines, rhythms and all kind of dialogical exchanges (Bertau, 2004; Lyra, 2006). This other constantly introduces novelty and imposes some structure on these exchanges. Thus:

> Since emotions are the essential regulatory factor in intersubjective contact, expressed emotions are fundamentally dialogic or between persons, in the same sense that Bakhtin (1981) treats all thought as dialogic—even monologue. (Trevarthen & Aitken, 2001, p. 18)

Consequently, from the very beginning there is a dialogical and affective organization self-other. The sense of self is coconstructed in the dialogical exchanges with others, especially the primary caregivers and affect is the main currency exchanged and regulated. This emergent self is a self-with-others, but this intersubjectivity does not mean fusion-with-other. The observed interconnectedness infant-caregivers is constantly permeated by a reciprocity that simultaneously unites and differentiates. Dialogicality is operative since the beginning. Following Stern (1998), this interpersonal relatedness is the background from which a core self is instituted, with a sense of volition, continuity and agency. Trevarthen (2001) clearly agrees:

> Self-other awareness is, even in the first months, colored and regulated by explicit relational states such as pride, coyness, shame, and mistrust. This accords with the observation that after four months infants are drawn to look at their mirror images, and after an initial period when they show staring as if fascinated, they may manifest momentary but complex "self-conscious" reactions to their reflected selves, including, besides looking away, both "coyness" and "showing off." (p. 108)

Consequently, these findings necessarily lead us to the consideration of some form of self-awareness in the early phases of life: a sense of self-with-other (or against-other) and it is not surprising that some results point to the early emergence of self-reflexive emotions and affects, such as shame, in a preverbal phase—indeed, in the first months of life (Trevarthen, 2001). This topic is still controversial (see Levorato & Donati, 1999), but the most interesting feature is the clear indication that emotions become regulated by non-verbal exchanges with others. In fact, the exhibition of signs of shame or guilt in a presymbolic phase of life is an indication that these emotions become mediated by the previous relational history of the infant with adults.[1] In another way, it is an indication that the mind of the other was appropriated in a nonverbal way, creating a self-reflexive state of mind and mediating the possible action. From this point of view, self-reflexive emotions (Valsiner, 2005, and in this volume) (e.g., shame, pride, jealously, resentment, empathy) necessarily involve otherness and through otherness a sense of self, that situates the person in regards with the others' view.

Therefore, if nonself-reflexive-emotions and affects are themselves relational (in the sense that they enable intersubjective attunement) and provide some orientation toward the moment, self-reflexive-emotions are clear indications of the interpersonal regulation of our affectivity. Pride may regulate joy by integration of the others eye's, jealously may regulate frustration by the same process. Moreover, the same nonself-reflexive-feelings may become directed to oneself (Valsiner, 2005, and in this volume), since the intersubjective field enables the reading of one's own mind. The nonverbal child—in some way, the child in each one of us—becomes increasingly self-aware of his or her own felt state. Anyway, the studies of social referencing give a great support to this reasoning, since they have gathered evidence that in ambiguous situations the child looks for the adult in order to read his or her own felt state (e.g., falling down and looking for the facial and bodily expression of the mother and consequently smiling or crying in face of her reaction).

We have good reasons to believe that all this processes remain as more or less implicit processes throughout life (Stern, 2004; Valsiner, 2005, and in this volume). However, it should be noticed that affectivity is not independent of symbolization. The development toward language acquisition implies a quantum leap to a higher level of organization of feelings (Valsiner, 2005, and in this volume; Zittoun, 2003) and relatedness (Stern, 1998). Bräten (1998, 2003) argues that language acquisition leads to a tertiary intersubjectivity, where the child becomes increasingly able to symbolically manipulate the others mind, reaching the point of incorporating others' beliefs in their mental operations. In a way, they develop a complete "theory of mind." This expands the ability of active understanding of others—and of oneself—but this also means an active incorporation of the symbolic resources of the surrounding community. Again, differentiation is simultaneous with communion: the child more easily understands the other, but lying and cheating emerge as possible route of action. This seems to be the apparent paradox of a dialogical approach: the more open to you, the more different from you.

This shift is a step to a new higher order of the felt mind, the step toward semiotic mediation (Valsiner, 2005, and in this volume). It may so happen that this semiotic mediation does not end the process of self-regulation of the felt mind. Following the fascinating possibility claimed by Valsiner (2005, and in this volume), the semiotic level may regulated by a hyperconscious level of regulation—a level of a higher generalization, in which no words apply.

The need of a higher level of organization may be implied in digital nature of symbolic signs. If the semiotic regulation introduces a higher level of organization, it must be taken into account that, if words may have epiphanic properties (Leiman, 2002, 2004) of illuminating our situation in the world, they also create zones of shade (Stern, 1998). The symbolic level is in relation with the experiential level, but they remain distinguished throughout life. Therefore, language "can thus fracture amodal global experience. A discontinuity in experience is introduced" (Stern, 1998, p. 176). The experiential flowing of the lived moment is always greater than our words can express. This does not go without consequences. The favorable or dominant modes of describing of the experience may cut off some affective experiences, as seems to happen with several clients in psychotherapy. This is not only a matter of what I am able to experience, but also of what I am able to put into words. Moreover, affects neither noticed nor verbally recognized are not completely experienced (Greenberg, Rice, & Elliott, 1993). Within a dialogical framework, we would say that a potential and different I position lays dormant.

Some Final Thoughts

The final picture is a rather unfinished one. This chapter only tries to contribute to a psychological conception of self that follows a dialogical epistemological/ontological stance. My main argument is that a full relational account of selfhood must elaborate the notion of a communicational and relational agency in face of the others. Moreover, I am also joining those who argue that a dialogical conception implies an evaluative relation with others. Therefore, some sort of "energetic" force must feed all this process, instead of a pure and reflexive consciousness capable of analytical thinking. Subjectivity—our psychic life—is a lived phenomenon. Human existence involves flesh and bones and our affective abilities are deeply rooted in our body energy. Therefore, our decisions and actions are not rooted in a disengaged and rational mind; instead these decisions and actions are always rooted in some kind of relational and energetic field. My suggestion is to consider our affectivity as the main currency of our exchanges with the world, as an implicit, energetic, and relational dimension that underlies all our conduct.

None of this is new. If anything is to be highlighted, in comparison with traditional approaches, I would have to say it is the turning of the spotlight onto the fact that a relational/dialogical perspective implies a stubbornness to see relations where we used to see entities, to follow the continuous changes and processes that shape the psyche. The job is still to be done, but when I refer to "emotions," "affects" and "feelings" my goal is to find an essential dynamic element of description of a self-in-relations—and not to start a search of our inner truth and emotions. With the help of those that insistently study the intersubjective field of a non-verbal child, we conclude that affects are essential elements that shape not only relationships with others (and consequently the relationship with the world of objects, since we are guided by others to that material realm), but also the human agency and subjectivity. But affects remain processes and not things, remain a matter of "how" and not a matter of "what."

Affects are also essential elements in the simultaneous differentiation and coordination with others. Indeed, in the stance I am assuming, they have the typical dialogical property of a Janus-like process: both looking to the self and to the other, uniting the present with the immediate future. We should not confuse ourselves by the apparent different directionality of feelings: "feelings that are possible only toward the other (for example, love), and feelings possible only toward oneself (i.e., self-love, selflessness, and so forth). (Bakhtin, 1979/1986, p. 147). Indeed, those "self-feelings" and "other-feelings" are always brought to being by relations and they are always the other face of the simultaneous centrifugal and centripetal movements of a human relationship. Take love, for example. I can probably only love others because I was loved in the first place; and I can only love me while engaging in a self-reflective and communicational act of relating with myself that carries my history of love with others. However, this ability of self-relating as if I were an *Other* does not exhaust the need of the novelty and affect that others carry:

> Self-related emotions and other-related emotions are inseparable in the economy of adult feelings. Well-being and enjoyment of life depend on how "private" experience is built into memories of events that have been shared. Pain or sickness in one's body or mind can be endured more peacefully if there is sympathy from the other for the awareness of it. Exuberant discovery and skilful mastery of object use gains value if it becomes part of a project that others value. (Trevarthen, 2001, p. 117)

As such, if self-feelings and other-feelings are two sides of the same coin, this perspective may allow us, in a near future, to reconfigure the antinomy between altruism and egoism, between autonomy and heteronomy. For, in the end, as a colleague of mine said to me while discussing this chapter, the more open a person is to the other, the more different from the other the person becomes.

ACKNOWLEDGMENTS

This manuscript benefited from critical reading and feedback by the members of GEDI (Grupo de Estudos em Dialógica e Identidade—Group of Studies on Dialogism and Self at ISMAI, Portugal), my real others on this journey.

NOTE

1. This allows the possibility of establishing a triadic structure for the dialogical self in the early phase of life. The infant is involved in a dialogical exchange with others or with the world (the Other-in-the-self), and all this exchange is mediated by the previous relational history of the infant activated by the present moment.

REFERENCES

Aitken, K., & Trevarthen, C. (1997). Self/other organization in human psychological development. *Development and Psychopathology, 9*, 635-677.

Bakhtin, M. M. (1981). *The dialogic imagination: Four essays by M. M. Bakhtin* (C. Emerson & M. Holquist, Trans.). Austin: University of Texas Press.

Bakhtin, M. M. (1984). *Problems of Dostoevky's poetics* (C. Emerson, Trans.). Minneapolis, MN: University of Minnesota Press. (Original work published in 1929, revised in 1963)

Bakhtin, M. M. (1986). *Speech genres and other late essays* (V. W. McGee, Trans.) Austin: University of Texas Press. (Original work published in 1979)

Bakhtin, M. M. (1993). *Toward a philosophy of the act* (V. Liapunov, Trans.) Austin: University of Texas Press.

Bertau, M. -C. (2004). Developmental origins of the dialogical self: Some significant moments. In H. J. M. Hermans & G. Dimaggio (Eds.), *The dialogical self in psychotherapy* (pp. 29-42). Hove, East Sussex, England: Brunner-Routledge.

Bräten, S. (1998). Intersubjective communion and understanding: Development and perturbation. In *Intersubjective communication and emotion in early ontogeny* (pp. 372-382). Cambridge, England: Cambridge University Press.

Bräten, S. (2003). Participant perception of others' acts: Virtual otherness in infants and adults. *Culture & Psychology, 9*, 261-276.

Coelho Jr., N. E., & Figueiredo, L. C. (2003). Patterns of intersubjectivity in the constitution of subjectivity: Dimensions of otherness. *Culture & Psychology, 9*; 193-208.

Damásio, A. (1994). *Descartes' error: Emotion, reason and the human brain*. New York: Putnam.

Danziger, K. (1997). *Naming the mind: How psychology found its language*. London: Sage.

Ekman, P. (1992). An argument for basic emotions. *Cognition and Emotion, 6*, 169-200.

Ferreira, T., Salgado, J., & Cunha, C. (2006). Ambiguity and the dialogical self: In search for a dialogical psychology. *Estudios de Psicologia, 27*, 19-32.

Ferreira, T., Salgado, J., Cunha, C., Meira, L., Konopka, A. (2005). *Talking about voices: Divergences and convergences on the dialogical self.* In P. Oles & H. J. M. Hermans (Eds.), *The dialogical self: theory and research* (pp. 121-130). Lublin, Poland: Wydawnictwo KUL.

Greenberg, L. S., Rice, L. N., Elliott, R. (1993). *Facilitating emotional change: The moment-by-moment process.* New York: Guilford Press.

Hermans, H. J. M. (2004). The dialogical self: Between exchange and power. In H. J. M. Hermans & G. Dimaggio (Eds.), *The dialogical self in psychotherapy* (pp. 13-28). Hove, East Sussex, England: Brunner-Routledge.

Hermans, H., & Kempen, H. (1993). *The dialogical self: Meaning as movement.* San Diego, CA: Academic Press.

Hermans, H., Kempen, H., & Van Loon, R. (1992). The dialogical self: Beyond individualism and rationalism. *American Psychologist, 47,* 23-33.

Holquist, M. (1981). Glossary (C. Emerson & M. Holquist, Trans.). In M. Holquist (Ed.), *The dialogic imagination: Four essays by M. M. Bakhtin* (pp. 423-434). Austin: University of Texas Press.

Holquist, M. (1990). *Dialogism: Bakhtin and his world.* New York: Routledge.

Izard, C. E. (1992). Basic emotions, relations among emotions, and emotion-cognition relations. *Psychological Review, 99,* 561-565.

Jacques, F. (1991). *Difference and subjectivity: Dialogue and personal identity* (A. Rothwell, Trans.) New Haven, CT: Yale University Press.

Josephs, I. E. (2002). "The Hopi in me": The construction of a voice in the dialogical self from a cultural psychological perspective. *Theory & Psychology, 12,* 161-173.

Leiman, M. (2002). Toward semiotic dialogism: The role of the sign mediation in the dialogical self. *Theory & Psychology, 12,* 221-235.

Leiman, M. (2004). Dialogical sequence analysis. In H. J. M. Hermans & G. Dimaggio (Eds.), *The dialogical self in psychotherapy* (pp. 255-269). Hove, East Sussex: Brunner-Routledge.

Levorato, M. C., & Donati, V. (1999). Conceptual and lexical knowledge of shame in Italian children and adolescents. *International Journal of Behavioral Development, 23,* 873-897.

Linell, P. (2005). *Essentials of dialogism: Aspects and elements of a dialogical approach to language, communication and cognition.* Unpublished manuscript. [Draft retrieved March 15, 2005 from http://www.tema.liu.se/tema-k/personal/perli./]

Lyra, M. C. D. P. (2006). Mother-infant communication development and the emergence of self: The contributions of dynamic systems and dialogism. In C. Lightfoot, & M. C. D. P. Lyra (Eds.), *Challenges and strategies for studying human development in cultural contexts.* Greenwich, CT: Information Age.

Marková, I. (2003a). Constitution of the self: Intersubjectivity and dialogicality. *Culture & Psychology, 9,* 249-259.

Marková, I. (2003b). *Dialogicality and social representations.* Cambridge, England: Cambridge University Press.

Moghaddam, F. M. (2003). Interobjectivity and culture. *Culture & Psychology, 9,* 221-232.

Ortony, A., & Turner, T. J. (1990). What's basic about basic emotions: Can conflicting criteria converge? *Psychological Review, 97,* 315-331.

Richardson, F., Rogers, A., & McCarroll, J. (1998). Toward a dialogical self. *The American Behavioral Scientist, 41,* 496-515.

Rommetveit, R. (1992). Outlines of a dialogically based social-cognitive approach to human cognition and communication. In A. H. Wold (Ed.), *The dialogical alternative: Towards a theory of language and mind* (pp. 19-44). Oslo: Scandinavian Press.

Rommetveit, R. (1998). Intersubjective attunement and linguistically mediated meaning in discourse. In S. Bräten (Ed.), *Intersubjective communication and emotion in early ontogeny* (pp. 354-371). Cambridge, England: Cambridge University Press.

Rommetveit, R. (2003). On the role of "a psychology of the second person" in studies of meaning, language, and mind. *Mind, Culture, and Activity, 10,* 205-218.

Salgado, J. (2003). *Psicologia narrativa e identidade: Um estudo sobre o auto-engano* [Narrative psychology and self-identity: A study of self-deception]. Maia, Portugal: Publismai.

Salgado, J., & Ferreira, T. (2005). Dialogical relationships as triads: Implications for the dialogical self theory. In P. K. Oles & H. J. M. Hermans (Eds.), *The dialogical self: Theory and research* (pp. 141-152). Lublin, Poland: Wydawnictwo KUL.

Salgado, J., & Hermans, H. J. M. (2005). The return of subjectivity: From a multiplicity of selves to the dialogical self. *Electronic-Journal of Applied Psychology, 1,* 3-13.

Stern, D. N. (1998). *The interpersonal world of the infant* (paperback edition). London: Karnac.

Stern, D. N. (2004). *The present moment in psychotherapy and everyday life.* New York: W. W. Norton.

Trevarthen, C. (2001). Intrinsic motives for companionship in understanding: Their origin, development, and significance for infant mental health. *Infant Mental Health Journal, 22,* 95-131.

Trevarthen, C., & Aitken, K. J. (2001). Infant intersubjectivity: Research, theory, and clinical applications. *Journal of Child Psychology & Psychiatry, 42,* 3-48.

Turner, T. J., & Ortony, A. (1992). Basic emotions: Can conflicting criteria converge? *Psychological Review, 99,* 566-571.

Valsiner, J. (1998). *The guided mind: A sociogenetic approach.* Cambridge, MA: Harvard University Press.

Valsiner, J. (2004, August). *Temporal integration of structures within the dialogical self.* Keynote lecture presented at the third international conference on the dialogical self, Warsaw, Poland.

Valsiner, J. (2005). Affektive Entwicklung im kulturellen Kontext [Affective development in cultural context]. In J. B. Asendorpf (Ed.), *Enzyklopädie der Psychologie: Soziale, emotionale und Persönlichkeitsentwicklung* (Vol. 3, pp. 677-728). Göttingen: Hogrefe.

Zittoun, T. (2003). The hidden work of symbolic resources in emotions. *Culture & Psychology, 9,* 313-329.

CHAPTER 4

AT THE BOUNDARY OF ME AND YOU

Semiotic Architecture of Thinking and Feeling the Other

Emily Abbey

...meditating in the dark in November by candlelight, listening to other people breathe and then having the breathing sounds recede is the closest I've even gotten to a mystical experience ... and you leave ... profoundly different, sometimes agitated, but different. There is one man who comes but he's on an oxygen tank so all you can hear is this "Seeeee" breathing in and out. You feel every life in the group...

The other is constantly in the process of flowing into us and ebbing out, and reaching different tide lines in each cycle. At some moments, you are there, entering into the realm of my awareness, you are a sound, a scent, a tactile sensation, and moments later, you may be gone, as my attention is called elsewhere. You come in, though not too far, and you recede. You may also linger in my awareness, even as I attend to other things. You are there, maybe even annoyingly so, and at some moment, concrete meanings may come, you are a man, a woman, a child. You may then recede.

Or you may extend into generality, becoming old, intelligent, a peace worker, a savior. And at this point, you may go, again moving onto something else. You come in, reaching higher, and you recede.

But if you do not go, you can even come closer, much closer. You can come into my subjective core, to the place where I am no longer using language to pinpoint you, and me, but *feeling* you. At this place, you are much more than noticed, or labeled. You become a being, integrated with me, and any meanings that otherwise form dimensions of difference between us are, at least temporarily, neutralized. Words are set aside. You come in, reaching as high as you can, and after moments or lifetimes, you recede.

THE IMPORTANCE OF *FEELING* OTHER PEOPLE

There are numerous places one might begin discussing this flow and ebb of the other, and the different qualities of relating—noticing, thinking and feeling—that accompany this movement. In this paper, I am particularly interested in comparing the feeling quality of relating with its alternatives. The movement into or moving out of *feeling* the other can be seen as crossing a critical threshold with respect to theoretical perspectives that view the other as a constituent part of the person's self and subjectivity. For instance, dialogical perspectives (Hermans, 1995; Hermans, 2001; Hermans & Kempen, 1993) suggest "*other people* occupy positions in the multivoiced self" (Hermans, Kempen, & van Loon, 1992, p. 29, emphasis added), and in such a perspective, "occupancy" is not because we notice the other person, or because we place the other person among layers of generalizations, but because we feel them. In comparing the feeling quality of relating with alternatives, I am then offering one possible way to distinguish the experience of *talking* with the other from being in *dialogue* with another.

It is the transition in and out of such feeling sense through which people extend beyond existing labels toward unknown spaces—despite a sometimes overwhelming amount of exchange with the collective world about what one should or should not do—or who one should or should not be. As the narrator's comments at the start of the paper indicate, feeling the other does leave us "*profoundly different,*" for we enter into an unknown space, reconstructing meaning in the process. There is something qualitatively unique that comes from feeling the other, as opposed to alternative kinds of relating.

As I walk down the street, for instance, I may become aware of a person there, maybe by sight or sound, but I am busy in conversation with a friend and continue with the business at hand. Or, I may begin the complex activity of surrounding the person with my labels, constructing gender, "it is a *man*," "and age, "he is *old*," and moving at some moment to "he is "*homeless*." I may even form some ideas such as, "he is the *victim* of a *selfish* world where *haves* care little for the *have nots*." And then I move on, and the "homeless man" recedes, and in neither case do *I* feel particularly *different*.

A similar set up characterizes the first few lines of the following passage, where the narrator is describing his experience as an aid worker in a homeless shelter:

> We took our first load of food to the kitchen and unpacked it on stainless steel counters, old fashioned deep sinks with rusted plumbing and windows that looked out on dark street corners. When I turned around to revisit the van, I was startled to see the pipes of a great organ. As my gaze lifted I realized that the scrolling woodwork and the expanse of the room signaled that we were in a church. This church, *filled with men* with *only a dream of today*, had no pews, no minister, and no liturgy. The text for the evening was written on the lined faces of those sleeping and those still awake. *This, a sea of humanity*, two hundred strangers in quiet sanctuary—a church to thousands. Surely, God's hand was at work in this place, though there would be no collection.

Noticing the presence of others, the narrator moves into a series of concrete statements, for example, "filled with *men*," each followed by a further abstraction, for example, men who have "*only a dream of today*" and "*This*" ("these men") as "*a sea of humanity*." In many instances, this might have been the end of the experience, a movement into relating with the other through thinking about them, and having them recede without any deeper movement—without much difference.

But here the narrator's words seem to indicate deeper movement. He goes on:

> We brought the remaining food to the church kitchen and walked out, to the thanks and goodbyes of several men sitting at small tables near the door. While the hall had been defined by twilight voices, the half-light masking what must have been great suffering, *the inside of me had grown completely still*. We drove west and out of the city in a close and companionable *silence*. *How is it that life connects us? I am not homeless, yet some part of me was in the streets that night*.

Here, seen in the sudden wordlessness that the narrator experiences: "we drove west and out of the city in a close and companionable *silence*," and the stillness, "the inside of me had grown *completely still*," the other has moved into his feeling space, momentarily transcending the verbal, and in doing so, creating the difference, the extension beyond mentioned above; he is *"not homeless"* and still *"some part of me was* in the streets that night." Through this *feeling* of the other, the narrator is momentarily "beyond" his own labels (see Abbey & Davis 2003; Abbey & Valsiner, 2005).

Of course, extension beyond labels can produce complexities in some contexts, especially those that demand one be X or its opposite, and not "a part of me *is homeless*, even though I am also *not homeless*." These demands may place the narrator in a position of awkwardness similar to that encountered by those who cross geographic and political borders (Bhatia & Ram, 2001). Yet seeing the other *beyond* their label—and in so doing, seeing one's self beyond one's own—may be the best hope of surviving such transitions, for it is where we see, or feel the humanness in the other.

LOCATING THE OTHER

"How is it life connects us?" The focus here echoes the narrator's own quandary—how is it possible that at one moment one can see themselves as an "aid worker" who is there to "help the homeless," that is, someone whose identity at the moment is defined on the basis of this core opposition, and at the next moment feel at one with them? In everyday conversation, one may say that it is "chance," or "whim," or even "fate" that lies behind movement of the other within the self, especially if one moves into the deep *feeling* quality of relating. In this paper, I offer otherwise, showing that people create and use higher-order signs that organize the intrapsychological context, making it open to the possibility of feeling the other or closed to such a possibility.

An Overview of the Self as a Series of Bounded Regions

Following Lewin (1936), my offering is based on the notion that intrapsychological space is a series of concentric regions determined to be part of the same structural whole on the basis of dynamic dependency on one another. These regions are linked to one another by boundaries, defined as "those points of a region for which there is no surrounding that lies entirely within the region" (p. 118). Lewin distinguishes the *motor-perceptual region* from the *inner-personal region*, positioning the former as an intermediary between the environment and *inner-personal* region (p. 177), and I maintain this distinction here. Such a positioning is justified, because anytime the environment has some influence on the inner region, there first must be some motor-perceptual processes, and anytime the individual has an influence on the environment, this influence is again exerted through motor-perceptual activity (pp. 177-178).

Activity in the motor-perceptual region begins as the outermost boundary between the person and the environment is crossed (boundary "a" in Figure 4.1) and one registers a sound, a touch, a smell. Upon being perceived, the other may simply linger in this region momentarily and then fade. In the example above, the narrator becomes aware that others are there, and yet this attention may be the entirety of the experience—never even moving to consider that they are "homeless." Yet, presence in the motor-perceptual region may also constitute the basis of further movement of the other into the self, and such movement *can* happen if the boundary between the motor-perceptual region and the peripheral/thinking region ("b" in Figure 4.1) is crossed.

Peripheral Region→Thinking About the Other

As one crosses boundary "b" which constitutes the edge of the inner-personal region broadly speaking, one enters into the peripheral area. In specifying the activities of the peripheral region, I follow Valsiner, suggesting it is the place where the individual begins to generate generalized meaning (Valsiner, 1997) about the other. This is the region where one labels the other as "homeless."

The important thing is that while meaning of the other is generalized in any number of ways, the other is not, in this region, integrated into the person's subjective core. That is to say, the feeling or affective quality has not been added. The homeless individuals, may be *passionately* spoken

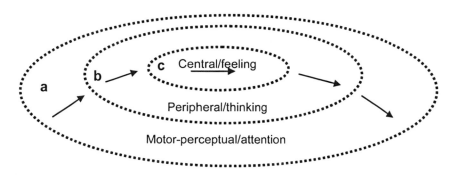

Figure 4.1.   Regions of the intrapsychological space linked by boundaries (a, b, c).

about, as above, yet are not yet *felt*; this only occurs when boundary "c" between the peripheral and central region is crossed.

Central Region→Feeling the Other

Boundary "c" joins the peripheral region with the central region— this positioning, again being in terms of dynamic dependency, as there is less communication to and from the central region to the outside world than to and from the peripheral region. This central region makes up the affective core of the person—it is in this region that the other is actually *felt*. Experience in the feeling realm cannot be well described—it is the place of "silence" and "wordlessness" that the narrator above enters in the homeless shelter. Conceptually then, as emphasized by the arrows in Figure 4.1, the process of internalizing and externalizing (Lawrence & Valsiner, 1993) the other is not an "all-or-nothing" event, but a *differentiated process* (Valsiner, 1997), where bringing the other into the *feeling* space depends on the passage of each boundary, in succession, (a→b→c), and passage out, the same boundaries in reverse order.

MOVING INTO THE BOUNDARY

As a series of bounded regions, the person plays a role in setting up certain qualities of relating with the other by constructing signs at each boundary of each region that serve as its regulators, making that boundary selectively open or closed to particular kinds of incoming and outgoing messages. Boundary regulators cannot determine what happens, in the sense that even when a boundary is open, it does not guarantee that meaning passes; however, they play a powerful role in setting up the person to be open to the possibility of such movement or closed to it.

This sense of the sign's role in boundary passage is similar to the notion of constraints (e.g., Valsiner, 1998), which do not completely control the direction of development, but serve as a guiding framework as the person moves forward with time. Valsiner describes a constraint as "a regulator of the move from the present to the immediate future state of the developing organism-environment system, which delimits the full set of ways of that move, thus enabling the developing organism to construct the actual move under a reduced set of possibilities" (Valsiner, 1998, p. 52).

Each sign is understood as a duality, a dialogical relation of voice and counter-voice that codetermine one another (Josephs, Valsiner, & Surgan,

1999). The counter-voice speaks as an oppositional complement to the focal voice, becoming any and all of the meanings that the voice is not but could become. Meaning, for instance, "I find this painting *beautiful*," is formed through its relation to what is non-beautiful. At times, it is possible to explicitly view the oppositional relation between the voice and counter-voice, yet in much of meaning-making this counter-voice remains hidden from view; it is, however, even when 'hidden," remaining active (Gupta & Valsiner, 1996). As the person moves through any given meaning-making event, he or she may make more distinctions, with these new signs building on previous signs. For instance, the previous sign "*beautiful*" can be further built upon by the notion of *childhood*, "I find this painting beautiful because it brings me back to my *childhood*." And, such metalevel semiotic reflection (Valsiner, 1998) is also a voice and counter-voice relation.

Semiotic Architecture: Sign Fields Structured by Metalevel Sign Fields

With each new sign comes the possible emergence of a *metalevel sign field* building on it. The function of each metalevel sign is to regulate the sign below it, and through such building, there develops a *semiotic architecture* for the boundary. Boundary regulation becomes an extended process of regulation of one sign field by a second sign field, which is in turn regulated by the next higher field. It is accepted axiomatically that there is no maximum limit to the number of higher-order structuring fields, yet it is probable that the semiotic regulatory system itself sets limits upon the extension of the sign field hierarchy (Valsiner, 1999). As seen in the example that follows, given this arrangement, a shift in dominance between the voice and counter-voice of a higher-order regulating sign creates a shift in the same relationship in the sign below it.

FEELING THE OTHER

To further detail how people create and use higher-order signs to regulate the boundary crossings between peripheral and central regions of the intrapsychological space, I now return to the same man whose comments about working in a homeless shelter were used above. The present section is a deeper exploration of his life story, a story that turns out to be as much about the other as it is about the self. Perhaps surprisingly, given the strong *feeling* sense of the other in the above excerpt, his life has been one where feeling the other was at best a tortuous process given the signs he constructed at the boundary between the peripheral and central region. I will first outline his story at the level of his own reflective narrative, pointing out the shifting qualities of relations with his feeling center, and how these shifts changed his quality of relating with others. I will then move back through the story detailing the different signs that appear around the boundary between the feeling center and the peripheral regions of his intrapsychological space.

Years 18-55: Closing the Boundary Encircling the Feeling Center

The man is 56 years of age at the time of the interview, and he speaks in the quiet of a summer morning from the screened porch of a seaside cottage. His voice is soft and melodic, and as he moves through the interview, his comments are sometimes rueful, sometimes humble, and increasingly populated by glinting humor.

He begins by returning to his 18th year of life, and the death of a brother 2 years his junior. The death occurred during the man's last year of high school, silently and without warning in the middle of one otherwise ordinary night. No cause of death was ever determined. The man describes this event as one that "put me into that place of long-term suffering," not only because of the pain the death itself created, but because the emotional aftermath was something his family did not process well, leaving him to fend for himself, and in the process, develop ways of coping that would turn out to create suffering for decades to come. As the man describes it, his family ritualistically mourned, yet never really dealt with the *feelings* surrounding the death: "We did all of the experiential things, but talked through none of the *emotional content*." The man recalls trying to compensate for others' lack of emotional processing by single-handedly comforting everyone; it seems this was quite a difficult task, for he describes it as a burden: "So I carried the *burden* emotionally for comforting my father, my mother, and my brother."

A critical period of time seems to be the summer that followed this death, where the man found himself completely alone. His parents and remaining older brother had gone away (no doubt trying in their own ways to cope), and so he was physically by himself. But he was also psychologically alone, so much so that even the darkness and silence of night were not easily tolerated, as he says, "I slept with all the lights on and the radio on because I couldn't stand the dark and I couldn't stand the silence because of the death." This summer, with its extreme sense of being alone, is the period where the man, reflectively, can see that he "began to withdraw."

The man started college, and reflectively, it is at this point that any ongoing emotional changes—withdrawal— begin to be apparent. As he began to construct his life, the man points out, "I got jobs right away, I got married right away, I was seen as a very promising young teacher" and yet his identity had little personal meaning, in the sense that it was devoid of feeling. Retrospectively, he describes this identity as a facade, a remainder of sorts left behind as emotion is drained out. He says, "so the people I met only saw the facade" and any relating was limited by it, "I didn't develop attached relationships with people, I was aggressive and antagonistic." It is hard to imagine, in some senses, the power of this shift during his 20s—where a person, who only years earlier, was ready to embrace his family in their profound pain and need, becomes unwilling (or unable) to form emotional attachments to almost any other.

These limits on emotional attachment were not only between the man and his coworkers; they extended into his first marriage. As he describes it, this union was founded not on the seemingly dangerous ground of emotional intimacy, but in being good "work partners," "we were great *work partners*, that's what we did really well together." He recounts that at 33 years of age he decided to leave this marriage, and reflectively, he can see the internal struggle to *feel* the other was ongoing. He points out that he remarried because of a yearning for feeling: "I actually remarried because I *craved this connection*," yet in the same breath, he points out the somewhat convoluted logic of this decision, "I thought *this woman* brought all this emotional content"; that is, he was in many respects trying to compensate for his own lack of emotion through an external source.

Through his 40s, the man continued this complicated mode of operation, where it seemed like he was "doing everything right," but in truth (as he will go on to point out), all of what he did was still part of the surface and not connected to his emotional center. The air of humility mixed with humor that he brings into so much of the interview deeply infuses the following quotation, where the man suggests that his favorite physical locations during these decades—ladders, roofs, mountain tops—formed a sort of metaphor for his life:

> I spent most of my free time on the roof because *you couldn't get me there*, on a ladder ... that is actually a good metaphor for my life, I was always seeking an elevated state, *where nobody could get at me*. Um, literally, I used to climb towers when I was young, climb ladders, walk on roofs, climb mountains, anything that would get me up and *away ... was important*.

At 55 years of age, perhaps catalyzed by the end of his second marriage, the man recounts that after so many years of living this guarded life, he felt a lack of will to continue: "I couldn't cope anymore.... I was literally drowning.... I didn't want to live." The man tells how, in the throws of confusion he packed up his things, mounted his motorcycle, and traveled the long distance to his brother's grave, a place he had not been in many years. At the grave, as he tells it, something critical happened—he sat and engaged in a tearful dialogue with his brother.

Years 55 Onward: Opening the Boundary Encircling the Feeling Center

This graveside experience has profound meaning for the man. It is as if by returning to the grave, he came full circle, and therein allowed him to start down a new path where emotions and experience could be linked to one another.

At the point of narrating, the man has been on his "new path" for a little over a year, and even in this short time, he points out differences in the quality of his life given the new possibility of linking his feelings with everything else. For one, contact with the feeling region allows him to embrace the Eastern notion of a collective consciousness: "Collective consciousness is that I really *am* linked to the people on the streets of Calcutta. And the people who sit in mansions in California, and I have to be open to how that connection works." This is seen quite clearly in the experience with the homeless men above, where it is truly possible for him to go beyond the labels "homeless," and for him "homefull," to feel the other.

An anecdote he gives offers another example of this deeper connection to the other that he now finds possible. In it, he describes a meditation session that he recently attended, where he was seated next to a parent in the school where he is the principal. He describes how, during the last 2 minutes of the meditation, he reached over and held this woman's hand, and in doing so, experiences a deep feeling connection: "You hold her hand and she appreciates it, and it's mutual, and it cemented the relationship between the two of us." He is still aware of how, at the level of labels, this act creates as much chaos as feeling the "homeless men" can: "I'm just the principal in the school, I have a nice relationship with her *but nothing other than that* ... if I did that in the workplace it would be considered "*sexual harassment*,'" and yet now he can also move beyond those labels for a moment, relating in his feeling center.

BOUNDARY PASSAGE

As I begin to outline a semiotic architecture of self-created signs at the boundary of the central and peripheral region, I return to the summer following the man's brother's death—a time when there is pronounced struggle around the boundary, and where the ambivalences that likely play a role in hidden form in the following decades are still visible.

Importantly, after his brother's death, the man is initially open to feeling. Returning to his comments above, he recalls the need to try and experience emotions, so much so that he tried helping everyone in his family. Yet, feeling quickly became complicated, because while on the one hand he wanted to feel, no one else did. And while he tried to help everyone else cope, no one tried to help him. Feeling became something that he wanted to do, yet simultaneously something he did not want to do, because no one was there to help him cope. At this point, there is clearly a deep penetration of the other in the self, of feeling his brother.

This ambivalence, seemingly in its infancy at this point, probably grew stronger on both sides during the summer of nights spent feeling alone. By the end of the summer, the man says: "then I just *packaged that all up and went to college, ... I suppressed my feelings.*" One can imagine an inner dialogue where gradually, over the summer, the sense that an ***okay to feel*** <> *not okay to feel* complex is taken over by its counter voice, ***not okay to feel*** <> *okay to feel*. The sense of "package that all up" is telling, where the feelings are "boxed up" as this sign closes the boundary between the central and peripheral regions for passage (see Figure 4.2). The boundary, as it becomes closed, keeps incoming material out, but can also be seen in these comments as keeping material in the feeling center "in" or "suppressed"; that is, the center is still active in some way, but

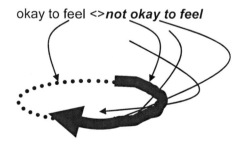

Figure 4.2.   Closing the boundary between feeling center and peripheral region as "not okay to feel" becomes dominant over "okay to feel."

these suppressed ideas—and others—are largely blocked from coming into contact with the peripheral region.

This sort of boundary modulation can be seen operating in many life contexts, allowing shifts between seemingly "heartless" and "heartfull" interaction. It is the one used by soldiers to block feeling (*not okay to feel*) for the enemy during times of battle, yet open to feeling (*okay to feel*) compassion for children of the enemy as he or she walks in their streets or fields. There are, of course, too many situations where this sign keeps the boundary *rigidly* closed, as in the case of massacres, where people are killed indiscriminately. In a less extreme sense, this basic regulation is also seen in the Western world, where men learn that it is "not okay to feel" and women learn that it is "very much okay to feel." Here too though, people may make their own choices, and different ones at different times, regarding this basic regulation.

It is in the dominance of *not okay to feel* that the facade finds seed, for any meaning-making about the self is directed away from the feeling core, where one's life choices can be felt—and therefore made rich with personal meaning. By going about life without feeling, not surprisingly, his identity feels like a facade, devoid of personal relevance, as feeling has been drained from it. At some point, perhaps early on, the *metasign 1 **not okay to feel** <> okay to feel* complex that is regulating *feeling* becomes further regulated by *metasign 2*, that stipulates emotions can be experienced in *private*, but not in public. He says, "I experienced most of them [emotions] passively and in a secondary way, so I would show them only to myself *in private*, um, I lived such a guarded life that it wasn't safe to show most emotions." Here it is possible to see a bit of the emerging *semiotic architecture* of the boundary:

Meta-2: PRIVATE-PUBLIC
Meta-1: OK TO FEEL/NOT OK TO FEEL (IN GENERAL)

FEELING X

Metasign 2, qualifying the first, is in some senses critical to our current focus, for contact with the other is necessarily not such an instance of "privacy." It is this sign's role to activate *not okay to feel*—restricting boundary passage into the feeling region—each time the other is encountered. And it is here that a sense of "protecting" the self seems to develop:

Once, somebody said to me, "I never know what you are thinking," I looked at her and said, "*You're not supposed to!*" That was like thirty years ago. I said this to a music teacher ... *she was very emotional* and *it* [her words] *felt like invasion into me* ... "*You are not going to find out.*"

In this quote, one sees an inner dialogue, where "*you're not going to find out*" and "*you're not supposed to*" appear as lower-order signs around the boundary between the peripheral region and the central. Invasions, as he mentions, can only be launched against closed territory, and for the man, the boundary to the feeling region of the self was one such area.

Organization and Interaction of Sign Complexes

Looking over the course of these decades, a semiotic architecture has begun to develop (see Figure 4.3 below), where **feeling only in private** **<>** **feeling in public** field regulates the lower sign field **not okay to feel** **<>** *okay to feel*. This sign, in turn, sets the general orientation and regulates the sign specific to the man's relation to others, making *protected self* the dominant voice in the **protected self** **<>** *defenseless* self complex,

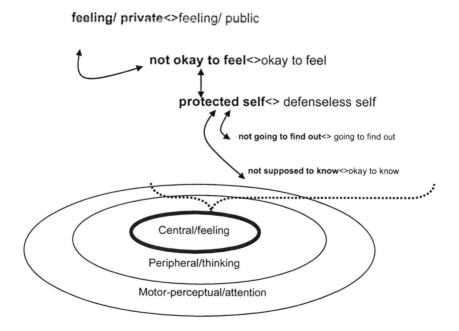

feeling/ private<>feeling/ public

not okay to feel<>okay to feel

protected self<> defenseless self

not going to find out<> going to find out

not supposed to know<>okay to know

Central/feeling

Peripheral/thinking

Motor-perceptual/attention

Figure 4.3.   Hierarchy of signs "closing" boundary between thinking and feeling region.

as well as *"not supposed to know me"* <> *okay to know me* and *"not sup-posed to find out"* <> *okay to find out.* Together, these signs function to close the boundary between the central and peripheral regions as the self comes into contact with the other.

Opening the Boundary to the Feeling Core

The trip to his brother's grave can be seen as an intense moment for the voice and counter-voice relation in the sign complexes he had con-structed. It is as if over the decades, the "okay to feel" voice had contin-ued to try and reassert itself, only to be shut out by metasigns that discouraged this. One can see the visit to the grave as an apex of the ten-sion between these voices, where at the point of total confusion, the *okay to feel* voice wins out.

In the weeks, months, and eventually years that followed this crisis, the man explains how he began saying the serenity prayer throughout the day; he would carry it around with him, sometimes written and other times simply going over it in his thoughts. He comments about the extent to which the prayer became part of his daily life: "the seren-ity prayer is so important ... I say it twice a day, 'let me accept the things I cannot change and [have] the courage and wisdom to tell the difference.' It defines my whole life." The man began to use the prayer not in a strictly ritualistic activity, but as a *symbolic resource* (Zittoun, Duveen, Gillespie, Invison, & Psaltis, 2003; Zittoun, 2005, in press) in a passionate attempt to resolve his crisis.

This prayer seems to contain quite a bit of relevant semiotic content. For one, it seems to speak to a need to "control" seen in many aspects of the man's thinking, including his restrictions on when it was or was not okay to experience feeling. The prayer seems to suggest he *"can't control everything"* and for him to *"think carefully about what can be controlled."* The prayer also suggests a metasign for *"can't control everything,"* which is *"accept what you cannot control,"* that is to say, bring it inside. Positioned above the *feelings in private* <> *feelings in public* complex, these signs regulate each other, and the signs below. Their action is clear in his comments, "well, *letting go* is important ... we think we have such authority to influence events around us when in fact we have very little." As these metasigns become positioned, they negate the whole feelings/public <> feelings/private complex (as this complex was about trying to control what one cannot) and make the still lower sign *okay to feel* become dominant. This in turn leads to a dominance reversal as *protected self* <> *defenseless self* becomes *defenseless self* <>pro-

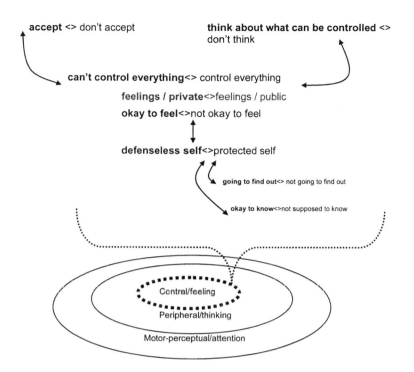

accept <> don't accept   **think about what can be controlled** <> don't think

can't control everything<> control everything

feelings / **private**<>feelings / public

okay to feel<>not okay to feel

defenseless self<>protected self

going to find out<> not going to find out

okay to know<>not supposed to know

Central/feeling

Peripheral/thinking

Motor-perceptual/attention

Figure 4.4.   Addition of "can't control everything" and its metasigns allows "opening" of feeling center.

tected self, cascading down to other signs and opening the boundary to the feeling center (see Figure 4.4).

It seems that saying the serenity prayer becomes for the man a ritualized activity, a critical element of internalization processes, constantly reactivating the signs at the top that allow the feeling center of the self to become open. He comes to some additional extensions, where there are almost explicit instructions about "how to" let meaning pass into the feeling area. He says, "I *take the value off* of everything." It is almost as if one can feel the value "peel off one's own and other's skin" and they do become not "homeless and homefull" but two beings. The man himself seems to have a sense that the inner core is a place of such deep relating, as he says, "It doesn't mean that I become emotionless, it actually means that I *become more deeply emotional about everything* there because I am not reacting *superficially* to everything."

This in fact is the opening of the self to the feeling region that provides a "space" for interaction with the other, where the elements of the periphery that "make" the homeless man different can be ignored; the other is only "homeless" on the periphery, and the man is only "homefull" on the periphery, but at the center, there can be the deepest relating, the feeling of the other.

Communication Between Regions

The critical point of this model is the notion of voice and counter-voice, such that even when a particular voice is dominating, there is the potential for the other voice to emerge at any point as he moves with time. As the man goes on to talk about his life *now*, it becomes clear that rather than achieving a new "monologicality" in these new ways of thinking, (e.g., going from one extreme nonopenness to an extreme of openness), the major emphasis is to try and make dialogical the relations between times when the feeling center is open and times when it may remain closed. He speaks of a "*finely tuned balance*" between the ways of making meaning: "So I try to live with *balance* between spiritual growth, which is more meditative and slower, and focused, and the world that I have to work in which is busy and sometimes chaotic" Here, both voice and counter voice come into contact with one another, and he is able to regulate the boundary in a flexible way, at times setting up a pattern where the core may not be open, and yet also (finally) being able to open it at some moments.

Here we see another metasign, "*watching my thinking*" appear in the semiotic architecture, designed to regulate "*can't control everything < > control everything*," as he says, "**watching your thinking** is what I work on all the time ... [when] what is going on in my brain is very different than what's happening in front of me... I try to **divert those thoughts**." As an example, he recalls a situation where he had begun to work in the periphery, closing the boundary and using labels to "judge" other people. And he "catches" himself in the process, saying "that's the same old thing in different clothing, that's believing that I am somehow in charge of the world. So I *redirected that thought, I let go of it.*"

Semiotic Reflexivity

As seen here, the individual is self-reflexive, not only making meaning to understand the here-and-now situation, but making meaning about that process and using such ideas to construct higher order regulators of the moment-to-moment interaction. This man's narrative offers many examples where this reflexivity makes him an active participant in his own development. Some of the more interesting aspects in the construction of architecture are the places where the man introduces new signs that seem reflexively motivated constructions where sensing something is "wrong," he creates a higher-order unit to fix the problem. This is first seen with the construction of *feeling/private* <> *feeling/public* to regulate below, for one can imagine it is impossible to never feel, and so this needs to be further regulated. Still higher in the architecture (decades later), there is the intense awareness of the problem caused by this first arrangement, and another move explicitly oriented toward positioning a new sign, "*not in control of everything,*" to take care of it. The further addition of "*watching your thinking*" is yet another example. Of course, what is seen here is a macro-oriented perspective of such constructions, and microgenetic studies of such construction would no doubt provide further clarity that is still needed.

TOGETHER YET *APART*, APART YET *TOGETHER*

Before closing, I want to move further toward the focus of this volume, *otherness in question*, by returning to the man as he narrates about being homeless and yet not so, "*I am not homeless, yet some part of me was in the streets that night.*" This statement is where, for me, otherness and selfness come into question together, as both other and self can be understood as composed of the duality of generalized abstractions and feelings that necessarily transcend these ideas. The other is not only the other, as we reformulate them using language and labels, they are also a feeling. Likewise, the self is also composed of labels—the "homefullness" of the narrator cannot be denied—yet the self is also there in a different way.

The statement, "*I am not homeless, yet some part of me was in the streets that night,*" reflects the reality that there are two others (or qualities of the other) and two qualities of the self. The men in the shelter, to some degree, remain homeless, but through the semiotic mediation of the boundary they also become part of the narrator's self. The narrator, likewise, remains "home-full" but he is also, through this transaction of feeling, somehow beyond these labels.

These dualities are where we see the beauty and complexity of cultural life—the ability of the self to go *beyond being who it is supposed to be* (Abbey & Valsiner, 2005) and for the other to go beyond being other. It is also where we see the real core of such a cultural self in these deeply detailed hierarchies, created (and recreated) in order to *distance from the feeling center and yet come back to it*. It is through these hierarchies of signs that we bring the other in and out, and in so doing, bring in the self, taking it to new places and taking it back out. We are together yet *apart* from the other, *and* apart from the other yet *together*, and the same is true of the self.

CONCLUSION

One goal here is to take the person <> world relationship (itself a boundary) and extend it through the notion of the intrapsychological space as a series of regions. In so doing, it becomes possible to see some of the intricate details of "boundary work" and the complexity of semiotic processes involved in opening or closing such boundaries. It is not only that layer upon layer of generality may build on (become part of) any transition (e.g., beautiful→because reminds me of childhood), but also that many different sign complexes operate at the boundaries of regions, and play a role in suggesting what meaning's next step *could be*. As such, trying to 'know what comes next' from a person (i.e, predicting), *even by that person*, with any certainty, becomes a tricky process when one considers the number of signs and the interplay between them that play a role in generating the field of potential in each act of meaning-making. What is more, given this one particular role they play of bringing the self in and out of feeling the other, we cannot say who we are for sure: the adult, the child, the mother, or the belly dancer.

ACKNOWLEDGMENT

The author would like to thank the interviewee.

REFERENCES

Abbey, E., & Davis, P. (2003). Constructing one's identity through autodialogue: A cultural psychological approach. In I. Josephs (Ed.), *Dialogicality in development: Advances in Child Development within Culturally Structured Environments* (Vol 5, pp. 69-86). New York: Elsevier.

Abbey, E., & Valsiner, J. (2005). Poetiken des Selbst: Zwischen Ambivalenz, Bedeutung, Formlösigkeit und Wandel [The poetics of the Self: Being, form dynamics, and change]. *Psychologie & Gesellschaftskritik, 115*(3), 133-149.

Bhatia, S., & Ram, A. (2001). Locating the dialogical self in the age of transnational migrations, border crossings and diasporas. *Culture & Psychology, 7*(3), 297-309.

Gupta, S. N., & Valsiner, J. (1996). *Myths in the hearts: Implicit suggestions in the story.* Poster session presented at the second conference for Socio-Cultural Research, Geneva, Switzerland.

Hermans, H. J. M. (1995). The limitations of logic in defining the self. *Theory and Psychology, 5*(3), 375-382.

Hermans, H. J. M. (2001). The construction of a personal position repertoire: method and practice. *Culture & Psychology, 7*(3), 323-365.

Hermans, H. J. M., & Kempen, H. J. G. (1993). *The dialogical self: Meaning as movement.* San Diego, CA: Academic Press.

Hermans, H. J. M., Kempen, H., & van Loon, R. J. P. (1992). The dialogical self: beyond individualism and rationalism. *American Psychologist, 47*(1), 23-33.

Josephs, I. E., Valsiner, J., & Surgan, S. E. (1999). The process of meaning construction. In J. Brandtstätdter & R. M. Lerner (Eds.), *Action & self development* (pp. 257-282). Thousand Oaks, CA: Sage.

Lawrence, J. A., & Valsiner, J. (1993). Conceptual roots of internalization: From transmission to transformation. *Human Development, 36,* 150-167

Lewin, K. (1936). *Principles of topological psychology.* New York: McGraw-Hill.

Valsiner, J. (1997). *Culture and the development of children's action.* New York: Wiley.

Valsiner, J. (1998). *The guided mind.* Cambridge, MA: Harvard University Press.

Valsiner, J. (1999). I create you to control me. *Human Development, 42,* 26-30.

Zittoun, T., Duveen, G., Gillespie, A., Invison, G., & Psaltis, C. (2003). The uses of symbolic resources in developmental transactions. *Culture & Psychology, 9*(4), 415-448.

Zittoun, T. (2005). Transitions. Development through symbolic resources. Advances in Cultural Psychology: Constructing Development. Greenwich, CT: Information Age.

Zittoun, T. (in press). The role of Symbolic resources in human lives. In J. Valsiner & A. Rosa, (Eds.), *Cambridge handbook of socio-cultural psychology.* Cambridge, MA: Cambridge University Press.

CHAPTER 5

THE SELF EXPERIENCE OF OTHERNESS AND THE SHADOWS OF IDENTITY

N. E. Coelho, Jr.

For the purposes of this essay, the notion of *identity* should be understood as the experience (conscious and unconscious) of self and the feeling of self, established by means of successive identifications, and which sustain the subject's sense of the continuity of the self; the identity of a subject who, while not remaining the same, nevertheless presents himself to himself as identical, in the temporal sequence which goes from past to future. *Alterity* is to be understood as all and any form of presence, within and before the subject, of the radically Other, of what is different, which demands a response and movement on the part of the subject.[1]

Among the greatest challenges for twenty-first century psychology is the need for a more profound theorizing of the impasses created by the identity←→otherness and sameness←→difference oppositions in the constitution of subjectivity. The main purpose of this essay is to make a contribution to the advancement of this necessary theory construction, establishing dialogues between a character in modern literature and the philosophies of Emmanuel Lévinas and Merleau-Ponty, as well as psycho-analytical theories and practice.

As a starting point, the self experience of otherness is discussed through the character of Vitangelo Moscarda, in Luigi Pirandello's novel *Uno, Nessuno e Centomilla (One, No One, and One Hundred Thousand)* (1926/1992). The literary work of Luigi Pirandello (1867-1936) is recognized for its special sensitivity to the processes of subjective constitution of identities and alterities, and to the aesthetic expression of the problem of the levels of reality and illusion which make up the spaces in which his characters exist. Pirandello understood that his vast literary output could be reduced to variations on three basic themes: the inevitable mistakes in mutual understanding, the multiplicity of our experiences of identity (we are one, no one, one hundred thousand), and the immanent tragic conflict between a life which moves and changes continuously and the different forms which fix it, which keep it immutable (cf. Silveira, 1999, p. 35). Needless to say, with these three central themes his work must be considered of great interest for psychological and psychoanalytical studies. Any reader accustomed to a psychoanalytical framework will feel a strange sense of familiarity when he encounters the refined descriptions of mental processes in Pirandello. Processes of identification, projections, introjections, splittings, dissociations, depersonalizations, disintegrations, and fragmentations appear in his texts with an elegance, elaboration, and smoothness which is rarely found in psychoanalytical texts. The mental conflicts which characterize the contemporary subject's experience are described in Pirandello's work by means of a refined irony and the tensions inherent in the tragicomedy which, to some extent, make him the heir of Cervantes' Don Quixote and Laurence Sterne's Tristram Shandy.

The novel *Uno, Nessuno e Centomila*,[3] which was published in 1926, 8 years before Pirandello was awarded the Nobel Prize for literature, tells of the sufferings of one character, Vitangelo Moscarda, caused by the tensions imposed by alterity on his experience of identity. Pirandello considered this last novel of his as the synthesis of all his work and also as the work in which can be found the most accomplished convergence of the themes which characterize his writing. From the outset of the novel, Pirandello confronts us with "the fragility of our 'I' in the face of the other's gaze," as Alfredo Bosi suggests in his preface to the Brazilian edition (p. 10). One day, Dida, Vitangelo Moscarda's wife, tells her husband that she thinks his nose leans to the right. The confirmation of this fact is sufficient to lead Vitangelo to make a series of important discoveries: "I was obsessed by the thought that for others I was not what till now, privately, I had imagined myself to be" (p. 7). This first discovery, far from being the realization of the obvious, causes a chronic conflict to arise in Vitangelo Moscarda, sowing doubts and anguish where hitherto there had been the safe serenity of an unquestioned identity. From a progressively more critical observation of himself, Vitangelo starts to live the experience of an identity which is fragmented into an infinite number of parts, or at least into as many parts as the eyes of the others who see him. Pirandello gradually constitutes the metamorphosis of a subject surprised by the infinite images of himself which are at the same time absolutely foreign and absolutely familiar. We follow Vitangelo as, cornered in the face of his discovery, he sets out in search of isolation, which, as will be seen, is not just an isolation in relation to the *external others*:

> I wanted to be alone in quite an unusual, new way. The very opposite of what you are thinking: namely, *without myself*, and, in fact, with an outsider *present.*... This is the way I wanted to be alone. Without myself. I mean, without that self I already knew, or thought I knew. Alone with a certain outsider, whom I already felt obscurely I would no longer be able to get rid of, as it was I myself: *the outsider inseparable from myself.* (pp. 11-12)

But how does one discover this stranger? How can one control the inevitable habit of always recognizing oneself as the same? We reencounter Vitangelo, and his *stranger*, in front of a mirror, with eyes closed and attempting to restrain "every sentimental and rational impulse":

> But a cursed voice inside me said that he was also there, the *outsider*, opposite me, in the mirror. Waiting, like me, his eyes closed. He was there, and I couldn't see him. He couldn't see me, either, because, like me, he had his eyes closed. But what was he waiting for? To see me? No. *He could be seen, not see me.* He was for me what I was for others, who could be seen and not see myself. Opening my eyes, however, would I see *him* as another? This was the point. (p. 17)

Drawn by his anxiety to discover everything, seeking to refind himself in this strange other, the outsider, which he knew to be himself, but still lacking the courage to open his eyes and not recognize himself in the very act of recognition provided by the mirror, Vitangelo Moscarda continues to express a slim hope: "I must see him and not be seen. Is this possible? The moment I see him, he'll see me and we'll recognize each other. Thanks a lot! I don't want to recognize myself; I want to know him outside of myself" (p. 17). He ends his painful soliloquy with the decision that he must direct his search: "not seeing myself *in me*, but in being seen *by me*, with my same eyes but as if I were another: that other whom everyone sees, except me" (p. 17). He decides to open his eyes. And what does he see? "Nothing: I saw *me*. I was there, frowning, charged with my same thought, with a very disgusted face.... As I lived, I never pictured any image of myself to myself. So why should I see that body there as a necessary image of myself?" (p. 19)

PIRANDELLO AND FREUD: COMRADES IN ARMS

It becomes inevitable, for us historians of modern subjectivity, to recognize in Pirandello's (1926/1992) text the clear presence of the crisis of the modern subject. With that we have to recognize him not just as a contemporary, but also as a companion of Freud in his struggle to show that the subject in the late modern age is not even master of his own house. As is known, projects in modern philosophy and science since the sixteenth century, as Figueiredo (1992) points out, have sought to construct a concept of the subject as an indissoluble unity, which remains the same at different moments of its existence and which has the ability to be transparent for itself. That subject which, not by chance, has been represented by the idea of *being a subject* who is *in control of* its consciousness, the source of all knowledge of itself and of the world.

Accompanying this notion of the subject is the notion of identity which was already present in Leibniz, for example, as individual identity and personal identity (cf. Lalande, 1956, pp. 455-458). It came to represent the experience of a unity which is the self in itself, recognizable subjectively and which, in principle, would also correspond to what is recognized objectively. It is against this backcloth that we must recognize Pirandello's (1926/1992) demands through the character of Vitangelo Moscarda, who, impelled by the force of his reflections, comes to question whether others do not experience things in the same way that he does, and proposes:

> Be sincere: it never crossed your mind to want to see yourself live? You pay attention to living for yourselves, and rightly, with no thought of what in the meanwhile you might be for the others; not because you care nothing about the opinion of others: on the contrary, you care a great deal; but because you live in the blissful illusion that the others, outside, must picture you to themselves as you picture yourself. (p. 23)

It is also this criticism of the dual illusion (the self's illusion about itself and about others), with its consequences for theoretical developments regarding the experience of communication between subjects and for studies of the processes of subjective constitution, that makes Pirandello an interlocutor of great interest in current debates in psychology.

In the second part of the novel we find Vitangelo Moscarda announcing his desire to annul his identity, seeking to eliminate his own name, to deconstruct every connotation present in his name. The experience of self and of others as a reality which can be shared comes to be questioned even more. With the lucid madness so characteristic of Cervantes' Don Quixote, Vitangelo Moscarda questions the very existence of so-called "reality": "If only there were outside of us, for both, a my reality and a your reality, both sovereign, I mean in themselves, and at the same time, unchangeable. There isn't" (Pirandello, 1926/1992, p. 32). And, a little further on, he questions what it is to know oneself and others:

> Do you believe that you can know yourselves if you don't somehow construct yourselves? Or that I can know you if I don't construct you in my way? And can you know me, if you don't construct me in your way? ... and for myself I have no other reality except in the form I can give myself. How? By constructing myself, in fact. (p. 41)

In the midst of the torments of a reflection that seemed as if it would have no end, Vitangelo Moscarda resolves to act. Bothered by his reputation as a usurer, which he had inherited from his father along with his great wealth, he decides to give one of his houses to a pauper, considered a little crazy by everybody, who was living free of charge in one of his houses. But to give his decision a greater public impact he first asks the police to evict the man and his wife from the house they were occupying. When this has been done, part of the population of the small town in Sicily where the novel takes place begins to yell: "Death to...! Down with...! Usurer! Usurer!" (p. 94) Thereupon, a clerk from the Notary Public's office informs everyone of the donation of a new house and a large sum of money to the poor couple who have just been turned out. Upon hearing this news, the crowd starts to shout: "Madman! Madman! Madman!", which leads Vitangelo to conclude, "all because I had wanted to prove that, for the others too, I could be someone different from the man I was believed to be" (Pirandello, 1926/1992, p. 95).

There can be no more doubt. Pirandello (1926/1992) constructs, step by step, yet another of his famous labyrinths in which extreme relativism leads us at first sight into a dead end, down the road to madness, already so well explored by writers such as the famous Brazilian author Machado de Assis, in his short story *The Alienist*. Between extreme relativism and the simple solution of portraying his character as a madman, Pirandello presents, with great clarity, the reflections of a man in search of himself:

> When the eyesight of the others doesn't help us establish somehow in ourselves the reality of what we see, our eyes no longer know what they are seeing; our awareness is confused, because what we believe to be our most personal attribute, our awareness, means *the others in us;* and we can never feel alone. I sprang to my feet, terrified. I knew my solitude; but only now could I feel and truly touch its horror. (p. 105)

But as he moves towards a life with "no conclusion" (the title of the last part of Book VIII, the novel's ending), Vitangelo Moscarda discovers that the limits between the "I" and the other, between inside and outside, between the same and difference, can find new meanings through absolute immersion in the vital flow of nature:

> The city is distant. From it, at times, in the twilight calm, the sound of bells reaches me. But now I hear those bells no longer inside me; but outside, rung for themselves, and perhaps they quiver with joy in their humming hollowness, in a fine blue sky filled with hot sun amid the shriek of the swallows or in the cloudy wind, heavy and high over their airy spires. To think of death, to pray. There are those who still have the need and the bells became their voice. I no longer have this need; because I die at every instant, and I am reborn, new and without memories: live and whole, no longer inside myself, but in every thing outside. (p. 160)

In spite of the meaning that each reader may give to these final sentences of the novel, which lose nothing by comparison with the best pages of some oriental philosophies, in which the "part" finds its vital meaning once more by means of reimmersion in the "whole," we have to recognize in the "solution" proposed by Pirandello one of the existential paths trodden by many individuals in our late modern age, saturated with individualisms and "subjectivities." This is not the place to analyze or interpret the meaning that Pirandello may have wanted to give by means of this ending, nor does it seem necessary to discuss whether a "lyrical pantheism" (cf. Bosi, 2003)[5] is the inevitable destiny of a consciousness which has deconstructed its certainties and followed the tortuous trails of relativism. However, I understand that many interpretations based on different frames of reference from psychology and psychoanalysis would be pertinent and certainly throw light on various aspects of this fascinating character, Vitangelo Moscarda, constructed by Pirandello. As will be seen, I will make my own choices which, of course, do not invalidate any others that may be made.

At the risk of reducing, perhaps excessively, Pirandello's penetrating ability to establish the successive steps in the process of transformation instigated by the confrontation with alterities coming from another and also from oneself, I make bold to propose some considerations, with the didactic purpose of highlighting central points in the identity←→alterity tension:

1. The other's look (a first mark of alterity) reveals to the subject something of himself that until then he seemed not to know; in this sense, the other's look can be considered simultaneously as

operating constitutive processes of subjectivity and destabilizing processes of an identity already constituted;

2. The effect of the discovery of the unknown in oneself is traumatic. We should understand "traumatic" as meaning that can not be assimilated into the set of images/sensations/feelings of oneself which hitherto sustained an experience of oneself which we have become accustomed to calling *identity*;

3. Something that is the subject, but that cannot be assimilated into the identity, causes conflict, threatening one's very identity, even going so far as to dissolve it;

4. The recognition of an *other* within what was until then a "monolithic subject" produces splitting, an element which, since Freud's initial discoveries, has been recognized by psychoanalysis as central in pathological processes, but also as fundamental in the development of creative processes of mental maturation (as is known in the work of M. Klein, D. Winnicott, and others).

The First Guiding Principle

With this, a first guiding principle for our exposition can be suggested: the other arises and erupts before the subject, challenges his capacity for assimilation, ultimately dislodging him and making the subject something other than himself, as a condition for contact. The other thus imposes the dislodging of the subject, imposes the impossibility of really being in contact with the radically Other unless one abandons the empire of the Same and accepts being dislodged by an Other which cannot be assimilated (cf. Lévinas, 1961). To be in contact with the other and only be able to assimilate what is similar, inevitably becomes the permanent maintenance of sameness. Lévinas' criticism to all "totalizing" vestiges in Western philosophy, which invokes the permanence of the Same in opposition to movement and the non recognition of the radical otherness of the other, reveals his unique conception of the identity←→alterity tension.

A Second Guiding Principle: Alterity is Necessarily Irreducible to Identity

The relation which manifests the singularity of another person cannot be constituted by means of a fusion. This is because if someone else is the Other in its radicality and not simply a relative other (an other who is not the subject), the relation can never be "totalized," taken in a whole which is common to both. There is always something that escapes, that exceeds, in the contact of a subject with the Other. It is in this sense that the Other cannot and should not be reduced to an other conceived just as someone with whom the subject interacts, since this interaction would indicate a symmetry in the relation. The relation will always be asymmetrical, with the Other preceding and anteceding the subject.

However, it is worth bearing in mind that although alterity precedes the subject, just as it does his anxiety for an identity, there is no alterity except for a subject, or rather, its full effect is produced in the necessary transformation which it imposes on a subject. There is no alterity in relation to nothing or alterity of a nothing. There is alterity as a constitutive force of subjectivity.

A Third Guiding Principle

It is necessary to recognize that we will always be subject to situations for which we have no organized mental defense, and we will thus be subject to the need to resort to more primitive mental processes of defense. This is a situation which, as we know, does not occur without consequences of a psychopathological order. Splittings, isolations, and defenses are often installed as last resorts in the face of dilacerating traumatic experiences, which continuously put us back face to face with the persistent enigmas produced by our forms of union and separation with others.

A Fourth Guiding Principle

It seems clear to me that alterity brings in the impossibility of full identification with an other. That is to say, there is always a lack of recognition, the strange in someone else, something that can never be reduced to the same. And, on the part of the subject who seeks through identifications to be the same as an other (an other that is generally idealized and has a constitutive function, in mental terms), there will always be the barrier, the impossibility of absolute identification. There will always be something remaining, something that escapes the possibility of the perfect superimposition of 'I' and 'other', something that makes the dream of the totality of sameness impossible. On the one hand we are faced with the traumatic presence created by this impossibility and, on the other, with the presence of the vitality of a coming to be, marked by difference, by alterity, which demands movement, a response and permanent struggle between the desire for sameness and the vital need for the gap produced by difference.

A Fifth Guiding Principle

It is in the tenuous mental limits between interiority and exteriority that one of the greatest blows has been struck to the modern notion of the subject as sole constitutor of his own contents and limits. With the empirical and logical confirmation of the proposal of the subject as constituted, greater importance becomes attached to the constitutive presence of alterity and of the differentiating elements in the processes of subjectivization. One of the inevitable consequences of these observations has therefore been the repositioning of the notion of *identity* in the set of psychological investigations. For many decades psychoanalytical theorists have sought to show that the identity may need to be thought of, more and more, as a mental refuge constructed on the basis of the demands placed by the intense, traumatic processes of affective and cognitive changes and oscillations produced in the subject's contacts with different alterities (internal and external). Thought of in terms of a narcissistic reappropriation in the face of the traumatic impact, the experience of identity gains new forms.

TRAUMATIC SIMULTANEITY OF THE STRANGE AND THE FAMILIAR[2]

I understand that intersubjective relations necessarily imply a certain displacement, a certain splitting or modification in the subjective experience of each one of the subjects involved, whether in its primary constitution or in subjectivities already constituted but in the process of reconstitution, as occurs, for example, in psychoanalysis. I go along with Lévinas, who believes there is, in every subjectivization process, alongside other experiences the inalienable experience of a radical passivity. Such passivity is one of the basic conditions for subjective constitution.

Subjective experience is thus seen as permanent and inevitable openness to the other, in its alterity. I also consider, once again in keeping with Lévinas, that this contact is in itself traumatic. Furthermore I understand that the impacts of traumatic experiences reveal the presence of alterity, as much in its "external" dimension (the impact of the difference produced by an other, external to the subject) as in its "internal" dimension (the other which inhabits the subject himself) (cf. Coelho & Figueiredo, 2003, pp. 193-208).[3] I will try to show, however, that what produces the traumatic impact is the simultaneity of strange and familiar elements.

I thus go on to describe the experience of alterity as something which disturbs the order of the world, which puts the subject in contact with that which exceeds and which escapes the possibility of apprehension, of immediate assimilation. And in addition to this, I intend to show that what is traumatic in this experience reveals the presence of familiar and strange elements inhabiting the same body in its permanent contact with the world and with other bodies.

Let us look at the following report by a patient who recently suffered what could be considered a traumatic experience:

> Suddenly I am overwhelmed by an excess of emotion, by an intense anguish. I no longer recognize the forms, the frontiers and barriers that protected me and separated me from the other and from the situation. I am overwhelmed by a strange sensation of terror: I simultaneously recognize and do not recognize the expressions and characteristics of an extreme situation that is imposed on me by the non-refusable presence of an emotional torment provoked by the impact of contact with another person. It is a person that I know, but in the state in which he is I do not recognize him. I perceive that it is something that at that moment I cannot assimilate and fully tolerate. I am taken over by terror of the moment, experienced as a great emergency alarm that demands action, and at the same time paralyzes me. That moment seems to last for ever, I experience the panic of never being able to be the same again, and I am anguished by nostalgia for how I was before, when everything was so good, without threats which it was impossible to face up to.

On returning to the experience after some time, the patient recognizes that he continues to have the feeling of deep discomfort and clearly perceives his great fear that it can all happen again and that the thought of the future (with the permanence of this state of discomfort) torments him in the same way, or even more, than the memory of the past. When he manages to distance himself a little and starts to include more elements into his reflection, resorting to a first level of possible abstraction, he begins to recognize that what seems to be the effect of a trauma or of the consequence of a trauma is *the simultaneity of the familiar and the strange, producing an nonassimilable emotional excess.* In other words, he comes to recognize the situation as human and belonging to his world, but, at the same time, he sees himself deprived of the resources which would allow full assimilation and metabolization of what he has lived. It is more than the impossibility of symbolization, of assimilation through the representational inclusion of the experience in his mental world. On the one hand, there is no possibility of assimilating in the flesh, precisely because what has been lived cannot be assimilated fully, which is why there is no way of assimilating it. But on the other hand it continues to be traumatic and cannot be discarded, excluded from the field of experience, because in something of what has been lived there can also be recognized a part which also is oneself (which is also part of his "internal" self), something to some extent familiar.

For some years I have thought about critical and controversial questions of psychology and psychoanalysis from the standpoint of the phenomenon of simultaneity. In this presentation my aim is to demonstrate the analytical potential of the notion of simultaneity, based on the trauma created by the experience of alterity. I take the concept of simultaneity from Merleau-Ponty. As I have already tried to show in other texts (cf. Coelho, 2002; Coelho & Carmo, 1992), Merleau-Ponty's philosophy, in its ontological concept, emphasizes the simultaneity of differentiation and nondifferentiation. In proposing a concept of the human being and his relation with other human beings and with the world, Merleau-Ponty looks to the idea of simultaneity as a form of overcoming both absolute differentiation, which implies irrevocably separate polarities, and complete nondifferentiation, which presupposes the elimination of the poles, the elimination of one and other (an "I" and another "I," or an "I" and the world). In his view there is no anteriority of nondifferentiation in relation to differentiation, nor the reverse. There is simultaneity: a simultaneity which Merleau-Ponty (1961), in *The Eye and the Spirit*, says was "a mystery which psychologists handle as a child handles explosives" (p. 84).

Is it the familiar which becomes strange, or, on the contrary, is it the strange that brings something familiar? The answer to this question, it seems to me, lies in the notion of simultaneity. There is no anteriority of the familiar over the strange, nor the reverse. There is simultaneity. The mental splitting described by psychoanalytical theory imposes the simultaneity of irreconcilable mental forms, not assimilable to one another. From this perspective, simultaneity characterizes the very pathological dynamics to be faced by analytical practice.

In the first part of this essay, by analyzing different levels and types of disturbance inflicted on individual identities by the impacts produced by otherness, I intended to focalize the dynamics of the identity⟷alterity tension. Subsequently, I have presented a determinant aspect of the subjective experience of otherness, that is, the traumatic impact experienced by a subject when confronted with radical otherness. Based on a clinical excerpt, I have tried to show that what is traumatic in the self's experience of otherness (alterity) is the particular simultaneity (in Merleau-Ponty's sense) of familiar and strange elements. Finally, concluding the second part of this essay, I emphasized the simultaneity of these two dissonant, or even opposite, elements in a subjective situation marked by trauma: the simultaneity of two elements which reveals as much the indissolubility of the elements as their effect of splitting and dissociation. This dual track principle is established originally by the presence of an other, of alterity, which necessarily ends up by exceeding the subject. Such a situation demands from the subject something which he is unable to offer. The traumatic situation arises with the impact of the familiarity and strangeness of the *other* and with the "internal" impact of the strangeness and familiarity regarding my own self. In conclusion, it could be stated that we as subjects will always face the impact of an *other* (internal and external) which is simultaneously familiar and strange and, therefore, traumatic. The traumatic impact is both constitutive of our capacity to deal with the movements and tensions required by existence and one of the sources of unbearable sufferings.

NOTES

1.   Definitions which, as can be seen, come close to those of Lévinas (1961, p. 25):

> Alterity, the radical heterogeneity of the Other, is only possible if the Other is really other in relation to a term whose essence is to remain at the starting-point, to serve as an *entrance* to the relation.... Being "I" is, beyond all the individualization which can be had from a system of references, possessing identity as a content. The "I" is not a being that always remains the same, but the being whose existence consists in identifying itself, in refinding its identity through everything that happens to it. It is identity *par excellence*, the original work of identification.

2.   Some of the aspects presented in this section have been developed in greater depth in another essay (Coelho, 2003).

3.   One of the intersubjective matrices, or one of the dimensions of alterity developed in this article, is the dimension that we call "Traumatic Intersubjectivity," which aims to embrace different forms of traumatic impact produced by "external" and "internal" experiences of contact with alterity.

REFERENCES

Bosi, A. (2003). Apresentação [Preface]. In L. Pirandello, (Ed.), *Um, nenhum e cem mil* [One no one, one hundred thousand] (p. 14). São Paulo, Brazil: Cosac & Naify. (Original work published 1926)

Coelho, N., Jr. (2002). Percepção e realidade nos diálogos de Merleau-Ponty com a Clínica Psicanalítica [Perception and reality in the dialogs between Merleau-Ponty and the psychoanalytical practice] In R. Pacheco Filho, M. Debieux Rosa, N. Coelho Junior, A. C. Lo Bianco, P. Endo, & T. Carignoto (Eds.), *Novas contribuições metapsicológicas à clínica psicanalítica* [New metapsichological contributions to the psychoanalytical practice] (pp. 55-71). Taubaté, Brazil: Cabral Editora.

Coelho, N., Jr. (2003). Trauma, cisão e simultaneidade [Trauma, splitting and simulataneity]. *Tempo Psicanalítico*, *35*, 75-91.

Coelho, N., Jr., & Carmo, P. S. (1992). *Merleau-Ponty: Filosofia como corpo e existência* [Merleau-Ponty: Philosophy as body and existence]. São Paulo, Brazil: Escuta.

Coelho, N. E, Jr., & Figueiredo, L. C. (2003). Patterns of intersubjectivity in the constitution of subjectivity: Dimensions of otherness. *Culture and Psychology*, *9*(3), 193-208.

Figueiredo, L. C. (1992). *A invenção do psicológico: Quatro séculos de subjetivação (1500-1900)*. [The invention of the psychological: Four centuries of subjectivity (1500-1900)]. São Paulo, Brazil: EDUC/Escuta.

Lalande, A. (1956). *Vocabulaire technique et critique de la philosophie*. [Technical and critical vocabulary of philosophy]. Paris: P.U.F.

Lévinas. E. (1961). *Totalité et infini* [Totality and infinity]. La Haye, Netherlands: Martinus Nijhoff.

Merleau-Ponty, M. (1961). *L'Oeil e l'esprit* [Eye and mind]. Paris: Gallimard.

Pirandello, L. (1992) *One, no one, one hundred thousand* (William Weaver, Trans). New York: Marsilio. (Original work published 1926)

Silveira, F. M. (1999). Sou aquele por quem me tomam [I am whoever they take me for]. In J. Guinsburg (Ed.), *Do teatro no teatro* [*Of theater in the theater*] (p. 35). São Paulo, Brazil: Perspectiva.

ALLUSION AND ILLUSIONS

Dynamics of Self and Otherness:
A Commentary

Nandita Chaudhary

If we accept human psyche as being primarily relational, communicative and contextual (Salgado, this volume), it becomes important to explore vital features of social life for the study of otherness. The discussion of social experiences, real or imagined, is likely to assist in unravelling the mystery of the self and the significance of the other. Alterity, the quality of being different, and sameness, the quality of being similar, are two sides of the same feature. The defining features of sameness often become the reasons for constructing alterity or otherness. This complementarity is important to recognize, since it is the presence of one that creates the idea of the other. Without sameness, there would be no "other" and vice versa. In these discussions, it will become important to reference the practical and the theoretical, functional as well as structural and personal as well as social dimensions of human activity. This commentary dwells on such issues that have emerged from the reading of chapters of Salgado, Coelho, and Abbey

Otherness in Question: Labyrinths of the Self, 107–121
Copyright © 2007 by Information Age Publishing

(this volume) as well as ensuing interviews and discussions with the authors on selected ideas.

ALTERITY AND THE LIFE-SPAN:
AUTONOMOUS INFANTS AND INTERDEPENDENT ELDERS?

Within the life span of every individual, sociality undergoes many changes. The relationships that we encounter (infant-mother, child-adult, adult-child, others) provide us with a range of possibilities with reference to self-other dynamics, in terms of interpersonal distance and intersubjectivity. The sense of having another person within the life space is essential for the emergence of subjectivity because it is an "inclusive" otherness that characterizes human psychological processes (Coelho & Figueiredo, 2003). It is not just knowledge of the self, but also knowledge itself that can be attributed to the human capacity for alterity (Mead, 1913), thereby engaging in reflexive dialogue with the self about the social world, self and otherness. This understanding develops through childhood with increasing awareness of others and a corresponding emergence of the self.

In all societies, the young infant is in the physical care of an adult, deeply dependent on her for survival. Although we find much variety in the structural arrangements of care, nurturing is an essential component. For instance, autonomy for the young baby, whether it is being able to sleep alone or soothe oneself, can only function within a limited range of settings with conditions like temperature control, safety devices, and soothers; otherwise, being away from an adult in early infancy can even be fatal. Some other questions also arise when we think of children: What characterizes the self-other immersion of a newborn? What about the adult in this relationship (with a newborn), what does it mean to be a mother or father of a young baby? How does alterity express itself in such situations? What about old age? Is it not true that the older person also would not survive without the support of others, whether these are members of the family or commune, or state health care facilities? Perhaps the difference between the dependence of the young baby versus that of an old person is precisely the knowledge of "otherness."

These age-related changes in alterity have generated much academic interest. Research efforts have been devoted to issues like autobiographical memory, attachment, individuation, egocentrism, infant amnesia, and more recently, theory of mind. In a nutshell, the baby has no sense of self, or paradoxically, has *only* a self, not even a sense of it. The body is everything, full blown solipsism, since it is not even aware of its self-centered-ness. The young child, Piaget tells us is not only self-oriented, but incapable of apprehending "otherness"; so dominant is the experience of the self. More recently, some of these claims have been questioned and intersubjectivity and responsiveness to another person have been discov-ered even in young infants, termed as primary intersubjectivity (Tre-varthen, 1993). The theory of mind research displays that the young child under 3 years of age does not have the realization that other people *have* a mind, just as themselves; a feat easily accomplished a year or two later. As we grow, we soon discover the quality of otherness and gradually we become aware of the degree and extent of alterity, even becoming capable of manipulating interpersonal distance and reflecting on the history of the self (see Abbey, this volume). However, most research on intersubjec-tivity is based on democratically organized relationships (Moghaddam, 2003), where awareness that others have the "same" kind of a mind may indeed be a culturally bound notion. It would be interesting to see if there are different degrees of awareness and knowledge that become attributed to putatively wiser categories of people like "elders," "parents" or even "god." In such situations, it may be possible to find a differently organized "theory of mind," perhaps one that is vertically organized. It seems possi-ble that the reverence that is expected in hierarchical societies may bal-ance on just such a belief.

To return to self-other study, the life span of an individual displays the cyclical journey from complete ignorance of the self and self-absorption as a newborn (and the corresponding dependence on another person) to the gradual awareness of otherness and intersubjectivity corresponding with separation-individuation. This pattern is universal, although the pathways chosen by communities may be rather divergent. Childhood is spent in learning and becoming aware of the self and adulthood perhaps in learning to live with others, whereas in old age, it seems that learning to live without others becomes key to happiness, at least in some societies.

The role of the other seems to be most intense and critical for sur-vival when there is least awareness; perhaps this is not coincidental. Gradually, awareness and interpersonal distance intersect as the child matures into adulthood. The difficulty of many older people may also be linked with the intersection of these two dimensions, where there is awareness of the "other," but survival depends on assistance from other people or institutions. In general, the provenance of alterity is sup-ported by the emergence of autonomy, although the relative degree to which these tendencies will be sustained is canalized by cultural con-straints.

Composite Selves and Group Identities

In order to fully explicate otherness, the self needs to be clarified. The notion of the self has received much attention from various fields of study. We find that science has often attempted to downsize human beings, either speaking about humans as a "gaggle of genes with their own selfish needs" (Achenbach, 2005a, p. 5), or a small detail in the cosmic scheme. More recently, we find that "Most of our cells aren't even human. If you had to count all the cells in your body, the vast majority—by a factor of ten—would be microbes. They're everywhere ... magnified they look like horror-movie monsters," we are a synthesis of species rather than a single organism; raising an interesting question about what it means to be "human" (Achenbach, p. 5).

At a psychological level, a person is believed to be a collection of selves created from the consolidation of perspectives gained in interaction with others. Going beyond the subject/object divide, the self can be construed as a fusion of intersubjective experience. During social encounters, interpersonal experiences force us to think intrapsychically (Coelho & Figueiredo, 2003) and we realize our own sense of self. The behavior of the subject toward others and the social meanings produced by such interactions are formative in the making of the sense of self (Mead, 1978). At the outset, the presentation of the social world takes place through the guided activity between an adult and child, rather than as a "trans-subjective" otherness (Coelho & Figueiredo, 2003, p. 203) that appears later in life. The social play of the "other" becoming *part of* the self and of the "self" becoming *other to* the self creates intrapsychic "dialogicality" and the formation of what Hermans (2001) calls the "dialogical" self.

Another dimension of otherness is the capacity for the formation of groups with a common identity. It is said that animals have a prewired ability to recognize others, especially their own kin. For instance, a sheep can remember 50 other sheep faces for more than 2 years (Achenbach, 2005b). Among humans, beliefs in group distinctiveness has cohered and divided people so intensely that the dynamics of social distancing is a matter of serious concern in social psychology and other disciplines. We are capable of creating groupings of human "kinds" that are "results of unspoken contracts between fickle minds and changeful reality," making human groupings highly mutable. We constantly "project our urges onto what we see" (Gee, 2005, p. 76). On occasion, affiliation with group identity can even become strong enough to dissolve a sense of self, resulting in overidentification with a group or a cause. Perhaps this is an instance of the "other" completely eclipsing the self. This can be displayed as an arrangement of two extreme possibilities, one of the self as all powerful, as in the notion of divinity or royalty, and the other end of a self that is completely consumed by the "sense" of another. It is critical to understand here, that in both instances, the other (or the self) still always exists. On account of the complementarity, the one cannot exist without the other, however insignificant it may be.

Some experiments have displayed the fundamentally divisive (and therefore also internally cohesive) tendencies in human beings, even young children (see A Class Divided, Public Broadcasting Service, n.d). Social dynamics among groups can also be seen to display similar principles of interpersonal relationships: primacy, communication, alterity, and contextuality (Salgado, this volume). Likewise, activity can also be visualized between a group and an individual. One can argue that individuals actually "create" societies by imagining them; ideology therefore, is an essential element of sociality (Kavanagh, 1990). A society becomes possible only because people carry around the image of such a grouping in their heads, a group toward which they carry an affiliation. In this regard, the introduction of the concept of "inter-objectivity" becomes pertinent.

There is a predominance of individual-orientation in discussions of otherness, at the expense of the shared understanding of social reality through dialogues within and between cultures where collective (rather than inter and intrapersonal) manifestations of social processes are addressed (Moghaddam, 2003). Dealing with power relations and social dynamics, Moghaddam proceeds to argue that the construct of intersubjectivity is based on misplaced assumptions of equality in social relations between and within groups. People's ideas about each other will be critically shaped by power relations between and within groups into "collaboratively constructed worlds outside individuals" (p. 230). It is the practical engagement with collectivity that orients the individual toward patterns of understanding otherness rather than the other way around.

Prevalent ideologies will therefore influence group dynamics and interobjectivity and thereby also influence patterns of intersubjectivity. Where individualism is central to personal organization, it would also be manifested in the construction of group identity. In fact this has been found to be so. In Western society, people from non-Western societies are often believed to be lacking the vital personal attributes of self-control and individual autonomy by Westerners (Said, 1978). Similar attributions are also ascribed to women (Glick & Fiske, 1996), children and mentally ill people (Jodelet, 1991). In these beliefs, marked overtones of a cultural inter-objectivity can be discerned. Cultural priorities thus become important defining labels for in-group membership and out-group distancing.

Alterity of Language and Language of Alterity

Language is a medium through which reality is constructed and not just discovered (Rowe, 1990). Through participation in language activity, the sense of self is juxtaposed with responses from others to create a "double attitude" that of the actor and the observer through "reflective consciousness" caused by self-appraisal; become the "other" to oneself (Gillespie, 2003, p. 218). Further confounding is supplied by the quality of language to correspondingly simplify and complicate matters of the mind.

Languages of the world display intricate taxonomy for social activity, using names, pronouns, kin terms, endearments, and other words to talk about themselves and others. It is important to understand that selfhood becomes constructed around factors that maybe technically "outside of oneself" (Chaudhary, 2003, p. 473) and therefore speech patterns of any community would exhibit prevalent patterns of interpersonal sociality. For person references, there are powerful strategies which facilitate the manipulation of responsibility, power and authority, perspective-taking, and indexing in conversations. As in the instance of pronouns, their "incurable subjectivity" (Buehler, 1990, p. 123) makes them particularly effective as conversational tools due to the flexibility that they provide. Person talk is especially designed for manipulations of perspective, permitting ambiguity or objectivity as required. It facilitates the variety that human conduct needs to survive the stipulations of collective living and interpersonal dynamics. The tasks of intersubjectivity as well as interobjectivity, both become facilitated by speech and other forms of symbolic activity, and can therefore prove to be a commanding source for unraveling self-other relations. Talk about other people, the forms of address used, or socialization patterns for language use would exhibit the implicit beliefs about otherness and also of the self.

Terminology of "otherness" has also been linked with group identity, within group cohesiveness and out-group distancing as we noted in the previous section. There is also a link with language here. For social phenomena, it makes little sense to define terms "as such," since these terms would refer to a relationship rather than the thing itself (Sollers, 1990, p. 288). A term like "ethnicity" is based on contrast, since if all humanity belonged to one ethnic group, there would be no need to differentiate within humanity. This is what Devereux (1975, p. 67) calls "dissociative character" where membership to one group would be defined by non-membership with another. In this manner, symbolic boundaries and ethnic contrasts are created that subsequently become rationalized as "reasonable" arguments for social cohesion, personal affinity, or social distancing.

Dealing with "other cultures" has often relied on the use of symbols or labels that have helped to perpetuate imperialism. For instance, wearing the *burqa* has become symbolic for Muslim women's subjugation in the eyes of Western society (Abu-Lughod, 2002) thereby reducing diverse circumstances and attitudes to a single item of clothing as the defining feature of the cultural "other" (p. 186). In colonial times in India, the British justified colonial rule and administrative reform on the basis of ethnic practices of local people; the White men attempted to release the "brown women" from "brown men" (Spivak, 1988).

Interestingly, the term ethnicity is derived from the Greek word "ethnos" which has two meanings, the inclusive one that means "people in general" and the exclusive one that means "other people." Interestingly, ethnicity was an obsolete word that was reintroduced as a more neutral term instead of "race" during World War II since the latter had become the label of oppression. Race too has both meanings like ethnicity, implying both "our race" and "that race" (Sollers, 1990).

Literary Otherness

The use of language for literary purposes is yet another domain for exploring the construction of self-other dynamics. Like the character Funes, created by Borges (1993/1962) who was capable of seeing everything as unique and therefore unable to objectify his experiences. Being unable to classify his encounters, Funes was completely unable to make any sense of the world. Vicarious participation in "otherness" characterizes human interactions from childhood onwards, whether it is pretend play, theater, or literary pursuits. Perhaps these illustrations allow us to develop characters in unconstrained directions inaccessible in real life or academic pursuit. In fiction, a harmonious relationship can be terminated, a dying person can be revived, and the very essence of alterity can be created out of nothing or destroyed beyond recognition. As a literary device, such an instrument allows the poet, writer, or even the artist to transform an outcome, thereby reaching out to the audience with imagined selves and fictitious others that often come close enough to real people and plausible outcomes to make the novel a story of (and for) the self (Nair, 2002). In the following poem, we are able to capture the psychological schism of a young woman who is confronted with her own "otherness" in a rather disturbing mirror image. Figuratively, one is able to apprehend the corresponding duality (or multiplicity) of the psyche.

The Virgin

by Amrita Pritam

When I moved into your bed
I was not alone-there were
two of us
A married woman and a virgin
To sleep with you
I had to offer the virgin in
me
I did so
This slaughter is permissible
in law
Not the indignity of it
And I bore the onslaught of
the insult
The next morning
I looked at my blood stained
hands
I washed my hands
But the moment I stood
before the mirror
I found her standing there
The one whom I thought I
had slaughtered last night
Oh God!
Was it too dark in your bed
I had to kill one and I killed
the other?

—*translated from the original Punjabi by Kartar Singh Duggal* (Pritam, n.d.)

Culture, Self, and Otherness

The search for solutions for otherness (and therefore the self) are not limited to fields of philosophy, psychology, and cultural studies. From ancient times, humans have attempted to unravel the mystery of existence, individuality, and social relationships. Often, the notion of the supernatural or divine has assisted in reducing uncertainty and fear and assuring people of beliefs about the self. Cultural patterns of sociality assist in organizing ideal "pathways" for development of personal relationships providing reassuring familiarity and comforting constraints for the otherwise unknown life course.

In the Indian family, for instance, one can find resonance of the traditional notions of collectivity in the understanding of self-other relations. It is "incorporation" of the group by the individual, as well as the individual by the group, rather than simple identification that prevails. The absence of family is often marked as a source of distress for an average Indian. In the case of childhood, for instance, the "embeddedness of children within the group" is an important feature of social life of Indians (Raman, 2003, p. 90). Family life and vertical heterogeneity is the norm in social situations. Even young people spend far more time with the family in India than in other countries (Saraswathi, 1999; Verma & Saraswathi, 2002; Verma & Sharma, 2003). Continuity between childhood and adulthood (Kumar, 1993), participation, presence, and significance of other people, the value of externality and sociality rather than inwardness, characterizes Indian communities. A child and the family are not merely associated by resemblance; the child's ego is constituted through being contained within the group. The child has a sense of his action taken on behalf of or even by the group contained within him. There is a simultaneous "encompassing and a sense of being encompassed" (Kurtz, 1992, p. 103). The group, and more importantly the family, is thus primary in the consolidation of the individual sense of self of a child (Roland, 1988).

Dumont also talks of the issue of "containing and being contained by" others as constituting principles of hierarchy in the Indian context (Dumont, 1980), as does Trawick (1990). There is comfort in the belief that the self contains the "other" in the self-structure, just as the individual is embedded into the family system, others are carried within them (Trawick, 2003).

Divinity, Self, and Otherness

I will now proceed to a rather contentious area in the enquiry into otherness, the discussion of divinity. The idea of a god is perhaps the equivalent of a theoretical construction of a self (or other, depending on which religion one is talking about) that is all-encompassing, omniscient. The boundaries of alterity are really put to test when we speculate about something/someone containing everything and everyone else. I will take the examples of Buddhism and Hinduism to reveal that attempts to understand otherness are as ancient as humanity itself.

Buddhism, which is recently being understood more as a philosophy "or a form of psychology" primarily because there is no notion of a supreme being, is nondogmatic, and urges people to understand the true nature of reality by empirical verification rather than belief (Garfinkel, 2005, p. 98). One of the primary teachings of the Buddha focussed on a single clause of the human proclivity: that of forming attachments, with other people, with things, places, and so on. These attachments are believed to be illusory and predispose a person to sorrow. *Vipassana* the "mindful" form of meditation through insight is basically oriented toward self-reflection on issues like "Who am I? Why am I here?" and the gradual realization of the transient nature of reality (Garfinkel, p. 99).

In this regard, the idea of the "no-self" (as in Buddhism), or the inclusion of the "self" in the other or "other" in the self (as in Hinduism) cannot be attributed simply to the ideology of "collectivism"; it is perhaps more fitting to recognize it as a "spiritual" belief in the inclusion of others in the self and vice versa as belonging to humanity (Chaudhary, 2004). Perhaps the construct of *advaita* or collective personhood in Hindu thinking may help to understand the particular essence of collectivity implied here. The notion of *advaita* is a nondualistic belief in the existence of eternal *brahman*, the source of everything and the *atman* or the unchanging consciousness of the self, which is manifestation of the quality of the eternal (Rajagopalachari, 1951/1999).

In the ancient Hindu epic, *Mahabharata*, we read that Lord Krishna urges Arjuna to take up arms against his own cousins for the fight against evil with a distinguished sermon, the *Bhagavadgita*. Selected extracts from the *Gita* display the profound speculations of existence that are attempted:

> Perceive the same self abiding in every being, and all beings abiding in the self. (Bhalla, p. 19)

In another source,

> I am the father and mother of this universe, and its grandfather too; I am its entire support. I am the sum of all knowledge, the purifier ... I am the goal of life, the Lord and support of all, the inner witness, the abode of all. I am the only refuge, the one true friend; I am the beginning, the staying, and the end of creation; I am the womb and the eternal seed. I am heat; I give and withhold the rain. I am immortality and I am death; I am what is and what is not. (Easwaran, 1985, p. 53)

It is important to recognise that the idea of divinity, god (or guru) may be created and sustained by the need to *look up to* someone or something in certain moments of one's life (see Abbey, this volume). This might seem rather unfamiliar to cultural minds that are dominated by the ideology of democracy, freedom, and equality; but there are parts of the world where inequality (not necessarily in subjugating), hierarchy (not necessarily dominating) and admiration (not necessarily uncritical) are inescapable elements of interobjectivity.

In Buddhist philosophy, the state of *anatta* or nonself is what characterizes human life. The five basic properties of this nonself which are
believed to be essentially changing are feeling, corporeality, consciousness, perception, and mental formations (including volition or will).
Whereas (unlike Hinduism from which Buddhism has emerged) the existence of a permanent selfhood and soul is denied, a person is believed to
be transformed at every moment. Holding on to any one of the five qualities is believed to be the source of suffering for humanity, since any one or
a combination of these five elements can be mistaken as the self (Giles,
1993). Further,

> In Buddhism, the consciousness that arises at conception is not the same as
> the consciousness of the individual at death but nor it is totally different. It
> is best to see the movement from this life to the next as a continuum rather
> than the passage of one self-contained essence into a new body. There is no
> transference of a permanent self as there is no permanent self. It's not that
> Buddhism denies the obvious fact that we, as individuals, exist. We exist, yes,
> but not in the way we think. (Flanagan, n.d.)

However, this must not be treated as a scholarly analysis of Buddhism or
Hinduism. The religions are adduced for the primary purpose of display
and discussion on the theory of self. As a matter of fact, many parallels
can be seen between Buddhism and Hume's theory of the fictitious identity (Giles, 1993). Both sources state that words like "self" and "I" are just
grammatical devices and one must not be confused into believing in the
existence of such a quality. Self-ness is challenged on the basis of "imper-
manence." Conventional referents for the self, names, pronouns, endearments, Buddhism believes, are accountable for the mistaken assumption
in a substantial entity. Indeed, introspection leads us to one of the elements or combinations thereof, the language of the self, in other words
"leads to its fabrication" (Giles, p. 197). This is the beginning of a lifelong journey of self-delusion and Buddhism promotes the discard of self-
oriented emotions like pride, envy, embarrassment, and humility through
meditation, during which the internal self is believed to become apparent. The principles of Buddhism advocate that the potentiality of enlightenment is contained in all living beings, "look within, thou are Buddha"
(Humphreys, 2005). Unlike the older Hindu belief in an essential soul or
atman which transcends lives in the ultimate path to salvation, Buddhism
denies such a belief.

This would be a disconcerting notion for those of us who have come to
believe in the self as a separate entity. However, we find the challenge of
just such a belief in Buddhism. The notion of the noself is quite distinct
from the idea of a reduced self where mental phenomena are merely com-
pacted to physical ones. Buddhist notion of the self is "eliminative" rather

than "reductive" (Giles, 1993, p.175). The project in Buddhism is phenomenological, without making any attempt to defend the existence of a personal identity on the assertion that the belief in something does not vindicate its existence. Hume too challenges such a belief in his writing. We also, claims Hume, do not have simplicity or even identity that is consistent; "the self or person is not any one impression, but that to which our several impressions and ideas are *supposed* to have reference" (Hume, 1978, p. 251, emphasis mine). Identity is according to him a fictitious construct.

Traveling through science and scepticism, faith, and fable, we find ourselves perhaps still searching for answers. Having been reared in a tradition where storytelling carries much influence, I find this a fortuitous moment to narrate one myself. This was a favorite tale of Sage Ramana Maharishi (1879-1950) when he approached the subject of the self with his disciples. The story itself is from the ancient mythological texts the *Puranas*, believed to have been completed by 500 A.D.

The Story of Ribhu

In the ancient Puranic texts, the story goes of a man, Nidagha who was a true disciple of sage Ribhu. The sage loved his disciple dearly, but Nigadha was not fully convinced of the path of wisdom and returned to his village for a life of ritual, service and ceremony. The sage kept a vigil on his disciple to observe his spiritual progress away from ritualism through visits, often in disguise. One day, dressed as a village rustic, Ribhu encountered Nidagha watching a royal procession. Unknown to him, his guru asked him what all the fuss was about. "The king's procession is passing," he informed the village lad. "Which one is the king?" The villager questioned. "Oh there, on the elephant" came the reply. "But which is the king and which, the elephant?" he persisted. "The king is the one above and the elephant is the one below of course, you fool!" But the queries did not end. "What is above and below?" Annoyed at the stupidity of the question, Nidagha then proceeded to teach the ignorant man a lesson.

"You see the king and the elephant, the one above and the other below. Yet you want to know what is meant by 'above' and 'below' " burst the angry Nidagha. "If things seen and words spoken can convey so little to you, action alone can teach you. Bend forward, and you will know it all too well." The rustic did as he was told. Nidagha got on to his shoulders and said: "Know it now! I am above as the king, you are below as the elephant. Is that clear enough?" Persisting in his apparent ignorance, the sage in disguise quietly replied, "No, not yet. You say you are above like the king, and I am below like the elephant. The 'king,' the 'elephant,' 'above' and 'below'—so far it is clear. But pray, tell me what you mean by 'I' and 'you'?"

Nigadha was quickly wrenched from his confidence and realized that this was in fact his guru before him, attempting for him to finally see the true nature of the "Self" (Anonymous, n.d.).

Is there something that we can learn from this passage? Is it possible that self and otherness is *designed* to be a fluctuating complementarity, thereby making it impossible to define according to any particular arrangement? This flexible alternation of self and other in different relationships over the developmental span, as well as those which are created in the imaginings of lovers and novelists may be the critical quality of intersubjectivity. Maybe the one thing we can conclude about self and otherness is that we cannot; since it will remain an eternally fluid arrangement of complementarity.

This elasticity will allow human beings to become learned men or their followers, devoted mothers or unknowing babies, leaders of countries or ordinary people, poets, or lovers.

REFERENCES

Abu-Lughod, L. (2002). Do Muslim women really need saving? Anthropological reflections on cultural relativism and its others. *American Anthropologist, 104*(3), 783-790.

Achenbach, J. (2005a). Growing on you: Our bodies are crawling with microbes. *National Geographic, 208*(5), 5-6.

Achenbach, J. (2005b). You're one in a million to me. *National Geographic, 208*(6), 1.

Anonymous. (n.d.). *The story of Ribhu: Spiritual stories as told by Ramana Maharishi.* (Published with permission of his nephew V. Ganeshan). Retrieved November 20, 2005, from http://sentient.org/story2.html.

Bhalla, H. (n.d.) *The Bhagvad-Gita.* Retrieved November 20, 2005, from http://www.hinduwebsite.com/chapters.asp

Borges, J. L. (1993). Funes, the *memorious.* In J. Sturrock (Ed.), *Ficciones* (pp. 83-91). New York: Alfred A. Knopf/Everyman. (Original work published 1962)

Buehler, K. (1990). *Theory of language: The representational function of language.* Philadelphia: John Benjamins.

Chaudhary, N. (2003). Speaking the self into becoming. *Culture and Psychology, 9*(4), 471-486.

Chaudhary, N. (2004). *Listening to culture.* New Delhi, India: Sage.

Coelho, N. E., & Figueiredo, L. C. (2003). Patterns of intersubjectivity in the constitution of subjectivity: Dimensions of otherness. *Culture and Psychology, 9*(3), 193-208.

Devereux, G. (1975). Ethnic identity: Its logical foundations and its dysfunctions.

Dumont, L. (1980). *Homo Hierarchicus: The caste system and its implications*. Chicago: University of Chicago Press.

Easwaran, E. (1985). *The bhagvad gita*. Berkeley, CA: The Blue Mountain Centre of Meditation.

Flanagan, A. (n.d.). *Anatta—The teaching on the non-self.* Retrieved November 19, 2005, from http://buddhism.about.com/library/weekly/aa070702a.htm

Garfinkel, P. (2005, December). Buddha rising. *National Geographic, 208*(6), 88-109.

Gee, H. (2005). Tricky, turbulent, tribal: Friend or foe is a mutable designation. (A review of Us and them: Understanding your tribal mind by David Berreby). *Scientific American, 1*(7), 76-77.

Giles, J. (1993). The no-self theory: Hume, Buddhism and personal identity. *Philosophy, East and West, 43*(2), 175-200.

Gillespie, A. (2003). Supplementarity and surplus: Moving between the dimensions of otherness. *Culture and Psychology, 9*(3), 209-220.

Glick, P., & Fiske, S.T. (1996). The ambivalent sexism inventory: Differentiating hostile and benevolent sexism. *Journal of Personality and Social Psychology, 70*, 491-512.

Hermans, H. H. (2001). The dialogical self: Towards a theory of personal and cultural positioning. *Culture and Psychology, 7*(3), 243-281.

Hume, D. (1978). *A treatise of human nature*. Oxford, England: Clarendon Press.

Humphreys, C. (2005). *Twelve principles of Buddhism*. Retrieved November 20, 2005, from http://www.budtempchi.org/12prin.html

Jodelet, D. (1991). *Madness and social representations*. Hertfordshire, England: Harvester-Wheatsheaf.

Kavanagh, J. H. (1990). Ideology. In F. Lentricchia & T. McLaughlin (Eds.), *Critical terms for literary study* (pp. 306-320). Chicago: University of Chicago Press.

Kumar, K. (1993). Study of childhood and family. In T. S. Saraswathi & B. Kaur (Eds.), *Human development and family studies in India: An agenda for research and policy* (pp. 67-76). New Delhi, India: Sage.

Kurtz, S. N. (1992). *All the mothers are one: Hindu India and the cultural reshaping of psychoanalysis*. New York: Columbia University Press.

Mead, G. H. (1913). The social self. *Journal of Philosophy, 10*, 374-380.

Mead, G. H. (1978). What social objects must psychology presuppose? In T. Luckmann (Ed.), *Phenomenology and sociology*. Harmondsworth: Penguin. (Original work published in 1910)

Moghaddam, F. M. (2003). Interobjectivity and culture. *Culture and Psychology, 9*(3), 221-233.

Nair, R. B. (2002). *Narrative gravity: Conversation, cognition, culture*. New Delhi, India: Oxford University Press.

Pritam, A. (n.d.) *The Virgin*. Retrieved November 22, 2005, from http://www.foundationsaarcwriters.com/indiawriter4.html

Public Broadcasting System. (n.d.). *Frontline: A class divided*. Retrieved November 21, 2005.

Rajagopalachari, C. (1999). *Mahabharata* (36th ed.). Bombay, India: Bharatiya Vidya Bhavan. (Original work published 1951)

Raman, V. (2003). The diverse life-worlds of Indian childhood. In M. Pernau, I. Ahmad, & H. Reifeld (Eds.), *Family and gender: Changing values in Germany and India* (pp. 84-111). New Delhi, India: Sage.

Roland, A. (1988). *In search of the self in India and Japan*. Princeton, NJ: Princeton University Press.

Rowe, J. C. (1990). Structure. In F. Lentricchia & T. McLaughlin (Eds.), *Critical terms for literary study* (pp. 23-38). Chicago: University of Chicago Press.

Saraswathi, T. S. (1999). Adult-child continuity in India: Is adolescence a myth or an emerging reality? In T. S. Saraswathi (Ed.), *Culture, socialization and human development: Theory, research and applications in India* (pp. 213-232). New Delhi: Sage.

Sollers, W. (1990). Ethnicity. In F. Lentricchia & T. McLaghlin (Eds.), *Critical terms for literary study* (pp. 288 -305). Chicago: University of Chicago Press.

Trawick, M. (1990). *Notes on love in a Tamil family*. Berkeley: University of California Press.

Trawick, M. (2003). The person behind the family. In V. Das (Ed.), *The Oxford companion to sociology and social anthropology* (Vol. 2, pp. 1158-1178). New Delhi, India: Oxford University Press.

Trevarthen, C. (1993). The self born in intersubjectivity: An infant communicating. In U. Neisser (Ed.), *The perceived self: Ecological and interpersonal knowledge of the self* (pp. 121-173). New York: Cambridge University Press.

Said, E. W. (1978). *Orientalism: Western conceptions of the orient*. London: Penguin.

Spivak, G. C. (1988). Can the subaltern speak? In C. Nelson & L. Grossberg (Eds.), *Marxism and the interpretation of culture* (pp. 271-313). Urbana: University of Illinois Press.

Verma, S., & Saraswathi, T. S. (2002). Adolescence in India: Street children or Silicon Valley millionaires. In B. B. Brown, R. W. Larson, & T. S. Saraswathi (Eds.), *The world's youth: Adolescence in eight regions of the globe* (pp. 105-140). Oxford, England: Cambridge University Press.

Verma, S., & Sharma, D. (2003). Cultural continuity amid social change: Adolescents' use of free time in India. In S. Verma & R. Larson (Eds.), *Examining adolescent leisure time across cultures* (pp. 37-51). San Francisco: Jossey-Boss.

Part III

STRIVING TOWARD THE KNOWN UNKOWN:
SELF IN MOTION

CHAPTER 6

OTHERNESS IN THE THERAPEUTIC CONTEXT

The Social Construction of Change

Marisa Japur, Carla Guanaes, and Emerson F. Rasera

Our experience on reflecting about the implications of social constructionist assumptions for the theory and practice of group therapy has motivated us to write this text in six hands. During our meetings to define the
argument to be developed, we searched for convergence. Up to that
point, to talk about the diversity over tense questions had been attractive.
Tension came from the interest in keeping dialogue with different constructionist authors bearing distinct perspectives and emphasis. The new
context invited us to search for commonalities and it turned out to be a
challenge bigger that we had imagined.

Considering social constructionism a useful discursive option
(McNamee, 2004) to the understanding of the realities constructed in
conversation, in prior research[1] we attempted to build up resources for
the analysis of the dialogical process in therapeutic groups. In this
chapter we will attempt, more specifically, to give visibility to the process of social construction of change in the therapeutic context, by ana-

lyzing conversations of two different groups (Guanaes, 2006; Rasera, 2004).

We will start by pointing our understanding of the implications of social constructionist perspectives for the emergence of an alternative description of otherness in this intelligibility field. We will be in dialogue with authors who are familiar to us (Gergen, 1985, 1989, 1992, 1997; Harré & Gillet, 1994; Harré & van GillLangenhove, 1999; McNamee, 2004; McNamee & Gergen, 1995, 1999; Shotter, 1993, 2000, 2003; Spink, 1999), but their proposals will not be inserted here with the complexity they have. It is just an invitation to the production of a shared intelligibility around positions that we take in analyses of conversational processes.

OTHERNESS AND ALTERNATIVE DESCRIPTIONS OF SELF

Based on the questioning of modern tradition in Western culture, contemporary contributions to the understanding of psychological phenomenon have favored the emergence of another epistemological approach. Like social constructionism, these contributions point to a relational view of the making sense process.

According to social constructionist perspective, language is a social practice that constructs our realities. This understanding draws our attention to language in use and emphasizes the social and historical character of making sense process. It focuses the language and not the mind, as well as the relationship and not the self. Some social constructionist versions[2] privilege the microsocial processes of conversation in the construction of the realities in which we live, and it is with these versions that we will be in dialogue.

Taking the Bakhtinian conception of dialogism (Bakhtin, 1984, 1986; Volosinov, 1973), different versions of social constructionism comprehend that utterances gain their meaning in the dialogue among interlocutors and other countless social voices. These utterances are always developed in response to previous ones, within the continuous flow of human communication. Thus, utterances are also referred to the dialogue among different social discourses available in our culture.

In this language conception, the person does not make sense alone (Gergen, 1997). It is always in a relationship with other(s) that the process of making sense takes place. It is only when there is a supplementation act that meaning becomes possible. The supplementation act enlarges the utterance, by assuring a meaning potential in a certain direction; and, at the same time, it constrains its potential, limiting other meaning possibilities. The supplement is also subject to further supplementation from the other, and then successively in the continuous process of human communication. Therefore, we take both utterance and supplementation as actions, assuming the performative (and not the representational) character of language in use.

We understand that this relational view of the making sense process does not deny that the utterance has a meaning to whom enunciate its. It points, though, that possibility of making sense is created within the relationship, in the dialogue between voices: voices of whom enunciates, which are derived from participation in multiple relationships in his/her lived time; voices of the *present other* in the short time of the interaction; anticipated voices of the present other and its future implications; and still, broader social voices, inscribed in the long time of the cultural history, that create and constrain the possibilities of making sense in any relationship. These notions of *lived time, long time,* and *short time* were proposed by Spink (1999) to refer to historical dimensions of the making sense process. Rossetti-Ferreira, Amorin, and Silva (1999) added to this proposition the notion of *prospective time*.

Thus, the action supplement is a reciprocal process that takes place in the short time of interaction, but it is a process that remains related to a more complex chain of speech communication. It involves dialogues between voices of long-term cultural memory—meanings that gain stability through the social discourses in which we are immersed. Also, it involves dialogues between voices of the emotional memory from the lived time—meanings in constant (re)construction, whose stability or change depends on our participation in multiple domains of action-supplementation, shaping us in every moment (Spink, 1999).

People live immersed in conversational forms of one culture and when they talk they take part in a (verbal and nonverbal) language system, sharing it. At the same time, it is in the *embodied use of language* (Shotter, 2000), from the within the relationship that their actions make sense. In other words, this way of understanding language question the conception that words can mean what people want. Meaning is an action that always involves others (in concrete or imaginary relationships). Thus, not only the relational, but also the unpredictable and non-intentional character of the conversational process is highlighted (Shotter, 2003). This questions the notion of the self as the only author of the making sense process and of the person as the locus of it.

In our point of view, this idea also questions the external character of the relationship I-other, usually referred to as two distinct and separate units. What social constructionist's emphasis on language in use suggests is the constructive power of the relationship I-other, within which descriptions of self and other are created. The social constructionist notion of self doesn't intend to be an ontological explanation. As any other descriptions, it is circumscribed to processes of negotiation of meanings, which serve to certain purposes in social life. From this perspective, I and Other does not exist in themselves prior to the processes of social construction of the world that makes any meaning possible (Japur, 2004).

On the other hand, it is expected that, in Western culture, people have some sense of self. Our challenge, then, is to understand this based in a social constructionist view. In Gergen's work, the self is considered a discourse from two distinct perspectives: (a) as a vocabulary social-historically situated and (b) as narrative forms that support certain relationships (Rasera, Guanaes, & Japur, 2004).

In the first perspective, Gergen (1992) analyzes the social-historical conditions that enabled the appearance of the modern discourse of the self (individual, unitary, coherent, stable); and, also, the emergence, in the so-called postmodern culture, of the relational view of the person. This invites an understanding of the self as a discourse, "as the intersection of multiple relationships, local and immediate manifestation of relational histories" (McNamee & Gergen, 1999, p. 22). As a discourse, its legitimacy is not referred to the truth of an essential self, but to the social processes of negotiation of meanings, through which certain versions prevail over others. That is, the legitimacy of the discourses of self is derivative of its maintenance in the social network that gives them a sense of reality as they become consensual.

In the second perspective, Gergen (1997) no longer considers the relation between social discourses about the self, but the pragmatics of self-narratives, analyzing it as a conversational construction, as a linguistic resource that we use in social life to raise, to widen, to limit, or to constrain certain actions/descriptions of self and other. This focus on the pragmatics of self-narratives, shifts our attention from ontological descriptions and points to the discursive processes of construction, maintenance or change of the self and their implications. Described this way, the self is always multiple—descriptions made possible in the interactive moment, and related to the short, lived, long, and prospective time. Thus, self can be considered as the capacity to language and narration, being defined in each moment of the interaction through the different ways in which people describe themselves (and are described by others) in their conversations (Guanaes & Japur, 2003).

In social life, both perspectives are articulated—the one of the self as a discourse and the one of the pragmatics of self-narratives. On giving a self description, the person highlights and articulates, in a specific way, fragments of multiple descriptions that momentarily constitute him/her. This description, created within the narrative conventions culturally available, turns itself into the self, for the person her/himself and for his/her conversational partners. A personal description gains a sense of reality when it is legitimated both by the culturally available discourses of self and the pragmatics of self-narratives in the context that it takes place.

Our cultural insertion in a tradition that shares a deep understanding of self as unitary, stable, and coherent, requests self descriptions to be organized in a temporal sequence and, usually, in a causal and coherent logic. If the descriptions-of-self do not obey the narrative conventions culturally available, they may not produce intelligibility and be dysfunctional in the relationships. In the modern discourse of self, this lack of intelligibility would be considered a symptom of the disorganization of the logical capacity of the person who gives this description. In the perspective of the relational self, the lack of intelligibility can only be considered as a conversational achievement of the relationship.

Finally, we want to consider that this view of the pragmatics of self-narratives also implies other descriptions of otherness. In the present text, otherness is described as: *other selves*—the multiplicity of potential self descriptions; *present others*—interlocutors present in the interactive moment of a conversational; *referred others*—those who are mentioned to by the interlocutors of a conversation. We understand that it is in the relationship with this multiple others that the self is socially constructed.

THE SOCIAL CONSTRUCTION OF CHANGE

To focus the change, in reference to a social constructionist discourse, is by no means an easy task due to the plurality of possible descriptions of it. It would also be contradictory to have a single description, through which we could define what change really is.

Along the reciprocal game of relationships, people go on creating certain identity versions, which are sustained by themselves and others in everyday life. The process of conversation (action-supplementation), always multiple, dynamic, and unpredictable, demands a continuous process of negotiation of these identity versions, once they are anchored in a network of reciprocating identities (Gergen, 1997). A self description also contains a certain identity version of the *present other.* When a person makes use of the actions of this *present other* to make his/her self description intelligible, the other person can or cannot agree with the description made of her/his actions. Thus, the sustenance or change of any self description depends on the negotiation made possible in the reciprocal game of the relationship.

In Gergen's words

> this reliance on others places the actor in a position of precarious interdependence, for in the same way that self-intelligibility depends on whether

others agree about their own place in the story, so their own identity depends on the actor's affirmation of them. An actor's success in sustaining a given self-narrative is fundamentally dependent on the willingness of others to play out parts in relationship to him.... Identities, in this sense, are never individual; each is suspended in an array of precariously situated relationships. (Gergen, 1997, p. 209)

As we understand it, the notion of a network of reciprocating identities enables the understanding of change as a social achievement of dialogue. Change involves a continuous process of (re)construction of meanings of world and self. And, based on Gergen assumptions, an alternative self description would also depend on the willingness of others to sustain it.

On the other hand, the discourses about psychotherapy in Western culture promote it as the proper context for the emergence of problems and self narratives. Maybe for this reason, the clinical practice, based on social constructionist, has also inspired a discourse about change as a specific conversational achievement. This has favored the emphasis on ways of talking in the therapeutic context and on the construction of alternative self-description and problems (Guanaes, 2004). It has also enabled the understanding of group therapy as a context which favors the questioning of meanings, the acceptance of indeterminacy and the comprehension that there is not a single and definitive personal history (Rasera & Japur, 2003).

Besides, self-descriptions always include identity versions of referred other(s) mentioned by the interlocutors in a conversation. The sustenance or change of these self descriptions will also depend on its intelligibility to the present-other. Typically, in the therapeutic context, the stories of problem involve not only the narrator's action but also the action of this referred other and, in many cases, it is the latter that vitally contributes to the description of the events as being problematic. Also, in a therapeutic group, some descriptions that are not described as a problem in a given narrative can be constructed as one, in the relationship with the *present other* (Rasera, 2004).

From this dialogical and discursive focus, the problem is considered a social construction, once it is described as such in local contexts and sustained by broader social discourses. That is, there are no problems outside the shared descriptions of problems. Thus, considering the constitutive power of our conversational realities, the descriptions of problems do cause suffering for those who organize their lives around them. As we see, the therapeutic context can promote conversations about self-descriptions and the expansion of its domains of supplementation, thus creating possibilities for change.

With these conceptual tools, we intend to broaden this dialogue by inserting moments of therapeutic conversations that took place in two distinct groups. In the first case (Guanaes, 2006), we will illustrate the importance of *present others* in the construction of Estela's change, by legitimating self-descriptions that were not dominant in the story first told by her in the group context. In the second (Rasera, 2004), we will illustrate how the change process of Pedro's self-description, coconstructed with the *present others* in the group, also changes the referred other's self-descriptions (his wife) in the events narrated by him. By doing this, we hope to contribute to the understanding of the process of change of self-descriptions as a social construction that takes place in a network of reciprocating identities negotiated in group therapy.

ESTELA'S CHANGE:
IMPLICATIONS TO THE PRESENT OTHERS IN THE GROUP

Aiming to illustrate the importance of otherness in the conversational construction of change, we will present an analysis of some interactive moments experienced by some participants in a support group offered in a mental health ambulatory in Ribeirão Preto (Brazil). This group had 16 weekly sessions of around an hour and a half each and was coordinated by a psychiatrist. The group consisted of 10 patients, who had different clinical diagnoses and history of psychiatric treatments.

For the purposes of this chapter, we will describe an analysis of the narratives coconstructed in the group about the problem presented by one of the participants (Estela). Our aim is to give visibility to the centrality of otherness of in the conversational construction of change, here conceived as the possibility of emergence and sustenance of alternative *self*-descriptions, *in* conversational exchanges among group participants. More specifically, we will focus on the participation of the group *present others* in Estela's narrative change, favoring the recognition and sustenance of other selves present in her narrative, which was not part of her prevailing discourse of self so far. By analyzing the net of reciprocating identities that was articulated in the group's conversational process, we intend to show how the relational construction and sustenance of some meanings of self, problem and change became possible to Estela and to the other participants in the group (Guanaes & Japur, 2005; Guanaes, 2006).

At first, we show a short description of Estela, aiming to contextualize her participation in the support group. Estela was 42 years old when she looked for the mental clinic for the first time. She was divorced, unemployed, and she was living with her daughter. She mentioned having thought about committing suicide when things did not work out well and she complained of tiredness, inaptitude, and weight loss. In this situation, she received a diagnosis for generalized anxiety and was invited to participate in the support group. It is interesting to point that Estela did not refer to these initial complaints during her participation in the group. However, in this context, Estela told the group part of her life story, emphasizing happenings and difficulties she had experienced in the past, instead of mentioning her complaints and symptoms.

Estela's verbal participation did not start until the sixth group session, when Ana Maria invites her to talk about her problems. This event takes place after a group discussion on "mental diseases," in which the participants tried to keep distance from the identity of mental ill people, through the alternative description of themselves as "people with difficulties in life."

In this context, Ana Maria invites Estela to talk about the "problem" that led her to look for treatment. Estela accepts the invitation and starts telling her personal story, after making sure that the group was a confidential and reliable setting. Thus, the construction of a story about the cause of her problem starts taking place in this relational setting.

Ana Maria:	This one probably doesn't have any problems isn't it, doctor? (poking Estela, seated on her left). She doesn't say a word!
Estela:	(speaking quietly) I'm waiting for the right day to say...
Therapist:	Wait for what... [...]
Ana Maria:	She said she was waiting for the right day to open her mouth. She already has, now it's just to go on! (She laughs)
Estela:	Yeah...
Therapist:	Do you have any problems?
Estela:	We do have problems, don't we? (Silence)
Therapist:	Isn't it like hers—that is to do different things
Estela:	Hein?
Therapist:	Isn't it like hers—that is to different things at the same time?
Estela:	No!
Terapeuta:	So, it's easier...
Estela:	hmm!... As you say, that we can open up, that nobody knows us here, everything, you know, and that we can tell our story, can't we?
Therapist:	Our talks belong to this group only.
Estela:	Maybe if I open up and tell what I've been through, I hope I'll feel better...
Therapist:	So do I...
Estela:	We have to know if there is enough time, don't we?

Therapist: There is plenty of time... (Session 6, p. 18, L. 16a p. 19,
L. 04).

In this interactive moment, it seems that the description offered by the
therapist, in which he suggests that Estela might have a less "serious problem" strengthens the sense of self previously negotiated among the participants that they are not "mentally ill." At the same time, in the dialogue
with meanings previously negotiated in the group, the therapist's utterance propitiates the construction of the problem as being related to "difficulties in life."

To this group movement, Estela replies by anticipating that she will tell
a long story ("We have to know if there is enough time, don't we") about a
past experience ("maybe if I open up and tell what I've been through"),
from the understanding that the fact of speaking about her past may help
her to feel better. Her action of speaking in the group is embedded in a
sense about what can be therapeutic for her ("I hope *I'll feel better*").

It is based on this description of problem (difficulties in life) and on the
possibility of change (talking cure) that she will start her self presentation,
developing a long narrative, sustained, at first, only by the therapist, by
means of reiterations, questions, and investigations.

Estela: Before getting married, I met my ex-husband and then I
            got engaged, then after some time, we were going to get
            married, I was going to have a wedding dress made. My
            mother was a sort of person who enjoyed to play cards,
            you know. Our wedding day had already been arranged.
            It was about 3 or 4 months before the wedding when on a
            Saturday my fiancé went to my house and my mother
            invited us to play cards but he didn't want to. Then I hap-
            pened to say a word that I didn't seem to know what it
            meant. When I said the word, he slapped my face in front
            of my mother.
Therapist: Him?
Estela: Yeah. Then my mother, then he left, and my mother said:
            "This marriage won't work out."
Therapist: Because of this event...
Estela: "It's not going to work out, because he beats you in front
            of me, it won't work out." I didn't care. I stayed with him.
            Then my father was against my getting married to him. I
            kept on meeting him in secret. Then the situation came
            to a point that I wanted to run away with him. But my
            mother had suffered from heart problems, so I couldn't
            make her get nervous, and I decided to get married at the

<u>registry office only.</u> <u>I got married, but kept on being</u>
<u>beaten.</u> (Session 6, p. 19, L. 5-21)

Estela's narrative is constructed as a dramatic plot, which has in it a
clear evidence of a suffering story. In her relationship with an aggressive
husband (the referred other in the event narrated), Estela constructs herself, in the interactive moment with the other group participants, as a victim of a violent relationship.

Thus, her fiancé (and husband-to-be) becomes a central character in
Estela's description. It is the discursive construction of her husband as an
aggressor that enables her own description as a victim, in this specific
interactive moment of the group. In other words, Estela's self descriptions
occur in the relationship with the referred other.

Estela: I got married and I was already pregnant a month later, and
he gave me a beating after another. Then it was the period I
had a small child, and other things, and then after some
time, I went to live with my mother in law, his mother.
There he started fighting again.... Then I told him we'd
better break up, it wasn't working out anyway, was it? Then
my father in law came to us and said: "I'll find a place for
you, a house for you to live—perhaps if you live far away,
you'll stop fighting." Then we rented a house. There, we
started fighting again. After some time my husband traveled, then I, he bit me. I ran away to her house (my mother-
in-law's), I only had the elder boy. He then threatened to
kill me if I didn't come back to him. He threatened to kill
me and I was scared and took the stupid decision of coming
back. I came back to him and then I was pregnant—the
younger girl. There I was again living with my mother-in-
law, but then we had our house built at the back of hers.
Then, pregnant, I had my younger daughter, and after
around five years, he was dating another woman and wasn't
providing food for the kids back at home. At this time, I
didn't use to work. Things went on and I ended up trying to
find a job, because the kids didn't have any milk, any tea to
drink—they didn't have enough food....Then, one night he
arrived at home, I came to him and said: "so, you have
another woman, don't you? He said it was none of my business and started beating me right away. He beat me so
much that I had my leg broken. I ended up in hospital.
Then I stayed there for a week and the next 4 months with-

<u>out going out of home</u> (Session 6, p. 19, L. 21a p. 20, L. 08).

Thus, in the group interaction, Estela builds up a detailed narrative, in which she reports how much she suffered along the period she was married. Her narrative follows a chronological order, in which she describes happenings, separations and reconciliations. Despite considering leaving her aggressive husband, she always postponed her decision because of external events: moving houses, pregnancy, young children, and so forth. In her self description what prevails is Estela as being subject to the events of life and to *others' decisions* on how she should/could live.

On telling her story to the group, Estela describes herself in the relationship with a diversity of many *others* (husband, daughter, father, mother-in-law, attorney, judge, sheriff, etc.), involved in her identity construction, co-authors of her possibilities of action in the world. It is from within the relationship with them *(referred others in the narrated event)* that Estela constructs a story of herself, in which emerges the dominant identity of a suffering woman, victim of the violence of an aggressive husband.

The description of the intensity of the husband's aggressiveness is the central core of this process. In one violence episode, she has one of her legs broken. In the relationship with *the present others in the short time of the group interaction,* this story gains sense of reality from the perception of Estela's body itself—she carries along the inscriptions of such suffering (she limps).

From now on, the possibility of construction and recognition of this as a "problem" emerges in the group interaction. As we pointed before, the construction of the group as a special setting guaranteed to her telling a therapeutic sense. In the relationship with otherness (voices from the present others and, also, from social discourses about psychotherapy) Estela has her narrative legitimized as a problem, which justifies her need of treatment/group therapy.

On continuing telling her story to the group, Estela reports how a series of later events helped her to get divorce. Estela has an abortion—to have a baby would have made her stay longer with her husband—and, her father, who was ill, passes away. Then, she prepares herself, "waits" until "she gets really better" and leaves her husband. However, this possibility of managing her life by herself is threatened once again. As she says, she "took the stupid decision" of getting married to someone else, that similarly to the first husband used to drink and beat her. A new cycle of suffering starts from then on. However, it is broken by Estela's decision of leaving him in order to live with her daughter.

> Estela: I decided to go and live with him and I suffered a lot—I
>   lived with him for 2 years. Then he didn't want my daugh-
>   ter and <u>I left him</u>. He left for work, you know, and I got my
>   things and moved right away. <u>I moved, I found a room
>   where I am today</u>—<u>I picked up my daughter</u> and she's been
>   with me ever since (Session 6, p. 22, L. 21).

Thus, in her relationship with her first and then with her second husband *(others)*, Estela constructs herself as a victim, who cannot change the
events of her life. In her relationship with the other group participants
(present others), her story can be legitimated and Estela constructs herself
and is constructed as a victim of conjugal violence.

The richness of details present in her narrative, the possibility of legitimacy of this/her account in the context of social discourses about violence
against women[3] and the embodiment[4] of her suffering in the immediate
context of the group, guarantee relationally a sense of legitimacy and
veracity to her narrative. Estela's construction as a victim is sustained, this
way, in relation to otherness—present others in the group, referred others
in her account and social voices present in broader social discourses.

The description of Estela as a victim starts changing when she tells the
group about her decision of leaving her second husband *("He left for work,
you know, and I got my things, you know, and moved right away. I moved—I
found a room there where I am today—picked up my daughter and she's been with
me ever since").* By recovering aspects already present in her narrative, the
utterances of some of the group participants will allow the emergence of
new meanings of self and the conversational construction of change.

This movement starts with the therapist's speech, in which he investigates Estela's present condition, seeking to construct a speech of "problem" and a meaning to the support group's immediate action, thus
favoring the construction of the group as "therapeutic" setting. He tries
to better understand what Estela's present "problem" is, once in her story
her past is apparently overcome.

> Therapist: But these <u>situations you told</u>, this <u>crisis</u>, did you feel <u>they
>   caused you any grief</u>—<u>did they disturb you a lot</u>, <u>did they
>   affect your feelings</u>? <u>Why are you here? Why did you
>   come here after all</u>?
> Estela: <u>Because all these things fill up my head. I didn't have
>   anybody to whom I could open up.</u> (the tape ends). *(She
>   says that she asked for help <u>she didn't have anybody to whom she
>   could open up</u> and because she felt the need to <u>open up to differ-
>   ent people</u>. She also talks about <u>her life with her daughter</u>, saying
>   that she doesn't feel comfortable depending financially of her*

> *daughter's support, that she gets_worried about her debts_ and* *then she ends up having too much to think about).* <u>It's not easy,</u> <u>you know. I had always been the breadwinner, I gave her</u> <u>everything.</u> I don't think she's giving me things...

Therapist: But this is how things should be, isn't it? If you are unemployed...

Estela: <u>Yeah, but I have bills to pay, then I get worried.</u>

Therapist: Have you managed to pay them?

Estela: Not at all. I've stopped paying them!

Therapist: <u>But you can find a solution to that.</u> As far as I can see,
<u>despite all your difficulties, you went on struggling to</u>
<u>have a little bit of peace.</u> And then with this guy now, who
knows? He doesn't beat you, does he?

Estela: No, he doesn't drink alcohol.

Therapist: Did the other one use to drink?

Estela: My husband? My goodness! Both of them did... [...]

Therapist: Do you remember that story we were talking about the
other day, <u>that no one here has problems?</u> <u>I mean, we</u>
<u>have to start listening to her stories in order to figure out</u>
<u>the emotional load in her relationship with her husband.</u>
Two relationships that didn't work out! How long did you
stay with him? *(Asking sympathetically)*

Estela: Fifteen years...

Therapist: <u>Fifteen years of you life...</u>

Ana Maria: If her older daughter is 21 years old, <u>this has lasted 21</u>
<u>years, isn't it?</u> (Session 6, p. 23, L. 29a p. 24, L. 23).

At the same time that the therapist investigates Estela's understanding of her necessity of treatment, he also presents a possible reason for her presence in the group. He questions if the "situations" or *"crisis"* experienced by her in the past, and revealed in her reports to the group, disturbed her or caused her any emotional problem that might justify her search for assistance. By doing so, the therapist introduces, in the short time of interaction, an explanation of "problem" that is coherent to the psychological discourses over the role of the therapy (about psychotherapy)—social voices referred to the long time of interaction. In this relational context, Estela's participation in the group therapy can only be justified if she has any emotional difficulty that she wishes to have "treated." Thus, the possibility of problem and self descriptions in this context is also influenced by the social discourses on what means to have psychological problems.

Considering that therapeutic conversations are usually constructed around *narratives of problems*, the therapist's question circumscribes the possible conversations in this context. On building the problem in a certain way, it is also possible to create possibilities for change it. In this direction, Estela's answer to the therapist brings two dimensions: first, she states that past story of suffering "fills up" her head, when she sees the group as an appropriate context "to open up" and to talk about her past. However, this "theory" about what makes her ill seems to be associated also to a "theory" of how she can get better. She understands that she needs to talk about it (she needs to open up) and the group is the place for that. Besides, Estela mentions to be worried about her financial condition and her economically dependence on her daughter, with whom she lives. Here, money problems appear as a possible explanation to the difficulties she experiences at present.

In response to Estela, the therapist circumscribes some possibilities for the dialogue in the group. Taking into consideration the therapeutic context of the group—meaning that it is a space for the discussion of psychological/emotional issues—the therapist chooses the discourse that her difficulty is a result of past experiences of suffering, related to the "emotional" field. Thus, the therapist participates actively in the construction of an emotional discourse on the origin of Estela's problem. In doing this, he presentifies a legitimated discourse in the area of psychology, in which more personal and individualist descriptions, centered on (past or present) emotional experiences, are privileged in detriment of explanations sustained in social and economical aspects.

Apart from that, also in this interaction, the therapist focus on the future, giving voice to the hope that Estela will be able to construct other possibilities of life (*despite all your difficulties, you went on to have a little of peace. And then with this guy now, who knows He doesn't beat you, does he?*). The break with the cycle of violent relationships, by which she saw herself imprisoned, is signified by the therapist as a personal accomplishment. Despite the difficulties, Estela "struggled" to have a little of peace and quiet. Meanings of a future self, not affected by the prevailing narrative of the problem, appear as possibilities.

In this moment of the interaction, the therapist's answer—signified, above all, according to the affective tone in which it is verbalized—propitiates the construction of Estela as a strong woman, who has overcome her difficulties. This meaning is pointed in Ana Maria's utterance as well: *"If her older daughter is 21 years old, this has lasted 21 years, hasn't it?"* Estela has problems because she suffered a lot in her past. The intensity of her suffering justifies her "problem" and places it in the category of "emotional difficulties" (*"Do you remember the story we were talking about the other day— that no-one here has problems?* I mean, we have to start listening to the stories in order to figure out the emotional load in her relationship with her husband. Two relationships that didn't work out! <u>How long</u> did you stay with him?").

Thus, in this moment of group interaction, the therapist's the other participants' speech acts increasing the possibilities of descriptions of Estela. In the relationship with *the present others*, Estela is gradually constructed in different ways; her efforts gain recognition and she changes from the position of victim to the position of winner. It is in the relationship with otherness that both the legitimacy of Estela's "problem" and the possibility of her changing take place.

As far as this centrality of otherness is concerned, an important aspect to be considered in the making sense process is the network of reciprocating identities that is created in the conversational process among the group participants. With the relational construction of Estela's problem as having an emotional core, the debate *"problem/mental disease"* that occurred in the first moments of this session emerges once again. Now, the discourse of "past suffering" starts being used to replace the notion of "mental disease." The construction of a certain explanation about the problem's cause allows the emergence of an alternative personal identity for both Estela and the other group participants.

Valter:	I don't know if you've understood. What I meant is that <u>people perhaps don't have mental problems. They have problems.</u>
Therapist:	Yeah, this story of disease...
Valter:	<u>The guy suffers from depression, sometimes it's the consequence of a problem.</u> Because<u>, in my opinion crazy is the guy who tears money and goes on setting fire to it, you know.</u>...
Ana Maria:	(laugh) <u>You won't find any one!</u>
Valter:	As she told <u>about a relative of hers</u>, that one, I don't know, that shouts and things... [...] <u>It's frightening, isn't it, the guy may have, I don't know, a devilish temper</u>, I don't know... [...]
Therapist:	Look, <u>coming back to her story. It doesn't necessarily mean that she is crazy. She's lived almost half of her life</u> ... How old are you?
Estela:	42.
Therapist:	<u>Half of her life getting emotionally involved with people who only caused her pain. How this has affected her we'll see ahead.</u> Now that she's managed to get some peace. But now, it's not peace with her husband. It's peace with her daughter...that's being the breadwinner. (laugh). So you see, if it's only her, you'll have to <u>put up with it, for a</u>

> while, till you start working again. What's wrong about it?
> (Session 6, p.24, L.22 a p.25, L.14).

From Estela's discursive construction as someone that has problems only, the other group participants also construct themselves as "not being mentally ill," as people who have difficulties or life problems only. In other words, Estela's construction as "not-ill" also brings identity implications to the others. Like her, they *have problems*, not *a disease*. Here, otherness and identity construction appears strongly related—self identities are constructed in dialogue with the narrative of others.

Moreover, the above vignette can be an example of what constructionist authors usually refers as "the social construction of problem." Helping to deconstruct the more traditional, individualistic and essentialist notion of "problem," Goolishian and Anderson (2001) presents the following description of "problem": problem is what a person and the system in which she/he participates describe as such. Thus, problem is a description (or descriptions).

It is important to consider, though, that, according to the social constructionist view of language (language as a social practice), descriptions are not representations of reality. Rather, they constitute our realities. When used by people to make sense of their selves and lives, they construct them as people of "some kind," with some features.

It follows that to be described or to describe someone as having a problem means also to live in a world in which this description defines and creates forms of life and relationship to the system involved on it. Thus, a problem is not an entity, but a social constructed reality that is sustained by people as they coordinate their actions, in language practices. Quoting Anderson (1997), a problem is a position adopted, a meaning constructed or a narrative that is developed.

Another aspect to be considered is the centrality of otherness in the conversational construction of change, referred to the participation of *the present others* (group participants) in the construction of alternative versions of self to Estela.

Having legitimated Estela's story of suffering, a new movement starts in the group, in which the participants debate on how Estela overcome the difficulties that she experienced. An interesting process of construction of Estela as an agent of her own life results from this, from the recognition of meanings not integrated to the description of self so far.

Therapist: Half of her life getting emotionally involved with people who only caused her pain. How this has affected her, we'll just see ahead. [...] What's wrong with it?

Irene: It means that <u>her mind is good</u>, isn't it, doctor? Fortunately, you know, <u>it's not everybody who has a good mind</u>, don't you think? Sometimes a man goes through a small problem and it seems that a lot of worse things come up. <u>At least she has overcome it</u>, isn't it?

Marta: <u>She was very resilient…</u>

Therapist: <u>How did you put up with it for so long?</u>

Estela: <u>Faith in God,</u> don't you know?

Therapist: <u>Was it God's work to solve that</u>?! *(Ironic, provocative tone)*

Estela: Ah, I don't know!

Therapist: Or was it you who solved it, when you said: "<u>I'll leave</u>." <u>You said that</u> to your father, <u>didn't you?</u>

Estela: <u>I did.</u>

Therapist: <u>You said</u> you'd broke up…

Estela: <u>I was tired of being beaten. I couldn't put up with it anymore!</u>

Therapist: Fifteen years! I think you waited for too long! You had a broken leg—you had to undergo an operation… […] *(Therapist remarks that Estela waited for too long, and Estela said that the judge had asked her not to break up for the sake of the kids).* Because it didn't depend on anyone else, <u>it was up to you</u>. And then you might have waited for too long…

Estela: So, <u>I have faith in God,</u> because I told him (physician): "<u>If I were to be on a wheel-chair, I'd rather die!</u>" Then he asked: "Are you sure?" I said: "I am." And the physician said: "Don't give up your faith and you'll overcome it." And thanks God.… I don't walk perfectly well. I walk with a limp, but thanks God. I'm able to work…

Ana Maria: <u>Impressive, isn't it?</u>

Therapist: <u>You kept living this ordeal for a long time</u>, either with one or with the other…

Estela: <u>Yeah … yeah</u> (brief silence, from then on Maria starts her story) (Session 6, p.25, L.10 a p.26, L.16).

In this interactive moment, it is possible to perceive the recognition of Estela's other selves through the group *present others,* who start describing her as someone strong, resilient, who has a "good mind" and that has managed to overcome difficulties that she experienced.

It is interesting to notice that these meanings of "strength" and decision making ability are not promptly recognized by Estela. To the therapist's question on how she managed to overcome her difficulties, Estela replies by saying that it was her *"faith in God,"* somehow contradicting his expectation of personal strengthening. Even so, the therapist highlights

Estela's action, again positioning her as the agent of her own change: it was her who decided to break up, so it was her who succeeded in overcoming that.

It is also possible to understand that in Estela's response she creates her own agency and that of God (the powerful other) (Valsiner, 1999). It seems that the therapist did not recognize that Estela's personal strengthening could be achieved through her discourse about "faith in God" and then he insisted on promoting a certain individualistic discourse of autonomy and self-government.

Despite agreeing with the therapist, Estela does not value this description as much as him. She made decisions because she was *"tired of being beaten"* and not, as the agency discourse suggests, because she became aware of her role in the construction of change possibilities and, as a result, more self-government of her own life. Despite this, the conversation goes on legitimating the suffering that she has gone through, and asserting her resilience and strength on tolerating such suffering for so many years. In dialogue with the group participants, Estela is introduced to new descriptions of herself that had not been recognized by her yet. So, different meanings of self are constructed gradually along the group conversations.

Estela will only talk about herself in session 14, when asking the therapist to share his evaluation about her present condition. First, she says that she won a plot in a raffle and will not need to pay for rents any longer. Until the present moment, she has been living in a small house that she had built in her sister's backyard. Now, she fears that her sister will not refund her the money she spent on the building, once the plot does not belong to her. However, despite describing this apparently conflictive situation, she says she is not worried. Indeed, she is very optimistic towards her future: *"But it's alright. What really matters is that I'm alive! Ahead now."* (laughing). (Session 14, p. 04, L. 18)

After reporting the accomplishment of this *"dream,"* Estela questions about the end of the group and asks for her assessment. In this moment, she establishes a dialogue with the therapist, in which she explains her view of the treatment and creates, in her relationship with him, a discourse of change. Based on it, she describes her therapeutic process in the support group.

> Estela: How long is it before we finish?
> Therapist: Two weeks.
> Estela: And how does it work—it finishes here—or you'll see if the person—if the person did well?

Therapist: I think that in our last meeting we should have an evaluation, which out of our session, <u>to talk about everybody's
impressions.</u> [...].

Estela: Do you think I am any better? [...] Have you noticed any
change?

Therapist: <u>I don't know. You are the one who has to tell if things
have changed...</u>

Estela: Ah, because at the beginning I almost said nothing, did I?

Therapist: <u>If speaking is the case, you speak much more now. But, is
it better?</u> Do you think it is better? <u>You can talk about
some things now—at least here in the group.</u>

Estela: <u>I didn't talk before, now I do.</u>

Therapist: She didn't speak and now she does. And <u>it's better</u> for
her. *(Estela and the therapist laugh)*

Therapist: <u>I don't know whether it's better or worse. I don't have my
crystal ball here</u>. *(He says that in a funny, amiable but not confronting tone)* (Session 14, p.05, L.25 a p.06, L.14).

In this interaction, Estela confirms her improvement through a rather
unusual definition for this context, in which change is usually related to
the absence of the symptoms or complaints presented at the beginning.
In Estela's point of view, she has improved *"because at the beginning she
almost said nothing"* and now she does.

Although she seems to be sure about her improvement, she seeks to
have the therapist's approval of her evaluation. However, he does not
seem to be sure about the criteria of evaluation that she brought, and
expresses his doubt or uncertainty about it *("If speaking is the case, you speak
much more now. But, is it better?")*.

Despite expressing his doubt verbally, through his body posture and
through his affectionate tone of voice, the therapist shows himself to be
not worried towards such explanation. An amiable tone is added to the
contents of his speech, what reduces the uncertainty of this "diagnosis"
and legitimates Estela's opinion that she is better: *"She didn't speak and
now she does. And it's better for her."* In this way, the therapist assesses Estela's
condition based in what she told him and she told him a story of success.
This is an important assessment, considering the "specialist" position
socially attributed to him and which sustain his assessment.

It is interesting to notice that, when she mentions her problem for the
first time, Estela refers to her expectation of changing, which is sustained
in her own action of speaking ("Maybe if I open up and tell what I've been
through, I hope I'll feel better"). In the same way, in session 14, she evalu-
ates her condition at the end of the group employing the same criteria: "I
didn't talk before, now I do." She considers her ability to talk as the

"result" of her participation in the group, as some learning acquisition. For her, the very problem was to not be able to talk, even if other explanations could be ascribed to it.

It is also worth noticing that, Estela did not describe herself, at no time at all in the 6th session of the group, from the same dimensions presented to the therapist at the selection interview. In that moment several complaints were referred to (suicidal idea, inaptitude, de-motivation, weight loss, etc.). The difference of the way that Estela constructed herself and was constructed in these different contexts also exemplifies the centrality of otherness in the discursive construction of self—otherness referred both to the relationship with the *present others,* and with several social discourses which, bringing the mark of the long time history of a culture, sustains some discursive possibilities among the interlocutors, in the interactive moment. For Estela, when requesting for assistance, to describe herself from narratives and complaints about problems was a way to guarantee her own assistance and a space to be heard by a psychiatrist doctor. Differently, in a specific moment of negotiation of an identity version with other group interlocutors, to talk about difficulties instead of complaints and symptoms guaranteed a position of not mentally ill to her and to the group, thus legitimating her story of suffering and victimization. In this way, in the simplicity of her own evaluation at the end of the group, Estela refers to a meaning proposed by the constructionist discourse that it is in the conversational process that we construct our realities and ourselves. As she experienced in the group, her past story, that used to be a repetitive "monologue" in her mind, when taking part in a context of dialogical and responsive relationships, could be reorganized and resignified, thus favoring the emergence of alternative meanings of world and of self, sustained in the relationship with otherness.

In the group interaction, the importance of otherness can be seen in different ways, calling our attention to the centrality of others in the construction of meanings of self, problems, and change: present others (group participants); multiple selves (constructive multiplicity of her own self); referred others (people mentioned in her stories and also other social voices of the long time of interaction). It is in the relationship with these multiple others that the possibility of construction of alternative meanings of self for Estela (strong, resilient woman) and for the others participants in the group (not mentally ill people, but people who have experienced difficulties in they lives) takes places.

Based on notion of *"network of reciprocating identities"* proposed by Gergen (1997), we understand that this is an example of the participation of (present or referred) others in the sustenance of an identity description—a process that enables a narrative to be legitimated within certain social and relational contexts. In the case of Estela, not only was her story legitimated as being a true story of suffering, within the group interaction, but it was also resignified, favoring a number of features. First, there was the emergence of alternative meanings of self; secondly—the conversational construction of Estela's change; third—the concomitant construction of the other group participants as not mentally ill; and, finally, the construction of the group as a therapeutic resource.

PEDRO'S CHANGE THAT CHANGES MILENE

Aiming to analyze empiric situations that give visibility to the change process in therapy from a reading that focus on the network of reciprocating identities that is articulated in each moment of that process, we will show excerpts from conversations carried out in sessions of a therapeutic group about the difficulties in the conjugal relationship of one of the participants. The analysis of several excerpts will enable us to track the numerous changes in self-descriptions negotiated among participants, as well as in others referred to in such descriptions, and the implications of this process to the relationships that are constructed in the sessions.

The group conversations to be analyzed took place in a short term support group to HIV carriers, conducted in Ribeirão Preto—Brazil, which aimed at promoting dialogical conversations that could lead to the construction of other ways to live with HIV. The therapist attempted to build up a conversational partnership marked by reflection, negotiation, and coresponsibility with the other participants. Apart from two or three individual sessions for selection and preparation for the group, it had 10 weekly group sessions of 1½ hours, a final conversation and a follow-up conversation with each participant 3 months after the end of the group. The group consisted of five participants and the therapist: Pedro, 45, who had known about being HIV carrier for 9 months and looked for the group so that he could have someone to talk to, "to open up" and to feel better; Marina, 53, who had known to be HIV positive for 5 months and needed to talk about her revealing this to her family; Tiago, 30, who had known to be HIV carrier for 9 years and searched for a happier way to live with HIV; Ricardo, 31, had known to be HIV seropositive for 4 months and wanted to know more about the disease, how to face prejudice and how to tell his family about his being infected; and Emerson, the therapist, 29, psychologist and researcher, who had worked with HIV carriers for 6 years, and he is one of the authors of this chapter.

We have selected for analysis the conversations about Pedro's difficulties in his conjugal relationship. They were present in several moments of the therapy, however, due to the lengthy task of bringing all the self-descriptions brought for/to Pedro and to Milene (Pedro's wife) in conversations about that topic, we will keep ourselves to the analysis of some descriptions related to moments of session 2, 4, 5, 6, and 10. These moments have been selected because, by analyzing them, we will be able to visualize the different ways through which such descriptions were negotiated in the group as well as how the descriptions of Milene changed in Pedro's discourse and the other participants'.

The self-descriptions which were presented represent different perspectives, being them, I to myself, I to the other and the other to me, while they can be referred to different times, either past, present, or future. They can be explicit or implicit, imposed or suggested, being defined from the relationship with the other. Many of them are suggested by the complement to a description openly expressed in the conversation. As we will see, the look towards the self-descriptions constitutes an analysis level that is always possible in any conversation in the group context.

On starting the analysis from the group's second session, the first in which Pedro participates, we can notice that, after his introduction to the group, he describes himself as being married, having a child and fearing they had been infected. In this moment this description does not expands. This will only happen later in the session. In this situation, Pedro is talking about his difficulties towards the antiretroviral medication, when Marina asks him how his wife helps him in such a situation. Taking for granted that Pedro has to take the medication and being this the very first moment they talk in the group, Marina investigates Pedro's life. This is the first time that Pedro's description as being rejected by his wife has come up.

Marina:	But didn't she tell you: "oh, you have to take your medicine"? Doesn't she cheer you up? Is she so quiet?
Pedro:	Not at all. She says she doesn't give it a damn. It's all the same to whether I live or not. She really doesn't give it a damn...
Emerson:	What was that Pedro? I didn't get it.
Pedro:	She said she doesn't give it a damn. It's all the same whether I live or not. (...)
Emerson:	Did you understand Pedro's answer to Marina's question? What do you think about his answer? (Silence)
Tiago:	Well, very radical, isn't it, Pedro?
Ricardo:	You caused the problem, you solve it? It's somehow like this, isn't it?
Emerson:	Yeah...
Marina:	I don't think so...
Emerson:	What did you say Tiago?

Tiago: Hmm, you see, quite radical. I don't know—on one side, you know? Perhaps if he had talked over it better, I think … it's not his wife's opinion, is it? Hmm, well…

Marina: To listen?

Tiago: Yeah…

Marina: To talk over it, isn't it?

Tiago: To talk more—try to explain it better to her, you know. I think they'll get on better with each other, don't you think? Because I think she is disappointed at him, as a person, isn't she? (…) You're married, you have kids together. I think you'll … you … she takes part in your life. I'm sure that, that she wants what is better for you. She has a, a kind of duty to be there in hard times too (S2, p. 17/18).

This self-description of Pedro as being rejected by his wife comes up from a question of the present other (Marina's, specifically), in the context of a conversation with specific topic (compliance with medication), but from its appearance it starts progressing in the conversation and broadens into new developments. It does not appear as a complaint, a claim, a problem because which Pedro searches for help. Pedro's passivity and his disillusionment with his life make it difficult to him even to point out his very problems.

In this session, Pedro takes the place of the different one, both in the relationship with his wife and in relation to the narratives produced in the group up to that moment. Such difference brings in it the difficulty in comprehending, in understanding the meaning of what is going on, in knowing how Pedro's accounts must be interpreted. There are doubts, impressions, fears and preoccupations. The description produced by Pedro threatens and disturbs the other participants.

In the relationship with *present others,* Pedro's description turns into something that has to be changed. The silence of the group, Tiago's assessment, Pedro's wife's position imagined by Ricardo and Marina's suggestion construct such a description as a problem. A problem that is built up in the dialogue with social voices that synthesize one of the most threatening suffering narratives about AIDS: the rejections on the part of the closest people when they learn about the person's contamination. It was difficult to the others to think about such situation. Everybody was moved by Pedro's description. Milene's (Pedro's wife) reaction brought silence to the group. They could not accept the fact that someone could do that. It was difficult to blame her, as Pedro's description would suggest. *Social voices* about marriage, as the union of spouses marked by mutual care, make it difficult to comprehend Pedro's speeches in this moment of the group conversations.

They try to figure out what Pedro did wrong. And, then, they almost blame him, by trying to build him as being responsible for Milene's rejection, because if Milene were like what Pedro had suggested, any change would be difficult. It was easier to imagine that he was not communicating with her adequately. It was the group's first attempt to help Pedro in this situation.

Tiago and Marina try to help him to construct himself as someone who talks to his wife, supposing that there is some kind of disagreement between them and that it is his responsibility to clear it up. In the dialogue with *present others*, *other selves* of Pedro and Milene are built.

> Marina: She might be suffering much more than you. Because of your behavior, don't you think? As you keep to yourself, she gets nervous, but if you come to her "Dear, sit down here, let's talk" The way you do, I don't know. "Sit here, let's talk, oh, I don't want to die, I won't..."
>
> Pedro: No I don't talk about it.
>
> Marina: So, then the willingness to live dies out. Now, you don't take your medicine. You're too radical. You're not protecting her this way.
>
> Pedro: Her, I'll, I don't talk about it. I don't talk about it to her. At first I did, but I don't anymore, you know. That I'll die, of nothing. But, every now and then she says: You damn! You've got AIDS! Go and die in hell". So, if I keep talking about it, what is it going to be like?
>
> Marina: Yeah, it gets complicated, doesn't it? But you know her better than anyone else. You know how you can approach her. (S2, p. 20)

The dramatic tone of this conversation touched everyone. At the same time, Tiago and Marina were desperately trying to do something. In the conversation that followed, the therapist invites the group to think about this situation which one has to deal with the reaction of close people, when they get to know about one's condition of being HIV positive. It was not only Pedro who needed help. The problem was not Pedro's difficulties in talking to his wife, but the shared effort to deal with AIDS in relationships with family and friends. The social voices of AIDS constituted the group participants as the "different" in the relationship with HIV negative family members. In this very question, Pedro and the other participants saw each other as fellows. The difference constitutes itself as such and vanishes in the turns of a conversation. It does not present itself as a natural fact, but as being relationally built.

Along these conversations, Pedro describes Milene as if she did not care about his fate. The *present others* in the group, however, based on certain social discourses, describe her as a woman who has her duties in marriage and as person to whom Pedro did not give a chance to understand his disease. The group does not accept the description of Milene that is brought by Pedro and suggests that he should change his behavior towards her so as to support her. He has nothing else to do but be more open and optimistic to explain his health condition and motivate Milene. Pedro is seen as someone "reserved," radical and that does not protect Milene. In this session, it seems that Pedro's place in the group is strongly marked by the description of relationship with his wife. The *reciprocity in the construction of* Pedro's and Milene's *identities* expresses itself in this understanding.

In session 4, the issue regarding Pedro's difficulties in his relationship with his wife comes back. After previous talks in the session about the acceptance of an HIV positive person in the family and at work, they talk about the possibility of a sexual life and again descriptions associated to Pedro's wife rejection towards him come up.

Marina: Can I ask something? You don't have a relationship like, like a couple, do you? You know.

Pedro: No, no.(…)

Marina: She might be afraid of catching it, she must have been…

Pedro: (puzzled)

Marina: I don't know if he retreated into his shell, you know…

Emerson: Ask him.

Marina: … isn't it, Pedro (…) you were rather quiet when you came here, now you are talking a bit to us, but you came "No, no, I will die," maybe it's you who should change a little, don't you think? Because maybe she is a simple woman like me, maybe even simpler, isn't she? She is afraid, maybe you say "No, there is no problem, it's this, like this"—Have you already tried to say it to her?

Pedro: I've already said it to her. M (social worker) has too and so has Doctor A (physician)

Marina: To her?

Pedro: To her, yes, but not even God can make her understand.

Marina: Ah, so you'll have to find another partner, what can one do? (…)

Marina: So, so I think you need, I think you need to impose a sense of union, you either stay or not to talk is not like this, it's to orientate her.

> Pedro: I've got something for me. I don't like to force ... to force
>   anyone that wants, doesn't want—stay where you are and I'll
>   stay where I am, that's over. (S4, p. 8/9)

It is the first time that Milene has also been considered possibly responsible for the relationship difficulties that she and Pedro live. The opening to dialogue represents the minimum condition for the marriage sustenance. Milene does not listen to anyone. This conversation starts changing Pedro's description both in his relationship out of the group (with Milene) and his relationship with the other group participants. A new description of Pedro starts being built, in which he is no longer the one who was doing everything in an inadequate way, but, on the contrary, who was trying to deal with a difficult. By saying that he does not like to "force anyone," he describes himself as someone who respects Milene. Milene starts having her description of misunderstood wife threatened. She also finds it difficult to talk and she does not listen to other people's opinions. Gradually, in Pedro's relationships with the *present others* in the group, the descriptions of Milene (*reffered* other) change.

This new description, however, is not comfortable to Pedro in the group conversations, either. The descriptions about him, implicit in the descriptions of others, do not fit perfectly in his other self-descriptions. Considering that Milene is, to a certain extent, responsible for the situation they live, Pedro has to justify the reason why he is still married to her. The reason why the relationship is maintained appears then through Pedro's concerns with his son. Other self-descriptions of Pedro appear to justify the fact of still being married. In this moment, the otherness has nothing to do with *present others* or *referred* others, but it is related to the *other that exists in him*. It does not invite to the change, but sustain the persistence of certain self-description.

> Pedro: I talked to her and she said that, after learning about the
>   result, "From now on, we won't have any relation," I said
>   "No problem."
> Emerson: Who said that?
> Pedro: She did. I said then, "You take care of your own business, I
>   keep to myself, you keep on doing the house chores and I
>   keep to my duties as a man, (it's not because you don't want
>   to stay with me any longer that you won't live anymore, is
>   it?), I am responsible. I won't leave you because I have a
>   son. My son doesn't have to pay for the mistakes of ours—
>   grown-ups" (S4, p. 10).

Such decision of Pedro's on keeping married because of his son is questioned then by Marina. In the dialogue with other *social voices* about marriage and gender relationships she seems to contribute to the reflection about a possible separation. Milene is no longer described as someone who needs to be protected and cared for by Pedro.

> Pedro: Before we learnt about this problem, we were going to split up; we were going to split up. I was going to live with another woman (…)
>
> Marina: So, see how complicated it is. That's what I say. Can I say that? I'll be straight forward, Pedro, (…) one day you get fed up. We end up getting fed up. The kid will grow up. The kid needs father and mother. He doesn't need the spouse. You're not a spouse—you're a father—you'll have to help the child (S4, p 16).

After this conversation, reacting to Marina's comments, Pedro repeats his self-description of a man that is still married because of his son. The dialogue is tense, marked by small changes. No new description is produced or anything that can serve as a conclusion or solution, but there is a sincere involvement of the participants. Marina tries to show Pedro that he has the right to be happy with other people. He tries to explain his fears related to living with another woman and not staying with his son everyday. His self-description of a man who has duties towards his son and towards not infecting his wife seems to guide the possibility of negotiating a new self-description in his relationship with Milene.

In session 5, the topic related to his relationship with Milene appears again. Pedro reports the failure of his attempt to talk to Milene:

> Pedro: The conversation we had here and that I took home. I tried to solve the problem about us, and I tried in a certain way and it didn't work out. I tried another way. It didn't work out, either. Then the conversation was over, (?), "Get out. Haven't I told you —it's over, if you fall ill in hospital, you can die there because I won't see you there. I can call the ambulance to take you. Why don't you die at once," then this is what came to my mind—then I said, "I have to die soon, if I die soon, the problem is over."
>
> Emerson: Did you understand that Tiago? What do you think about this story?
>
> Tiago: It's difficult, isn't it? …
>
> Pedro: If I happen to come to you every, everyday and say to you, "You're causing too much work" and this and that. "The

work hasn't started yet. It'll come." I said—One's already
low ... so why not die soon ... why wait for a problem to
appear—you'd better finish this up soon and the problem is
over.

Tiago: I think this way, Pedro. You, as a person, should love yourself—try to love yourself and not worry too much about
what she might end up telling you, right (...) look for God
(...), then, take these silly thoughts out of your mind—you
have to live—you're a healthy guy—I don't imagine you ill,
I see you... (S5, p. 2/3).

Pedro tried to talk to his wife, but it did not work out. However it was
an attempt in which Pedro got involved searching for a new kind of
relationship with his wife. He was trying to do things in a different way.
He was not only complaining about his life, but also trying to make it
better. It is a significant change in his descriptions about his life in the
group conversations. Pedro has a problem, but he is not only justifying
why it is not possible to solve it. Now he tries to take actions. From
Tiago's remarks, the descriptions of Milene in the group conversations
also change. From someone about whom Pedro should worry and shelter and explain things, Milene is now someone who Pedro should not
listen to, about whom he should not worry. Trying to sustain Pedro's
other future selves, Tiago's speeches outline and highlight Milene's other
selves. After this moment, the participants start to talk about the
group's suggestions, the search for solutions, and limits to tolerate certain situations.

In another moment of this session, that conversation about the limits
to tolerate certain situations leads Pedro to describe himself as being married to Milene and he, then, reports how he made her a last proposal:

Pedro: I know it—I can't stand it anymore (nervous laughter), I'm
getting to the last drop, already. That's what I told her—
"Oh, I'll try another week, if it doesn't work out (coughing),
if you don't change a thing," but there is no agreement, no
way to come to an agreement (S5, p. 11).

Such last proposal, that contributes to a self-description contrary to
that of keeping married because of the son, seems to be inspired by the
differentiation between spouse and father, proposed by Marina in the previous session. This difference leads Pedro to a reflection over his role, his
rights and duties. A new self-description of Pedro comes up, one in which
he wants to separate from his wife because of his son.

Pedro: In the conversation we had, what came out—we left here
talking about the extend to which a kid—since when you'll
have to pay alimony—you'll see your kid—up to which
point you'll suffer for your kid who has, who has his mother
—the mother doesn't want anything bad to happen to her
kid—so I've got these things in my head—Am I going to be
alone, because of the kid? I think I can help better—
because if he grows up under that speech—"Ah you're like
this because of this and that"—he'll grow up to be revolted,
won't he? So If I get out, he won't see this argument (…)
(S5, p. 13)

After this speech, Tiago and the therapist talk how serious this decision
is and how careful Pedro should be, setting himself free to take whatever
decision he wants, trying to show him that he did not have to do anything
due to that conversation in the group. However, trying to put into practice what Tiago and Marina had suggested, Pedro encountered even more
difficulties and then he felt that a new decision was needed. It is interesting to observe Pedro's description as a father in the attempt to justify his
separation from Milene. It is because of his son that he decides either to
stay with Milene or to separate from her. It is not the case of directly
searching for a happier conjugal relationship, as suggested by Marina.
Probably this change is associated with Pedro's description as a responsi
ble man. However, for this new possibility it was necessary a transformation of Milene's description as well. She is now a good mother who will
take proper care of her son. It is her validation as a good mother that
enables Pedro to describe himself as a good, responsible father, worried
about his son's future, even being separated from his wife.

Along these conversations of session 5, it is possible to observe how the
descriptions of Milene change as well as the descriptions of Pedro. The
constructions of other possibilities of self-description for Pedro imply
transformations in the descriptions of Milene. It is not possible to change
on one's own. From the comprehension of the self-description as taking
place in a *network of reciprocating identities*, the change in this description
depend on the others reported in it. It is necessary to redescribe Milene
so that certain descriptions of Pedro become possible and sustainable.
This process does not happen only through Pedro's statements, but also
through the questionings and judgments of the other participants
(present others).

In the following session, the sixth session, after they had talked about
some of Marina's questions and about Pedro's adaptation to the medication, Marina questions Pedro on his relationship with his wife. In this conversation we can observe how the description of Pedro, who has conjugal

difficulties, is still a problematic description to the group. It is not Pedro who brings the issue to be discussed among the group members. It is Marina who questions him, who invites him to talk about it, as if it were something that one should worry about. His description in the previous session was not considered as end, but as something that demanded developments. His consideration towards the *present others* and his opening to their contributions, are marks in the conversational dynamics proposed and constructed in sessions of group therapy.

In reply to Marina's questions, Pedro says that he is no longer arguing because he has been working all day long.

> Marina: What about your wife and these medicines—does she know what you've taking? (...)
>
> Pedro: I arrived the other day—that day I'd been talking. I came the other day ... I came to her and said: "I think I'll leave – It's the best thing for me—you stay at your place, I stay at mine," "But you can't go away—what will I do if you go away? I said, "So, you're worried about your life—that's what you're worried about, then?" I said, "No, the two of us in the same place, under the same roof, doesn't work out at all. You stay at your place and I stay at mine. I'll be taking care of you and you'll be taking care of me. Let's stand it a little longer and consider it better." (...)
>
> Emerson: And you made your decisions—you said this—ah, you said you were going away. After she said that, then you decided to stay—why did you decide to stay?
>
> Pedro: Because now I'm saying, "If only stop swearing, talking like this (...) you stay quiet at your place, I stay at mine, mine, I go on, the way I used to be, I'll go on, but I ask you—where there are three, four talking, you don't come closer," if the person has to say something, I'll wait for everybody to leave and then I'll speak (S6, p 14).

This conversation allows the continuation of the process of redescription of Pedro and Milene's places in the construction of the description of Pedro as having difficulties in his conjugal relationship. Pedro describes himself as the one who takes the decision of staying at his home. He is no longer someone completely rejected by Milene. She wants him to stay. He agrees, but imposes conditions. The therapist points out the difference, and then expand this description of the relationship between Pedro and Milene. The strengthening of that self-description of Pedro is an invitation to other descriptions in which Pedro succeeds in taking new decisions and taking care of himself. This situation points the clash of the numerous self-descriptions and the hegemony of some of them. The otherness represented by the other in himself also takes part in the same game of negotiations in the conversations with present others.

The analysis of this moment in the session points out that the process of construction of new self-descriptions for Pedro does not end in the group conversation. The descriptions suggested and constructed there must also be used in Pedro's other relationships, in this case, with his own wife. It's essential that Milene accept this new description of Pedro and the place spared for her in it so that such description can be sustained.

In the group's last session, when there is a reflection over the participation in the group, Pedro reports again a new decision on his love relationship. The construction of a description of Pedro as someone who has found a new girlfriend is established:

> Pedro: What I can say is that it was good for me—It made me want to live. I've already been to the attorney to talk about the alimony (and another thing I'd like to talk—?), I'm considering getting married again—I don't think about dying anymore—I think about getting married again. (...)
>
> Emerson: What do you think about taking this decision? How are you feeling?
>
> Pedro: I feel much better, you know, you have to take, it's a decision you have to take. Let's supose, a year ago—I should have taken this decision a year ago but I didn't. You see.

After Pedro's stating this, the participants talk about what happened to the group that contributed to that change. In this final session, this self-description of Pedro contributed to the construction of his position in the group as someone who achieved his aims regarding what he had looked for in the therapy. At this point it is possible to identify the sensibility towards the context of any relationship with one's self and with others. By thanking the group for the help he received, Pedro shows the importance of love relationships in his life. This is a question that is contrary to the wish to die. For him, to search for a new girlfriend is to search for living. It is no longer the question of something to solve in relation to Milene, but in relation to himself and maybe to his new girlfriend. It was not this particular conversation that promoted such a change, but as in other situations, the group was a place where he could legitimate some of his actions outside the group. It is through the relationship with *present others* that other self-descriptions can sustain themselves and gain stability.

Judging from this last report, the description of Pedro as someone experiencing difficulties in his marriage seems to have changed so much that he could stop experiencing it as a problem. However, by the time of his follow-up interview, Pedro is still living with Milene. His plans did not work out as he had expected. However, it was no longer the case of Pedro keeping the marriage because of his son. The description of Pedro who searches for another girlfriend still remains. This self-description, non-existing in the group at its start, seems to mean new possibilities to be built by Pedro along his future. Four months after the follow-up interview, Pedro reports that differently from the way he used to take his decisions previously, he had separated from Milene and was living alone in another house, despite having a new love relationship in his life. The other's place and the self's place in his decisions seem to have changed.

As we can see, along the group conversations there is not any linear or accumulative construction of one description for Pedro in his relationship with his wife, but a series of attempts build up from the invitations, demands and possibilities created in certain conversations. This last description was only a momentary outline in his narrative about his life and the new descriptions that can follow.

The new descriptions negotiated in the group start building conversational resources that will be used in new conversations with different people, as well as with oneself in one's reflections. It is an exercise of possibilities in which the group serves to strengthen the appearance of these new descriptions, by questioning, suggesting, rejecting, or validating certain descriptions.

The change in the description of Pedro as living conjugal difficulties did not happen as a change related to something that depended only on him. Considering that from these descriptions and narratives that we live we create *networks of reciprocating identities*, to negotiate a new self-description involves creating a new description of other people, in the group and outside the group and for the person herself.

This relational analysis of the construction of Pedro's description invites us to seriously consider the multiple descriptions of the participants about themselves and the others with whom they construct their lives. A certain change for one participant is possible only from the transformation of a network of descriptions that involve both self-descriptions and the descriptions of the people with whom he/she has relationships (*referred* others).

By reflecting on Pedro's multiple descriptions, we see that the change of a description involves changing other self-descriptions. To change Pedro's description as someone living problems in his conjugal relationship involves changes in his description as a father. In each moment of the conversation, a specific articulation of these several descriptions is formed and it delimits negotiation possibilities.

The transformations of Milene's descriptions in conversations along the group sessions are representative of relational implications of this process. It is important to emphasize that these changes did not occur only through Pedro's speeches, in his attempts to justify and explain certain events, but also through other participants' speeches when suggesting certain actions and ways of perceiving the situation. They emerged, however, from something dynamically negotiated in the group discussion among the participants.

The transformations in Milene's descriptions associated to Pedro with difficulties in conjugal relationship did not happen in a linear, progressive way and they also involved other descriptions of Milene, besides that of a wife. Moreover, along the group conversations, the transformations in Pedro's description as someone who is rejected by his wife into someone who looks for a new girlfriend can be compared to the description of Milene as someone who rejects/who is not understood by Pedro into a new possibility of description of Pedro, in which Milene's description becomes less representative.

This relational analysis enables us to reflect on the descriptions that emerge from the group conversation that become a conversational resource to Pedro. In the analysis of several moments shown before, we can notice that the descriptions of Pedro as someone who talks to his wife and that finds a new girlfriend, mentioned by the group in session 2 and 5, come back in session 5 and 10 respectively, in Pedro's voice, though, in his description of his life.

The transformations of the descriptions of Pedro about his relationship with other group participants also enable us to think about other aspects of the relational perspective of this change process related to the immediate conditions of the conversation, its situational character. Along the sessions, we can notice how Pedro changes from a posture of responding promptly to the proposals of the *present others*, sometimes, rejecting them, to one in which he actively bring/tell his new attempts to solve the proposed problem. At first, Pedro's description as someone who had difficulties in marriage is not even considered by him as a problem. The group actively contributes to involving him into defining it as being a problem, and as such, something that he has to deal with. The group then tries to support him, questioning him and offering alternatives to him. Pedro's involvement in such a form of relationship makes him anticipate and bring to the group his new solutions, giving a new dimension to what the group participants had said in previous sessions and widening it.

In conclusion, we can consider that the analysis of the social construction of Pedro's change in the group shows that: (a) there are self-descriptions that change along the conversations and others that keep on being used; (b) there is a network of self-descriptions that articulate at each moment in the relationship with the *present other*; (c) the self-descriptions support each other and they can sustain different possibilities of action;

(d) they are negotiated by people in interaction—informing, suggesting, validating, questioning, sharing pave the way to other self-descriptions; (e) a new self-description gets stability from the moment it stops being questioned by the participant himself/herself and by the *present others* in the group; (f) the self-description transformations involve different relational dimensions whether with other self-descriptions (*other selves*), with the descriptions of people involved in these descriptions (*referred others*) and with the descriptions of other group participants (*present others*).

FINAL CONSIDERATIONS

Contemporary psychological discourses have propitiated a more relational view over human being and, with them, the idea of otherness become more and more central. In the therapeutic context, to talk about otherness sounds familiar. Although it has always considered the importance of difference and of others (whether the therapist or the group participants) for the achievement of change, this issue has also been more emphasized in the present discourses about psychotherapy.

In this chapter, while sharing this perspective, we also seek to widen the understanding of otherness, pointing to what we have been calling the social construction of therapeutic change. For us, to propose the *social* character of this process leads to several implications, and, in our analysis of Estela's and Pedro's change, we focused on two of them, that we will outline here to finish it.

On presenting Estela's change, we wish to show that it emerged as an achievement of the conversational context in which it has occurred. Estela's narratives were situated. First, in terms of the immediate conversation, her silence along the six previous sessions could not be sustained. She was invited to participate with the other group participants in the negotiation of their identities as participants of a therapeutic group. Second, her narratives were also situated within broader social discourses that establish what can be considered as a legitimate narrative in this context. While Estela's narrative was being reconstructed within the relationship with the present others in the group, thus favoring the construction of another identity version for her, the group participants were also implicated in this process. Thus, the negotiation of meanings around Estela' story, also enabled for the others conversational partners alternative and acceptable descriptions of self. They were also relationally constructed as not being mentally ill. That is, Estela changed with the participation and collaboration of others.

Concerning Pedro's narrative, it was also the supplementation of other participants that enabled the construction of Pedro as someone who has difficulties in conjugal relationship. For the *present others*, Pedro's identity as being passive when facing his wife's rejection, invites the negotiation of this description. It was not possible for the present others in the group to remain silent before the prejudice that also threatened them. Jointly with Pedro, they will search for other possible selves, which Pedro will negotiate with Milene as well. Whether Milene's self-description changed or not for her remains an open question. But we understand that Pedro's change implied a concomitant change of his descriptions of Milene.

The analysis of the process of the social construction of change pointed to how otherness is present at the context of group psychotherapy in many ways (present other, referred other and other selves) and also works in different ways, supporting certain self descriptions and challenging others. Otherness represented by other participants has an important role in the process of change.

Otherness is present in our self descriptions as well as in the other's. However, the recognition of otherness is a joint action, a relational achievement. In the same way that there is not only one self description, there is not only one description of the other. The otherness of the other and of ourselves emerges from those conversational spaces that invites the difference. In our view of the psychotherapy change process, otherness is denaturalized and the interdependence of the construction of self descriptions and of the descriptions of others is emphasized.

NOTES

1. Under tuition from the first author, the other two got their PhD degrees, sharing the same research group for years. They also took part in a training program at University of New Hampshire, Durham, NH (USA), being in dialogue with professors Sheila McNamee and John Shotter, in 2002.

2. Danziger (1997) proposes a distinction between light constructionism and dark constructionism. The texts referring to the light constructionism privilege the microsocial level for the study of the construction of knowledge emphasizing the opening to the multiplicity of discourses for the transformation of social life. In contrast, the texts referring to the dark constructionism privilege the macrosocial level emphasizing nondiscursive aspects of human relationships, specially those related to the issue of power.

3. For beyond the immediate relationship I/other, there is also the possible recognition of the group that the stories of conjugal violence are not unusual in Brazilian context, historically influenced by the hegemony of patriarchal and chauvinist culture.

4. We emphasize here language as an embodied making sense activity, once we understand that when one speaks about something one also speaks through a body that communicates and that has its own ways of expression.

REFERENCES

Anderson, H. (1997). *Conversation, language and possibilities:* A postmodern approach to therapy. New York: Basic Books.

Bakhtin, M. M. (1984). *Problems of Dostoevsky's poetics* (C. Emerson, Ed. & Trans.). Minneapolis: University of Minnesota Press.

Bakhtin, M. M. (1986). *Speech genres and other late essays* (V. W. McGee, Trans). Austin: University of Texas Press.

Danziger, K. (1997). The varieties of social construction. *Theory and Psychology, 7*(3), 399-416.

Gergen, K. J. (1985). The social constructionist movement in modern psychology. *American Psychologist, 40,* 266-275.

Gergen, K. J. (1989). Warranting voice and the elaboration of the self. In J. Shotter & K. J. Gergen (Eds.), *Texts of identity* (pp. 70-81). London: Sage.

Gergen, K. J. (1992). *The saturated self.* New York: Basic Books.

Gergen, K. J. (1997). *Realities and relationships: Soundings in social construction* (3rd ed.). Cambridge, MA: Harvard University Press.

Goolishian, H. A., & Anderson, H. (1996). Narrativa e self: Alguns dilemas pósmodernos da psicoterapia [Narrative and self: Some postmodern dilemmas of psychotherapy]. In D. F. Schnitman (Ed.), *Novos paradigmas, cultura e subjetividade* (pp. 191-203). Porto Alegre: Artes Médicas..

Guanaes, C. (2006). *A construção da mudança em terapia de grupo: um enfoque construcionista social* [The construction of change in group therapy: A social constructionist perspective]. São Paulo, Brazil: Vetor. (The title and year of this reference was changed)

Guanaes, C., & Japur, M. (2003). Construcionismo social e metapsicologia: Um diálogo sobre o conceito de self [Social constructionism and metapsychology: A dialogue about the concept of self]. *Psicologia: Teoria e Pesquisa, 19*(2), 135-143.

Guanaes, C., & Japur, M. (2005). Sentidos de doença mental em um grupo de apoio e suas implicações [Implications of mental illness meanings in a therapeutic group]. *Psicologia: Teoria e Pesquisa, 21*(2), 227-235

Harré, R., & van GillLangenhove, L. (Eds.). (1999). *Positioning theory: Moral contexts of intentional action.* Oxford, England: Blackwell.

Japur, M. (2004). Alteridade e grupo: Uma perspectiva construcionista social [Otherness and group: A social constructionist perspective]. In L. M. Simão & A. M. Martinez (Eds.), *O outro no desenvolvimento humano: Diálogos para a pesquisa e a prática profissional em Psicologia* (pp. 145-170). São Paulo, Brazil: Pioneira Thomson Learning.

McNamee, S. (2004). Social construction as practice theory: Lessons for practice and reflection in psychotherapy. In D. Pare & G. Larner (Eds.), *Collaborative practice in psychology and therapy* (pp. 9-21). New York: Haworth.

McNamee, S., & Gergen K. J. (Eds.). (1995). *Therapy as social construction.* London: Sage.

McNamee, S., & Gergen K. J. (Eds.). (1999). *Relational responsibility.* London: Sage.

Rasera, E. F. (2004). *Grupo como construção social: Aproximações entre o construcionismo social e a terapia de grupo* [Group as a social construction: Soundings in social construction and group therapy]. Ribeirão Preto, Tese de Doutorado - Programa de Pós-Graduação em Psicologia, FFCLRP-USP.

Rasera, E. F., Guanaes, C., & Japur, M. (2004). Psicologia, ciência e construcionismos: Dando sentido ao self [Psychology, science and constructionisms: Making sense of self]. *Psicologia: Reflexão e Crítica, 17*(2), 157-165.

Rasera, E. F., & Japur, M. (2003). Grupo de apoio aberto para pessoas portadoras do HIV: A construção da homogeneidade [Open support groups for persons living with HIV/AIDS: The construction of its homogeneity]. *Estudos de Psicologia, 8*(1), 55-62.

Rossetti-Ferreira, M. C., Amorin, K. S., & Silva, A. P. S. (1999). Comment: The network of meanings which structures and canalizes interactions, interpretations and comment. *Culture & Psychology, 5*(3), 337-349.

Shotter, J. (1993). *Cultural politics of everyday life.* Toronto, Canada: University of Toronto Press.

Shotter, J. (2000). *Conversational realities: Constructing life through language* (Inquires in social construction). London: Sage.

Shotter, J. (2003). *Inside the moment of speaking: In our meetings with others, we cannot simply be ourselves.* 2003. Retrieved May 7, 2004, from http: pubpages.unh.edu/~jds/Tornio.htm

Spink, M. J. (Ed.). (1999). *Práticas discursivas e produção de sentido no cotidiano* [Discursive practices and meaning making in daily life]. São Paulo, Brazil: Cortez.

Valsiner, J. (1999). I create you to control me: A glimpse into basic processes of semiotic mediation. *Human Development, 42*, 26-30.

Volosinov, V. N. (1973). *Marxism and the philosophy of language* (L. Matejka & I. R. Titunik, Trans.). Cambridge, MA: Harvard University Press.

CHAPTER 7

TIME, SELF, AND THE OTHER

The Striving Tourist In Ladakh, North India

Alex Gillespie

What is the relation between the dialogical, or social, self and the goal-directed self, and how might this relation be theorized? On the one hand there is a growing body of literature that has established the self as social and internally differentiated (e.g., Laing, 1960; Rowan & Cooper, 1999), or to paraphrase Hermans (2002), a "landscape" of I-positions which have their origin in the social world. On the other hand, the idea that the self is goal-directed is well established (Burke, 1969; James, 1878/1992; Wertsch, 1998). While the dialogical self literature draws upon a spatial metaphor of the self, the striving self literature draws upon a temporal metaphor of the self. The question is; what are the conceptual linkages between these two substantial strands of theory in cultural psychology? How can these two root metaphors, or *themata* (Holton, 1975), the spatial and the temporal, be combined? The present chapter contributes to the integration of these two traditions by showing how concepts relating to the social and dialogical nature of the self can be extended to account for

Otherness in Question: Labyrinths of the Self, 163–186
Copyright © 2007 by Information Age Publishing
All rights of reproduction in any form reserved.

the striving self. Specifically, it is argued that other people are essential to understanding the striving self because self is often striving to occupy the position of the other. The starting point for this theoretical proposition comes from Mead's (1927, 1932) work on time and space.

THE EXTENDED ENVIRONMENT

For Mead (1927, 1932) the mind is a more or less integrated system of perspectives. Perspectives, for Mead, are temporal relationships between the organism and the world. The entire world, as known, can be described in terms of perspectives, because everything one knows about the world implies some relation to the world. One consequence of this line of thinking is that we cannot separate mind from the environment: a person's beliefs about the environment are a constitutive element of the person's environment. The paths of action open to a person are, in part, a function of the persons' conception of the environment. Moreover, the person's conception of the past and the future also enter into the present, altering the possible paths of action. Taking this idea to its logical conclusion Mead argued the radical proposition that mind can be conceived of as the temporal and spatial extension of the present.

First, consider mind as the spatial extension of the present. For Mead (1927, p. 170), reality is that which lies within the present manipulatory area—the things we can immediately act upon. Within the manipulatory area, ideas can lead to actions that succeed or fail, thus establishing the future reality, or falsity, of those ideas. But what about phenomena beyond this manipulatory area? One might see an apple on the table. The reality of this apple remains a possibility until one takes hold of the apple and bites into it. Only at that point does the apple become real, because on approaching the apple, one may realize that it is a plastic apple, used only for decoration. Before this phenomenological moment, when the tasty apple turns into the replica apple, Mead argues that the all the qualities of the apple (e.g., the perceived tastiness) are sustained in mind; they are part of the minds spatial extension of the present. From the perspective of the researcher the apple is a semiotic construct within the mind of the person. From the perspective of the person, the apple is an object in the environment. Thus, when Mead describes the mind as the spatial extension of the environment, he is more precisely stating that the mind of the individual, as studied by the researcher, is the environment as perceived by the individual.

But, what about things that are outside of the perceptual field? For example, what about the knowledge that there is an apple in the closed box? Believing that the apple is in the box, while not being able to perceive the apple, means that the apple is purely a possibility, and this possibility is not actualized until one opens the box and takes a bite of the apple. Thus we can say that before opening the box the apple is part of the environment that is sustained by mind—it is a semiotic construct. This is not to say that the apple is not real: the idea of the apple may be very real in its consequences of mediating ongoing action. For example, one may get hungry and, purposively, open the box to get the apple. In order to explain this movement of opening the box one would have to rely upon the motivating idea of the apple. The motivating power of this idea remains real regardless of whether the apple turns out not to be in the box or to be plastic. The key point, then, is that the apple in the box, which motivates self, is also part of the mind's spatial extension of the environment.

Second, consider mind as a temporal extension of the present environment. Both the past and the future, like the apple in the box, are also beyond the perceptual field. Yet both past and future can become active mediators of action and thought *in the present*. That is to say, both the past and the future are also semiotic constructions in the present. This radical idea, which destabilizes our common sense notions of time, originates in the writings of St. Augustine (Adam, 1990, p. 33). To say that the past and future only exist in the present does not make the past or future "unreal." Again, these ideas may have very real consequences. Possible pasts and possible futures can change events in the present even if they have never occurred or will never occur. Consider, for example, a student who is highly motivated for an exam because she hopes, and believes that she can obtain, a high grade. The belief may be fallacious, and she may obtain a low grade. The future outcome, however, is not the issue. The point is that the belief in the possible future of obtaining a high grade makes her work harder in the present. The future possibility (which does not transpire) can still be a very real semiotic mediator of action in the present. Indeed, in order to understand the striving of the student we need to understand the student's imagined possible futures. These possible futures, then, are not "in" the future, rather they form part of the temporally extended present and they are sustained through what we, as researchers, call semiotic constructions, or what Mead called mind. They constitute the paths of action that are open to the individual, or what Boesch (1991) calls the individual's action potential. Exactly how this temporally extended environment is constructed, and motivates human purposive action, is the topic of the present chapter.

The distinction between the spatially extended and the temporally extended environment actually breaks down under the full force of Mead's analysis. For Mead all reality is in the future (i.e., in the completion of the act). Even the apple within the perceptual field gains reality from the future act of holding and eating (though it is imagined on the basis of past holding and eating). In perceiving the tastiness of the apple one is perceiving the future act of eating the apple through one's prior experience of eating apples. Thus the spatially extended environment implies a temporal extension of the environment. Each object in the spatial environment implies a path of action that leads into the future, and that path of action is constructed out of past experiences and memories. This insight is important because it overcomes the opposition between spatial metaphors and temporal metaphors, and, as we will see, points toward a way of integrating the dialogical self with the striving self.

From a Meadian perspective Self inhabits an environment that extends into many possible futures. Paths of action lead off around every corner leading to numerous expectations and goals. Striving, or any purposive action, can be understood in terms of these possible futures. When the self is striving, the spatially and temporally extended environment is active, as a semiotic construct, in the present. Possible futures always imply both a temporal and a spatial extension of the environment. The present chapter asks the following questions: where do these images of the future come from? Where does the motivation for striving come from? The proposed answer lies in an integration between the dialogical self and the striving self. In order to illustrate the proposed integration, the chapter will analyze tourist striving in Ladakh.

Striving Tourists

Tourism is an ideal subject through which to unpack the construction of the future. Tourists often decide to go to places where they have not been before. The obvious, but important, fact is that even if tourists have never been to a destination before, they nevertheless have expectations concerning the destination. They can imagine what their destination will be like. Indeed, they are investing considerable time and money in this expectation. Once abroad, the tourist is striving to actualize some aspect of the imagined future. Tourists are looking for that which made them travel in the first place. The first question to ask is, how has this future image been constructed? The mass media, John Urry (1990) argues, is central to this construction:

> Places are chosen to be gazed upon because there is an anticipation, especially through daydreaming and fantasy, of intense pleasures, either on a different scale or involving different senses from those customarily encountered. Such anticipation is constructed and sustained through a variety of non-tourist practices, such as film, TV, literature, magazines, records and videos, which construct and reinforce that gaze. (p. 3)

The close relation between the mass media and tourism is evident in the growing number of "location guidebooks." For example, the tourist can travel to Scotland with the guidebook, *Scotland the Movie* (Bruce, 1997). This guidebook presents the tourist with the main set locations for films like *Braveheart*, *Chariots of Fire*, and *Trainspotting* among many more. The guidebook provides maps, itineraries, and background details about the films. Some guidebooks even provide GPS (global positioning system) positioning, so that tourists can get within five meters of the "actual" location of fictional events. It is now widely established that attracting a blockbuster movie to film in a given local can, overnight, create a long standing tourist attraction (Tooke & Baker, 1996). For example, the Stirling Tourist Association has reported that the film *Braveheart* has caused a significant increase in visitors to the Wallace Monument (which honors William Wallace on whom the film *Braveheart* is based).

The extent to which the mass media extends our environment, nurturing our imagination of places and times beyond our immediate experience, is also evident in the fact that most people have associations to places such as the Amazon, Egypt, Antarctica, and Tibet, despite never having been there. When thinking of such places, where do these associations and expectations come from? The most likely answer is in vicarious experiences through the mass media. To paraphrase McLuhan (1964), the mass media are an extension of our perceptual field. Moreover, they are a semiotic support structure enabling an unprecedented extension of our spatial and temporal environment. The mass media are fundamental to creating the global village by enabling people, anywhere in the world, to participate in all global, and local, events from the comfort of their armchair. Less optimistically, Anderson (1993) has argued that the mass media are fundamental to nationalism. Without the mass media it would be impossible for the members of modern nation states to imagine themselves as belonging to a nation among other nations.

The mass media not only extend peoples perceptions of different places and times, but are also fundamental to peoples' imagination of themselves (Beeton, 2001). Fiction provides people with ideals that they can aspire to, and thus with potential future selves. The mass media offers identities and extends recognition to certain actions and practices. The recognition the mass media bestows upon certain celebrities is recognition that consumers can strive for. Consider the tourist boom created in New Zealand by the *Lord of the Rings* trilogy. "Lord of the Rings Tours" (2005), one of many companies offering treks to the movie set locations, claims on its Web site to be "the only tour in New Zealand which gives you the opportunity to handle and try on items featured in the movies." On the tour, tourists get to wear helmets and armor, and to wield swords, all of which were used in the movies. The tour, then, offers tourists the option of ceasing to observe the films and instead to take the place of a hero within the films. The film, *Lord of the Rings*, has created an imagined landscape that merges with tourists' own possible futures. Lord of the Rings Tours prospers through actualizing the possible future selves that have been imagined through the film.

An alternative to traveling to film locations is to simply enact aspects of films or books in imagination. For example, the book *Lord of the Rings* stimulated the development of role playing games (see Guimarães & Simão, in this volume). These can be played in small groups, on a computer or accross the Internet. In all cases the players take the place of a hero in an imaginary landscape. Through the course of the game the player triumphs over evil, develops new skills and abilities, and gains power and prestige. Guimarães and Simão dissect the fabric of intersubjectivtiy in these games, showing how people move positions within the game; my concern, however, is with the fact that people are striving to take the place of a fictional other.

In order to further theorize the role of the mass media in constructing and extending the spatial and temporal environment, the concept of symbolic resources (Zittoun, in this volume; Zittoun, Duveen, Gillespie, Ivinson, & Psaltis, 2003) is useful. Symbolic resources provide a conceptual bridge between the collective and the individual. At the collective level there are cultural elements (such as books and films), artifacts (such as tools, languages, and heuristics) and social representations (shared definitions of an object within a group). These semiotic forms become symbolic resources in the moment of being used by an individual within a particular context and to a particular end. According to Zittoun (2004), symbolic resources are used to serve practical, identity, and emotional functions. The present chapter identifies another function of symbolic resources: tourists use symbolic resources to extend their spatial and temporal environment and to imagine possible future selves. That is to say, symbolic resources can offer individuals new subject positions that are worth striving for and by thus opening up new paths of action they expand the individual's temporal and spatial environment.

The Case Of Ladakh

Ladakh is a region in the northernmost part of India, bordering Tibet and China. It is on the high altitude Tibetan plateau, and culturally has much in common with Tibet. The majority of Ladakhis are Buddhist, they speak a variant of the Tibetan language, and have many similar customs. Tourists travel to Ladakh in order to experience Buddhist culture and the Himalayan mountain peaks. Once in Ladakh, tourists go to cultural festivals and trek to remote villages. Many choose to travel to Ladakh as a substitute for going to Tibet, which, they say, is less accessible.

The association of Ladakh with Tibet is evident in several ways. The *Lonely Planet* guidebook (Mayhew, Plunkett, Coxall, Saxton, & Greenway, 2000, p. 210) refers to the palace in Leh, as "a miniature version of the Potala in Lhasa." In Leh's market, vendors appeal to tourists with "*Tintin in Tibet*" T-shirts and copies of the film *Seven Years in Tibet*. Another association that is evident in the tourist mind is with Shangri-la. Shangri-la is the name of a fictional location in James Hilton's (1933) popular novel *Lost Horizon* which in 1937 was made into a film that won two Oscars. In the book and film, Shangri-la is a hidden idyllic community nestled in the high Himalaya (Tibet is implied, but not mentioned). Since the film the image of Shangri-la has sedimented into the environment of tourists, who now often assume that Shangri-la does exist. Indeed, in an effort to boost tourism the Chinese government has recently declared that a small village in Yunnan province is Shangri-la (British Broadcasting Corporation, 1998). Similarly, in Leh many Ladakhis try to cash in on the association. In Leh one can find the Shangri-la restaurant, Shangri-la trekking company and a Shangri-la bookshop.

The data used in the present chapter are from 25 naturalistic group discussions and 10 interviews, all with tourists in Ladakh. The naturalistic group discussions were broad ranging, covering all aspects of tourists' relation to Ladakh. The interviews were based on tourists' own photographs. Before the interview, the interviewer collected rolls of film from the tourists, arranged for them to be developed, and then used the photographs as stimulus material for the interviews (the tourists were given a free set of prints for participating in the interview). On average each tourist provided 46 photographs. In total 462 photographs were collected. However, each tourist only saw and responded to their own photographs. Both the group discussions and the interviews were audio recorded. In neither the group discussions nor in the individual interviews were tourists asked explicitly about the mass media or the role that it plays in shaping their expectations.

The data were coded for the spontaneous invocation of the mass media by tourists. This yielded 116 instances. Across these instances, a broad range of mass media elements were invoked, including guidebooks (usually the *Lonely Planet*), the *National Geographic*, books on India or Ladakh (e.g., *Are You Experienced*, *Karma Cola*, and *A Journey in Ladakh*) and a variety of films (e.g., *Ancient Futures*, *The Beach*, *Lost Horizon*, *Seven Years in Tibet*, *Himalaya*, and *Easy Rider*). These symbolic resources serve three main purposes in tourists' discussions of their experiences in Ladakh: providing "facts" about Ladakh, providing ideals toward which tourists strive, and facilitating reflective criticisms of tourism. The following analysis focuses only upon the first two uses (the third has been discussed in Zittoun et al., 2003). The first analytic section explores how tourists use symbolic resource to extend the spatial and temporal environment. The second analytic section examines how symbolic resources provide ideals (possible future selves) towards which tourists strive.

The Mass Mediated Environment

Tourists arrive in Ladakh with expectations. For example, they may expect mountains, Buddhist people and a rich traditional culture. Once they get off the plane, or bus, these expectations are not likely to be completely fulfilled. The capital Leh, is surrounded by high mountains, but they are not the most spectacular mountains in Ladakh. The people tourists meet in Leh are not likely to appear particularly Buddhist or traditional. In Boesch's (1991) terminology, there may be a disjunction between the "should-value" and the "is-value." Tourists, however, are rarely disheartened. They say that Leh is not the "real" Ladakh, and that in order to experience the real Ladakh one has to trek to remote villages that are cut off from roads and the telecommunication infrastructure. In this sense, even while the tourist is in Leh (where most tourists spend most of their time), the Ladakh that they talk about is still beyond their immediate experience (i.e., it is part of the symbolically extended environment).

The following excerpt is from a discussion that I had with an American tourist, Matt,[1] who had just arrived in Leh. The discussion took place in the courtyard of a guesthouse with several other tourists joining in the discussion. Although Matt had never been in Ladakh before, and had not yet been to any remote villages, he still spoke admiringly of Ladakhi village life. Accordingly I asked him if he would have liked to have grown up in such a village:

Matt: As long as you are not hungry, not starving, I mean its a tough life, but you are more with nature than you are in the States, you are really living by the seasons, and by-

Me: Is that a good thing?

Matt: Yeah, I think so, its how we are meant to be, its how we started out as human beings, living with nature, its like the divide between the settled and the nomad world, they are sort of more the nomads, they herd sheep [...] We have so many things in America that distract us, there are so many things we buy, like, televisions, radios—you are so worried about money, it just affects how you are, but here, when you

are out on the mountain pass with the shepherds, and all
you are thinking about is just like getting your sheep back
to home, and getting a getting a good night's sleep and getting up in the morning

Matt is invoking one of the iconic images associated with Ladakh,
namely, the nomadic shepherd. There is a postcard series on Ladakh
titled *Nomads* that contains several postcards of Ladakhis with animals.
Also, in the guidebooks Ladakhis are often portrayed herding animals on
mountain passes (e.g., Mayhew et al., 2000, opposite p. 273). For Matt,
this image crystallizes the utopia of a simple, authentic, and stress-free life
that is the opposite of contemporary American society. The point to be
made about Matt's observations is that he has never been to the villages
and he has never experienced the life of a Ladakhi herder. The life of the
Ladakhi herder, however, is a real part of his environment. It is real
enough to make him criticize his own country, and real enough to motivate him to go trekking in the mountains. The image of the nomadic
herder is what he will strive to find. But where has this rich image come
from? The answer to this question emerges as the conversation continues:

> Matt: I'm thinking about, I read a really interesting book about
> this, by Bruce Chatwin, did you ever read anything by him?
> [Orienting to me]
>
> Me: Don't think so
>
> Matt   [...] His last book *Songlines*, its like half fiction, half nonfic-
> tion, there is a whole section on nomads that is really inter-
> esting, things he witnessed and talking to the nomads, how
> they lived (pause) I guess that is why Ladakh interests me,
> it's that nomad life, it's life that has been going before set-
> tled civilization, its how people were, going from place to
> place when the weather changed

Part of the origin of Matt's imagination of Ladakhi village life comes
from the book *The Songlines*, by Bruce Chatwin. This book concerns Australian Aborigines, and Matt fuses this into his imagination of Ladakh. In
Matt's mind Ladakhis and the Australian Aborigines are equivalent
because they participate in "life that has been going on before settled civilization." In actuality, there are only a few seminomadic populations in
Ladakh and Ladakh has had "settled civilization" for over a millennium.
But Matt is not talking about Ladakh as such. The idea of nomadic life
"before settled civilization" would exist in Matt's mind, even if Ladakh did
not exist. This is part of Matt's extended environment. This image is sustained not just in Chatwin's book, but in innumerable other mass media

products. The image is part of our collective imagination, or social representations (Moscovici, 1984), of traditional life. Matt, then, lives in an environment that has been collectively and culturally extended.

The experience of Ladakh cannot be clearly separated from the mass mediated images that tourists bring with them. Events, places, or ways of life read about in guidebooks and seen in films organize the ongoing experience of Ladakh. So many aspects of the tourists' environment are mass mediated, from factual information about where the bus station is and the height of nearby mountain peaks, to less consensual information about the character of the Ladakhis and their place in the modern world. The experience and the mass mediated image blend together, each supporting the other.

For example, one young British student was explaining in a discussion that the Ladakhis "have a strong sense of community." However, she had not been outside of the capital Leh. Leh is far removed from the ideal image of Shangri-La; it is a bustling city, with shops, hawkers and persuasive souvenir sellers. Leh is in the throws of "modernization" as demonstrated by a massive increase in cars, concrete houses, and rubbish. The tourist industry has proved so lucrative that migrant workers from across India arrive in Leh for the summer months to work—almost doubling the population of Leh. Given this state of affairs, I asked the young British student where she saw evidence of this "sense of community" in Leh. She replied: "if I had not seen that film [*Ancient Futures*], I would not know how community it is." This quote betrays the way in which symbolic resources, like the film *Ancient Futures*, flesh out tourists' experience of Ladakh and extend the environment that the tourist inhabits.

When Experience Coincides With the Ideal

Ideals are an important part of the mass mediated environment. Ideals, in this sense, refer to ideal possible future experiences and ideal possible future selves. Tourists invest considerable time and money travelling to Ladakh, and once in Ladakh, they spend more time and money trekking to remote villages. These tourists are striving after some ideal experience—a possible future that they feel is within their grasp. Tourist striving is motivated by such ideals. Analyzing the interview data, which uses tourists' own photographs as stimulus material, reveals the nature and origin of these possible ideals.

Tourists often take photographs at exactly the moment when their ongoing experience coincides with the ideal towards which they are striving. Consider, for example, Figure 7.1. This is a photograph taken by a couple from the United Kingdom. They had taken a scooter and traveled

Figure 7.1.   A tourist's photograph of Thiksey *gonpa*.

out of Leh, up the valley to see Thiksey *gonpa* (a Buddhist monastery).
When they arrived at the *gonpa*, they took this photograph. I asked the
woman why she took the photograph, and she replied:

> They [the Buddhist monasteries] look incredible, because I had a book on
> Ladakh, and it was all the pictures I had seen and now I was there!

This photograph is a very typical representation of Ladakh, and similar photographs can be found in postcards (e.g., Figure 7.2) and in
guidebooks. Looking at the photograph, the monastery, with its white
washed buildings and red temples on top, resembles the Potala Palace
in Lhasa, in Tibet, where the Dalai Lama lived before going into exile.
The Potala Palace is often featured in books and film (e.g., Figure 7.3)—
maybe it was an image of the Potala Palace that this tourist brought to
Ladakh? However, it does not matter for our purposes exactly which
book provided the imagery. The point is that the woman brought to

Figure 7.2.   A postcard of Thiksey *gonpa*.

Figure 7.3.   A still of the Potala Palace from the film *Seven Years in Tibet*.

Ladakh images from Western culture, conveyed through the mass media, and that she uses these images as criteria by which to judge her own experience. She took the photograph *because* what she saw was just like in the book: her experience conformed to her ideal expectation. The image of the Buddhist monastery existed, via books, before she ever arrived in Ladakh. This tourist's striving was, in part, an attempt to actualize this image which she achieves both in her experience and in the photograph.

The ideal image that tourists strive toward can be very general. This is evident in several references to the *National Geographic* magazine. Although the *National Geographic* has had several articles on Ladakh, there is nothing to suggest that any of the tourists I interviewed had actually seen these articles (the last major article was in 1978). Instead, the *National Geographic* is used by tourists to refer to a particular genre of the exotic. And it is towards this type of exotic that tourists strive. For example, when a young tourist from the United States of America saw, for the first time, her photograph of a dancing monk (Figure 7.4) she exclaimed "*National Geographic*, here I come!" The photograph has no tourists in the way, the colors are bright, the subject matter is exotic, and the dancer is clearly in motion. The photograph appears to provide a window on an ancient ritual. The indication of this exclamation is that she had achieved the ideal that she desired and had been striving for. This is not to say that she is reproducing an image that she saw in the *National Geographic* (though one can find very similar photographs in the magazine, for example, Figure 7.5), but rather that she felt her photograph was as good as those presented in the *National Geographic*.

Books and films are also be used to position the tourist's own experiences of Ladakh in the minds of significant others—to answer the question "what would significant others think about this particular experience?" Figure 7.6 is a photograph taken by Leo, another tourist from the United States of America. Leo had done a 20-day trek. Figure 7.6 is a photograph from this trek, and when he saw the photograph he said:

> That's a picture of the trail, going down into this gorge, and this bridge was at the bottom, [...] I took that picture for friends back home, they are going to ask me like, "so you walked through the Himalaya, were there photos like in the movie *Himalaya*?" For the most part there weren't cliff hangers, but some were pretty extreme, so I kind of took this picture to show people back home you know that, although this does not look terribly dangerous, it does look very raggedy and steep

In the photograph we see a deep gorge with turquoise water and an archaic looking stone bridge. In the film *Himalaya*, the deep gorges, tur-

Figure 7.4.   Tourist's photograph of a dancing monk.

quoise water and stone bridges are by most accounts remarkable. Figure 7.6 thus captures some of the most vivid aspects of the film *Himalaya*, and is distinctly similar to many images in guidebooks (e.g., Figure 7.7). Moreover, rather than just reproduce these images, the photograph shows clearly that this is the trail that Leo trekked on. The photograph is evidence that Leo has had an experience equivalent with that which is merely presented in the film *Himalaya*. Leo knows that his friends have seen, and were impressed by, the film *Himalaya*. By anchoring his own experiences and photographs into this imaginative landscape, he is able

Figure 7.5.   An image of a dancing Ladakhi monk from the
National Geographic (Abercrombie, 1978).

to claim a desired position in their eyes. In this sense, Leo is not just striving for a certain ideal experience, but simultaneously he is striving for
social recognition from the other.

One surprising ideal that several tourists have regarding Ladakh concerns motor biking. The *Lonely Planet* guidebook makes considerable
mention of the fact that to get to Leh from Delhi by road one must cross
the earth's second highest road, and that if one drives north from Leh,
one crosses the earth's highest road (5,602m). Many tourists speak of
these roads with awe: there is desolate scenery, very few people and high

Figure 7.6.   An image from Trekking in Ladakh (Loram, 1996).

mountain peaks. For some tourists the scenery, and the guidebook fact about the height of the roads, raises expectations of an epic road journey. Several places in Leh cater to this type of striving by renting motorbikes and scooters to tourists.

Figure 7.4 presents a photograph from a middle aged Italian man, Simone, who, along with his two companions, had rented two scooters. The highlight of Simone's experience of Ladakh concerned this scooter trip. Over half of Simone's photographs are not only of this scooter trip, but are of the road. In Figure 7.4 one can see the scooters, the desert and the blue sky. The tourists are wearing sunglasses and one has a baseball cap worn backwards. When Simone saw this photograph, he said:

> This was the first stop, just outside of Leh, you know, we just wanted to have an *Easy Rider* picture.

Figure 7.7. Leo's photograph of the trail.

Easy Rider is a cult film in which two counterculture bikers travel from Los Angeles to New Orleans. The *Easy Rider* image is one of freedom, the open road, and adventure. It appears that this film helped to structure Simone's ideal expectation of riding on a scooter in Ladakh. The utterance "we just wanted to have an *Easy Rider* picture" reveals the way in which the film *Easy Rider* crystallizes and objectifies the ideal being strived for. Again, the photograph is taken at the moment when the ideal coincides, to some degree, with the experience.

The ideal of traveling over the Himalaya on motorbikes is surprisingly common. There is even a trekking company that caters to tourists who have this striving. They specialize in taking groups of tourists on motorbikes from Delhi up to Leh. The journey takes several days, and the company provides Enfield motorbikes, a mechanic and a guide. The following excerpt is from a discussion I had with one group of tourists who had just completed this journey:

> Me: So what was the highlight of this epic journey?
> Paul: Just amazing places

Figure 7.8.   Simone's *Easy Rider* photograph.

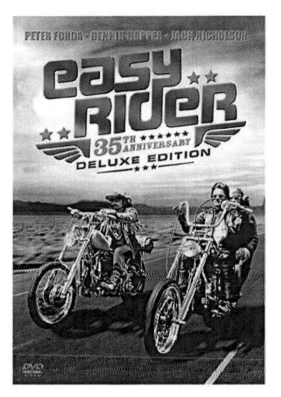

Figure 7.9.   The film *Easy Rider.*

Mark: Riding through the desert, absolutely unbelievable, the
         scenery, and just, I don't know
Etgar: For him it's the first time to be in a desert
Mark: Yeah, first time in a desert, so that on a bike is unbelievable
         Herb: There is something about that *Easy Rider,* long road
         kind of thing
Mark: But its true, its amazing, its not just on the film it looks
         good, it bloody is good, it really is good [...] you are going
         through flat desert, and you just see these huge mountains
         with snow, and you are like just there, it's boiling hot, and
         there is snow, its just like a postcard.

Easy Rider is used as a vivid image that situates the experience. The
phrase "it's not just on the film it looks good, it bloody is good" is particularly revealing. The film concerns a road trip in the United States of
America during the 1960s. These tourists have traveled on motorbikes

over the Himalaya. However after this latter experience, the tourist implies that he has had the former experience. He says that it "is" good. The implication is that he has done the same activity and had the same experience as depicted in the film. Rather than just watching the film, he has been in the position of the actor in the film, and has experienced the same as the hero in the film.

Striving: The Role of the Other

The invocations of *Easy Rider* and *Himalaya* point towards a way of reconciling the dialogical and social aspect of the self with the temporal and striving aspect of the self. In both cases the image that tourists are striving to actualize is the experience that they have observed in the other. First they see the other trek through the Himalaya or ride motorbikes across the United States of America. The experiences and actions of these heroes in the mass media are admired and given recognition by the tourist and the community in general. Theoretically, we can say that a zone of preferred development is established (Valsiner, 1998). In the landscape of future possible positions that people can occupy, these positions become privileged by the community. Accordingly, the tourist then strives to become like the hero, to engage in the same actions as the hero, and to have the same experiences as the hero. Much scholarship on Mead has focused upon taking the perspective of the other, which has become an increasingly cognitive concept (Gillespie, 2005). I am pointing to something much more material. The tourists are not trying to "take the perspective" of these heroes, *instead they are trying to take the social position of these heroes,* and thus to enact and live out the experiences of these heroes —to be these heroes. Taking the social position of the other, compared to taking the perspective of the other, is embodied and experiential. It is in part due to the inadequacy of simply taking the perspective of the other that tourists strive to become the other.

Striving to become the hero, or other, is evidenced in the following excerpt from Katie, a young British student. In a group discussion, Katie was talking about the journey up to Ladakh on the bus. She was particularly struck by the "dramatic" scenery. After a pause in the conversation she said:

> I have to keep pinching myself that it's actually real, because its the kind of scenery that you see in *National Geographics*, you look through and its like "wow imagine being there" (pause) I can't believe I am here seeing it!

The interesting thing about this utterance is that it illustrates the switch of social position that I argue is fundamental to the striving tourist. She begins by saying that Ladakh has the kind of scenery that "you" see in the *National Geographic*, and that "you" look through and say "wow imagine being there." After the pause she says "I can't believe I am here." This is interesting because the "you" in the first part of the utterance refers to the general gaze of her community, and to her in the past. She uses the pronoun "you" because she is no longer the viewer of these books. As the second part of the utterance reveals, her "I" is now in Ladakh, and is "seeing it." She no longer has to "imagine being there." The "there" has become the "here." The recognition that Katie and her community bestow upon people who have such experiences, is now bestowed upon Katie. That which was imagined through the mass media has become a real experience. The mass media offered the future possibility, and travelling through Ladakh has actualized this possibility. The important point, however, is that by virtue of having this experience, Katie has changed position. Katie has become the other (i.e., equivalent to the photographer for the *National Geographic*) that she so admired.

The change of social position experienced by Katie, is experienced by other tourists as well. One young Israeli tourist, David, had gone on a scooter trip and had arranged for a photograph of him on the scooter to be taken. When David saw this photograph in the interview, he exclaimed: "that's me on the bike! I cant believe it, at home I don't do that!" David's utterance reveals a degree of surprise and astonishment, which is also evident in Katie's utterance. Previously it was the other who trekked in the Himalaya, and it was the other who rode on motorbikes. The striving tourist occupies these social positions, and thus, becomes the other. This change of social position means that the admiration and recognition previously offered to the other, now returns and becomes a form of pride in self.

CONCLUSION

Conceiving of striving as striving to become other, provides a way of integrating the dialogical self with the striving self. According to Hermans (1999) the self is a landscape of I-positions. Some of these I-positions self identifies with, while other I-positions self does not identify with. Hermans (2001) calls these self-positions (e.g., me-as-a-woman, me-as-Italian, me-as-a-tourist, etc.) and other-positions (e.g., those-politicians, those-heroes-in-the-movies, those-terrorists, etc.). Now the interesting thing with both Katie and David is that during the course of their travels, some other-positions become self-positions. Specifically, for Katie those-photographers-in-the-Himalaya becomes me-in-the-Himalaya, and for David, those-people-on-motorbikes becomes me-on-a-motorbike.

The proposition being advanced is that the distinction between self-positions and other-positions, within the dialogical self, can be used to help understand the striving self. The assumption is that self-positions and other-positions can be inter-related such that one I-position can give recognition to a second I-position. A simple example is the tourist who admires, or gives recognition to, the hero in *Easy Rider*. The hero in *Easy Rider* occupies, within the tourist's dialogical self, a privileged other-position. The hero objectifies, or crystallizes, a zone of privileged or preferred development (Valsiner, 1998). The interesting thing about this interrelation is that the motivating dynamic is structure of recognition established within the dialogical self. The recognition offered by self to this other-position is motivation for self to self to strive to occupy the position of the other (e.g., hero in *Easy Rider*) and thus to make this other-position a self-position. If this is achieved, then the recognition extended to the hero becomes reversed and is extended toward self. Abstracting from this toward a more general statement, one could say that, the recognition that self gives to the other is simultaneously recognition promised, or extended, to self (if self manages to occupy the position of the other) and thus constitutive of self's motivation for striving.

This general statement manages to link together the dialogical and social self with the temporal and striving self. Within the dialogical self there is a system of I-positions, which include both self-positions and other-positions. The point being made concerns the other-positions. All of these other-positions, whether they are privileged or denigrated are not just different "parts" of a "spatialised" self, they are also possible future selves. These other-positions within the dialogical self constitute an important aspect of self's temporally extended environment. Each of these other-positions is a possible future self. Moreover, the attitude that self has to these other-positions (e.g., the admiration of the hero or the scorn for the villain) sets up a system of recognition that motivates self to strive to occupy some social positions, and to avoid other social positions.

NOTE

1.   All the names have been changed.

ACKNOWLEDGMENT

I would like to thank Claudia Catacchio, Deepika Sharma, and Jason King for discussing the tourist photographs with me and Tania Zittoun, Lívia Simão, and Jaan Valsiner for making useful comments on an earlier draft.

REFERENCES

Abercrombie, T. J. (1978). Ladakh: The last Shangri-La. *National Geographic, 153*(3), 332-359.

Adam, B. (1990). *Time & social theory*. Cambridge, England: Polity.

Anderson, B. (1993). *Imagined communities: Reflections on the origin and spread of nationalism*. London: Verso.

British Broadcasting Corporation. (1998). *Promoting paradise in Shangri-La*. Retrieved November 24, 2005, from http://news.bbc.co.uk/1/hi/world/asia-pacific/164902.stm.

Beeton, S. (2001). Smiling for the camera: The influence of film audiences on a budget tourism destination. *Tourism, Culture & Communication, 3*(1), 15-25.

Boesch, E. E. (1991). *Symbolic action theory and cultural psychology*. Berlin, Germany: Springer.

Bruce, D. (1997). *Scotland—The movie*. Palm Desert, CA: Polygon.

Burke, K. (1969). *A grammar of motives*. Berkeley: University of California Press.

Gillespie, A. (2005). G. H. Mead: Theorist of the social act. *Journal for the Theory of Social Behaviour, 35*(1), 19-39.

Hermans, H. J. M. (1999). Dialogical thinking and self-innovation. *Culture & Psychology, 5*(1), 67-87.

Hermans, H. J. M. (2001). The dialogical self: Toward a theory of personal and cultural positioning. *Culture & Psychology, 7*(3), 243-281.

Hermans, H. J. M. (2002). The dialogical self as a society of mind. *Theory & Psychology, 12*(2), 147-160.

Hilton, J. (1933). *Lost horizon*. Delhi: Book Faith India.

Holton, G. (1975). On the role of themata in scientific thought. *Science, 188*(4186), 328-334.

James, W. (1878/1992). *Remarks on Spencer's definition of mind as correspondence: Writings, 1878-1899*. New York: Library of America. (Original work published 1878).

Laing, R. D. (1960). *The divided self: A study of sanity and madness*. London: Travistock.

Loram, C. (1996). *Trekking in Ladakh*. Surrey, England: Trailblazer.

Lord of the Rings Tours. (2005). Retrieved November 24, 2005, from http://www.lordoftheringstours.co.nz

Mayhew, B., Plunkett, R., Coxall, M., Saxton, P., & Greenway, P. (2000). *Indian Himalaya* (2nd ed.). London: Lonely Planet.

McLuhan, M. (1964). *Understanding media: The extensions of man*. London: Ark.

Mead, G. H. (1927). The objective reality of perspectives. In S. Brightman (Ed.), *Proceedings of the sixth international congress of philosophy* (pp. 75-85). New York: Longmans, Green.

Mead, G. H. (1932). *The philosophy of the present*. La Salle, IL: Open Court.

Moscovici, S. (1984). The phenomenon of social representations. In R. Farr & S. Moscovici (Eds.), *Social representations*. Cambridge, MA: Cambridge University Press.

Rowan, J., & Cooper, M. (1999). *The plural self: Multiplicity in everyday life*. London: Sage.

Tooke, N., & Baker, M. (1996). Seeing is believing: The effect of film on visitor numbers to screened locations. *Tourism Management, 17*(2), 87-94.

Urry, J. (1990). *The tourist gaze: Leisure and travel in contemporary societies*. London: Sage.

Valsiner, J. (1998). *The guided mind*. Cambridge, MA: Harvard University Press.

Wertsch, J. V. (1998). *Mind as action*. Oxford, England: Oxford University Press.

Zittoun, T. (2004). Symbolic competencies for developmental transitions: The case of the choice of first names. *Culture & Psychology, 10*(2), 131-160.

Zittoun, T., Duveen, G., Gillespie, A., Ivinson, G., & Psaltis, C. (2003). The use of symbolic resources in developmental transitions. *Culture & Psychology, 9*(4), 415-448.

CHAPTER 8

DYNAMICS OF INTERIORITY

Ruptures and Transitions in the Self Development

Tania Zittoun

Als das Kind Kind war,

warf es einen Stock als Lanze gegen den Baum,

und sie zittert da heute noch.[1]

—Peter Handke, *Lied Vom Kindsein* (1987)

How does one become, who one is? What are the events who have given a person shades and shapes, who are the others whose voices have become one's own, what are the events that redefine one's trajectory? Here, I will only examine the role of poems, novels, and images, and other objects made out of signs in the fabric of self. I will also examine only one life story; and I will only focus on its moments of ruptures and possible transformations. Through this one case study, I will propose conceptual tools which might enable to examine other lives in the making.

Otherness in Question: Labyrinths of the Self, 187–214
Copyright © 2007 by Information Age Publishing

DIFFERENT LIVES OF A MAN

The life story we will examine is the following. It is that of a man called alternatively Hans-Peter, Peter, Juan Pedro, Uri[2] and Professor U. Uri is the name that I will use here unless I am referring to particular periods of his life. Uri was born in Germany in 1928, from a Jewish upper middle class family, liberal, and assimilated. He grew up as the first child, brother of two girls. His childhood happens in the shadow of political events: the National-Socialist Party takes the power in 1933, and relatively quickly Jews start to be the object of discrimination and persecution. Uri's parents decide to move the children away from Germany as often as they can. In 1938, Hitler annexes Austria; pogroms and arrests become constant; Uri and his sisters are sent to Switzerland, before being joined by his parents; the family then moves to South America. From 1939 to 1948, Uri grows up in Argentina. His childhood and youth happen in the contact with European refugees, who are antifascists, socialists, Jewish immigrants, some of them Zionists. Uri tries out various professions—he starts medical studies, works as a clerk, engages an apprenticeship as a carpenter, sells advertising spaces for cinema, and eventually learns agriculture.

Uri moves to Israel in 1949, where he stays until 1957. He becomes one of the founders of a Kibbutz—cooperative farms—where he works as a tractor driver, and becomes general secretary. As a soldier, he protects the frontiers and participates to the war in 1957. In that year, though, Uri leaves Israel and moves back to Switzerland. He registers in an applied center for psychology, joins the University, and becomes a guidance counselor. He creates a group for educational research and planning, which questions the dynamics of school selection and social inequalities. In parallel, he studies sociology and trains to become a psychoanalyst. In 1967, aged 39, he marries his first wife, with whom he has two sons.

In 1971 Uri becomes head of educational research in a Swiss canton, president of the pedagogic commission of the Swiss Conference of Ministers of Education, while he practices as a psychoanalyst. He becomes an expert for planning and evaluation of teaching, works for the World Bank and for various organisms supporting development in Asian countries. He divorces, and marries his second wife in 1991. Officially retired since 1992, Uri still works as an expert for national research programs, educational reforms, theoretical explorations for the OECD, and for the first time teaches at University—he becomes professor U.

Uri's life course is striking by its richness and diversity. It is constructed through ruptures, radical changes, and life reorientation. Some of these ruptures are imposed—the war, the emigration—others are chosen—marriages and professional moves. Each rupture has required an important work of transformation. Uri had to redefine himself in each new situation, had to acquire new languages, skills and expertise, and had to maintain a sense of continuity through time. What supported such transformations, and how could such changes be facilitated? Or how can we, as psychologist, describe such changes and highlight developmental dynamics?

LOOKING FOR THEORETICAL MODELS

The study of development of self in the life course is still searching for its theoretical frame. Major contributions have been given by the patient study of life courses, and various theoretical sketches have been proposed to capture the dominant shape or patterns of such life development (Smelser & Erikson, 1980). However, for each model that can be proposed, other voices raise to signal the cultural, moral, or social blind spots of researchers. Hence, thinking life in terms of growth and decline supposes a clear sense of what is the "maximum" of a human's life (a person's physical strength?); stages models are quick to be read as norms (one is expected to get a professional position, and then to have children). Even models that propose general principles—physical and biological sources are progressively supported by cultural ones—tend to suggest that there is a maximization of a person's possible uses of resources (Baltes, 1997).

It is a common place to say that development is constrained by biological, psychical, material, social, and societal forces. Change, however, is constant—for consciousness and activity are a stream (James, 1892/1984), and experiencing the world is ever moving; the transactions between a changing person and her changing world, is what we can study. Change has no particular direction in itself (Valsiner, 2000). If it is so, should we say that development is change, or rather, that every change is developmental?

Ruptures and Transitions

The unit of analysis given by the pair *rupture-transition* might help us to analyze the flow of change, and thus to clarify this point. The model is inspired by biological or mathematical models suggesting that a given system, with its normal changes, might be disrupted by a catastrophe—a brutal modification of its environment or its functioning (Thom, 1975). In order to subsist, the system must be rearranged or modified until it finds a relative stability. Similarly, ruptures can be seen as "catastrophes" in people's lives; transitions are the processes of restructuration that follow. The pair rupture-transition thus corresponds to the processes identified by Piaget and Inhelder (1966/1969) as disequilibration-equilibration, with this main difference that the former apply to cognitive structures, while ruptures-transitions can affect a great variety of human conduct.

Ruptures

Ruptures are interruption of the normal flow of events. Humans have a sense of being specific and themselves, and of having some continuity through time (Erikson, 1968; James, 1890). Consequently, the first criteria to consider an event as a significant rupture, is that it is subjectively, consciously or unconsciously, perceived by a person as questioning her sense of self and sense of continuity. From a person's perspective, a rupture is felt when her representations and understandings of a part of the world are not anymore adequate to apprehend and organize the given of her experience. Ruptures can thus wake emotions and have unconscious prolongations—each rupture, even the happiest one, always supposes a loss, and mourning (Bowlby, 1980; Bridges, 1980/1996).

Ruptures can be very diverse. Humans have a wide variety of experiences in various spheres of their life. Some ruptures affect the whole sense of who one is, as do crises (Erikson, 1950/1995, 1968), challenges (Smelser, 1980), or turning points in the course of a life (Rutter, 1994). Other ruptures can be more local, and affect only one sphere of experience, without dramatic desequilibration of the whole person. As we will see in the case of Uri's life, ruptures are at times caused by a single event—as when Uri moves place—and at other, by an accumulation of events—as when the Nazi power progressively modifies the environment from a familiar, to a hostile anti-Semitic one. Some ruptures are actively initiated by a person—such as when Uri moves away from his country; others are imposed, either being culturally set (such as being sent to school), or being accidental. Ruptures also have various scales. Some ruptures are caused by changes at the scale of the societal conditions, as it is the case with the *Anschluss* of Austria. A person's immediate sphere of experience can be changed, as it is the case when Uri is taken away from his family or they all move country. Interpersonal relationship can be modified—Uri gets married, has children. Finally, some changes are internal, such a when Uri enters in adolescence.

If ruptures are defined as events questioning a person's sense of taken-for-granted, they do not necessarily overlap objective changes. For example, moving place as a child might be a major rupture; but in Uri's adult life, moving place has become a normal event, which requires some arrangements which have become routine, or for which he has some expertise.

Transitions

Transitions are the processes that correspond to re-equilibration subsequent to ruptures. These might involve processes going in a direction of assimilation or accommodation. They aim at restore one's sense of continuity and integrity of self beyond the rupture (Carugati, 2004; Erikson, 1968; James, 1892/1984; Palmonari, 1993), and to allow a person to define conduct and understanding for the new given. Processes of transition thus reduce uncertainty by creating normality.[3] Note that this definition of transition as processes contrasts with approaches that see transitions as period between well-defined stages (e.g., the school to work transition).

Transition processes can be seen as belonging to interdependent classes of events, that have usually have been analyzed under three different headings: processes of identity change and repositioning; process of learning and skill acquisition; processes of meaning making, including emotional regulation and elaboration of the unconscious processes awaken by the rupture (Perret-Clermont & Zittoun, 2002).

Repositioning and identity change imply social and subjective change. For example, as a young man arriving in Israel, Uri was confronted to a new space, new persons, who would react to him very differently than he was used to. In terms of social positioning, his relatively privileged upper class identification is replaced by that of newcomer not speaking the shared language. The others' gaze also brings one to perceive oneself in a different manner, which might, or not, harm one's self-perception. Transition obviously involve *new forms of knowledge*: acquiring new languages, becoming a South American youngster, becoming a tractor driver or an academic professor require some learning, In turn, we see how these will be part of the identity transformation just identified.

Transition also include *meaning-making*. How will one give sense to such incessant changes? Consecutively to each major rupture, Uri had his first names changed. Name changes signal transformations of self for oneself and for other, and are the crystallization of various streams of meaning (Zittoun, 2005a). Meaning is established along two axes. On one side, it is fabricated by the linking of time: by maintaining a sense of the past, and, in the present, by working toward a future (Vygotsky, 1925/1971). On the other side, meaning is built thanks to a system of orientation—an organized system of values and criteria that are used as a basis of thinking and actions, as "piloting system." For example, one might think that Uri has, quite early, defined a "socialist-humanist" project, which has taken various forms through his life: a Zionist project in his early adulthood, a work of educational counselor, and then, as expert in education in developing countries.

Ruptures and Transitions in Development

Rupture and transitions are, for humans, motivational: disruptions of life self-evidence in irreversible time bring people to move away from what has been, and tenses them toward what will be. The work of transition is the activity in which one is engaged by moving away form a just-lost past, in order to create a better future.

With this model of ruptures and transitions I can now attempt to define development as *a sort of change*. Rupture call for transition processes, which are catalyzed periods of changes. Changes might be good enough to enable a person to restore a sense of self consistency and continuity, as well as a good enough adjustment to her environment. Changes might however leave the person with a sense of alienation—loss of self, loss of continuity, or loss of contact with her environment. A senseless self become highly problematic for further changes, for it reduces human striving, and limits possible agency in finding resources when facing ruptures. Consequently, transition processes might become minimal self-maintenance processes, often of a repetitive nature. In situations of self alienation, distancing becomes problematic, and it might be difficult for a person to apprehend the nature of a rupture, to realize the novelty of a situation, to explore its possible requirements; social alienation might limit access to means likely to be used as resources for transitions.

On this basis I will say that change in ruptures and transitions is developmental as long as it enables the person to generate new conduct, and therefore, to address new transitions with renewed possibilities. Change is not developmental when it prevents the person to engage in new transition processes, thus rather taking the form of mere repetition. However, life is often surprisingly flexible, and change which leads to apparently repetitive conduct (such as repetitive games in children) might in some cases be part of a temporary phase of reinforcement of some aspect of the person, which might then lead to more openly generative changes.

Resources and Symbolic Resources

Cultural systems are classically organized so as to provide people with support for transitions required by canonical or expected ruptures, on social or biological grounds. Traditional adolescence "rites de passage" are culturally organized supports for transitions processes required by the rupture caused by biological maturation, itself followed by the rupture of a social status change. In contrast, societies which have not developed collective representation or cultural means to address a given type of rupture leave people with the need to create, or to define support for their transition processes.

Constrains on Resources

The work of transition can be supported by the use of social, symbolic, and material. The availability of means to be used as resource is bounded by the nature of the rupture at stake. A rupture caused by an unexpected war might leave people with very little means to support transition, while a deliberate and local rupture, such as deciding to attend a chess club to learn to play, provides the person with resources to facilitate the transitions (other players, instructions, a setting, etc.). If sorts of ruptures bond possible resources, they also canalize the work of transition that can take place.

Four Main Resources—Uri's Case

What are the resources that support Uri's work of adjustment in new situations, which trigger, guide, and reinforce the emergence of new conducts reducing uncertainty? Four main types of resources can be identified. First, social support and interpersonal relationships are of major importance: parents, relatives, refugee help groups, are fundamental in the survival and the relocation of Uri's family. Material resources are equally important—one has to have financial means, clothes, food, in order to overcome ruptures such as the one the family lived. Third, one can mobilize various forms of knowledge and experience: social, cognitive, technical knowledge, skills, or strategies that might enable to overcome this or that aspect of the new demanding situations. Fourth, to support the work of meaning making, people need cultural resources—cultural constructs that carry meanings that other people found in their experiences. Social representations, shared beliefs, patterns of conducts might be used as cultural resources. One particular subgroup of cultural resources are these made on the basis of objects of fiction—novels, poetry, music, films. When these are used to illuminate some aspect of one's real or inner life, I will call them symbolic resources (Zittoun, 2004b). A *symbolic resource* is therefore here: (a) a configuration of semiotic units; (b) which are bounded, materially (as a symphony is "bounded" by a CD) or socially (as a religious ritual is "bounded" by a religious institution); (c) which requires an imaginary experience.

Interiority

To say that a cultural experience can mediate thinking or mind and the making of the self, requires a certain definition of self. The subject, the person, and her inner world, have been the great losses of some streams of social and humans sciences at the end of last millennium. As dialogical approaches have shown, interactions with others require for a person a form of decentring—a partial imaginary move to the position of the other, as if one would see the world from that perspective (Gillespie, 2006, in this volume). A person's experience can be seen as a story of subjective de-location and relocation (Benson, 2001). Some of these positions are evanescent and adopted once; others are taken on a regular basis. They thus progressively become the armatures of the "architecture of the self" (Gillespie, 2007; Zittoun, 2005a). The architecture of the self is the imaginary structure offering guiding lines for the moves of the center of one's consciousness and attention. The *center* is not as much a place, as a constantly changing moment.

Fiction and cultural experiences are techniques for guiding such relocation of aspects of self. Cultural experiences offer to a person an imaginary semiotically constructed world. To render a cultural experience meaningful and alive, a person has to mobilize her past memories and embodied experiences. One understands an English novel because one has memories of castles, woods, aspirations, and sadness. The memories are reorganized and composed following the narrative line; they are however arranged in a new fashion. In that sense the might bring the person to adopt new perspective on woods and sadness, and experience new feelings. Cultural experiences offer "vicarious experiences" (Nell, 1988)— they bring in a time and space beyond the here and now, but also, they might transform one's apprehension of this shared reality subsequently (Zittoun, 2005b). Cultural experiences are powerful because they suppose the meeting of one's unique embodied feelings, memories, and experience, and symbolic objects made out of sign designating or containing other possible human experiences. Having a cultural experience supposes the blending of two realities—inner life and the social, or an embodied first person perspective and a distant third person perspective (Gillespie, 2005b, in press). It is this mixed interface that can be called "interiority."

Interiority is thus not a place that needs an eye to be seen. It is a moment or a quality of human experience. It is the moment "between" one's reading, hearing, watching of cultural elements, and one's subsequent reflection, expressions or forgetting of it—it is between internalization and externalization. It is also, as psychoanalysts underline, between the socially shared reality (language, rules, coded) and the innermost private thoughts and desires; it is "between the found and the created" by the person (Green, 2002/2005; Winnicott, 1971/2001). Interiority thus enables us to conceptualize an architecture of self constantly reshaped by the meeting of one's embodied memories and the given of a particular cultural experience or its memory. Uri could thus be moved when hearing Israeli songs for the first time—crystallizing the emotions and the expectations of leaving one's country, and of being one among young people with infinite freedom and possibilities in a new land. Later on, he can think back at these melodies, and remember the emotions he had at that time; this might trigger thoughts related to his present position, such as nostalgia or disillusionment. The process of moving through these self-positions will lead Uri to a new emotional state, which is a composite of embodied memories and thoughts, from different times and places, crystallized around a symbol (Janet, 1926, 1928; Zittoun, 2004c).

Otherness in Ruptures, Transitions, and Resources

In a model of development through ruptures and transitions, otherness acquires an important function. Personal or general others can cause ruptures. Other can shape transitions, by providing means to facilitate them, or by limiting access to these. Also, others can become symbolic; crystallized experiences of others might become resources for transitions, by implementing voices and echoes of others within the person in the making (Bakhtin, 1979/1986). If transitions and ruptures are part of the movement of a striving self, otherness is likely to dynamize, shape, or enable that movement, from within and from without self.

Methodology

There are various ways to study ruptures and transitions in a life course. Here, we decide to examine one single life story, and to identify various ruptures and transitions through time. Our analysis is enabled by a model developed through previous comparisons of equivalent life trajectories (Valsiner & Sato, 2006). Here, the question examined is, what are the changing resources a person uses to support the work of transition though his life?

The present paper is based on a case study. Case studies have a long history in the study of adult development (see the works of Freud, Janet, Erikson, among many others). They enable to identify the evolution of some lines of change, having the complexity of human lives as a background. They can maintain complexity as they can be constructed through a multiplicity of perspective. Here, I present some chosen episodes within the life story thus reconstructed, as exemplary material to illustrate some insights on the work of transitions in development.

The data have been produced as follows. Uri has been a psychoanalyst for 25 years. This means that he has developed an "expert" self-reflectivity, which is the main tool of analytical practice. He was also eager to engage in autobiographical writing. I proposed him to do so by picking up moments of his life that he remembered as a rupture, with its feelings of loss or eagerness facing uncertainty. During a few months, Uri has sent me autobiographical sequences. We have then closely discussed each of them. We have identified 15 ruptures and transitions, for which I have proposed analyses in terms of resources. In each case, we have thus questioned: what is the rupture, what has been used as resource, is it of social, experiential, or symbolic nature? What was the outcome of these uses? In what sense where such uses constrained or facilitated, by whom or by what? (see Table 8.1).

Uses of symbolic resources suppose that one has been exposed to cultural elements, and has, somehow, internalized them. Methodologically, the only way to know what symbolic resources have done "in the mind" of the person, is to observe externalizations that carry traces of the initial cultural elements. Such externalizations are conducts implying communication through one or the other mode of symbolization: discourse, nonverbal language, bodily expression, music, and so forth (Tisseron, 1998, 1999). Letters written, decision taken, action, discussions one had with others, can thus be shaped or tainted by earlier cultural experiences. These appear as "voices" making one's discourse, either being directly quoted, or adding echoes or harmonics to current experiences (Bakhtin, 1979/1986). Traces of voices are testimonies of the steps that have brought the person to the standpoints from which she currently expresses herself. Hence, observing and analyzing externalizations (which are symbolizations), one can identify cultural elements relevant to that person, and measure the transformation of the latter into the former. One can induce how that cultural element has been used as a symbolic resource.

Thus, on the basis of Uri's writing, we have tried to identify cultural elements that once were meaningful for him. I have tried to read or hear them. I have also gathered secondary testimonies about situations similar to these described by him (for example, stories of the German Jewish community in Argentina). Comparing transitions in his life and mentioned cultural elements, I have made hypothesis on the nature of their uses as resources. Each of these analyses has been discussed with Uri. We have then presented our work to a group of graduate students, mature learners and colleagues, who have discussed it. Data and its analysis are thus the product of a reiterative process and a multiplication of perspectives. The training of Uri has brought him to develop a particular awareness of his memories and inner life, and a strong reflectivity. Sequences

Table 8.1   Transition in Uri's 35 First Years

Historical Time	Factual Events	Age	Significant Ruptures and Transitions
1928	Birth of U in Germany	0	
1929		1	
1930		2	
1931		3	
1932		4	
1933	Nazis take power	5	T1. U. is let alone in the garden, he plays with a carriage U. has to take the train by himself, plays with timetable
1934		6	T2. U. is rejected by other children as a Jew
1935	U. starts school	7	T3. Family excluded from usual restaurant because Jewish; U. discovers positive contents of Judaism T4. Rejected by school mates, U.'s first love, finds beautiful papers
1936		8	T5. U. and sister are sent to school in Italy, U. writes fictional letter
1937		9	
1938	Anschluss, Kristallnacht	10	T6. Children are hidden in Switzerland; U. explores it by bike
1939	Family to South America	11	T7. Family crosses ocean to Uruguay, U. imagines it through fiction
1940	Children in colony	12	T8. U. in house for immigrant children; U. reads on trees, listens to music T9. U. initiated to politics and songs
1941	Family settles in Montevideo	13	
1942	World discovers concentration camps	14	T10. U. and friends start philosophical education
1943		15	
1944	U. starts medical studies	16	
1945		17	T11. U. wants to define possible socialism; after traditional Jewish experience, opts for Zionist project
1946	U. starts carpentry	18	
1947	U. works as accountant	19	
1948	Creation of Israel U. learns agriculture	20	
1949	U. moves to Kibboutz in Israel	21	T12. U. arrives in Israel; learns language thanks to novel
1950		22	

Table 8.1 continues on next page

1951	U. is general secretary of Kibboutz	23	
1952		24	
1953		25	
1954		26	
1955		27	
1956		28	
1957	U. soldier at war	29	T13. U. leaves Israel to study in Switzerland
1956		30	
1958	U. goes back to Israel	31	T14. U. becomes a school psychologist
1959		32	
1960	U. gets psy. diploma	33	
1961	U. creates research group on school planning	34	
1962		35	T15. U. redefines professional identity, studies sociology, and psychoanalysis

presented here are the product of a long work of remembering practiced over years, triggered by me, and jointly interpreted. Data has thus a particular, exemplary status.

BECOMING PROFESSOR U

In what follows I present ruptures, transitions, and uses of resources in sequences of Uri's autobiographical narrative. These are organized around three periods of his life, corresponding to his childhood, youth and adulthood. These periods have not been defined on the basis of age, but of his given or chosen first names. His first name changes clearly follow major ruptures in his life. As symbolic entities, names reveal (or enact) identity repositioning; they designate associated memories and fantasmatic resonance; they have a poetic force, for their sound and shape; and they have a projectual dimension (Zittoun, 2004a, 2005a). Here, after each rupture, changing first names expresses, or externalizes, identity repositioning, associated ideas and feelings and thus reveal that some work of transition has taken place.

The questions I will examine are: What are the cultural elements used as resources in this life story, for what results, in what constraints? What are the experiences that have enabled a person to turn cultural elements into symbolic resources? And do uses of symbolic resources change across a lifetime?

Childhood: From Presymbolic to Symbolic Resources

Uri was named Hans-Peter by his mother, after her brother Hans. As a child, he rejects the name "Hans"—he dislikes the uncle, and other association to the name, such as the children's songs depicting a weak "Hänschen" (little Hans) exposed to the world. His mother, he was said, wanted to have a little virile, brave sporty son:

> At that time, modern educational techniques dictated children not to be spoiled; they have to become hard. The father was ill, and this cult of "health" culture was even reinforced. They let him in the immense garden, in a little enclosure in the snow, in the winter, for hours: Peter shouts his lungs out. Desperation. Cold. His mother carries him in her arms. Warm.
>
> Peterchen (little Peter) is obedient, talks beautifully, and learns quickly what others want from him. At 3 years, he discovers the game of the "Leiterwagen" (wagon). During hours, he walks up a pathway in the garden, and from the top, drives quickly down the way that has a "dangerous" curve. Go up, down, and up, and down. The more times, the better. Peter drives his little wagon. Aged 6, Peter is sent to take the train from Frankfurt to Zurich on his own. He is given a watch and a train schedule. The most important is to watch (and write down on a piece of paper) each stop, to check whether the train is punctually entering the station, leaving the station. He watches the train and the landscape that moves backward. He knows, yes, yes, he is the one moving. Why couldn't one think that the trees are? He is asked to write [a letter to his parents] about his trip. He is proud to write "we arrived in Darmstadt 9:32 (3 minutes late) and left at 9:40 (on time), at Mannheim we arrived at 10:15 (on time) left at 10:25, Karlsruhe … and we arrived in Zurich at XXX hour with 15 minutes delay." Peter is proud of his letter. Later he is told, "You did not have much to say in this letter of yours." He vaguely feels it is unfair. Close to the aunt's house there is a streetcar terminus, where the carriage have to make a beautiful circle. The 7 comes every 6 minutes. It is beautiful to see them come and go; one knows when they will come and go. Peter stays there for hours. "Today I have seen 20 of them!" The aunt seems to understand the importance of these streetcars. "You liked it, little Peter?"

The ruptures little Peter has to face are separations, losses of his everyday, familiar environment. In various ways, he is removed from the warmth of his home and the attention of his loving mother and ill father. The trip to Zurich is exemplary. Here, little Peter is dragged away from his normal sphere of experience and forcefully immersed in uncertainty: a train station, a train. He does not know what it is to be alone in train, nor does he understand why he has to do this trip by himself. However, Peter is not free to be scared, for others expect him to be a brave young boy.

Peter finds resources to manage the displacement: the train schedule and the watch are used to transform the whole trip in a very special kind of "game." Using the train schedule as resource has multiple advantages. It offers a new definition to the situation: the trip is no more immersion in uncertainty; its meaning is now "controlling precision of trains." It gives an active role to Peter: instead of being a passive victim of adult's decision of moving him away, Peter now plays being the chief of the train, who "instructs" trains to be more punctual by registering departures and halts and their deviation from the norm. It enables emotional regulation: fear and anxiety are turned into the emotions related to the game: the excitement before the next station, the joy of arrival on scheduled time. Instead of fading out in a forgotten past and an unthinkable future, time is mastered: future is the next station, past the previous one. Uncertainty is canalized: the whole trip becomes a suite of redundant events. Strangeness is not totally deleted from the picture: there is still some uncertainty focused in his evaluation of the reverse trip of the trees.... Train schedule and objects are symbolic objects; yet, normally speaking, they are not the best objects to open imaginary spaces. Yet, they are the props that enable Peter to deploy the space of role-play, which is an imaginary "as-if" experience, that enable Peter to maintain himself through the rupture-experience (Josephs, 1998; Winnicott, 1971/2001).

Peter's uses of schedules to regulate his own fears are given some chance to be externalized, and socially acknowledged when he is asked to write a letter about his trip. For Peter, this is also a mean to communicate about this important experience to his parents. Unfortunately, the parents do not legitimize the content of the letter and do not recognize the value of Peter's experience: his conquest of fear and his acquisition of a self-technique are dismissed. Luckily, when Peter applies his techniques on the streetcars—rendering mechanical events masterable—his aunt will become the social other who acknowledges the personal importance and sense of such resource.

A few years later, in 1936, Peter and his younger sister are sent to a private boarding school in Italy. There, Peter accommodates to the new situation by doing his school work properly, avoiding other young boys, and succeeding in being admired by his teachers for his ability to recite poetry. A few were particularly striking, among which a poem by Theodore Fontane, *John Maynard*: a captain on the Eerie Sea saves his boat on fire at the price of his own life. In German history, Peter is impressed by dramatic descriptions of landscapes. Also, Peter and his sister have a wooden trunk that links them to home; they receive letter, packs, and salami, but not enough to feel comforted. Peter's sister cries often. Peter decided to write a long letter to his parents, in which he invents a dramatic story.

We, children and our teachers, went for a day trip on the sea, in rowing boats. The weather was splendid. We left the shore. Little by little, the weather started to change, clouds, not small anymore, turned black. Suddenly the wind rises. Waves are growing and growing. We fight to come closer to the shore, but the tempest creates chaos. A child falls in the water and is saved by the teacher, and I, who knows how to swim, save a little child. What a day!" (My story was much more detailed). I give the letter (which I forgot to close) to my preferred teacher for him to post. The boarding school had instituted information meetings on Sundays, ending with the distribution of delicious pastry. The following Sunday I attend the meeting as usual. One of the teachers starts a communication saying: there are among us pupils who don't bother writing stupidities about our institution. He reads my letter. See, children, this is very serious, very serious. After the first words, I wanted to disappear under earth. My preferred teacher had betrayed me ... and that Sunday I did not have the usual pastry.

The rupture Peter has to deal with is relatively similar to the previous ones. He arrives in a new setting, where he has a new position: the lonely bright boy who has the responsibility of his younger sister. Older, having access to more cultural elements than when he was 6, he now finds new resources to deal with the transition.

First, he and his sister use the wooden trunk—an object—as a way to maintain continuity with their life at home, and some of its warmth (Habermas, 1996/1999). Second, he develops social and cognitive strategies: a bright student, Peter uses his facility to be admired by his teachers and thus recreate his position of preferred son. And third, Peter has new cultural experiences: history, poetry—and they do move and touch him; he uses them as symbolic resources to work though his anxiety and sadness. How can we say so? We have the access to an "outcome" of such uses: the letter addressed to his parents and, accidentally, to the institution. It can be seen as an externalization of poems and texts that moved him. One might say that Peter did memorize and internalize them, because they made sense to him: they touched him, or rather, they seemed to echo, or represent him with feelings he was living, now symbolized under a poetic form. Such resonance can be based on structural, semiotic, or emotional resemblances: the lonely boy in the stormy wild world, taking care of a sister, is like a captain in the tempest, taking care of innocent passengers. This material is remobilized and used to say something new. The story written by Peter is indeed a transformation of the initial poem: in both cases, a tempest endangers travelers; the hero is dedicated to weaker than him; but now, he does not have to die. The space of the imaginary—the poem, the fiction-letter—is framed. It welcomes Peter's feelings, contains, represent and transforms them to him: unfocused anxieties become clearly attached to a clear danger—the tempest—and finds a resolution in the joy of the rescue. The imaginary also enables Peter to define a new role: from passive and powerless in front of his sister's despair, he becomes an active hero. He thus explores possible roles for himself. And, finally, his appropriation of poems is part of developing his literary sensibility. The poem used as a symbolic resource thus participate to a work of transition, to render manageable a new position, new responsibilities, in a new context.

Peter's use of resources might seem successful, since they enable to transform complex feelings that have no space in the socially shared reality (the despair of a displaced, precocious child). However, as with the train schedule resource, the use of the poetic resource partially fails, as it is not socially acknowledged. Uri indeed explains that he probably wanted, with this heroic letter, to call attention (because he is a drowning child) and sympathy (because he is literary gifted) upon him. Yet the adults do not acknowledge that letter, neither as a call for help, nor as a good student's work. Again, following their own definition of truth or of appropriateness, they deny the importance of the letter and its sense for the child. With this nonrecognition, the communicative potential of the externalization is denied, no socially shared meaning is established, and the efficiency of the use of the symbolic resource is not socially validated. As a consequence of such events, Uri comments, he learned to save his privacy, to stay by himself, and recline on himself.

These two childhood ruptures are quite similar. They imply physical relocations, and endanger the sense of continuity of the child. In both cases, Peter uses resources that enable maintaining a sense of self (through the regular time checking; through the heroic image), aiming at gaining recognition from adults; they also enable emotional regulation, and a redefinition of the situation. The resources Peter uses are changing: they are proto-symbolic in the case of the train schedule, and thus enable a repetitive control, but also, probably, are reinforcing some inner sense of self or thinking scheme (Tisseron, 1998, 1999). The resources are fully symbolic in the second example. They enable the creation of a complex world, out of the here and now, where events and feeling cannot only be regulated, but also deployed, contained, symbolized, and transformed.

Youth—Symbolic Resources to Transform Oneself in one's World

A few years later, in 1939, Uri moved with his family to South America. He asks Spanish speakers to be called Juan Pedro, to avoid the diminutive "Pedrito" for Peter, which sounds for him too much as a dog name ("perrito," little dog). In Argentina, Peter and his sister are first placed in a children's house directed by German antifascists. There, life is much more simple and rude than they are used to, and there is no space for him to play the "gifted child." It takes him some time to find a new balance—new organization of time, new role, and new resources. Eventually he finds books, which he reads perched on trees, and discovers that a room with a gramophone and discs offers a refuge of a new sort which, after all, reconnects him to the ambiance of his family home in Germany. Later on the children are placed in a public day school, where their childhood takes a more smiling face again.

Between 1942 and 1943, out of the feeling that school and family fail to answer the questions raised by the events in Europe and the world, Peter and his friends start to meet weekly at the house of a German man, whom I will call Thomas, creating "the Dienstagsgruppe" (Tuesday group). The adolescents ask the adult to teach them some knowledge, not ideology. Juan Pedro's ambition is to develop his rationality and to avoid the seduction of sentimentality.

> We will have to discover how Good and Bad are shaped in history and through the becoming of societies, and define where my (our) place is in the world, and how I (we) might contribute to it. We are aware—or rather, it is an omnipresent state of mind, troubling and deep—that we are there because we have survived that terrible tempest that brought us here. But now, I want to navigate, I want to find my light, and I believe in my lucidity. We start with the Greek Polis: with Thomas, we look at maps of houses in Athens and try to imagine how people used to live.

The "Dienstagsgruppe" explores from antiquity to enlightenment, Kant, and then Bernard Shaw, Feuerbach, and of course, Marx—and here Peter discovers the beautiful rhythm of Hegelian dialectic. The members of the group define their stance: they decide to fight for the ideals of the French revolution: freedom, equality, fraternity. They realize that capitalism and nationalism have led to the war, and that future is international socialism. But now that such a set of ideas and commitments have been defined, how to implement them? In 1944-45, the group reads about the persecution of the Jews, anti-Semitism, the Dreyfus affair, the history of Zionism, and of the Jewish labor movements. They are Jews, although they did not have a religious education. They realize that communism, which might be a political solution, excludes Jews: Rosa Luxembourg has been assassinated, and Trotsky was forced to exile. Juan Pedro realizes that, as he comes from a German higher-class Jewish family, there is no proletariat in Argentina that would see him as one of them. What options are then left? Zionism appears as a possibility—but it appears first as a negative choice. Is there any positive reason to be committed to Israel, when one is not religious (see also Finkelkraut, 1980/1997; Sartre, 1946/

1995)? Peter eventually meets traditional and religious Jews coming from Eastern Europe, and is introduced to Yiddish literature and songs, as well to religious ceremonies. These ritually organized, emotionally intense, saturated with meanings, and accompanied by songs that deeply move him. This participation, the intensity of his emotion, the sense of belonging structured around symbolic action, in the whole context, suddenly give to Uri that "positive" content to his Jewish identity. For him, it is a revelation: "suddenly," he writes, "I knew that I am Jewish, because who I am." Hence, through the mediation of new cultural and religious experiences—or, with the use of ritual actions as symbolic resources—the new set of values, commitments, and principles given by international socialism finds a concrete possible road for action: the Zionist project.

The ruptures of Juan Pedro's youth are partly due to his growth, maturation, and the development of his thinking capabilities, that create the need to define a set of values and orientation (Erikson, 1968; Piaget, 1951; Zittoun, 2005b). The societal context is also part of these ruptures: his adolescence is marked by the world's discovery of the atrocities of Nazism in Europe, the war, and the concentration camps. Altogether, the normal and reassuring world of school and family breaks down to reveal infinite absurdity and loss of meaning. The need to define values, common in youth, takes a particular intensity in the context, and this is why the enterprise of the *Dienstagsgruppe* appears as a "genealogy of moral": if the world collapses, where to ground values?

The resources used here are directly symbolic. Historical and philosophical texts offer the space and the perspective to rethink the world. They are used with the objective of changing the understanding and the knowledge of young people, and therefore, their identity, their system of orientation, and their projects. Thomas is at the beginning the person who mediates their relationships to the texts, and who supports and legitimize this use of texts. Although the project is to define a "rational" analysis of the world, the group creates a strong emulation, friendship, and emotional container for each of the adolescents. They used these resources to address the world, each other, and each one's own understanding of the world. The resources are used to contain emotions—give an articulation to fear and revolt; they help to understand local events; they also enable to define categories to analyze the world. Finally, they are used to define overarching commitments and ideas.

In the youth transition of Juan Pedro, these texts support identity changes; they provide him with a knowledge of history of thought, and with new thinking heuristics. Finally, these uses of resources provide him with a time perspective and a set of values that will enable conferring meaning to history and his place in the world. Yet this is not enough. These new understandings still need to find a possible application, and it is Jewish rites, religious texts and songs, the remembrance of the Yiddish culture of the Shtetl (the traditional village) which flesh out a very abstract project and belonging. They create a space out of the here and now, where life gets richness and an emotional quality that transcends matter. It is this mystical cultural experience that enables to turn a very abstract system of value elevated through symbolic resource, into an applicable project. Thus, as in many other cases of "illumination" or "insights," a symbolic, relatively hermetic form crystallizes a very complex equation that rationality pains to solve (for example, when choosing first names for children, Zittoun, 2005a, 2005c).

Adulthood—Transformative Uses of Resources

In 1948 Juan Pedro makes his Alyah—he "goes up" to Israel. There, he asks to be called Uri—a Hebrew name, which he describes as short and strong. He arrives in a country where Hebrew is the spoken language, as a mean to unify people of different origins. As many newcomers, Uri does not speak it. This leads to hectic experiences: to be taken seriously and be in charge of responsibilities, which will position him, he tricks people and make them believe he is competent. Yet he fails learning the language in classes aimed at newcomers. Uri and a group of comrades decide to create their own Kibbutz; once there, exhausted by the physical work, he still is very far from mastering the language. Until he realizes that, if he wants to be able to be able to play a full role in the community, if he wants to be able to speak a perfect language (as he used to do in German and Spanish), and if he wants to charm the beautiful young girl he has met, he has to learn Hebrew—and so he decides to define his own way of doing so. He thus chooses a book he loves, the *Legend of Uelenspiegel in Flanders and elsewhere*, by Charles de Coster (1922/2003). He finds two versions of the book: a German one, and a Hebrew translation, by the Israeli poet and writer Abraham Shlonsky. He decides to work through a page a day, learning by heart words he does not know, identifying their roots, and understanding verbal declinations and grammatical rules. Which he does, sitting far from the housings in the grass on the top of a hill:

At the end of each day I want to hear the music of Shlonski's language. It pleases me. It is like climbing on a an high tower everyday, from which one can contemplates the view from above, and then go down. The tower is narrow, it is hazardous, it will be enlarged later. The daily rhythm—so hard to keep – work the land, shower, get enclosed in the little exclusive world of my spiritual acrobaty—almost becomes a drug. More and more, the structural beauty of the language fascinates me, the main families of word rooted in three letters groups, feminine forms everywhere, often more beautiful that the masculine, the richness of the conjugations, the syntax, and all this in a crystalline structure.

And so he learns Hebrew. Of course, his girlfriend is very surprised to receive letters in a complex and poetic Hebrew! Here, the rupture is obviously that of arriving in Israel—a new country, with different climatic, material, economical political conditions, in which people gather with particular projects, and where activity is organized and justified under very different principles than the ones to which Uri had been used. In this country, the mean to communicate is Hebrew. Uri, not speaking it, is also excluded of the position he used to give himself, that of talented young literary person, and he can not apply its usual social strategies. He then realizes that he is powerless without mastery of the language, and, in the mid of the fields, chooses a personal mean to learn it. He chooses an epic novel as resource for learning Hebrew. Is that choice random? It is not so sure.

First, it is a story in German, that Uri new on the past; the novel reconnects him with his past and his previous, literary self, thus reinforcing his sense of continuity through change. It creates a known zone in this new and uncertain world. Second, looking at the novel, we can see how it might have "spoken" to Uri. It is the story of Till the mischievous, an errand and good-for nothing, who scares crowds, fools wises, and courts girls. The narrative line thus seems a comic figuration of Uri's own situation in Israel, where he is a good-for nothing, falling in love with young women, and getting involved in absurd situations in which he finds his ways through tricks and bright inventions. The story of Till also provides Uri with the metaphor of the tower, which condensates various of his lines of thinking: Uri sitting on the top of the hill to read, is the same person than Juan Pedro reading in the tree in his antifascist home; Uri on the hill is, like Till in his tower, distancing himself form a world than he hopes to master; and the heights of the hill are like the tower of language, mean to both escape the world and mastering it. Third, the novel is used for the esthetical pleasure it provides—in German, and through it, in Hebrew.

Eventually, thus use of the resource is successful. On the one hand, it enables indeed Uri to speak Hebrew—that is, to acquire a specific knowledge. With it, he triggers an identity change: he is now a speaker, who can fully communicate, participate to the Kibbutz's life, and take on responsibilities. On the other hand, the use of the novel as resources is validated by others: the girlfriend is indeed charmed by the eloquence of Uri's letters; and the Kibbutz, recognizing Uri's abilities and aspirations, decides to be lead by him.

About 9 years later, Uri has lost his illusions about the Kibbutz. For various reasons, he decides to study and emigrates back to in Switzerland, where he now will sign his work Uri Peter—an interesting compromise between the "leader" Uri and the sensible child he once used to be. Uri Peter chooses to study psychology, and this has various reasons. Practically, it is a mean to build up on his earlier studies in South America. But on a more abstract level, psychology can be seen as a choice consistent with Uri Peter's previous commitments: it is the way for implementing social level at a microlevel, whereas his previous action was aimed (and failed?) at a collective level. Uri describes his choices at that time as being guided or supported by the image of the "Zauberer," the magician "who, with his clear sight, will illuminate the drama of the psyche." The image of the magician seems to be a crystallization of various literary figures. It mostly refers to the work of Thomas Mann with which Uri had a lifelong familiarity. Thomas Mann is a German writer from the higher upper class; his children used to call him the Magician. Two of his novels are titled after this image: *Mario and the Magician*, and the *Magic Mountain*. Both refer to exceptional men, having access to genial dream worlds, thanks to which they are distinguished from all others. In Uri Peter's personal culture (Valsiner, 1998), the image of the magician also refers to the shows of the mime Marcel Marceau, whose mime of the lifecycle deeply impressed him in those years.

Here, the personal rupture is coming back to academic life. The symbolic resource that is used here is a condensed image—or rather, is used a *symbolic image* that crystallizes a whole network of cultural elements functioning as resources. On the Thomas Mann side, there are emotionally invested images that refer to Uri Peter's past—his past as member of the German upper class, his feeling of being particularly talented, but also, alienated from the world of others because of his ability to generate poetic world. The image of the mime refers to the normal gains and looses of the lifecycle. Uri mentions the extreme lightness and delicacy of this mime, and its contrast with the heavy, laborer's life in the Kibbutz. Leaving the Kibbutz implies losses—losses of one's illusions, loss of what one has constructed, of one's life, of one's identity. The mime of the lifecycle might enable to reintegrate the loss in a narrative of development—one looses part of self, to become another one. The use of such resources then also enabled to confer a new coherence to Uri Peter's life. His past dreaminess, often cause of Uri Peter's rejection, is now fused with a social commitment —improving the world. A crystallizing symbolic image thus guides his investment in new learning and a new self-position and experience—that of a psychologist. Eventually, psychology will then enrich the image itself. Uri Peter will define his practice of psychology as the art of a magician: as a counselor psychologist, he manipulates projective texts which reveal the hidden "true" potential of his young patients.... Later on, reunifying his social and political projects and his care for the individual person, Uri Peter will become both psychoanalyst and a nationally and internationally known specialist in education. But this is another story. Let me now come back the uses of symbolic resources.

USES OF SYMBOLIC RESOURCES IN THE DEVELOPMENT OF SELF

Based on an autobiographic exploration, I have tried to indicate some of the turning points, or the transition processes through which a young boy playing in a snowy courtyard became a professor of education. What makes such a life story is weaved in complex streams of historical and political events, contextual affordances, interpersonal relationships, but also, as I have suggested, through one's uses of symbolic resources.

Fully aware of the reduction I am imposing on a life story, I have highlighted three main transitions, and for each of them, the resources mainly used. Through his childhood, adolescence and adulthood, Uri learned to develop social strategies—being recognized and admired by adults, or being estimated. This went along with Uri's development of cognitive abilities—learning by heart literature, developing heuristics of learning and thinking (so as to acquire new languages or to understand philosophy), and acquiring various skills (such as writing, singing, etc.). Uri's experiences also become resources: having traveled as a very young child becomes a past experience on the basis of which to apprehend the next ones. Additionally, there where social, cognitive, and experiential resources do not suffice to apprehend new situations as such, Uri mobilized available objects of culture and used them as symbolic resources. I have discussed the developmental issues in uses of symbolic resources elsewhere (Zittoun, 2005b, in press).

Methodological Advantages of Life Stories

This chapter has proposed to come back to life stories, as basic material for expanding developmental theories that account for the complexity of life in worlds of culture. I have offered a set of theoretical tools which enable to highlight various dynamics of change in a life story. Of course, Uri's life story has been particularly thought through and his memories have a reconstructed accuracy which is probably above average. It might be that other life stories will lack precision about early childhood memories. Nevertheless, life stories can also be reconstructed with a multiplicity of sources, as when Gillespie confronts archives, biography and letters for reconstructing the life of Malcolm X (Gillespie, 2005a). Theories can then be expanded through a confrontation of comparable analyses of the development of self. Comparability is given by two minimal conditions. The first one is a shared set of basic theoretical assumptions underpinning analyses: assuming the ever-changing nature of the person, the semiotic and dialogical nature of the psyche, and the role of the contexts. The second condition is the comparisons of trajectories or events which can be theoretically considered as equivalent (Valsiner & Sato, 2006). Transition and ruptures in development give a simple unit of analysis that greatly facilitates the comparisons of particular stories. The notions of resources and symbolic resources and their use give a mean to follow the role of others and culture in the development of self. The notion of interiority finally provides with an attention to emotional and unconscious dynamics.

Symbolic Resources: Bringing Otherness in the Making of Self

Facing a new situation or a problem, people can rely on their personal experience and knowledge, or on the experience or the presence of others, as when one asks for cooperation or help. In contrast, using a symbolic resource might seem a more solitary experience, where one relies on cultural objects as helpers or enabling means.

Yet sociality is not absent in such uses. For one part, using a cultural element is of social nature, since one mobilizes the experience or the knowledge of others, which is concretized and symbolized in the cultural object, in a specific social situation. For the other part, if we examine the origin of Uri's symbolic resources, or the structure of the situation in which these are used, the presence of others is striking.

Let us go back to the situation in which a train schedule is turned in a symbolic resource. Here, Peter is sent alone away. Yet adults give him the train schedule and the watch, which then become invested of their presence. Once alone, these objects are the sole link Peter has to his parents. Holding to these, is also holding to them. Additionally, one might think that these have been given to him with a special solemnity and intensity (parents telling him that is going to behave like a little man, trying to reassure themselves while worrying for their son, etc.). This emotional load might have been felt by Peter, which has then given a stronger importance to the objects. Thus, adults transmit a double message to the child: on one side, the objects have a socially simple shared meaning—they are meant for ensuring to be on time; on the other side, the same objects have a particular dramatic sense for them—possibly linked to feelings of responsibility, guilt, and fear. The objects Peter receives are thus constituted as resources in this particular social-emotional configuration.

Constructing a simple object meant to "be on time" is captured by the emotional charge, and thus hijacked. Even if Peter manages to use it not only as a way to regulate his own emotional state, but also according to the socially shared meaning, the latter will be charged with this strange intensity. Finally, once the object is used as symbolic resource, the parents' nonrecognition of the importance of this control for Peter is a nonrecognition of this double value; in contrast, the aunt acknowledges the emotional sense of these. Later in Peter's life, the use of fiction as resource is also dependent on an emotional valence given by others. His investment in learning and writing appears as a direct function of adults' recognition of his giftedness.

In adolescence, Juan Pedro invests music as a way to become closer to the Headmistress, and discovers philosophy with his friends and with the estimated Thomas.

What I am suggesting, is that any transformation of a cultural element into a symbolic resource requires two moments of social presence. First, to become involved within a cultural element is an emotional dynamic; it is, most of the time, enabled by the presence of an other, acknowledging the object, or one's link to the object (that is, sharing its meaning, or acknowledging its sense for self). Second, mobilizing a cultural element as resource is possible when one is authorized by such others, in the concrete situation where others legitimize such a use, or in one's mind, when others and their reactions (and one's own reactions to these) have been internalised. Constructing a cultural element into a symbolic resource, or using a symbolic resource, thus always put one in the presence of others. This is the configuration I propose to capture in a semiotic prism (Zittoun, 2005b). The pole of the prism are the self, the cultural object, the social meaning or/and the personal sense it has for others, and the sense it has for self, or the meaning one perceives of it. Consequently, the relations between these poles are both representational and emotional (Fonagy, Gergely, Jurist, & Target, 2002), based on knowledge and affects or feelings. At times, these two aspects find a balance, and one knows that there is a distance between the socially shared meaning of objects (what is the usual function of a watch) and the personal sense they have for self (the vicarious presence of a worrying mother) (Vygotsky, 1934/1971). At other moments, the latter captures the former, and objects become "mad" objects. If they are mad in that, that their uses can not be acknowledged by the community, they remain social in the sense that they can still carry the shadow of others (Zittoun, Duveen, Gillespie, Ivinson, & Psaltis, 2003).

Such analysis thus suggests a basic configuration enabling a person to turn a cultural element into a personally meaningful symbolic resource, and describing the presence of Other in the background of any later use

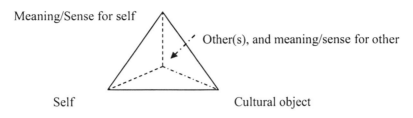

Figure 8.1.   Semiotic prism.

of symbolic resources. The development of uses of symbolic resources can thus be described as sedimentation of semiotic prisms, either when constructing the usage of a cultural element as symbolic resource, or when mobilizing it. Through time, poles of the prisms are replaced by new realities. For example, the "other" who gives a train schedule to Peter is his mother, the "other" who recognizes its usage is his aunt; the "calming object" is a carriage, and then a train schedule. Thus, others, objects, as well as sense for self change, and can eventually become more distanced from the here and now (see Zittoun, 2005b for a developmental account); one's others can become a generalized Other. Finally, the semiotic prism gives a structure to analyze the process though which cultural elements can become used symbolic resources, and thus cultural technique for the development of self. And what this analysis reveals, is that Other is never absent of the use of symbolic resources.

ACKNOWLEDGMENTS

I thank Uri of accepting the challenge of offering his life as a case study, for letting me use some passages of his autobiography and some of our joined reflections here, and for his comments on this manuscript. This chapter is dedicated to him. I also thank Anne-Nelly Perret-Clermont for her support in such an adventure. I am grateful to Alex Gillespie and the editors for their comments on this text. The redaction of this chapter has been enabled by a Research Fellowship from the Swiss science foundation.

NOTES

1.   "When the child was a child, It threw a stick like a lance against a tree, And it quivers there still today." Peter Handke, "Song of Childhood." (Unpub-

lished in English, translation available at http://www.wim-wenders.com/movies/movies_spec/wingsofdesire/wod-song-of-childhood.htm)

2. With the exception of these first names, all the other name and places mentioned in this chapter are masked.

3. Some authors seeing transitions as processes have attempt to describe sub-sequences in transitions, including the acceptation of the loss, a period of exploration, and a new beginning (Brammer, 1991; Bowlby, 1980; Bridge, 1980).

REFERENCES

Bakhtin, M. M. (1986). *Speech genres and other late essays* (V. McGee, Trans.). Austin: University of Texas. (Original work published 1979)

Baltes, P. B. (1997). On the incomplete architecture of human ontogeny. selection, optimization and compensation as foundation of developmental psychology. *American Psychologist, 52*(4), 366-380.

Benson, C. (2001). *The cultural psychology of self.* London: Routledge.

Bowlby, J. (1980). *Loss: Sadness & depression, in Vol. 3 of attachment and loss.* London: Penguin books.

Brammer, L. M. (1991). *How to cope with life transitions: The challenge of personal change.* New York: Hemisphere.

Bridges, W. (1996). *Making sense of life's changes.* London: Nicholas Brealey. (Original work published 1980)

Carugati, F. (2004). Learning and thinking in adolescence and youth. How to inhabit new provinces of menaing. In A. -N. Perret-Clermont, C. Pontecorvo, L. Resnick, T. Zittoun, & B. Burge (Eds.), *Joining society: Social interaction and learning in adolescence and youth* (pp. 119-140). Cambridge, MA: Cambridge University Press.

De Coster, C. (2003). *Legend of Ulenspiegel and Lamme Goedzak and their adventures heroical, joyous and glorious in the land of Flanders and elsewhere* (F. M. Atkinson, Trans.). Kila, MT: Kessinger. (Original work published 1922)

Erikson, E. H. (1968). *Identity, youth and crisis.* London: Faber & Faber.

Erikson, E. H. (1995) *Childhood and society.* London: Vintage. (Original work published 1950)

Finkelkraut, A. (1997). *The imaginary Jew* (Texts and contexts series) (K. O'Neill & D. Suchoff, Trans.). Lincoln, NE: University of Nebraska Press. (Original work published 1980)

Fonagy, P., Gergely, G., Jurist, E. L., & Target, M. (2002). *Affect regulation, mentalisation, and the development of the self.* New York: Other Press.

Gillespie, A. (2005a). Malcolm X and his autobiography: Identity development and self-narration. *Culture & Psychology, 11*(1), 77-88.

Gillespie, A. (2005b). G. H. Mead: Theorist of the social act. *Journal for the Theory of Social Behavior, 35*(1), 19-39.

Gillespie, A. (2006). Tourist photography and the reverse gaze. *Ethos, 34*(3), 343-366.

Gillespie, A. (2007). *Becoming other to oneself: A Meadian study of culture tourism in Ladakh*. Greenwich, CT: Information Age.

Gillespie, A. (in press). *Becoming other to oneself: A Meadian study of culture tourism in Ladakh* (Advances in cultural psychology series) (J. Valsiner, Ed.). Greenwich, CT: Information Age Publishing.

Green, A. (2005). *Key ideas for contemporary psychoanalysis: misrecognition and recognition of the unconscious* (A. Weller, Trans.). London: Brunner-Routledge. (Original work published 2002)

Habermas, T. (1999). *Geliebte Objekte: Symbole und instrumente der identitätsbildung* [Loved objects: Symbols and tools for identity construction]. Frankfurt, Germany: Suhrkamp. (Original work published 1996)

Handke, P. (1987). *Der Himmel über Berlin*. Ein Filmbuch. Mit Wim Wenders. Frankfurt/M: Suhrkamp.

James, W. (1890). *Principles of psychology*. London: Macmillan.

James, W. (1984). *Psychology: Briefer course*. Cambridge, MA: Harvard University Press. (Original work published 1892)

Janet, P. (1926). *De l'angoisse à l'extase* [From anxiety to ecstasy] (Vol. 1). Paris: Librairie Félix Alcan.

Janet, P. (1928) *De l'angoisse à l'extase* [From anxiety to ecstasy] (Vol. 2). Paris: Librairie Félix Alcan.

Josephs, I. E. (1998). Constructing one's self in the city of the silent: Dialogue, symbols, and the role of "as-if" in self-development. *Human Development, 41*, 180-195.

Nell, V. (1988). *Lost in a book: The psychology of reading for pleasure*. London: Yale University Press.

Palmonari, A. (Ed.). (1993). *Psicologia dell'adolescenza* [Psychology of adolescence]. Bologna, Italy: Il Mulino.

Perret-Clermont, A.-N., & Zittoun, T. (2002) Esquisse d'une psychologie de la transition [Sketch for a psychology of transitions]. *Education permanente. Revue Suisse pour la Formation Continue, 1*, 12-15.

Piaget, J. (1951). *Play, dreams and imitation in childhood*. London: William Heinemann.

Piaget, J., & Inhelder, B. (1969). *The psychology of the child*. New York: Basic Books. (Original work published 1966)

Rutter, M. (1994). Continuities, transitions and turning points in development. In M. Rutter & D. F. Hay (Eds.), *Development through life: A handbook for clinicians* (pp. 1–25). London: Blackwell.

Sartre, J. -P. (1995). *Anti-Semite and Jew: An exploration of the etiology of hate*. (G. J. Baker, Trans.). New York: Schocken Books. (Original work published 1946).9

Smelser, N. J. (1980). Issues in the study of love and work in Adulthood. In N. J. Smelser & E. H. Erikson (Eds.), *Themes of work and love in adulthood* (pp. 1-28). London: Grant McIntyre.

Smelser, N. J., & Erikson, E. H. (Eds) (1980). *Themes of work and love in adulthood*. London: Grant McIntyre.

Thom, R. (1975). *Structural stability and morphogenesis*. New York: Benjamin.

Tisseron, S. (1998). *Y a-t-il un pilote dans l'image?* [Is there a pilot in the picture?] Paris: Aubier.

Tisseron, S. (1999). *Comment l'esprit vient aux objets* [How spirit comes to objects]. Paris: Aubier.

Valsiner, J. (1998). *The guided mind. A sociogenetic approach to personality.* Cambridge, MA: Harvard University Press.

Valsiner, J. (2000). *Culture and human development.* Thousand Oaks, CA: Sage.

Valsiner, J., & Sato, T. (2006). Historically Structured Sampling (HSS): How can psychology's methodology become tuned in to the reality of the historical nature of cultural psychology? In J. Straub, C. Kölbl, D. Widenman, & B. Zielke (Eds.), *Pursuit of meaning. Advances in cultural and cross-cultural psychology* (pp. 215-252). Bielefeld: Transcript.

Vygotsky, L. S. (1962). Thought and word. In E. Hanfmann & G. Vakar (Eds.), *Thinking and speaking.* Cambridge, MA.: MIT Press. (Original work published 1934). Retrieved January 20, 2005, from http://www.marxists.org/archive/vygotsky/works/words/vygotsky.htm

Vygotsky, L. S (1971). *The psychology of art.* Cambridge, MA: MIT Press. (Original work published in 1925)

Winnicott, D. W. (2001). *Playing and reality.* Philadelphia: Bruner-Routledge. (Original work published 1971)

Zittoun, T. (2004a). Preapprenticeship as a transitional space. In A. -N. Perret-Clermont, C. Pontecorvo, L. Resnick, T. Zittoun, & B. Burge (Eds.), *Joining society: Social interaction and learning in adolescence and youth* (pp. 153-176). Cambridge, MA: Cambridge University Press.

Zittoun, T. (2004b). Symbolic competencies for developmental transitions: The case of the choice of first names. *Culture & Psychology, 10*(2), 131-161.

Zittoun, T. (2004c). Janet's emotions in the whole of human conduct. In R. Diriwaechter (Ed.), *From past to future* (pp. 25-29). Worcester, MA: Clark University.

Zittoun, T. (2005a). *Donner la vie, choisir un nom. Engendrements symboliques* [Giving life, choosing a name: Symbolic begetting]. Paris: L'Harmattan.

Zittoun, T. (2005b). *Transitions. Development through symbolic resources.* Greenwich. CT: Information Age.

Zittoun, T. (2005c). Uses of cultural resources in the transition to parenthood. In A. Gülerce, A. Hofmeister, I. Steauble, G. Saunders, & J. Kay (Eds.), *Contemporary theorizing in psychology: Global perspectives* (pp. 327-334). Concord: Captus Press.

Zittoun, T. (in press). The role of symbolic resources in human lives. In J. Valsiner & A. Rosa (Eds.), *Cambridge handbook of socio-cultural psychology.* Cambridge, MA: Cambridge University Press.

Zittoun, T., Duveen, G., Gillespie, A., Ivinson, G., & Psaltis, C. (2003). The uses of symbolic resources in transitions. *Culture & Psychology, 9*(4), 415-448.

STRIVING TOWARD NOVELTY IN A SCIENTIFIC DIALOGUE

Alexander Poddiakov

INTRODUCTION

A combination of target articles and the subsequent interviews in the same volume seems a very fruitful format for the issue on otherness and selfness. Such a format seems a cultural tool for explication of idea of interaction between selves and others. One may modify Zittoun's semiotic prism (Zittoun, this volume) for that special case in the following way (Figure 1).

Accordingly to Valsiner (2005), a value of a scientific journal in the digital age, when a reader can get e-copies of almost any article via Internet, is determined rather not by a value of an individual article published in the journal, but a value of composition (or a pattern) of articles, reading of which provides a reader with an opportunity to create a new wholeness of understanding. To say metaphorically, not a separated tone, but new whole chords are more interesting.

A main goal of a researcher in a science is novelty: novelty of theories, methods, data, their interpretations, and so forth. Lotman proved that a very important source of emerging novelty and creativity is dialogue

Otherness in Question: Labyrinths of the Self, 215–226

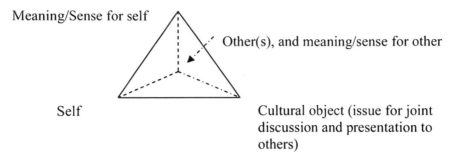

Meaning/Sense for self

Other(s), and meaning/sense for other

Self

Cultural object (issue for joint discussion and presentation to others)

Figure 1.   The modified semiotic prism of T. Zittoun with a cultural object for joint discussion and presentation to others as the fourth element.

based on overlapping (neither absolute equivalence nor absolute differ-ence) of zones of understanding of participants of the dialogue (Agger, 1999; Lotman, 1990). Such overlapping creates uncertainty, incomplete-ness, and contradictions, which stimulate creativity.

A feature of scientific dialogues is that their participants' aims and experiences concern operating with so-called methodological cycles (Branco & Valsiner, 1997) (Figure 2).

Naturally, different researchers have different intuitive experiencing, different theories, methods, get different data, and so forth. One can see a part of such differences in the articles presented to that chapter. Over-lapping of these components (theories, data, etc.) provides with an opportunity of emerging novelty in a dialogue between participants, and creating novelty by readers-researchers while reading the dialogue in the journal. Directions of the novelty creation may increase in case of the sub-sequent interviews.

Different strategies of asking questions in interviews are possible. In this volume, from point of view of the issue discussed, one may think interesting to ask such questions to Alex Gillespie, Tania Zittoun, Marisa Japur, Carla Guanes, and Emerson Rasera, content of which would over-lap with content of their articles and could provide overlapping and dif-ferentiation of the answers themselves.

Questions for the Interview

My questions concerned issues of novelty, uncertainty, stimulation, and inhibition of selves in relations with others, and beliefs about universality of some laws of development. Namely, I asked the authors the following questions.

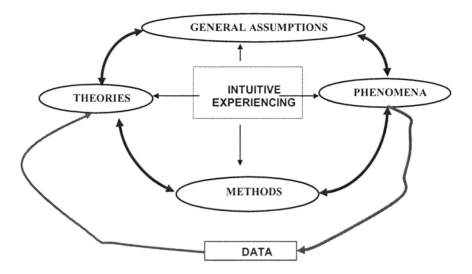

Figure 2.   The methodological cycle (Branco & Valsiner, 1997).

1. What is creation of novelty in motion of striving self? May one say about giftedness and a pattern of special abilities of (different) selves in their relations (interactions) with real and symbolic others?

2. What is meaning of known—unknown (certainty—uncertainty, predictability—unpredictability) in dynamical dimensions of real and symbolic interactions between striving self and other(s)?

3. What does stimulate and what does inhibit motion of striving self in context of relations with other(s)?

4. Accordingly to the orthogenetic principle (Goethe, Spencer, Werner), a main law of development of any wholes (organisms, individuals' mentalities, societies, etc.) is "a tendency to move from a state of relative globality and undifferentiatedness toward states of increasing differentiation and hierarchic integration" (Werner, cited by Franklin, 2004, p. xxv). Respectively, regress is related to decrease of differentiation and integration, and increase of diffuseness and non-clarity. Considering development of striving self and its relations with other(s), may you agree with this law?

I am very grateful to Alex Gillespie, Tania Zittoun, Marisa Japur, Carla Guanes, and Emerson Rasera for answering the questions. The answers are given below completely and without any changes and the subsequent comments.

The Authors' Answers to the Questions

Answer 1

What is creation of novelty in motion of striving self? May one say about giftedness and a pattern of special abilities of (different) selves in their relations (interactions) with real and symbolic others?

Alex Gillespie

From my point of view, the creation of novelty within the striving self is not about individual ability or giftedness, but rather about intraindividual dialogicality. The terms ability or giftedness do not seem to explain the creation of novelty (novelty simply emerges because the person is gifted). On the other hand using a dialogical approach means that we can explain the emergence of intraindividual novelty in the same way as we can explain the emergence of novelty between people, for example in a conversation. In both cases novelty emerges from the meeting of different perspectives. Each perspective is necessarily different to the other, each perspective sees both more and less than the other, and thus in interaction each draws novelty out of the other.

In my chapter on tourists I argued that the motivation for striving comes, in part, from an image from the mass media, that the tourists try to reproduce. The tourists have seen something that appeals to them, they have an expectation that they can actualize this, and then they are motivated to travel, and as travelers they are striving to make real their expectations.

Tania Zittoun

The question is, what do you consider as novelty? Minimally, one might say that novelty is any new way of apprehending a new event—novelty would be what is not mere repetition (that is, not the bare repetition of a conduct indifferently to the change of the environment and self—for example, therapeutic narratives in Japur, Guanes, and Rasera (this volume), where one woman keeps repeating her role as victim of abusive husbands). On another extreme, novelty might designate the emergence of new stable patterns of conducts, or higher level abilities, or structures. Between these two extremes, in my sense, novelty can be described as the emergence of a new self-other-meaningful object-personal sense configuration (the semiotic prism). In that sense, and as we see in the three papers in this section, novelty has to do with specific conjunctions of the person's interaction with others, the person's interaction with some semiotic or material objects, and the others' interactions with the person's interaction with the object.

Yet what *causes* movements and change within such configurations might be very diverse (an inner, or an outer event); when a configuration is challenged and under transformation, the way change is canalized or guided (or enabled or constrained) depends on interpersonal, social, cultural, symbolic, personal dimensions; the new state of the configuration can be more or less acknowledged by the person or/and others.

In that sense, some people might, in some situations, feel more eager to provoke or carry out such transformations. Some might have specific ways of handling novelty: have an eagerness to create ruptures (e.g., Uri creates the rupture of going to Israel, tourists create their being in an unknown world), an ability to find and use resources or social support to canalize new elaborations, or a trust in the fact that newness will emerge out of unknown and uncertain situation. Such a form of trust would thus turn any form of new configuration as a mean to create new questions or new transformations; the self would keep striving. "Giftedness" might thus designate an extreme self orientation toward change. However, these processes occur in everyone, with various intensities; and the emergence of novelty in the striving self is not an exception, it is a condition for being a human.

Marisa Japur, Carla Guanes, and Emerson Rasera

In the therapeutic context, the creation of novelty is related to the process of *change* of self-descriptions (McNamee & Gergen, 1995). From a constructionist perspective, change is a *self-narrative* constructed in the relationship with the therapist and other participants. While such, it is constrained by the context and people in relationship. It is something that is recognized as new depending on the relationship with the other, not presenting an essential characteristic itself. Change can be understood only from the discourses constructed about it, not being a steady, individual and internal acquisition.

In therapy, many times, novelty is something that *was already there* as a discursive possibility, but that is recognized as such from the invitation of the other. In our text, the description of Milene as a good mother, that was essential for the process of change of Pedro, appeared as novelty in the group context; however, it was supported by previous descriptions of the relationship of Pedro and Milene. The same occurred with the description of Estela as being strong and having "good head." In this way, novelty is based in something that already exists. However, from the moment that it is constructed as such, it reorganizes the meanings brought by the client providing a new narrative of the self and of the situations that he/she faces.

Considering a *relational definition of the construction of novelty*, it does not depend exclusively on individual abilities, being always constrained by the particular relationships in which people are involved. Consequently, the easiness of somebody's change in his/her relationship with his/her spouse may not be observed in his/her relationship with other people.

However, to the constructionists, the definition of novelty and change may be questioned. After all, people are daily describing themselves, as well as the world where they live in, in different ways according to the context and the people involved. In what sense these different descriptions can be considered as novelty? When a difference turns to be considered novelty? In the therapeutic context, the work of the therapist consists on an active coconstruction of narratives marked by a *sense of authorship and freedom*. Novelty, therefore, is the result of a *negotiation* between therapist and client and it varies according to the people involved.

Answer 2

What is meaning of known—unknown (certainty—uncertainty, predictability—unpredictability) in dynamical dimensions of real and symbolic interactions between striving self and other(s)?

Alex Gillespie

In terms of tourists in Ladakh the real issue is expectation-experience, that is the opposition between expected future experience and actualized experience. Ordinary people decide to travel to Ladakh and become tourists because they expect something—usually an image provided by the mass media. For example they expect mountains, Buddhist people, and remote villages. The dialogical tension emerges when they arrive in Ladakh and their experience may be different from what is experienced—the mountains may not be as steep, the locals not pious, and the villages electrified with televisions.

When expectations are not confirmed, tourists are most likely to classify the unpious local or the electrified village as "not the real Ladakh," and thus the striving continues. Tourists will keep striving after their expectations until they are fulfilled.

Tania Zittoun

The movement between known-unknown (etc.) is the oscillation which is motor and result of the creation of novelty as described above. Both are created through the evolution of the relationship between a person's semiotic means (mean to apprehend the world or herself), and the given of her experience. One might say that "knowing" is reducing the mismatch between these, and "un-knowing" is increasing it.

The striving self is provoked by, and provokes, a constant transformation of knowing into unknowing and unknowing into knowing—unknowing is the condition of knowing (as forgetting is the condition of learning, etc.), and inversely.

Others can either disrupt the known and generate uncertainty, or provide with means to support the making of known. A person's impression of knowing about X can be reinforced by others approving of the person thinking knowing that X. This can forbid the person to unknow, such as in orthodox thinking about X. If unknowing X is impossible, the dynamics of striving are blocked in the person's X sphere of experience.

Marisa Japur, Carla Guanes, and Emerson Rasera

To begin a dialogue about this question, we will take as reference Shotter's contribution to social constructionism (Shotter, 2000), once we consider his description about the making sense process, sustained by the dynamics of the interactive moment, very useful to the understanding of *known/unknown, predictability/unpredictability, certainty/uncertainty* dimensions in the social construction of reality and *self.*

In his responsive-rhetorical version of social constructionism, strongly supported by Bakhtin's ideas, Shotter proposes a focus upon the *contingent flow of continuous communicative interaction between people*, in which they are continuously making sense of themselves and their surroundings. Based on the notion of *language in use*, this perspective shows the predictable and unpredictable character of making sense process.

Accordingly to Bakhtin, an utterance acquires its meaning in the relationship with the different *voices*, present or presentified in human interaction. A relational emphasis sustains this understanding of the making sense process in language, showing its dynamism and unpredictability. However, the dynamism of this dialogical principle does not deny the influence of the context and the presence of some *stabilities* of meaning, which allow people to anticipate some understandings and to coordinate their actions around meanings supposedly consensual. This stability is given by the use of *social discourses* and *speech genres*, which are related to the social, cultural and historical context, and to the relationships among social groups. Although allowing our participation in a relatively known field of meanings, the use of *social discourses* and *speech genres* does not guarantee the meaning of an utterance in a specific interactive moment. It can not predict the result of a human interaction. Meaning will be always a momentarily achievement, an outcome of the dialogue among different voices, in a situated time and context. This *unpredictability* and *non intentionality* of making sense process can be summarized in the notion of *join-action* (Shotter, 1994). It's in the uncertainty of the interactive moment, in the boundaries between what one person speaks and what the other one responds, that the make sense process takes place.

On the same way, the making sense process of *self* will be marked by *certainty and uncertainty, stability* and *change, predictability* and *unpredictability*. This dialogical and relational construction of the person can be realized, for instance, by noticing that we compose ourselves differently accordingly to whom we address our utterances for. In this universe of relational possibilities, what makes a person unique is the discursive positions that she (and just she) assumes in an interaction, as well as her ability to defend these positions and to be responsible by them in front of others. Remembering, once more, that the possibilities of discursive construction of someone as being a person of some kind also depends on others *(network of reciprocating identities)*, on the context and on the interactive moment dynamics.

Answer 3

What does stimulate and what does inhibit motion of striving self in context of relations with other(s)?

Alex Gillespie

As mentioned above, the striving self, in my analysis of tourists, is motivated by an image of a hero in the media, and the tourist then is motivated to become that other, and thus to actualize that image. In striving the tourist needs a role model, someone, or some social position, or some set of experience to strive toward. Self sees the other and admires the other. Then self strives to become the other, by traveling to Ladakh, and, for example, having a similar adventure.

The inhibition of the striving self, for me, has two dimensions. First there is the individual's self-representation. While they may see and admire the other, the individual may be unable to imagine that becoming like the other. Self may see the hero in the film hike across the mountains, but never come to have that expectation because self does not identify with that image, or does not think that self is capable of such a feat. Thus for self to be motivated to become the other self must admire the other and then think that self can become the other. Second, inhibition may come from outside the self. Self's reference group or family may not offer self recognition for striving in a certain direction. For example, they might think that traveling to Ladakh, and climbing mountains is an idle pursuit, thus not extending any recognition. This again could inhibit the striving tourist.

Tania Zittoun

As mentioned before: any dynamic within the configuration described under (1) (the prism) or within the frame or the context of that configuration is likely to modify the motion of the striving self.

More precisely, a condition for the self to keep striving is: experiencing a rupture; interacting with others and objects, in a frame which enables free exploration; conferring personal sense to the situation; distinguishing shared meaning from personal sense; finding some form of acknowledgement by others, within that frame (this can be applied for the three papers).

Marisa Japur, Carla Guanes, and Emerson Rasera

Psychotherapeutic process can be understood as an opportunity of creation of new self-narratives through conversations among the group members and of these with the therapist, in which the expansion of meanings of self is possible. This understanding of therapy supports a discursive perspective of self construction, in which certain *conversational forms* restrict and stabilize the meanings of self while other ones expand and invite their change.

According to constructionist authors, some specific conversational forms can favor the generation of meaning. When promoting this kind of conversation, therapists usually try to act in a nonevaluative atmosphere, giving voice to the clients and their own descriptions of the problem and of themselves. This atmosphere creates an appropriate context where the therapist and the client are relationally engaged, being responsive one to the other and paying attention to the small details of the meeting. Over all, it is the *responsiveness* of the therapist to the client who guarantees the openness of the dialogue to new meanings.

Proposed by Shotter (2000), this notion is related to a special kind of relationship in which people are engaged in an embodied and dialogical form of conversation, speaking to each other from their own discursive position and conversational history. For him, the notion of *responsiveness* favors an understanding of the "quality" of the relation I-other. *Dialogical conversations* are responsive because they acknowledge the relationship that is established with another voice or conscience. They respond to something that is presented as different from them. In contrast, *monological conversations* lack a sense of responsiveness, given the difficulty of answering to the other as otherness and of establishing a relationship where new possibilities of meaning can be jointly constructed.

Moreover, the construction of new meanings of self is constrained by the *network of reciprocating identities* in which a person participates. Thus, a self-narrative always holds a description of others that must accept it so that it can be legitimated. In the same way, beyond the immediate conditions of the conversation, such self-narrative is constructed from the social discourses associated to certain forms of life. In our text, the influence of the network of reciprocating identities and of the social discourses in the construction of self narratives can be seen in the analysis of Estela's and other group member´s narratives. When describing Estela as "only having problems," the participants allow themselves to be described as not being mentally ill. At the same time, these new self descriptions locally reorganize the social discourses about mental illness.

Answer 4

Accordingly to the orthogenetic principle (Goethe, Spencer, Werner), a main law of development of any wholes (organisms, individuals' mentalities, societies, etc.) is "a tendency to move from a state of relative globality and undifferentiatedness toward states of increasing differentiation and hierarchic integration" (Werner, cited by Franklin, 2004, p. xxv). Respectively, regress is related to decrease of differentiation and integration, and increase of diffuseness and nonclarity. Considering development of striving self and its relations with other(s), may you agree with this law?

Alex Gillespie

I agree with the orthogenetic principle, and I think that it is relevant to a dialogical model of the striving self. From my point of view the striving self comprises many different self positions and other positions. These positions are offered various degrees of recognition (by both self and society). Some of the positions may also be stigmatized. My argument is that striving comes from self striving toward the social positions that have high recognition and away from those that have low recognition or even stigma.

It follows from this model, that if the self were undifferentiated there would be no striving, because there would be no differentiation of social positions. The more social positions are differentiated the more potential avenues for striving—the more different social positions that self can strive toward (and strive away from). However, numerous differentiated social positions is not sufficient. Integration is also necessary. The social positions are integrated in the sense of forming a structure of recognition, with some social positions being highly privileged, and others being stigmatised. It is this integration which provides the motivational aspect of striving.

Tania Zittoun

Yes and no. Take the example of Uri. His uses of symbolic resources are first based on the mobilization of extremely simple, preverbal means (train schedule); later on, through his development, he starts to use more differentiated means (novels, philosophical texts). Here the changes are along the orthogenetic principle.

Yet in his more expert uses of resources, Uri uses highly complex representational mean (the image of the magician), which is a synthesis of other resources. It is thus nondifferentiated, yet integrated. It is a very fuzzy resource, which can be used thanks to Uri's "expertise." Thus, there is a hierarchy, there is progress, yet high-level mediational means are undifferentiated (see also Valsiner, 2001 on this point).

Marisa Japur, Carla Guanes, and Emerson Rasera

According to social constructionism, this law, as any other theoretical description, is a *discourse* constructed under specific cultural conditions. Its effect of truth depends on broader social agreements, which position science as a social practice that produces truths. Thus, to agree or disagree with this law, in the construction of self and of its relationship with others is not to claim or deny its veracity, but it is an invitation to reflect on its intelligibility in other discourses, inside the same social practice. We will focus on the description of *self-narrative*, proposed by Gergen (1994), although noticing that this is not the only one in the social constructionism field. This description constructs self as the narratives and accounts people develop about themselves, in their attempt to create a story that made them intelligible to themselves and to others. These self-narratives are used as cultural resources, with different social purposes.

Our participation in a given culture exposes us to multiple forms of narratives. Also, it invites us to certain self descriptions, while constrains others, once we are always being evaluated based on the intelligibility and reality of the personal stories we construct. The possibility we have to construct and sustain some of our stories depends on our relationship to others and on their self-narratives, in the interior of specific cultural settings. This narrative interdependence results in an important social life feature that is the construction of a *network of reciprocating identities*. That is, an identity can be sustained only if (real or imaginary) others assume supportive roles in its construction and maintenance. Thus, the development of a self-narrative is always a process of coauthorship. The intelligibility of this coconstruction is based on shared social conventions, which circumscribes what will be considered as a well-formed narrative account, warranting to our personal stories a sense of reality.

In Western culture, in the last centuries, what gives our stories the rhetorical effect of veracity and reality is the temporal, linear, and causal ordering of events, as well as the linkage between them, producing an integrate, unique, and stable identity across time. In sustaining a comprehension about the cultural and local forms of description, as well as about the relational, dynamic, and flexible character of the self, this understanding *does not deny* that, in our development, we are strongly encouraged to coconstruct personal stories with and an increasing sense of differentiation and integration.

Thus, we consider that social constructionist's perspectives only question the universality of this law and the effects of its naturalization on legitimating some normative and excluding social practices.

REFERENCES

Agger, G. (1999). Intertextuality revisited: Dialogues and negotiations in media studies. *Canadian Aesthetics Journal/Revue canadienne d'esthétique* (Vol. 4). Retrieved from http://www.uqtr.uquebec.ca/AE/vol_4/gunhild.htm

Bakhtin, M. M. (1986). *Speech genres and other later essays* (V. W. McGee, Trans.) Austin: University of Texas Press.

Branco, A. U., & Valsiner, J. (1997). Changing methodologies: A co-constructivist study of goal orientations in social interactions. *Psychology and Developing Societies, 9*(1), 35-64.

Franklin, M. B. (2004). Prologue to the Percheron Press edition. In H. Werner (Ed.), *Comparative psychology of mental development* (pp. vii-xxv) . New York: Percheron Press.

Gergen, K. J. (1994). *Realities and relationships: soundings in social construction.* Cambridge, MA: Harvard University Press.

Lotman J. (1990). *Universe of the mind: A semiotic theory of culture.* (Ann Shukman Trans., introduction by Umberto Eco). New York: I. B. Tauris.

McNamee, S., & Gergen, K. J. (1995). *Therapy as social construction.* London: Sage.

Shotter, J. (1994). Making sense on the boundaries: On moving between philosophy and psychotherapy. In A. P. Griffiths (Ed.), *Philosophy, psychology and psychiatry* (pp. 55-72). Cambridge, NY: Cambridge University Press.

Shotter, J. (2000) *Conversational realities: Constructing life through language. (Inquires in social construction).* London: Sage.

Valsiner, J. (2001). Process structure of semiotic mediation in human development. *Human Development, 44*(2-3), 84-97.

Valsiner, J. (2005, December). *Culture and psychology.* Lecture delivered at Department of Psychology of Moscow State University Moscow.

Part IV

SELF IN COLLECTIVE OTHERNESS

CHAPTER 9

OTHERNESS IN HISTORICALLY SITUATED SELF–EXPERIENCES

A Case-Study on How Historical Events Affect the Architecture of the Self

Alberto Rosa , Jorge Castro, and Florentino Blanco

"You may roughly divide the nations of the world as the living and the dying ... the weak states are becoming weaker and the strong states are becoming stronger ... [the] living nations will gradually encroach on the territory of the dying, and the seeds and causes of conflict among civilised nations will speedily appear"

These words of Lord Robert Cecil Salisbury, Prime Minister of Queen Victoria, were stated in a speech made on May 4th 1898 before the gathering of the Tory Primrose League at the Royal Albert Hall in London. When listening to them many thought of China, Turkey, or Portugal, some Italians and French chose to take offence, but the Spaniards were certain that they were unmistakably referred to them. Three days earlier Commodore George Perry, in command of the U.S. Navy Pacific Squadron (adding together 19.362 tons and 33 heavy guns), had sunk all the Spanish Far East naval force (12,029 tons, 9 heavy guns) in the Philippines. Two

Otherness in Question: Labyrinths of the Self, 229–255
Copyright © 2007 by Information Age Publishing
All rights of reproduction in any form reserved.

months later the last nail on the coffin of Spanish imperial pride was hammered in by William Sampson's fleet at Santiago de Cuba on the eve of July 4th. His nine armored cruisers sunk all the four armored cruisers and three destroyers under the command of Admiral Pascual Cervera. Together the two encounters produced 912 Spanish casualties and 10 Americans (all of the latter not caused by enemy fire but because of accidents when operating their own guns). Rather than naval battles, the encounters resembled shooting drills. The Spanish Navy could not even claim a tragic but glorious defeat such as at Trafalgar. The feeling was that they had been sent to a hopeless slaughter. When 5 months later the Treaty of Paris brought peace, Spain was stripped of all its overseas possessions. A Spanish word changed its meaning: for decades *The Disaster* came to be synonymous with the year 98. This very same figure (98) gave its name to a generation of Spanish intellectuals who played a major role in the building of contemporary Spanish national identity.

The consequences of this loss were mixed. Surprisingly there was no social unrest in spite of the previous activism of republican and anarchist movements. The strenuous effort of keeping hundred of thousands of conscripted troops very far away from the metropolitan territory was suddenly released. The repatriation of capital and a quick and efficient fiscal reform rescued in a few years not only the war bonds, but also all the state debts accumulated for nearly a century. Fifteen years later the navy was rebuilt and the Spanish economy, although still lagging behind their immediate European neighbors, was better than ever before. The last imperial possessions proved to have been a burden rather than a resource. But the shock had been terrible and the morale of the country had sunk deeper than the vessels of the navy.

It may be surprising that the relatively small loss of several islands came to be such a shock when 75 years earlier a whole continent under the rule of the Spanish monarchy became independent, practically with no apparent harm to the national pride. But in the 1820s the independence of the American countries was the result of a civil war between Spaniards from the two sides of the Atlantic and, what is more important, a Spanish nation still did not exist. In contrast, *The Disaster* happened in the middle of the high tide of Western Imperialism, when Spencerian philosophy popularized the so called "Social Darwinism," and when the very issue of what sort of nation Spain was to be (if it had to be at all) was centre of a heated debate among the Spaniards themselves.

The Spanish 19th century had not been uneventful. Apart from the involvement in the Napoleonic Wars and the Wars of American Independence, there were three civil wars between liberals and partisans of the *ancienne régime*, one revolution, a change of dynasty, one republic (that lasted 11 months), a Bourbon restoration and several military coups d'etat. What is more—this took place within the process of transforming an ailing monarchy into a modern nation. This was a process in which the idea of "nation" appeared first as a liberal concept. It was fought against by the Church and the absolutists who defended that Catholicism and the monarchy were to be kept as the core of the legitimacy of the State. Still, it ended up being appropriated by the conservative forces. By the end of the nineteenth century there was no discussion that Spain was a nation rather than merely a Catholic monarchy, but the national identity was still very weak. There was heated discussion about what had gone wrong to make the country to fall into such decadence, whether it was a consequence of a withdrawal from the real self of the country (whatever that was), or the failure to accept modernity. As Álvarez Junco (2001) puts it, when England pictured herself under the image of the opulent *Britannia* ruling over the waves, or France appeared in the figure of the beautiful and resolute *Marianne*, the image under which Spain was pictured was that of a *Mater Dolorosa* crying for her dead sons and abandoned in her disgrace and helplessness.

A CAST OF CHARACTERS

There was a general feeling of pessimism, though this was not a sole consequence of *The Disaster*. Decadence was a persistent theme within the Spanish literature from the seventeenth century onwards, that reached its peak in the years before and after the defeat in 1898. Pessimism was widespread even among the elite. When the 1876 constitution was being drafted in Parliament and the article defining who was to be entitled to Spanish nationality was being discussed ("Spanish nationals are those born in Spain, those born from Spanish parents," etc.), the conservative Prime Minister Antonio Cánovas del Castillo said, as a sort of half joke, that "Spaniards are… those who can be nothing else" (Álvarez Junco, 2001, p. 573). If this was the feeling of the main political figure in Spanish politics at this time, that of those who attempted to imitate the French model of the *intellectual* was much more bitter. They were highly critical of the political system of the Restauration headed by Cánovas, and despised the whole political class. At the end of the century an avalanche of books appeared (see Table 9.1 for a selection of some of the best known), whose titles are eloquent. They conform a literary genre, known as *Regenerationism*, that developed at the turn of the nineteenth to the twentieth century, and their authors form a group, know as *Regenerationists*, in spite of the differences among their views.

Regeneracionism books are of a mixed origin and content. Some were collections of earlier press articles and others were originally written for

Table 9.1.   Books on *Regenerationism*

Title	1st Edition	Author	Political Tendency	Theorical Tendency	Professional Field
España tal como es [*Spain as it is*]	1889	Valentí Almirall (1841-1904)	Liberal	Positivist	Politics
Los desastres de la patria [*The Diseases of the Mother Country*]	1890	Lucas Mallada (1841-1921)	Liberal	Positivist	Scholar
El delincuente español: Hampa [*The Spanish Criminal: Underworld Life*]	1896	Rafael Salillas (1854-1923)	Liberal	Positivist	Scholar
Idearium español [*Spanish Idearium*]	1897	Ángel Ganivet (1865-1898)	Conservative	Idealistic	Politics
El desastre nacional y sus causas [*The National Disaster and its Causes*]	1899	Damián Isern (1852-1914)	Conservative	Eclectic (idealist)	Politics
Las desdichas de la Patria [*The Misfortunes of the Mother Country*]	1899	Vital Fité (?)	Liberal	Eclectic (positivist)	Journalism
El problema nacional [*The National Problem*]	1899	R. Macías Picavea (1847-1899)	Liberal	Eclectic (positivist)	Scholar
Hacia otra España [*Towards another Spain*]	1899	Ramiro de Maeztu (1874-1936)	Liberal	Eclectic (positivist)	Journalism
La moral de la derrota [*The Moral of the Defeat*]	1900	Luis Morote (1862- 1913)	Liberal	Eclectic (positivist)	Journalism
Recontitución y europeización [*Reconstitution and Europesation*]	1898	Joaquín Costa (1846-1911)	Liberal	Eclectic (positivist)	Scholar
Crisis política de España [*Spain's Political Crisis*]	1901				
Oligarquía y caciquismo [*Oligarchy and Petty Tyranny*]	1901				
En torno al casticismo [*About Traditionalism*]	1902	Miguel Unamuno (1864-1936)	Liberal	Idealist	Scholar
Psicología del Pueblo Español [*Psychology of the Spanish People*]	1902	Rafael Altamira (1866-1951)	Liberal	Eclectic (idealist)	Scholar

publication. Their authors were mainly members of the then scarce professional middle classes or university professors. Practically, none of the Regenerationists had connections with the political and the economical elites. Most were civil servants who supplemented their meager wages from what they got from writing in newspapers and giving public lectures. They complained bitterly of not being taken into account by the powers in the country, proclaimed proudly their independence, and rarely got involved in real politics at this time. But all shared a sincere personal concern about their country and took its ailments personally. As Miguel de Unamuno said, "I feel the pains of Spain" ["*me duele España*"]. They delved in the causes of the national sickness not only in the hope of reaching a diagnosis, but because they were searching for their own identity. They were as much searching for their country's psychology, as for their personal self within it. It is this struggle that made them an interesting case for study. Each of them got enmeshed in a web of identifications and counter-identifications which had to be navigated and disentangled in order to figure out the identity they were looking for. They were not very successful in their attempts, since they only managed to make clearer two opposing figures (the *Two Spains*, see Juliá, 2004), that 40 years later set the country ablaze in a civil war, where the two opposing views were killing each other as Francisco de Goya depicted in one of his "black" paintings 120 years earlier.

What interests us here is not what this group achieved, but how some of them carried out their task. They were professional writers who had a considerable store of knowledge and when facing the problem that most concerned them, simultaneously produced a theory about their nation's identity and put their own selves into play in the process. While doing so, they also set some of the foundations of the current predominant views on the history and identity of Spain. Whether their ideas were more or less valuable does not concern us here. What is the matter of our interest now is how they dealt with the public events they lived through, how they elaborated their theories, and the role otherness had in this process. And above all, how they envisioned the way in which they—and their fellow countrymen—should shape their own identities.

An Agent Feeling the Pains of the Mother Country

Perhaps the most illuminating case for our purposes is that of Rafael Altamira (1866-1951) a discrete but renowned scholar and one of the many exiled intellectuals after the Civil War (1936-39). He was an outstanding jurist, historian, literary critic, professor at Madrid University, Justice at the International Court of The Hague (an institution created by the Society of Nations following a project he authored) and candidate for the Nobel Peace Prize. He authored over 70 books, among them one titled *Psychology of the Spanish People*, published in 1902 (2nd edition 1917), the forewords of each are worth quoting:

> I wrote this book in the terrible summer of 1898 which left such a deep mark on the souls of true patriots. Between sorrowful tears and indignant rage—prompted by the ineptitude of some, the perfidy of others and the indifferent passivity of the majority,—I was filling sheets of paper, inspired not by the huge discouragement that any one would have then found justified, but by the hope, or better, by the urge that a movement would arise, as a reaction to the horrid disaster, similar to that which made the defeated Prussia of 1808 the strong and glorious Germany of today. That is why I also started then the translation of Fichte's *Discourses*. I was not contemplating a military revenge or a renaissance of imperialism…. What I was dreaming of was our interior regeneration, the correction of our faults, the vigorous effort that might take us from the deep national decadence, seen and felt for a long time.
>
> There is no doubt that our colonial problem and that of our international affairs is dependent on other internal and deeper problems, relating to the psychology of our people, to the state of our culture, to the conception that other nations have about us, and to the conception that we have of ourselves and the social entity in which we live and belong. (Altamira, 1902/1997, pp. 53-54)

> The two enemies I fought against … [before] have not disappeared…. In the first place Hispanophobia has not totally disappeared, and even less so the ignorance about our past, our present and the conditions of our people. There are still plenty of people outside Spain under the influence of blindly accepted traditional judgments … there are also parties and groups of people that think as a patriotic ideal to *de-Spanish* their country, that is, to erase even the smallest trace of tradition or Spanish influence, because they consider it to be deadly harmful, as a complete expression of backwardness, tyranny or intransigence in every moment of their past and in current reality.
>
> On the other hand, even if it is true that 1898 pessimism has been mended, it is also indubitable that it continues to be a burden in our psychology. Perhaps it is often unconfessed and one may have thought that it was defeated; but in the spiritual depths of many Spaniards' souls it keeps coercing activities, disheartening and shortening hopes…. [Sometimes] scepticism is allied with political passion, that makes some to reject everything that is supposed to remove the so-called traditional regimes and that instinctively hates everything that comes from those considered as enemies.
>
> However, our *practical* problem nowadays and for the future does not reside in whether or not to acknowledge the existence of a greater or lesser feeling of a Spanish national unity, but *in making an effort for it to exist* and to reinforce it increasingly, since this is something we lack and it should not be lacking. (Altamira, 1917/1997, pp. 49-51)

The Purpose

These excerpts make clear not only Altamira's purposes when writing this book, but also the addressees he had in mind, and the others he was thinking of when trying to picture *the* "Psychology of the Spanish People," others that were both outside and inside the country. His purpose was the *regeneration* of the country, rejecting the pessimism about the "essential capacity of the race to adapt ourselves to modern civilization," and supporting "the hope for a better future, which, more or less consciously, carried in its bosom the belief in fundamental qualities of our spirit suitable for every progress" (Altamira, 1902/1997, p. 45). He was attempting to disentangle the fundamental elements of the identity of *the* "Spanish people" in order to put it to work for "regeneration." An endeavor that required, first to look for the existing seeds useful to his purpose, and to separate them from the weeds that were an impediment for progress. Something that could not be done without identifying the others in con-trast to whom the existent "fundamental qualities" could become the resources upon which to build a national identity. Because the purpose hidden behind the label which gave the title of this book was unmistakably to develop a Spanish national identity, even if he chose to view it as the task of unveiling the psychology of the people of his country, a task that was not totally uncommon among the European social scientists of the time:

> Everywhere the hollow humanism of many internationalists—not the real humanism compatible with group differences, proclaimed by Herder,—and the petty egoisms of regions and local groups have been totally defeated. National patriotism, that before the war [first World War] was suffering in many parts an acute crisis, has overcome it and prevailed. Every country has felt, with the grave eloquence of suffering, that it can only save itself through a strong solidarity among every one of its members, which widens the social body and gathers both mass and strength for the beatings of today and tomorrow. (Altamira, p. 51)

Who were then the addressees he was talking to?, Who were the Others from whom to disentangle for *the real* self to be constructed? These are questions to be answered in due course.

From the Agent to the Agencies

Altamira was himself—as any social activist—a product of history and a producer of history. How he chose to present himself as an individual has to be inferred from the specific manner in which he was affected by the events of his time, the self-regulatory means he put into play, and the ways in which he chose to participate in the production of historical effects.

Altamira composed his discourse about the "national disaster" not only from his individual feelings, but also from a affectively committed collective approach. When he writes the foreword of *Psychology of the Spanish People* 4 years have passed after Cuba, Puerto Rico, and the Philippines were lost, and most of its content had already been published as separate articles throughout 1898 and 1899, but even so he chooses to appear before his audience with tears in his eyes. His voice transmits suffering, pain, rage, and determination to act for changing the state of affairs of his country.

Tragic feelings of pain and moral rage are perhaps among the affections most difficult to fake. Suffering is taken to be something unequivocally personal, private, only possible to feel in the first person. To appear as a suffering person—besides the authenticity of the affection or the intention—is a safe rhetorical device to be listened to, to make the addressee to be receptive to the message conveyed. To some extent to show one's emotions is to open oneself to others, to show one's intimacy, and so facilitate an empathy that increase the rhetorical force of the diagnosis and the solutions the author presents.

The Regenerationists' texts pretend to be "scientific," as their authors liked to say, but in fact they are the affectively committed answers of individuals who believe they have enough symbolic power to put their reflections on the national disaster on the market and so to be instrumental in the shaping of public opinion. Nevertheless, if we take a look at the main body of the texts, the attempt at keeping a personal distance from the events, required by the scientific ethos, is achieved in most of the cases; and also in Altamira's book, showing himself to be a rigorous and devoted academic. The author's feelings are systematically repressed, maintaining an impersonal tone at all times and making the force of the argument rely on reported facts (historical ones, in Altamira's case). Forewords are the only space in which they allow themselves to be explicit on how they transit between motives and reasons, between values and facts. Forewords (perhaps with the sole exception of Unamuno's *About Traditionalism*, that only comments on the origin of the materials gathered) appear as a rhetorical space where the self can show the genealogy of its motives, its purposes and the way they relate to the book's task. It is within such a space that Altamira, with a subtle calculated literary ambiguity, says:

> my pen logically rushed to write, before anything else, about the concept of the mother country and the need of the division in nations, in order to

affirm, if this should result from the scientific analysis of historical and sociological data, our right to live. (Altamira, 1902/1997, p. 54)

These forewords appear then as a sort of transitional zone between the individual self and the impersonal and collective discourse required by the scientific ethos. Forewords attempt to specify the particular ways in which the author commits himself to a task that transcends his own life, offering himself as a sort of medium that condenses the sense (or perhaps the nonsense) of his country's tragedy, sacrificing, if necessary, his own dignity. The self might have chosen to withdraw, to leave this task to somebody else, to allow himself to be drifted by the fatality of the stream of history; but it is the love for his country—an impetuous and savior feeling—that leads him to take his own responsibilities.

> evil reached even the healthier elements of the country, the youth, on whom everybody naturally trusts. Shall we keep our arms crossed and fall into the fatalism of the belief of the *races,* and leave destiny to carry us off? I, who am among those who start to mistrust everything, would consider myself as a coward if I laid down my arms when faced with this painful struggle, full of sorrows. In spite of the sadness and deep fear that often invades my soul, I continue working, and so I believe should anyone who truly love his country. (Altamira, 1902/1997, p. 56)

The task is so huge that it seems to point towards a collapse of the self onto the others, as if one may only aspire to a horizon of sense by taking upon oneself the collective task. The abdication of a space for personal interest is vindicated by the sense of the task of eradicating a pessimism that eventually gears itself towards egoism:

> [It is pessimism that] in the intellectual depths of many Spaniards keep coercing activities, dismaying nerves and shortening hopes. There are cases in which it has allied with the scepticism that often comes together with individual egoism and sacrifices everything on the altar of profit for a sole man. (Altamira, 1917/1997, p. 48)

It seems clear that Altamira puts into play an affective energy that arises from a deep rejection of three basic attitudes which define the profile against whom he derives his own specifity: the pessimists, the sceptics and the egoists. He is not very specific about the names of the people he is referring to, but it is not difficult to guess. They match with a part of the political sociogram of the Ultramontanist Spain, a group who managed to derail the train of progress in Spain and ruined the progressive projects that Altamira identified with. This generic "other" against whom Altamira reacts has one foot inside and another outside Spain, and forms a rhetorical alliance that has to be attacked at its roots.

There are still plenty of people outside Spain under the influence of blindly accepted traditional judgments. We have recently heard that some fellow countrymen of ours have been asked in a European capital city, whose name I will not mention, whether typing machines were known in Barcelona, or pianos in Madrid. There are still people who carry shotguns when coming to the Peninsula to remedy the lack of personal security that they assume to exist even in big towns. There are also parties and groups of people who think it as a patriotic ideal to *de-Spanish* their country." (Altamira, 1917/1997, p. 49)

Altamira was no bigot—nor a chauvinist. He was intellectually socialized within the Free Institute for Learning[1] (FIL), the flagship of Spanish intellectual progressive liberalism in the hinge of the nineteenth and twentieth centuries. Related to the FIL were figures such as Ramón y Cajal, Ortega y Gasset, Salvador Dalí, Luis Buñuel, and Federico García Lorca, among many others. The FIL also had as its aim to educate an elite able to produce a profound shift in the historical path of the country, and to hook it into the train of modern progress and Europe (see Blanco, 1997). These two sides of the FIL mission—education as the only and true means for producing a genuine, reliable, and definitive long-term change, and the idea that this task was to be carried out by a small number of agents of change—show a radical confidence in the individual, and are clearly apparent in Altamira's regenerationist program (see Asín, 1997).

The Action

Education is second to nothing for Altamira. Everything that is wrong with the country comes from a shared representation of what *to be Spanish* means, a completely out-of-focus view of the future of Spain, that causes a low collective self-esteem. Political, social, or economical problems are more the consequence of this distorted—or even perverse—representation rather than its cause. When Altamira writes about the "psychology of Spanish people" he is mainly referring to the logic and the historical dynamics of these representations, making the purpose of his book that of mending these distortions by resorting to historical and sociological data that seem to point towards the elimination of the motives for pessimism. As he clearly states:

my thesis and my argument unavoidably laid on an inquiry into the past and present psychological qualities of our people. I preached for overcoming our disheartment and effective decadence in many realms; I was fighting the unproductive pessimism; I was attempting to show that one of the most fertile means (shall I risk saying the only one?) is in educational reform, in strengthening and diffusing culture.

But, in order to fight against pessimism, … I needed first to show the lack of scientific value of the several *Psychologies* that pretended to define the Spanish soul as unappealingly incapable of civilised life, and therefore of any renaissance. (Altamira, 1917/1997, p. 46)

The only reasonable way to change these representations was by purposely and systematically handling the data in the proper way in order to slowly build a representation better-fitted to creating a higher collective self-esteem, a firmer identity and, in the long run, better social well-being. Education was the vehicle for change, and particularly the teaching of history. His book was intended to play a role in this endeavor since "there is no possible education without a foundation on the psychology of the subject" (Altamira, 1917/1997, p. 54).

Altamira's position was made possible by his choosing of (1) an affective approach to his motives for thinking (feeling "the pains" of the country), (2) the problem of Spain ("the injury"), something that can only be mended by (3) an educational reform ("the remedy"), that makes the country move towards the recovery of an almost lost self-esteem ("the healing"), and so open a future of social, cultural, and economical progress ("health"). Many elements of this argument were ready for use in Altamira's intellectual milieu, including this sickness-health allegory (Castro, 2004). An allegory he exhausts in the conclusion of his foreword to the 1902 edition of his book.

However, if he managed to put to work everything he called for

it was still to be seen whether the remedy arrived timely or it was already late; whether the good natural constitution [the psychology of the Spanish] was still strong enough to respond to the medicine and cast the sickness out of the organism. This is a question that only the future will answer. (Altamira, 1902/1997, p. 57)

The same allegory shows a more dramatic turn in Macías Picavea's text, where reason and science appear as having a therapeutic value.

we are perfectly aware that the straight, inconsiderate and sharp words of science … are a pure and shocking medicine, of the sort that produce a rush, a purge, or cut and burn the flesh of the patient…. I am a professor, and the reader shall see how I cut myself, how I cut all professors, and cut the educational system of the State where I live and teach…. Is this so required by the scientific conclusions that, deafening myself to everything else, I am seeking here?… Then, too bad. And whoever is found to be an abscess or pus, has to put up with being expelled and cleansed way.

Aren't we facing a deadly threat? Isn't it that we have to save a dying patient?... Then.... It is now or never when we have to make the exception of asking and allowing science to speak with its inexorable and truthful voice in the present, as well as in past history, submitting ourselves to her sentence, learning her teachings, and redeeming ourselves in the severe doctrine of her august rulings! *Veritas liberabit vos.* (Macías Picavea, 1899/ 1992, pp. 34-35)

Life, History, and the Self: The Drama Lived Through

The argument developed so far has not been gratuitous. Kenneth Burke (1945) was aware that there is no way human action can be described without a dramaturgical logic. No human action can be made sense of outside a grammar, a dense, and recursive combinatory of cases. An ordered and credible combination of agents, actions, sceneries, purposes, and agencies (the dramaturgic pentad) is a minimum condition, not only for the description of action, but also for the very existence of any significant action. Distal ("real") action and symbolic ("described") action are really the same. We may even consider that the specification of a self in a culture, vis-à-vis the world and the others, calls for shortening the distance between the action and its symbolic description. This is something that is particularly true, when one is talking about the action (writing in this case) of professional intellectuals, whose way of life lead them to construct their selves within the horizon of a progressing self-consciousness of the very conditions that make this construction possible. The self then appears as a chimera, as a belief. The realization of this idea is a painful increase of the awareness of the relative value of each case within a particular pentadic combination. The self ends up watching itself as another case, it could not be otherwise. That is why the agential part of the self in relation to the other elements of the pentad (action, scenery, purpose, and agency) has to be always subject to review.

Our purpose here is to reflect on the painful process of putting together a toolkit, which can be instrumental for the construction of the selves of a group of intellectuals, who also believe themselves to be tools for the construction of the collective identity of their country. The rest of the chapter will centre on showing some of the basic elements they contributed in the construction of a coherent collective discourse on the Spanish nation, and describing the grammar that regulated this process. We will see how the Regenerationists' discursive identification of some "others" came together with a fascinating dramatic performance of imputations of blame, or at least of a sharing of responsibilities, for the historical failure of a project of a Spanish nation. Every one of the Regenerationists thought of his own contribution as genuinely personal, but our analysis will show how they were actually merged in a collective task.

"The Other" in the Construction of Spanish National Identity: Polymorphic Otherness

Altamira's *Psychology of Spanish People* appeared in 1902 after the most significant titles of *Regenerationist* genre were published. This allowed him to devote some chapters to examining the previous opinions of his colleagues and modeling an intertextual space of discussion. In this sense, Altamira's book shows us clearly the programmatic goal of the *Regeneracionists*: to design the collective identity of the Spanish people in contrast to several disquieting others. Logically, this target also tacitly involved the unraveling of the identity and activity of the *Regerationism* as a group.

The Spanish Regenerationists were themselves a group caught in an identity crisis they believed to be the crisis of the national identity of their country. They took upon themselves the task of devising a new identity that, on the one hand, had to preserve the real self of the country, and on the other, had to be able to put it on the track of the progress they sought (see Tuñón, 2000 and Tusell, 1998 for reviews). In order to do so they had to select their addressees, to draw a suitable picture of the past and present, and to choose some Others from whom to disentangle themselves. This was not an easy task. They had to negotiate the past of the nation (the historical self and other), the social structure of the country (the social self and other), the diversity within the nation (the intranational others), and place their country within the international realm (the international other). Table 9.2 maps the web of identity tensions the Regenerationism genre dealt with.

All these tensions had to be negotiated in order to create a plausible national narrative identity suited to the desire of this group. Altamira was a historian and part of his attempt was to anchor the Psychology of the Spanish People on events of the country's past, creating a sort of narrative self. This required the invention of a set of suitable Others.

The "Historical Other"

The Regenerationist literature typically pictured the Spanish imperial past as the historical other, following the path of liberal historians of the time (see Fox, 1997; Morón, 1998; Wulff, 2003 for reviews). The Habsburg dynasty—particularly Carlos V and Philippe II, who exerted an aggressive military policy on Europe and America—and the Bourbons, from the eighteenth century onwards, were portrayed as conducting their imperial policies without taking into account the interests of the country.

**Table 9.2. Fields of Identity Tensions
Within Spanish Regenerationism**

		Identity Tensions Before the Other	
Fields of Experience	Profiles	Positive: Addressees (Acts of Identification)	Negative: Against Whom (Acts of Counter-Identification)
The Historical Other	Empire	Nostalgia of the lost collective Golden Age.	Rejection of the obsolete structures of the *ancienne régime*.
The Social Other	Elite	Proximity to the social groups capable of leading reforms.	Competition with the ruling classes.
	Masses	Confidence in the qualities and capabilities of the common people.	Uneasiness before the revolutionary potential of the lower classes. Mistrust of their ignorance and alienation.
The Intranational Other	Regions	Diversity as a potential asset of varied features of the collective.	Uneasiness before the potential claims of the regions for home rule or independence.
The International Other	Nation-state	Proximity to other collectives related by history, race, culture, etc. Imitation of foreign strategies and features in order to reach modernization.	Uneasiness before other potentially invasive national collectives. Colonial competition.
	Colonies	Desire to rule *savage* peoples in order to bring them to civilization.	Mistrust of former colonies because of their independence or their protection by foreign powers.

It was often thought that the glorification of the imperial past had the effect on the people of creating a sort of dreamy state of fascination with a glorious past that made them to be removed from the needs of the present.

However Altamira (1917/1997) pointed out that a sharp rejection of this past may be paradoxically counterproductive, since it could be the result of an uncritical acceptance of the "black legend," invented by the enemies of the Spanish Empire (see García Carcel, 1992, for a historical account). If that was the case, to assume the thesis that cruelty and fanaticism were features of the Spaniards would have a deleterious effect on the self-concept of contemporary Spaniards, producing a sort of morbid identification, which may be one of the causes of the decadence. He even went as far as criticizing some of his colleagues for having been carried away by this pessimism in their texts.

An alternative history had to be written. The classical protagonists of Spanish history (monarchs, ruling classes) had to be removed from the forefront, the people had to be rescued as the protagonists of the national history, and a strategic place had to be secured for the intellectual and commercial classes. Miguel de Unamuno (1895/1996) coined the term intrahistory (*intrahistoria*) in order to articulate a construction of the past fitted to this purpose. It was a sort of social or internal history fluctuating between the so-called dormant qualities of the race and the romantic literary genre of customs and manners, in which the common people appeared as the identity hinge between the past and the present of the national community. Most Regenerationists took for granted that, after expelling the Arabs from the Peninsula (1492) and the reign of the Catholic royals (Ferdinand and Isabella, 1479-1516), the outstanding qualities of the people were wasted in conquests and military adventures. What is more, the Spanish people, either unaware or naive, stoically suffered the errors, excesses, and incompetence of their rulers.

Macías Picavea (1899/1992) and Luis Morote (1900) believed that the irresponsible direction of the Austrian and French dynasties ruling Spain (still in the throne following the Bourbon Restoration of 1875) was foreign to the real national identity: they were exemplars of the anti-Spain. A strong man or a new class had to arise in order to remove the current remains of the *ancienne régime* and to rescue the people from their historic lethargy and put them on the path of progress. Joaquín Costa (1898-1901/1981) went as far as to identify his coetaneous intellectual classes as the heir to those who had to leave the country because of religious or political prosecution. The history of Spain, as he saw it, had been a sort of "reverse natural selection," since corrupt and unproductive ruling classes exploited the population, condemning the country to moral misery and decadence.

In sum, the Regenerationist projection of past history onto their present took them to perform three types of acts of identification: (a) to counter identify the national collective against the Habsburg monarchs and their Bourbon heirs; (b) to identify the people as the intrahistorical other, with their mixed features of hardworking capabilities and political infantilism; and (c) to present the Regenerationists as the assumed heirs to those who in the past had cultivated science and fought for freedom with the frustrated hope of making Spain to progress. This historical picture, if it managed to get stabilized in the collected memory of the Spaniards, would insure their group a key role in the future of the country. But this never happened.

The Social Other

These historical others are but presentist projections on the past of coetaneous others. The preferred antagonistic other were the ruling classes of the time: the politicians, industrialists and land owners of the Bourbon Restoration (1874-1923). This was a period of political equilibrium, where under a democratic facade, disguised fake election results and protected the interests of the wealthy classes, at the price of the political and economical marginalization of the broad majority of the population. A system whose workings were eloquently pictured by the title of one Joaquín Costa's books: *Oligarchy and Petty Tyranny* (1901/1998). Lucas Ma-llada (1890/1989) pictured this régime as a state of "public immorality" and "social mess," which he took to be a direct consequence of government corruption, political egoism, and the bad moral example of the ruling classes. Costa (1898-1901/1981) and Macías Picavea (1899/1992) also extended their criticisms to the parliamentary system that they viewed as unfitting to the type of reform required.

The common people is the second Other in this game. These people, at the end of the nineteenth century lived mainly in rural areas, most of them were illiterate, and some cases were also severely undernourished, a state of affairs that most of the time was born with a stoicism that the Regenerationists admired. Altamira (1902/1997), hoped that under this stoicism the potentialities of the historical race were still hidden so that they could be awakened by the proper agencies. However, there were also some disturbing signs. In spite of the scarcity of literacy skills that could facilitate the widespread diffusion of socialist messages, there were significant anarchist rootings in the country, that sometimes produced outburst of violence—mostly viewed as irrational and primitive reactions to abusive labour conditions (Salillas, 1898). Nevertheless, the most mentioned features of this part of the population were pauperization, malnutrition, illiteracy and unhealthy living conditions.

This made the burden of the responsibility fall to the so-called "neutral classes" (Costa, 1898-1901/1981), that is, those capable—because of their attitude, sensitivity and knowledge- to lead the reformation. They were the smaller businessmen, the intellectuals, scientists, and other social agents that—as the Regenerationists themselves—were ready to leave aside their personal interests to collaborate in a reformation addressed to the country as a whole. Costa again managed to provide a successful slogan for the needs of the time. "School and larder" was a motto that called for effective action in the areas of the professional expertise of Regenerationists: economics and education.

Altamira was adamant in calling on the responsibility of the enlightened elites for leading the dispossessed, and was also the one who most emphasized education as the main goal. He meant not just the reformation of the public system, but also the development of the so-called University Extension, in which university students will travel around the country carrying cultural activities for the education of the workers that he though would be as effective as "the school and the workshop to prepare them for the social, national endeavour that needs their concourse" (Altamira, 1902/1998, p. 183).

Education was to be the main road to nationalization. The different social others depicted in the Regenerationists' discourse should eventually join in the final stage of a harmonic Spanish nation state. But education was a political battleground in which the different ideological and political agents of the Restauration period were fighting to enlist the new generations.[2] As a result, rather than closing the gap, the split between these different "others" grew bigger. Their differences, now enplotted with arguments of the discourses of the new ideologies of the first decades of the twentieth century, was the feeding ground for the development of the conflicting identities of the two Spains that fought the Civil War (1936-39).

The Intranational Other

The Regenerationists could tailor their particular historical anti-Spain without risking their view of the nation state. It may change its shape but its integrity was not at risk. They thought the danger may come from a different quarter: the attempts to build other national entities within the Spanish territory. At the same time that the Regenerationists were struggling to make use of European nationalist ideas in order to make a modern state from the ruins left by the old Spanish Empire. There were also some Basque and Catalan writers, such as Sabino Arana or Prat de la Riba, who were attempting the same in their home regions (see Juaristi, 1997; Ucelay-Dacal, 2003). If they were to succeed the national integrity would be threatened, and Spain at the best would be a nation of nations, and in the worst a nation different to that of the Basques and the Catalans.

The construction of this particular other was particularly complex. It has to be said that all the Regenerationists were from peripheral regions of the country. Some of them were even native speakers of their vernacular languages (e.g., Basque for Unamuno, and Catalan for Altamira). They claimed that regional peculiarities were a sign of the differences within the nation state, not only in customs and manners but also in socioeconomical and moral development. However, these differences should be bridged by a common program. All the regions should

> get together in the beautiful and great common labour of reviving the common mother country; Aragon will give its indomitable impulse, Castille its

tireless endurance, Cantabria its energy, Galicia its patient laboriousness, Andalusia its tonic humour, Valencia its agility, and Catalonia and the Basque Country their guidance and leadership, since they are better equipped for this enterprise. (Macías, 1899/1992, p. 335)

Besides the regional diversity, and the possible centrifugal forces that could be unleashed, there was another disturbing other: the so-called Spanish individualism,—pointed out by Ganivet (1897/1996), Morote (1900) or Ma-llada (1890/1989)—which carried within it an antipathy and enmity to the neighbouring regions. The loss of the last colonies had loosened the interregional ties, providing an opportunity for some regionalist agents to design new collective identities and promote egoistical political interests. Altamira (1902/1997) was particularly concerned by this issue and, together with Maeztu (1899/1997) and Morote (1900), warned about the dangers of historical and anthropometrical arguments geared to the promotion of regionalisms. It was here where there was another Other which could produce the braking of the nation.

When taking into account the international front, the Regenerationists realized that only a strong nationality could survive. Some of them suggested that this role could be played by the political entity created by the Catholic Kings (Ferdinand and Isabella) centred around the Kingdom of Castille. But it was only some years later when some literary authors— mainly Azorín, Machado, and the late Unamuno,—the philosopher Ortega y Gasset, and the historian Menédez Pidal, came to idealize Castille as the central core of the country (see Morón, 1998). But this was a deviation from the original Regenerationists' idea of forging a common identity.

The International Other

Western Europe was the mirror in which the Regenerationists wanted their country to be reflected. England, Germany and France were taken as the model of modernity, progress, and social welfare, the summit of Western civilization. Thus a substantial part of the reforms they posed had the goal of reaching the level of development in these countries. In addition, this general goal was intertwined with a personal biographical dimension: they admired the social acknowledgement and relevance that scientists and intellectuals enjoyed in these countries and the international projection they had. But this admiration was not blind. They took as their task to preserve what was peculiar of Spain as the cement to keep together the elements of the identity they were attempting to devise. Thus they warned as much against the temptation of dissolving the country's identity and merging with this Other in a sort of vague cosmopolitism—under the name of humanity, socialism, fraternity, or whatever—as against a blind imitation of imported political, administrative, or educational models. They took some institutions and ideologies (self-government, democracy, liberalism, etc.) as possible useful tools for their purposes, but never beyond their applicability in the contemporary state of the country. Some aspects of the international Other were worthy to be used as a model, but never at the price of loosing one's own soul in the process. That is why Altamira advocated for the creation of grants that facilitated young Spaniards to study abroad, rather than employing imported methods and professors. He recommended these grants to be awarded not too early in the students' career, and to be long enough so they could thoroughly acquire useful knowledge, but limited in time, so that an excessive adherence to foreign Otherness could be avoided.

The international Other had aspects to be admired, but it also had to be resisted. It was a dangerous competitor in the international sphere, as well as a possible threat to the national identity. This threat showed itself acutely vis-à-vis the colonial question. This was the time of the high tide of imperialism. The prestige of the main powers was played in a colonial race, justified by the Spencerian philosophy that placed on the hand of the civilized the responsibility of bringing "the primitives" to a better state. To be cast away from the colonial race was an insult to national pride. It was not only that the Spanish Pacific Archipielagos (Marian and Caroline Islands) had to be sold to Germany (1899), because of the impossibility of defending them, or that the United States took advantage of the weakness after the defeat, also adding Guam and the Philippines to their bounty. It was also that Spain was left aside in the colonial distribution of Africa, with only a tiny colony in the Guinean Gulf (Equatorial Guinea). Even the Spanish interests in its immediate neighbor, Morocco—within the Spanish area of influence since the beginnings of modernity—were threatened, first by the Germans (Tangiers crisis, 1904) and then by the French. The Algeciras Conference (1905) solved the crisis splitting the Moroccan sultanate into a French protectorate (the South with rich agricultural lands and all the main cities), and a Spanish one (the small, poor, mountainous, and bellicose Rif). However, the colonial question was not a motive of great concern to the Regenerationists, since they were advocating in favor of an internal retreat in order to put matters in order at home. It was a part of the political, ideological, and economical struggles of the time, when the Spanish army was looking desperately for a war to clean their name after the 1898 defeat. The result was a long and bloody colonial war in Morocco, that eventually finished off the Bourbon Restoration régime, fed a growing Republican opposition and helped to pave the way to the Civil War (1936-39). But these events belong to the first third of the twentieth century.

Before and after the Cuban War (1898) the Regenerationists shared with the rest of Spaniards a dislike for the Anglo-Saxons, who were portrayed as materialists, egoistic and exploiters of their colonies, features that were taken to belong to Protestantism, that then acted as a sort of synonym to the Anglo-Saxon culture. In contrast, the Spanish were pictured as idealist, generous, and detached, characteristics that the most conservative regenerationism (Ganivet, 1897/1996; Isern, 1899) took as typical of the ecumenical character of Catholicism. Anglo-Saxon colonization was considered as predatory by the Regenerationist, while the Spanish disposition towards colonization was presented as giving concern to education, to the expansion of culture and, therefore committed to a truly civilizing enterprise. It was this view what contributed to the fact that many decades after the loss of the American empire, there was still hope that

> our language, culture, art, genius and spirit of the race, will prevail and be the *raison d'être* within the Planet of a Spain, the greatest Spain, mental and moral mother- country of eighteen nationalities, of nearly a whole continent, of a world politically separated from us, but which thinks and cherishes the same things as their Augustus mother, because when speaking, writing, laughing, singing, loving, they have to use the Castillian language. (Morote, 1900, p. 570)

This quotation is representative not just of an identity that goes beyond the borders of a particular political entity, it also concealed a concern for the survival of a wider identity. Many Regenerationists identified themselves with other Latin countries defeated at war, such as France was by Germany at Sedan (1870). What was at risk was not only the loss of colonies, but the annihilation of the Latin culture by the Anglo-Saxons. But the advocated strategy may seem naïve. Altamira (1902/1997), Morote (1900) or Unamuno (1895/1996) discredited warmongerism as incoherent with the *Zeitgeist* of modernity. Morote even resorted to Herbert Spencer (an Anglo-Saxon) when calling for the supremacy of the rule of law, the market and science in order to counter-attack some Spanish militarist tendencies, which were pictured as belonging to a barbaric sociohistorical stage already overcome.

But this naivety may be more strategic than sincere. On the one hand their linking of scientific and technological progress with success at war was not infrequent. It was a generally-agreed opinion that the Spanish Navy was sunk by American schools rather than by the guns of the U.S. Navy. This may be the reason why the Regenerationists were concerned in leaving aside past imperial glories and performing a strategic retreat to look for the real self of the country. As Ganivet said, paraphrasing St.

Augustine, *"Noli foras ire, in interiore Hispaniae habitat veritas"* (Ganivet, 1897/1996, p. 131).

It seems that Lord Salisbury's words hit their target, in spite of the explicit protests of Maeztu (1899/1997) and Morote (1900) against them. The international Other was too strong to be opposed. The only possible tactic was to follow the ways of the law, the market, science and education, which were the only way out of their current problems, international as well as national. This view had the added value of securing them as the only group able to lead the country into the future.

By Way of Conclusion: The Nineteenth Century Intellectual and the Construction of the Modern Nation-State

The Renerationists' crisis, that merged personal biographies with the national collective, rather than unusual, was typical of the nineteenth century intellectuals. They were placed within the identitarian crossroads where the new nation-states were being shaped. This is what makes this period a privileged landscape for the study of Otherness in historic situated self-experiences.

The nation state was the then preferred sociopolitical model for the social agents that attempted to get rid of the old absolutist monarchies and empires. Every social reorganization that followed a revolutionary (or anti-revolutionary) outburst resorted to theoretical contributions which putted together concepts borrowed from new disciplinary fields (*Geist*, collective psychology, race, etc.) and the emerging nationalistic ideology (nationality, state, people, etc.) developed by authors such as Fichte, Renan, or Sergi.[3] The new disciplines provided new genealogical and ontological arguments (the history of humanity and the national histories displaced Sacred History, and divine intervention changed into the spontaneity and continuities of natural evolution), which facilitated the exploration of subjectivity, and therefore opened the floor for its manipulation. The result was the "invention" of the subject and its management (Foucault, 1966, 1975). On the other hand, the emergent nationalism claimed for a defence of the singularity and integrity of a collective self that had to face some possible others, which so appeared as counter figures for the design of one's own collective identity. In sum, a new social model emerged, one that had to be carefully designed to manage the mismatches between specialization and homogenization that arose within a system that favoured the free exchange of material and symbolic commodities.

This makes us to believe that the nation state provided the discursive and practical laboratory where the self could take some historical-cultural depth and, at so was able to start thinking itself as an Other (see Ricoeur,

1990), or rather as a set of some possible others. This new scenery multiplied the fronts for experiencing otherness, and so making possible a fragmented subject or, as Gergen (1991) puts it, the "saturated self" that social sciences—and psychology—have been dealing with since the beginning of the nineteenth century. In other words, Western modern development produced a subject in a permanent state of crisis (Blanco, 2002).

There are many fronts for Otherness and the fragmentation of the modern subject; we will focus here on three of them: the breaking of empires into nations; the braking of states into social classes; and the braking of individuals into sociocultural roles. Each of them defined different subjective-identity alternatives as zones for experiencing life, and so have a potential for the estrangement of the individual. It is in the intersection between these three fronts, where the situated experience of Otherness we had been exploring so far—that of the nineteenth century intellectual—shows its significance. They were interesting characters, their sociocultural position placed them in a peculiar experiential position where they had to negotiate the consciousness of the interlink between their personal biography and identity with that of their collective, and consequently devise strategies to manage this connection. When dealing with these three fronts of Otherness, their particular position took them to (a) produce a theory of the nation state – to which they belonged; (b) to claim for the substitution of the old ruling elite for a new technocratic class—of which they were a part; and (c) to assume the distribution and management of the new sociocultural roles—that they shared. Their position in this crossroad left some traces in their identity which were as apparent in their public activities as in their private lives.

These intellectuals felt compelled to play the social role of the collective consciousness of their country, so much in the analysis and diffusion of knowledge (cognitive) as in a directive (executive) function. They felt responsible of the (performative) creation of a wide identity zone, an "imagined community" (Anderson, 1983). To reach this goal with no harm to the social structure, they deployed a wide set of mediational means (Cole, 1996; Wertsch, 1991) for the interpretation of their social world, for disseminating and implementing the views they developed, and for calling to a collective identification and action in the direction they signalled. These mediational means were taken from the realms of politics and education, and their effective diffusion should be done through the press and the publishing industry, which then were the main instruments for the creation of the "imagined community." However, being illiterate the great mass of the population, this strategy failed. Thus, the collective self that had to be instilled, and the Others from which people had to learn to distinguished themselves, never came to be known by the public to whom these products were addressed. As happened during the Peninsular War against the French (1808-1814), the experience of Otherness was only possible before an immediate physical presence, and not just by purely symbolic means (Álvarez Junco, 2001). Spanish intellectuals had to fight with huge communication difficulties, in addition to competing with the alternative identity offered by another directive elite with a more immediate communication with the common people: the Catholic Church.

However, it is the private dimension what is our major concern here. It is in the intellectuals of this period where we find the most interesting case of identity crisis in modernity. We believe that the kaleidoscopic nature of the identity they had to negotiate, can be disentangled following Ricoeur's (1990) dialogue between *selfhood* and *sameness*: self as identical to the others, and self as identical to itself.

When referring to self as identical to the others *(selfhood)*, the great variety of possible groups of belonging has to be taken into account. The intellectual viewed himself as a member of a harmonic community, at the same time that believed he belonged to an elite, to an intelligentsia that claimed a leading role before two different Others: the ignorant populace, and the traditional ruling classes. But this dual adscription needed to be included within a longer trajectory spanning into the past and the future; that is, he had to identify himself with agents of the historical past and hoped that in the future other people will continue his task. As Bruner (1990) says, narratives are the best way to decant acts of identification, to incorporate and reject the relevant Others.

When looking at the self as identical to itself *(sameness)*, we can see how the intellectuals changed his actions throughout his life span. They played different sociocultural roles and wore different persona masks in diverse circumstances. In the case of the Spanish Regenerationists we can see continuities when press articles are compiled in monographic volumes (Almirall, 1889/1983; Altamira, 1902/1997; Unamuno, 1895/1996; Maeztu, 1899/1997), or when revised editions of old books appeared (Altamira). But there were also discontinuities, when some of them rejected a part of their own production because later on in time they considered them as immature, banal or simply wrong (Maeztu, Unamuno). In the latter cases, they did not recognized themselves in what they said before, and forced their original discourses to adapt to a new life perspective.

When these two sides of the self are taken into account, it seems clear that the nineteenth century intellectual is not just one more of the different social roles and functions that Adam Smith linked to the growing complexity and specialization of modern culture. This intellectual is a character whose added value is in his pretended capability to be aware of the braking of classical subjectivity and the collapse of the individual. From his watch tower he seemed to glimpse the crossroads between the historical, the national, the social, the local, or the professional realms as arenas on which selfhood and otherness clashed in different manners. The very idea of the subject, the unified experiential self, appeared as affected by an unsolvable crisis. The impossible task they took upon themselves was that of mending the rips that the criss-cross of different Otherness had caused on the intimate, transcendental or psychological subject of the Kantian tradition.

Paradoxically, these intellectuals were the epitome of the saturated self. They volunteered to produce new foundations for subjectivity, but they were not able to unleash their own lives and identities from the enterprise they endeavoured. Their attempt could not succeed in a time when social roles and functions exponentially increased as new identity zones intersected, and so the number of professional managers of private and public identities (politicians, professionals of the health and educational services, the leisure industry, etc.) also did. In any case, the nineteenth century intellectual is indubitably one of the braking points in the genealogical theorization of Otherness.

The purpose of this chapter has been to examine how Otherness emerged in a particular historical time when other selves started to be objectified and theorized; when the estrangement before what it is not *me* began to produce hypothesis for action. This was a phenomenon with a long tradition of study in philosophy that goes as far back as Aristotle, but it was in the nineteenth century, when a new existential unrest marked the appearance of the modern individual, and collective subjectivity came to the forefront. Otherness appeared in the center of the crossroads between intersubjectivity and the encounter with the Other, and this made theorizing about Other to become a culturally relevant issue. It will be in the twentieth century when G. H. Mead's and Vygotsky's psychologies—as well as Schütz's, and Berger & Luckman's phenomenological sociologies —addressed the generalized presence of the other and its interiorization through socioinstitutional strategies devised for this purpose. But there is still a long journey ahead to map the genealogy of Otherness as a theorization of the culturally relevant Other. A task that requires the detection of relevant dimensions of Otherness in critical moments of the past (e.g., vis-à-vis the development of nationalism) and the exploration of the transformations currently under way.

NOTES

1. Institución Libre de Enseñanza (ILE)
2. The conservative forces, and the Catholic Church were also very active in educational reform, although their worry was to reserve secondary educa-

tion for the upper class layers of the population and maintaining the ideological monopoly of conservative Catholic ideology (see Puelles, 1980 for a review).

3. These three authors are instrumental for mapping a quick genealogy on the role of the Other for the construction of the National. Napoleonic imperialism is the implicit Other for the Germany vindicated by Fichte (1808/1995). Renan (1882/1934) explicitly mentioned Prussian Germany pointing out the reason why this Other cannot take the place of French national self. Lord Salisbury could also occupy a place in this genealogy when he differentiated between living and dying nations, and so established an asymmetrical Other. However there is not a perception of an Other dangerous enough to put at risk the survival of one's own nation until the Italian Sergi (1900/1901) proclaimed the degeneration of Latin nations.

REFERENCES

Almirall, V. (1983). *España tal como es* [Spain as it is]. Barcelona, Spain: Anthropos. (Original work published 1889)

Altamira, R. (1997). *Psicología del pueblo español* [Psychology of the Spanish People]. Madrid, Spain: Biblioteca Nueva. (First edition published 1902 and second 1917)

Álvarez Junco, J. (2001). *Mater Dolorosa: La idea de España en el siglo xix* [Mater Dolorosa: The idea of Spain in 19th century] Madrid, Spain: Taurus.

Anderson, B. (1983). *Imagined communities: Reflections on the origin and spread of nationalism.* New York: Verso.

Asín, R. (1997). La psicología del pueblo español: Introducción a R. Altamira [Psychology of the Spanish People: Introduction to R. Altamira]. Madrid, Spain: Biblioteca Nueva.

Blanco, F. (1997). *El lugar del discurso psicológico en la Institución Libre de Enseñanza: la psicología y la renovación de la conciencia nacional* [The place of the psychological discourse in the Free Institute for Learning: Psychology and renovation of the national mind]. In F. Blanco (Ed.), *Historia de la psicología Española. Desde una Perspectiva Socio-Institucional* (pp. 53-67). Madrid, Spain: Biblioteca Nueva.

Blanco, F. (2002). *El cultivo de la mente: Un ensayo teórico-crítico sobre la cultura psicológica* [The culture of the mind: A theorical-critical essay about psychological culture]. Madrid, Spain: Antonio Machado.

Bruner, J. (1990). *Acts of meaning.* Cambridge, MA: Harvard University Press.

Burke, K. (1945). *A grammar of motives.* Berkeley: University of California Press.

Castro, J. (2004). *La Psicología del Pueblo Español. El papel del discurso psicosociológico en la construcción de la identidad Española en torno a la crisis del 98* [The Psychology of the Spanish people. The role of the psychological discourse in the construction of the Spanish identity during the crisis of 1898]. Unpublished doctoral dissertation. Universidad Autónoma de Madrid.

Cole, M. (1996). *Cultural psychology.* Cambridge, MA: Harvard University Press.

Costa, J. (1981). *Reconstitución y europeización de España y otros escritos* [Reconstitution and europesation of Spain]. Madrid, Spain: Instituto de Estudios de Administración Local. (Original work published 1989-1901)

Costa, J. (1998). *Oligarquía y caciquismo* [Oligarchy and petty tyranny]. Madrid, Spain: Biblioteca Nueva. (Original work published 1901)

Fichte, J. G. (1995). *Reder an de Deutsche nation* [Discourses to the German nation]. Hamburg, Germany: Felix Meiner. (Original work published 1808)Foucault, M. (1966). *Les mots et les choses: Une archéologie des sciences humanes* [The order of things: An archaeology of the human sciences]. (Alan Sheridan, Trans.) París: Editions Gallimard.

Foucault, M. (1975). *Surveiller et punir* [Discipline and punish: The birth of the prison]. (Alan Sheridan, Trans.) París: Editions Gallimard.

Fox, I. (1997). *La invención de España* [The invention of Spain]. Madrid, Spain: Cátedra.

Ganivet, A. (1996). *Idearium Español* [*Spanish Idearium*]. Madrid, Spain: Biblioteca Nueva. (Original work published 1987)

García Cárcel, R. (1992). *La leyenda Negra: Historia y opinión* [The Black legend: history and opinion] Madrid, Spain: Alianza.

Gergen, K. (1991). *The saturated self.* New York: Basic Books.

Isern, D. (1899). *Del desastre nacional y sus causas* [The National Disaster and its causes]. Madrid, Spain: Imprenta de la viuda de M. Minerva de los Ríos.

Juaristi, J. (1997). *El bucle melancólico: Historias de nacionalistas vascos* [The melancholic turn: Histories of Basque nationalists] Madrid, Spain: Espasa.

Juliá, S. (2004). *Historia de las dos Españas* [History of the two Spains]. Madrid, Spain: Taurus.

Macías Picavea, R. (1899/1992). *El problema nacional* [The national problem]. Madrid, Spain: Fundación Banco Exterior.

Maeztu, R. (1997). *Hacia otra España* [Towards another Spain]. Madrid, Spain: Biblioteca Nueva. (Original work published 1899)

Mallada, L. (1890/1989) *Los Males de la Patria* [*The Diseases of the Mother Country*]. Madrid, Spain: Fundación Banco Exterior.

Morón, C. (1998). *El "Alma de España": Cien años de inseguridad* [The "Soul of Spain": A century of insecurity] Madrid, Spain: Ediciones Nobel.

Morote, L. (1900). *La moral de la derrota* [The moral of the defeat]. Madrid, Spain: Imprenta G. Juste.

Puelles, M. de (1980). *Educación e ideología en la España contemporánea (1867-1975)* [Education and ideology in contemporary Spain (1867-1975)]. Barcelona, Spain: Labor.

Renan, E. (1934). *Qu'est-ce qu'une Nation?* [*What is a Nation?*]. París: R. Helleam. (Original work published 1881)

Ricoeur, P. (1990). *Soi-même comme un autre* [Oneself as another]. París: Éditions du Seuil.

Salillas, R. (1896). *El delincuente español: Hampa (Antropología picaresca)* [The Spanish criminal: Underworld life]. Madrid, Spain: Imp. G. Juste.

Sergi, G. (1901) *La Decadencia de las naciones Latinas* [Decadence of Latin nations]. Barcelona, Spain: Antonio López-Librería Española. (Original work published 1900)

Tuñón de Lara, M. (2000). *La España del siglo XIX* [*Spain in XIXth century*]. Madrid, Spain: Akal.

Tusell, J. (1998). *Historia de España en el siglo XX. I. Del 98 a la proclamación de la República* [History of Spain in XIXth century. I. From 1898 to the Proclamation of the republic] Madrid, Spain: Taurus.

Ucelay-Dacal, E. (2003). *El imperialismo catalán: Prat de la Riba, Cambó, D'Ors y la conquista moral de España* [The Catalonian Imperialism: Prat de la Riba, Cambó, D'Ors and the moral conquest of Spain]. Barcelona, Spain: Edhasa.

Unamuno, M. (1996). *En torno al casticismo* [*About Traditionalism*]. Madrid, Spain: Biblioteca Nueva. (Original work published 1895)

Wertsch, J. (1991). *Voices of the mind*. Cambridge, MA: Harvard University Press.

Wulff, F. (2003). *Las esencias patrias. Historiografía e historia antigua en la construcción de la identidad española (siglos XVI-XX)* [The patriotic essences: Historiography and ancient history in the construction of Spanish identity]. Barcelona, Spain: Crítica.

CHAPTER 10

CONTEMPORARY CHINESE COMMUNICATION WITH ITS CULTURAL OTHERS

Shi-xu

How particular cultures communicate about and to cultural others have often been conceptualized in nationalistic and therefore culturally relativist terms. Particularly, in the mainstream cross-cultural and intercultural communication theory, field research, and pedagogy, there seems to have been a dominant discourse that assigns a central role to cross-cultural and cross-linguistic differences on the one hand and to knowledge and skills in the target language and culture on the other hand. These two sets of objects consequently become the main focus of attention.

An important assumption underlying this discourse is that during intercultural contact, the different cultural and linguistic backgrounds and differential or deficient cultural and linguistic knowledge and skills in the target language are likely sources or causes of misunderstanding, miscommunication, or even conflict among the participants in the communicational event. Conversely, cross-cultural and cross-linguistic "understanding" and ultimately "competence" in the intercultural communication are supposed to be the most important mechanisms for

Otherness in Question: Labyrinths of the Self, 257–276

smooth intercultural communication. From this point of view, the more knowledge and skills members of different cultures share, the more chances of success they stand in intercultural communication (e.g., Gudykunst, 2003; Gudykunst & Ting-Toomey, 1988; Hall, 1990; Kluckhohn, 1953, 1961; Schwartz, 2001, 2002).

In this chapter, I shall argue that such discourse of intercultural communication, call it the discourse of difference, is inadequate on several interrelated accounts. First, it takes linguistic and cultural difference as necessarily negative—a handicap as it were. Instead of seeing them as something to learn from, to engage with and to draw upon as resources for expanding human cultural space and enriching human cultural experience, this discourse portrays linguistic and cultural difference as something to unlearn, to guard against, and to overcome. This is a problem in the social scientists' attitude towards linguistic and cultural difference, though, more fundamentally, this may have to do with their underlying notions of culture and communication.

Second, the competence view oversimplifies the processes of intercultural communication and of human communication and relation more generally. For, it sees communication as merely a transparent medium or conduit for the flow of information between participants. According to this view, then, problems can arise when "mismatches" of information from two cultural perspectives occur. But this overlooks the fact that during (intercultural) communication members interact with and upon each other and socially coconstruct meaning. This is a problem in theory.

Third and perhaps more seriously, it fails to take note of the crucial historical and power-saturated nature of intercultural communication. Intercultural communication takes place in actual, concrete historical circumstances, including especially the context of European and American colonialism (hence also, ethnocentricism, orientalism) and Western cultural hegemony. It is this particular historical context actually that has led to the often taken-for-granted and implicit notion of the West as the centre, the standard or the norm in science as well as in everyday life. This explains why it has been the American-Western models of (intercultural) communication that have held sway in the relevant international scholarly scene. Otherwise, exposing and confronting the cultural imbalance and prejudice will also reflexively shake the foundations of existing theory, research, and education as professional and profitable institutions for intercultural contact and communication. This dimension of the discourse of difference is a problem in institutional power and politics.

I want to make an opposite call here: in order to study intercultural communication adequately and helpfully, we must view intercultural communication both globally and holistically on the one hand and locally and historically on the other hand (Shi-xu, Kienpointner, & Servaes, 2005). By this strategic move, I hope we can avoid the pitfalls of universalizing intercultural communication and understanding it a-historically. Further, I want to focus on a particular, Chinese, case, namely, contemporary Chinese intercultural communication. Thus, from the first, broad and general perspective, I shall argue more specifically that intercultural communication should be seen as joint, power-oriented and multicultural activity. From the second, particular and specific perspective, I shall try to suggest that it can be seen as oriented towards achieving cultural equilibrium vis-à-vis the (American) West.

Analytically, the local-global and so multicultural framework implies that we should approach intercultural communication in terms of, not merely individual, grammatical-textual or cultural-psychological causes of intercultural failure or success, but what it is that Chinese intercultural communication is doing in relation to the Western "others" and how it achieves that. In other words, research questions should be directed at determining the nature of Chinese intercultural communication practices and identifying the verbal means and nonverbal circumstances whereby relevant cultural relations and interconnections are accomplished. With these perspectives in mind, I shall analyze samples of typical, recent Chinese intercultural communication, namely of print media events on the issues of human rights and Europe's arms embargo against China, respectively.

THE DIFFERENCE-AND-DEFICIENCY PARADIGM

It is generally assumed that intercultural communication rests, fundamentally, upon participants' knowledge and skill in the target language and culture, or "intercultural competence" as it is often called (Gudykunst, 2003; Gudykunst & Ting-Toomey, 1988; Hall, 1990; Hofstede, 1980; Kluckhohn, 1953, 1961; Schwartz, 2001, 2002; Trompenaars, 1993). Thus, failure or trouble is to be attributed to lack of such knowledge and skill. Quite related to this assumption is the notion that difference in linguistic and cultural backgrounds can be a barrier to smooth communication between members of different culture, too. More generally, in the area of intercultural studies, linguistic and cultural differences and deficiencies in the target language and culture are taken to be the likely causes of misunderstanding, miscommunication, or even conflicts between participants in communication across different cultures. Consequently, much energy has been devoted to investigating differences in linguistic structure (e.g., Wierzbicka, 1991), discourse structure (e.g., Scollon & Scollon, 1995), speech acts (e.g., Blum-Kulka, House, & Kasper, 1989), cognition (Gudykunst & Ting-Toomey, 1988; Kim, 1991; Ting-Toomey,

1999) and social systems (e.g., Hofstede, 1980; Trompenaar, 1993) between people of different cultural backgrounds. Pedagogically, for the same reason, relevant knowledge and skills become the main objective for students' performance and achievement (Cushner & Brislin, 1996). Take for example the book *Intercultural Communication*, where Scollon and Scollon (1995, pp. 11-13) assume that communication will proceed smoothly when members share the same background but it may go awry when the members come from different cultural backgrounds.

The difference-and-deficiency paradigm has largely been a derivative of the (especially North America based) positivist, semiotic-informational, individualistic and universalist model of communication. In this model, communication is merely a descriptive affair and speakers are in an equal relationship. The performative or social-action (e.g., speech act), social-interactive and power-oriented nature of communication is removed from the picture.

However, reducing or attributing problems in intercultural communication to linguistic and/or cultural differences or individual deficiencies obscures the unequal cultural power relations involved and diverts critical attention from acts of cultural prejudice, oppression, or discrimination in the process of intercultural communication and ultimately legitimates and perpetuate such relations and actions. This kind of blindness to cultural power may remind one of the apparent discourse of equality in North America that covers up the underlying reality of inequality. Here the so-called "gender wars" around feminism is a good example.

I think the reason for the oversights in the field of intercultural communication may partly have to do with the interests of the discipline itself. The removal of the socially organized and moral order from intercultural communication theory is consistent with maintaining a science of (intercultural) communication as a static, individual, and cultural product and consequently producing and consuming the knowledge and skills of intercultural communication. Also, the nature and consequences of the difference-and-deficiency paradigm may have to do with the property of the discipline itself: theory, research, and training are normally organized and conducted by the more "powerful," more "successful," more often than not American/Western White elite groups. Intercultural research and training projects and program are often funded and supported by multinational corporate organizations, the goals of which are in sharing but patenting.

I do not intend to deny the potential interest and use of cultural and linguistic competence. General knowledge of, and skills in, the relevant languages and cultures can be useful tools for intercultural communication. But what I question here is the cultural-theoretical basis, self-interest involved and especially the political consequences of such difference-and-deficiency discourse.

INTERCULTURAL COMMUNICATION AS POWER CONTEST

There has already been a fair amount of reflexive and critical work on intercultural theory, research, and education. Recent developments in journals such as *Journal of Language and Intercultural Communication* and *Studies in Intercultural Communication* are examples of this work. Drawing on this body of work and especially cultural studies (Ang, 2001; Bhabha, 1994; Hall, 1996; Said, 1978, 1993; Spivak, 1988), I shall outline, suggestively, an alternative, globally-minded framework of intercultural communication.

Let us start by considering an imaginary example. When the manager of a German Volkswagen company talks with members of a Chinese partner company, he (as the manager is most probably to be) is, from a cultural-historical point of view (i.e., the West/Europe vs the East/China relations), already situated in a historically formed position of power asymmetry. From a business point of view, as investor for example, he may be motivated to persuade his Chinese partners so as to make maximum profit for his company other than just achieve understanding. Unless both parties adopt a political policy and go out of their way, by trying, again and again, to respect each other and look after each other's interest, their encounters will more often than not be punctuated with cultural repression and cultural resistance and result ultimately in the defeat and loss on the part of the powerless and probably both the "winner" and "loser."

Human cultures are not in an equal relation with one another and have never been. Nobody today will believe that the international and intercultural communication between America, the only current superpower in the world, and countries like Iraq, Afghanistan, or any others in Asia, Africa, or Latin American is carried out on the basis of equality and mutual respect or that every act on the part of the United States is to maintain and extend that basis. The long and brutal European history of colonialism and the American tradition of neo-colonialism have set up the framework of intercultural communication as imbalance of and struggle for power, inequality, and injustice between the American-West and the rest. To pretend that these power relations and practices did not occur or are not there any more, or to reduce them to domains outside of discourse and communication, is to render intercultural communication research and training ineffective and ultimately to help to legitimate, consolidate, and perpetuate the powers of the currently powerful forces over others.

Obviously central to this "culturalist account" of intercultural communication is the underlying notion of culture. My understanding here draws on the cultural studies tradition where culture is not defined in linguistic, geographic, national, or ethnic or any other essentialist terms. Rather it is seen from the point of view of human practices and experiences in them. In characterizing the notion of culture in the dominant paradigm of cultural studies, Hall (1996) states that it has been defined as

> the dialectic between social being and social consciousness: neither separable into its distinct poles .... It defines culture as *both* the meanings and values which arise amongst distinctive social groups and classes, on the basis of their given historical conditions and relationships, through which they "handle" and respond to the conditions of existence; *and* as the lived traditions and practices through which those "understandings" are expressed and in which they are embodied. Williams brings together these two aspects—definitions and ways of life—around the concept of "culture" itself. (pp. 37-38)

It should be stressed at this juncture that the perspective in question emphasizes the oppositional nature of culture: "no 'whole way of life' is without its dimension of struggle and confrontation between opposed *ways* of life" (Hall, 1996, p. 36). Accordingly, cultural analysis must focus on

> where and how people experience their conditions of life, define them and respond to them, which, for Thompson defines why every mode of production is also a culture, and every struggle between classes is always also a struggle between cultural modalities; and which for Williams, is what a 'cultural analysis', in the final instance, should deliver. In 'experience', all the different practices intersect; within 'culture' the different practices interact—even if on an uneven and mutually determining basis. (Hall, p. 38)

However, in this paradigm there is still an undertone of over-generalization on "practice" and "experience." Consequently, there does not seem to be due attention given to the differentiated groups or communities who are the agents of such practices and experiences. In this chapter I suggest that culture be seen as a diversity of situated, competing, and self-critical ways of sense making that are associated with particular groups or communities. Such ways of making meanings are like the "games" in the Wittgenstein's sense (1968), which have a family resemblance but are essentially different from one another and therefore do not and cannot transcend each other (Shi-xu, 2005). It may be added that the cultural nontranscendence comes from not only the incommensurable difference in culture and history, hence power-goals, but also the intrinsic critical consciousness of human cultures to reinvent themselves.

Proceeding from this modified notion of culture, I wish to suggest then that intercultural communication may best be viewed as a process of interaction and power contest between two or more cultural discourses, or linguistic-symbolic ways of sense making. All of these are associated with particular groups or communities and actualized in particular types of situations. Such processes have existed from the earliest of human history, whether in the east or the west. This does not mean that active forms of communication occur from all sides; some groups may ignore others and other groups may fail to have a voice or be heard. But it remains true that they form a "third space" (Bhabha, 1994) where groups (dis)associate and contend with one another, transforming themselves and others.

It is important to note here that intercultural communication conceived of in the present approach is a dialogical and socially interactive and dialectic process. Thus, failures or for that matter successes cannot be attributed to one or the other party alone. They are joint productions. This relational notion of intercultural communication is best exemplified in our contemporary culture of globalization.

The importance of intercultural communication and interaction cannot be overemphasized in our contemporary culture that is characterized by the tension between at once interdependence and alienation. The incidence at which they happen (at all), the directions that they take and the outcomes that they achieve will all have strong relevance to the survival of human cultures and the quality of the human race.

It is therefore not difficult to see that intercultural communication and interaction is not simply a zone of communication where messages and messages of varied intentions are exchanged. Neither is it an arena where forces of dominance and resistance contend. Rather, it is essentially a moral space where norms and values are negotiated and transformed.

If we take a serious interest in intercultural communication theory, research, and pedagogy, then, we would have to turn attention to how relations of cultural power are constituted, how practices of cultural power are accomplished, how new and helpful relations of cultural power are established, what the "powerless" cultural members feel about (lack of) intercultural communication, what strategies may be useful to combat relations and practices of cultural domination, repression or exclusion, and, finally, what norms and rules for intercultural and international communication and critique need to be established. At the same time it may be pointed out, educationally speaking, that it is of vital importance to develop the willpower to continue to try to engage in egalitarian communication for common benefit. For, as is known from history, the fate of superpowers in the world has been inevitable loss of that status, as Changiz Khan, Alexander of Macedonia, Napoleon, Hitler have amply demonstrated.

CHINESE INTERCULTURAL COMMUNICATION AS COUNTER-BALANCE

In relation to and consistent with the broad, global framework of intercultural communication outlined above, I want now to proceed to sketching out a particular, local, that is, Chinese, perspective in order to guide study of contemporary intercultural communication in mainland China. While the local perspective that I present is informed by the global one and will in this sense be multicultural in nature, it will more importantly focus on the concrete properties of the case of contemporary Chinese intercultural communication. Further it will more specifically concern the hitherto neglected area of communication in the public, mass-mediated sphere, as research has generally concentrated in private, industrial, or otherwise institutional settings (Shi-xu, 2001).

In order to produce such account, we can draw upon a number of resources. First, there is the Chinese intellectual tradition on language and communication, which can provide an important source of information about the nature of Chinese intercultural communication. It would be ludicrous to describe and interpret Chinese phenomena without considering what the local scholarly community has to say about it. By the same token, second, ordinary concepts about and practices in intercultural communication in the contemporary scene must also be taken into account. Participants' own experience and practice are a valuable resource for theorizing about their discourse. Third, the past and current conditions or context of Chinese intercultural discourse need to be taken into account as well. For, context is integral part of discourse and any account of discourse therefore must pay attention to it. The outcome of such a reflection will serve as the basis for the intended new perspective on contemporary public intercultural communication in mainland China (see also Shi-xu, 1997).

Chinese Response on Humanity

Thus, to begin with, according to traditional Chinese scholarship, language, and communication are, not a form of representing the world, but essentially a mode of activity for the sake of establishing and maintaining a harmonious relationship with social others (Chen, 2001, 2004; Shi-xu,

1997). That is, it has the harmonious relationship between participants as its ideal state or ultimate goal, other than personal, group, or community purposes or functions. This notion can be traced back to at least the ideas of (*ren*, "humanity") and (*li*, "politeness") of Confucius. In this case, as may be noted, different from the Western general theory of language and communication which emphases individual, representational functions, the Chinese theory emphasizes the relational, dialogical, and interactive nature of language and communication.

From the point of view of Chinese local conceptualizations and practices, it may be observed, too, that Chinese have traditionally been receptive, tolerant, and inclusive towards foreign cultures and generally maintained a socially harmonious communication and relation with foreign cultures and communities, like many other Asian cultures where Confucianism has played a dominant role. Indeed, one might argue that Chinese, since the beginning of their rewritten history, have been culturally open and multicultural. In the pre-Qin Dynasty, for example, China was already composed of a variety of kingdoms with distinct cultures (Qi-Lu culture, Yan-Zhao culture, Ba-Shu culture, Jin-Chu culture, Wu-Yue culture, etc.). During the Tan Dynasty, Buddhism reached its heights in China and became intermeshed and unified with Chinese culture. Later, Islam, too, came in through the Silk Road and became well blended into Chinese culture. Of course there were exceptions—when imperial foreign powers forced open China's door, for example, the Mongolians during the Yuan Dynasty and more recently the European, American, and Japanese colonial adventures from the middle of the nineteenth century to that of the twentieth century. The "new cultural movement" (新文化运动) in earlier last century which introduced Western "science" and "democracy" into China as the beleaguered and besieged nation's "way out" and the economic reform in the 80s of the last century which opened China's door to the West are further evidence that it has often held an open attitude toward cultural others and is prepared to assimilate and incorporate cultural others. Especially in the past years China has repeatedly and persistently aspired to achieve a more distinct, positive, and assertive voice in the international arena, whether this concerns arms embargo, trade disputes, or the proposed United Nations reform.

For example, the issue of the European ban on arms sales to China, the Chinese government insists that it be lifted not because China necessarily needs the sales but because it represents a "political prejudice" against China. That this is Chinese cultural power resistance becomes clearer when one considers the contrastive fact that oppositional language and communication in Chinese public media with regard to non-Western, Third World countries is virtually unseen, except when issues over China's sovereignty over Taiwan arise. Mainland China's concept of the Western discourse may be clearly reflected in the following item in *Outlook Weekly* (May 2, 2005, Vol. 18, p. 5), an official Chinese magazine:

> *Be vigilant on foreign cultural erosion*: In recent years, all sorts of ideas flood from abroad into our country, lashing at the Chinese people's norms and values. In particular, overseas hostile forces have been plotting to Westernise and disintegrate China. They have been trying through all manners and means to erode our country's culture: some use magazines, journals and other publications; some reply on capital operation; others employ the internet and other new media; still others mobilise cultural industrial firms. Everybody should keep high alert on them.

Finally, the past and recent historical context of Chinese communication, intercultural communication included, must be considered. We need not go very far. Chinese history since the middle of the nineteenth century until the end of World War II had been one of Western imperial domination and brutalization. During this long period, China had been repeatedly pillaged, conquered, and divided up by European and American colonial powers and Japanese occupiers. Chinese also understand that this fate of China had also to do with the decaying Chinese feudalist system and the corrupt Chinese governments of the time. This tragic and humiliating history is engraved in the minds of the Chinese people (see also the chapter of Alberto Rosa in this volume). After the end of the Second World War, China's international relations and standing had somewhat changed but continued to be dogged in particular by American political and military policies toward Taiwan, which it regards as its inalienable part. More generally, like most other non-Western countries, China has been facing Western domination in politics, economy, military, diplomacy, science, education, and virtually every other area.

However, the history is leading to a change. Real changes have occurred on the part of mainland China only after it started the open-door policy and economic reform some 20 years ago. China has since achieved and enjoyed unprecedented, and internationally extraordinary, economic success (with its GDP in 2004 over RMB 13 billions or $1.6 billions and annual GDP growth rate over 8% since 2001) and, owing to this, gained increasing international recognition and position. During this time, too, Hong Kong and Macao became decolonized.

Given the brutalized past of Western aggression and exploitation and the regained international standing, mainland China is particularly conscious of the meaning of cultural subjugation and the continued unfair world order and aspires to a balanced and equal world order vis-à-vis the Western world. Considering the intellectual legacy, the broad historical and cultural context and the present, changed conditions of China, I would like to propose that public intercultural communication in present-day China be seen as geared toward achieving a cultural power balance in relation or response to discourses of domination and repression in the international arena. It does so because given its historical experience it sees cultural power imbalance as essentially unfair and detrimental. At this point, as may be stressed, the Chinese international and intercultural communicative orientation for cultural power balance is not isolated or independent, but must be viewed as closely related to the broader, external or contextual cultural power struggle. Put in a different way, Chinese contemporary public intercultural communication is an integral and dialogical element of a larger framework of global power interaction and contention in language and communication.

A CASE STUDY

In the above section I already alluded to some instances of regular and consistent Chinese counterbalancing acts of opposing cultural domination, discrimination, and exclusion in its media. In the following, I want to focus on the particular case of the Chinese public, mass-mediated and official political discourse—and explicitly intercultural discourse at that— on the topic of human rights involving both China itself and the United States. I choose this because it is a typical example of present-day Chinese public intercultural communication with the American West (but simultaneously of interaction with and feedback on China's self) when the latter acts as in a domineering or discriminatory way and because it is involved in an extended chain of events and exchanges between China and the United States.

To make sense of the Chinese communication in question, it will be important to describe the local-global, cultural-interactive, context. This has to do mainly with the United States State Department's annual report on the negative side of human rights on a large number of countries in the world, usually non-Western, Third World ones. For many consecutive years its reports have included China. This non-Western, Third-World cultures oriented practice of (negatively) evaluating their human right status is not intended for genuine intercultural communication and critique since it is officially concluded. The more immediate circumstance is the publication of "Country Reports on Human Rights Practices" by the U.S. Department of State submitted to its congress (http://www.state.gov/g/drl/rls/hrrpt/2004/ At the same time, the United States has also always linked its alleged issues of human rights of China, as of other countries, to its matters of trade, diplomacy, international politics, and so forth, regarding China. So the reports are also otherwise motivated. Further, the concepts, values and standards employed in the American reports are all self-righteously presented as universal and the issues raised as a matter of course. From these it may be claimed that the American State Department's human right reports form explicitly cultural-other-directed acts and that these acts constitute a culturally high-handed and highly-motivated practice that effectively creates cultural domination, control and discrimination.

Following this historical-contextual account, I will introduce below a series of acts on the part of China in the specific medium of the print media of the broadsheet newspaper *Guangming Daily*, which is oriented to Chinese academic and educational readerships. It may be mentioned at this juncture that the newspaper data I present below have appeared in other major and minor papers as well as in other (mass) media channels including the internet. Thus, the discourse we shall be looking at—contemporary Chinese discourse with the American West—is from one perspective in dialogue with Chinese cultural self. But my interest here is a qualitative analysis of the discourses in relation to the American West.

While I shall take into account both cultural discourses, my analysis below will focus on the Chinese discursive "turns" in order to identify, characterize and highlight the Chinese contributions to the intercultural "exchange." The questions I shall be trying to answer concern such issues as the construction of cultural selves and others, relationships and interrelations, the reconstruction or transformation of relevant, key concepts and the exercise of cultural power.

On March 3, 2005, *Guangming Daily* carries a small news text that reports that the U.S. State Department issued *Country Reports on Human Rights Practices* involving various other countries for the year of 2004 on February 28 (as alluded to above), titled "China Resolutely Opposes America's Unfounded Accusations of our Human Rights Situation":

Xinhua Newsagency, Beijing, March 2 The Foreign Ministry spokesman Liu Jianchao said in response to correspondents' questions on the 2nd [of March] that China **resolutely opposes** America's **unfounded accusations** of our human rights situation. It was asked: What is China's response to the American State Department's recently published Country Reports on Human Rights Practices?

Liu Jianchao answered that the **so-called** annual country reports on human rights practices by the State of Department of the United States **made unfounded accusations** about China's human rights situation. China **expresses strong dissatisfaction** and **resolute opposition**.

He said that over the human rights situation in China **the Chinese people have the most authority**. The Chinese government **holds the principles of** treating people as the starting point [以人为本] and of governing for the people and in the respects of expanding democracy and strengthening the law has done much work. The Chinese people are **enjoying a higher level of human rights in various areas**.

He said that hopefully the American side will **pay more attention to human rights problems on its own part** and **does helpful things for resuming** the Sino-American human rights **dialogue and exchange**.

This text contains a set of features that rebuff the U.S. report and further that advises the United States to take a different stance on the communication between the United States and China on the human rights. These include use of verbs and verbal phrases (e.g., "oppose" and "express strong dissatisfaction"), disqualifying definitions of the other's actions (e.g., "unfounded accusations," "so-called"), reclaiming authority (e.g., "the Chinese people have the most authority"), positive evidence (e.g., "holds the principles of " … and "enjoying a higher level of human rights in various areas") and recommendation (e.g., "pay more attention").

On the following day (March 4th), *Guangming Daily* files another report on the same issue of human rights but with additional developments and information:

This paper, Beijing, March 3 (Correspondent Wang Jiabo) The Deputy Chair of the China Human Rights Development Fund, Ling Bocheng, said today that China Human Rights Development Fund **firmly supports** the Chinese State Council Information Office's report, released today, *The American Human Rights Record 2004*, which condemned the unfounded accusations about human rights practices that the United States made against over 190 countries and regions including China.

Ling Bocheng said that the State Department of America published *Country Reports on Human Rights Practices 2004* on Feb 28 and **made unfounded accusations** about human rights situations against over 190 countries and regions including China. **We express resolute opposition and strong condemnation**.

He pointed out that 2004 is an important year in the history of China's human rights development. In this year, the Chinese people put into the constitution the clause of "the nation respects and safeguards human rights" and opened a new page in the annals of Chinese human rights development. The Chinese government upholds the principles of treating people as the root and of governing for the people and has made tremendous achievements in expanding democracy and strengthening the law and this has won international recognition. **In contrast,** the American human rights record in 2004 is one **full of blemishes and smudges**. Especially the insane abuses of Iraqi prisoners of war by America shocked the world and rocked human conscience; they were strongly condemned by the international community. America **made no single mention** of its own poor human rights record but **completely ignored** it. And yet it **rudely blamed** China and **paid no attention** to its achievements in human rights. The Chinese government published *The American Human Rights Record 2004* at an appropriate time. **The point is to uphold justice, provide right information and expose concretely and critique effectively America's human rights stains, power politics and hegemony and its double-standards in human rights practices, etc. It is "to fill up gaps" and "to give a reminder" on America's human rights performance.**

This second report and statement is harsher in dealing with the US. In addition to the devices we saw in the first item, there is here a larger space devoted to the wrong-doing in the human rights by the United States itself. It reveals the double standard and rude behavior of the United States. And it also provides a justification for its own current practice, legitimating its own oppositional activity.

On the same day of the publication of the foregoing news report, in the same newspaper, the Chinese State Council Information Office publishes a large report (March 3), which occupies a little over one page, with the title of "America's Human Rights Record 2004," enumerating America's human rights abuses both at home and abroad (see also *People's Daily Online*: Full text of Human Rights Record of the United States in 2004 http://english.people.com.cn/200503/03/eng20050303_175406.html).

A set of features in the report is worth noting. First, the report details human rights mishaps in six different areas of American social and cultural life (1) Life, freedom, and safety; (2) Political rights and freedom; (3) Economic, social, and cultural rights; (4) Racial discrimination; (5) Women and children's rights; (6) Violating other countries' human rights), and does this using a large space—a whole page. It opens with a mimicry, humor, and revelation:

> In 2004 the atrocity of U.S. troops abusing Iraqi POWs **exposed the dark side** of human rights performance of the United States. The scandal shocked the humanity and was condemned by the international community. It is quite **ironic** that on Feb. 28 of this year, the State Department of the United States once again posed as the **"the world human rights police"** and released its Country Reports on Human Rights Practices for 2004. As in previous years, the reports pointed fingers at human rights situation in more than 190 countries and regions (including China) **but kept silent on the US misdeeds** in this field. Therefore, the world people have **to probe the human rights record behind the Statue of Liberty** in the United States. (http://english.people.com.cn/200504/13/eng20050413_180786.html)

What is particularly unusual about this article is that it includes a list of 82 endnotes, offering the sources of the information used in the article—an extraordinary practice for just any ordinary newspaper. This shows effectively the carefulness and the documentary foundations of the report and therefore the credibility of the negative report. All the three devices referred to here serve to undermine the trustworthiness and respectful-ness of the Other and so the Other's report.

Then, according to *Guangming Daily* (April 1), the American State Department issued another human rights report, *Supporting Human Right and Democracy: The U.S. Record 2004-2005* (March 28), accusing China of human rights abuses. This constitutes an immediate, important contex-tual circumstance (http://www.state.gov/g/drl/rls/shrd/2004/) for the new act on the part of Chinese in question. Thus, this very piece of Chinese news report, titled, "China Opposes American Unfounded Accusations on China's State Of Human Rights" puts up a form of resistance. It presents an opposition similar to the two actions reproduced above but employs a stronger term for what the State Department has done, namely "abhor-rent practice."

Following that, over 2 weeks later, on April 14, the Chinese State Coun-cil Information Office published, again in the same newspaper, a one-and-quarter-page-long report, with the title of "China's Progress in Human Rights in 2004" (see also http://english.people.com.cn/200504/13/eng20050413_180786.html). It includes seven sections: Foreword; I. People's Rights to Subsistence and Development; II. Civil and Political Rights; III. Judicial Guarantee for Human Rights; IV. Economic, Social, and Cultural Rights; V. Equal Rights and Special Protection for Ethnic Minorities; VI. The Rights and Interests of the Disabled; VII. Interna-tional Exchanges and Cooperation in the Field of Human Rights. The opening section is particularly interesting in that it displays the intercul-tural orientation clearly when it says,

> To help the international community toward a better understanding of the human rights situation in China, we hereby present an overview of the developments in the field of human rights in China in 2004. (http://english.people.com.cn/200504/13/eng20050413_180786.html)

This huge newspaper presentation offers a wide-ranging and detailed account of the achievements that China has made in the year of 2004. It presents a completely opposite and positive picture of the human rights situation in China. Thus, the official, public, and explicitly interculturally-oriented display of the accomplishments on the part of China forms a direct counter and undermining act vis-à-vis the previous American, other-negating, turn/act.

Reconstructing Interconnection and Counter-Balancing

In the above I have largely concentrated on the singular moves and their chronological connections on the part of Chinese public communication. But as stressed in my earlier theoretical account, such moves must also be viewed from a historically situated, culturally interactive, and culturally competitive standpoint. Only in this way can we appreciate the cultural dialectic and power dynamic of group-based, institutional communication. If, however, one took the texts such as those above in historical and cultural isolation, then s/he might come to the conclusion that Chinese political discourse is ideologically (namely nationalistically) determined to paint a positive image of its own country and a negative image of other nations.

First, it may be ascertained that the set of moves on the part of the Chinese media occurs in the concrete contexts of the U.S. long-standing tradition of pointing fingers at the human rights issues of largely non-Western, Third World countries and of the specific case of *Country Human Rights Report 2004*. This tradition, it must be noted, is also highly motivated, namely, as an economic and political leverage of the United States against China as well as other Third World countries, rather than a platform for genuine, equal intercultural communication, and dialogue for the betterment of the human rights. Therefore, emphatically, I am not saying that there should be no criticism on the human rights between different nations but that the Chinese discourse is not isolated or merely subjectively or ideologically motivated, but inextricably linked to the external, American Western discourse of the Other's human rights and particularly to the fact that the United States has not chosen mutually acceptable means to engage in equal and self-reflexive exchanges (I will return to this point shortly).

Second, it may be observed that China could have chosen to keep silent, at least inside China, about what the U.S. State Department said and did in the report, as it might have done in a comparable situation a couple of decades before. But China does not and, quite differently from even some years ago, quickly takes up the charges from the United States every time it occurs and makes a response to them. The Chinese media reports are directed at not merely the domestic readerships, but also the American West. Each subsequent event constitutes a response to the previous American cultural institutional "speaker." Thus, when the Chinese media, and behind it the government institutions, join the "battle" on the "front" of the human rights, it may be said that intercultural communication and relationship between China and the United States at the cultural and political levels are established and sustained.

Third, the series of mediated Chinese institutional moves (over nearly 1½ months) constitute intercultural, particularly East-West and therefore power-oriented, communication with the United States, because the two parties involved have historically been embedded in political, military, economic, and other forms of contest and struggle as mentioned at the outset. This East-West and hence power-saturated character of the Chinese official intercultural communication can also be evidenced by the fact that the countries and regions that the American report launches accusations against mostly belong to non-Western, Third World cultures. Of course, the common features that run through all those news texts and events most clearly embody this cultural power dimension: in response to the American accusations, the Chinese media use verbs and verbal phrases of protest and opposition, irony, humor, admonishment, revelation, and *tu quoque* with respect to the U.S. government and positive re-description of self (e.g., report of China's progress in human rights).

Fourth, when we proceed from an in-between-the-East-and-West, culturalist stance—as we linked the Chinese discourse with the American and the global context under the first point above. If we take into consideration the high-handed nature of the American actions on the issue of the human rights toward China as well as other—more than 190 countries— we might see that the Chinese actions can best be understood as efforts to off-set, at both a domestic and global domains, the effects of discursive power games of "the cultural Other." In other words, the Chinese media acts are acts of cultural counter balancing in an international, global scene. Seen from still another perspective, "intercultural communication" so far as the case of the human rights issue between China and the United States is concerned is not totally dominated by the American West but a field of cultural contestation with Chinese mediated resistance/counter-balancing in particular. More generally it might be said that when we take a global, holistic, and historically conscious perspective, the discourse directed at the Other is a negotiable space.

The reading of the Chinese acts as counter balancing or resistance to relations and practices of American domination of course implies a moral judgement of the American contributions to the intercultural contest. Taking an in-between-East-and-West, culturalist position, I would like to make (explicit) a set of assumptions here. One is that any international and intercultural communication about human rights must first proceed from an agreed-upon definition of the very concept and its domains of specific application. Another is that if one party is to criticize the other on some moral ground then the former had better at a minimum show an equally critical awareness of one's own conduct in the same field, especially in an international context, for otherwise that party can be seen as using double standards. In addition, it might be expected that if an organization or community wishes another country or community to improve or correct its human rights situation, it should try to liase with that country or community in question first and come to a common understanding of the situation before making proposals as to its rectification. But none of these conditions or expectations had been met, when the U.S. State

Department publicized its *Country Human Rights Report* and *Supporting Human Right and Democracy: The U.S. Record 2004-2005* and presented to the American Congress. In fact the U.S. government uses the human rights reports as a device to fulfill its political, economic, and military goals.

All in all, the series of intercultural acts on the part of the Chinese mass media is but a dramatic example of a more general pattern of present-day Chinese public discourse vis-à-vis the American-Western discourses of its other. This is a pattern of resisting against, countering, and offsetting the (speech) acts of cultural hegemony, prejudice, or other forms of marginalisation. Taking the dialogical and competitive processes between the local, Chinese, and the global, Western discourses as a whole, we might say that the intercultural communication between China/East and America/West is not a totalized state of American/Western domination but rather a dynamic process of repression and counter-action, domination and counter-balancing.

CONCLUSION

I started this chapter with a critique of the linguistic/cultural-causal and cultural-relativist account of intercultural communication by the difference-and-deficiency paradigm. That forms the starting point for my reformulation of a thoroughly culturalist approach which stresses the importance of analyzing intercultural communication in terms of dynamic cultural interaction and contestation. In this culturalist account, I argued in particular that more attention should be paid to the historically concrete, local, forms of intercultural communication.

Proceeding from this particularist position, I canvassed a theory of the contemporary Chinese public communication with the cultural West. I proposed that, as part of its general discursive orientation toward equilibrium, it tends to resist repression and domination by the Western Other, constituting thereby part of a competing relation and process of the intercultural communication between the East and the West.

Guided by this perspective, further, I illustrated this approach by examining a series of Chinese media texts in response to the American official reports on the issue of China's human rights "abuses." I showed in particular that the Chinese official media responded speedily and in a sustained manner, in varied forms and through various linguistic and rhetorical means. These discursive activities and strategies not only enabled intercultural communication, but also constituted part of a larger, domination-vs-resistance communicative international order.

ACKNOWLEDGMENT

Jaan Valsiner's always thought-provoking and constructive comments are gratefully acknowledged.

REFERENCES

Ang, I. (2001). *On not speaking Chinese: Living between Asia and the West*. London: Routledge.

Bhabha H. K. (1994). *The location of culture*. London: Routledge.

Blum-Kulka, S., House, J., & Kasper, G. (Eds.). (1989). *Cross-cultural pragmatics: Requests and apologies*. Norwood, NJ: Ablex.

Chen G. -M. (2001). Towards transcultural understanding: A harmony theory of Chinese communication. In V. H. Milhouse, M. K. Asante, & P. O. Nwosu (Eds.), *Transculture: Interdisciplinary perspectives on cross-cultural relations* (p. 55-70). Thousand Oaks, CA: Sage.

Chen, G. -M. (2004). The two faces of Chinese communication. *Human Communication, 7*, 25-36.

Cushner, K., & Brislin, R. W. (1996). *Intercultural interactions: A practical guide* (2nd ed.). Thousand Oaks: Sage.

Gudykunst, W. (2003). *Cross-cultural and intercultural communication*. Thousand Oaks: Sage.

Gudykunst, W., & Ting-Toomey, S. (1988). *Culture and interpersonal communication*. Sage.

Hall, S. (1990). Cultural identity and diaspora. In J. Ruterhford (Ed.), *Identity: Community, culture, difference* (pp. 222-237). London: Lawrence & Wishart.

Hall, S. (1996). Cultural studies: Two paradigms. In J. Storey (Ed.), *What is cultural studies: A reader* (pp. 31-48). London: Arnold. (Also 1980, *Media, Culture and Society, 2*)

Hofstede, G. (1980). *Culture's consequences: International differences in work-related values*. Newbury Park, CA: Sage.

Kim, Y. Y. (1991). Intercultural communication competence: A systems-theoretic view. In S. Ting-Toomey & F. Korzenny (Eds.), *Cross-cultural interpersonal communication* (pp. 259-275). Newbury Park, CA: Sage.

Kluckhohn, F. (1953). Dominant and variant value orientations. In C. Kluckhohn & H. Murray (Eds.), *Personality in nature, society, and culture* (pp. 342-357). New York: Alfred A. Khopf.

Kluckhohn, F. (1961). *Variations in value orientations*. Evanston IL: Row.

Said, E. W. (1978). *Orientalism*. London: Routledge & Kegan Paul.

Said, E. W. (1993). *Culture and imperialism*. New York: Alfred A. Knopf.

Scollon, R., & Scollon, S. W. (1995). *Intercultural communication: A discourse approach*. Oxford, England: Blackwell.

Schwartz, S. H. (2001). Value hierarchies across cultures: Taking a similarities perspective. *Journal of Cross-Cultural Psychology. 32*(3), 268-290.

Schwartz, S. H. (2002). Cultural values, source of guidance, and their relevance to managerial behavior: A 47-nation study. *Journal of Cross-Cultural Psychology, 33*(2), 188-208.

Shi-xu. (1997). *Cultural representations: Analyzing the discourse about the other.* New York: Peter Lang.

Shi-xu. (2001). Critical pedagogy and intercultural communication: Creating discourses of diversity, equality, common goals and rational-moral motivation. *Journal of Intercultural Studies, 22*(3), 279-293.

Shi-xu. (2005). *A cultural approach to discourse.* Houndmills, England: Palgrave Macmillan.

Shi-xu, Kienpointner, M., & Servaes, J. (Eds.). (2005). *Read the cultural other.* Berlin, Germany: Mouton de Gruyter.

Spivak, G. C. (1988). *In other words: Essays in cultural politics.* Routledge: New York.

Ting-Toomey, S. (1999). *Communicating across cultures.* New York: The Guilford Press.

Trompenaars, F. (1993). *Riding the waves of culture: Understanding cultural diversity in business.* London: Brealey.

Wierzbicka, A. (1991). *Cross-cultural pragmatics: The semantics of human interaction.* Berlin, Germany: Mouton de Gruyter.

Wittgenstein, L. (1968). *Philosophical investigations.* Oxford, England: Basil Blackwell.

CHAPTER 11

THE GAME OF POLITICAL DEBATES

A Play of Social Representations and Beyond

Derek Richer and Jaan Valsiner

I want to point out first, that I have not conducted any war; second, that for years past I have expressed my abhorrence of war, and, it is true, also my abhorrence of war-mongers; and third, I am not aware for what purpose I should wage a war at all

—From a speech by a politician (White, 1949, p. 160)

Politics involves us all—whether we are personally taking part in it or pretend to remain beyond its realm. We do listen to the speeches of politicians, discuss politics in the cozy environments of our homes, bars, or at cocktail parties. We get rather emotional about it, and at times may sacrifice ourselves to ideals promoted to us by political discourse.

Politics is a social game—played differently in different societies and at different times. Politics is a game that is too serious to be considered seriously—as its impacts range from mass graves to mass demonstrations, and from economic poverty to that of excesses of affluence. It is glorious

Otherness in Question: Labyrinths of the Self, 277–295
Copyright © 2007 by Information Age Publishing
All rights of reproduction in any form reserved.

nonsense that matters prominently in human lives. For the latter's sake, we return to it, become involved in it, and play our games with it. And at times—such as this one—we try to make sense of its underlying processes.

DIALOGICAL NATURE OF POLITICAL PROCESSES

For a dialogical perspective, the phenomena of politics constitute a rich source that has largely escaped our focus in psychology. The whole process of politics is inherently dialogical—whether it entails the intrapsychological decision making by a Julius Caesar or a collective negotiation process dramatized in the British House of Commons. The display of political dialogicality on contemporary television screens adds a triadic component—political agents involved in debates on the screen are actually oriented towards capturing the irrational urges of the audiences. These audiences —if turned into voters, demonstrators, or vigilantes— may serve the purposes of the politicians. Hence the efforts to "capture" the souls of the audience become crucial for politicians.

In this paper we look at the dialogical nature of political processes as an interpersonal phenomenon, as we use the U.S. presidential election debates as an example of how political processes can be analyzed within a framework of dialogical social science. Conceptualizing the dialogical nature of political processes necessitates separating the participants into two obvious categories: dialogical **consumers** (voters) and dialogical **exploiters** (politicians). The dialogical exploiters produce ambiguous messages— sent to one another, and to the dialogical consumers—with the aim of capturing the support of the consumers.

The dialogical nature of the consumer self is one of dynamic stability, whereby existing I-positions (Hermans, 2001, 2002) perpetually reproduce themselves while working with the multivoicedness of the self to "understand" the novelty of experience. Different messages from exploiters arrive in the receptive field of the consumers in a myriad of versions. These set up a multivoiced space. Even as the consumers relate to politics via their daily life activities, ambiguous messages they gain from the exploiters provide them with a symbolic field that need not directly fit with their daily lives. Yet the exploiters insist—using all power of communicative rhetoric—that this linkage between consumers' daily lives and what they—politicians—consider to be that, is strong.

Hence the political tactics—particularly political rhetoric, which is the focus of this paper—are concerned with constraining the multi-voicedness of the consumers' selves. Out of the multivoiced plurality of a mixture of personal opinions and appropriated meaning complexes (political clichés) of the consumers must come not a novel solution (which may take a form of a revolution, or at least social reform), but in the form of "independent conformity" to the action plan the particular politician outlines. The consumers—voters—need to arrive at their decision to support politician A (over his/her rivals) in some election in ways that look *as if* they do it "on their own free will" (Valsiner, 1984)—while in actuality they have been coerced into it by the system of symbolic constraints of different vagueness or clarity, and of different levels of abstraction, of the communicative messages of the political rhetoric.

More specifically, in different political systems that limiting of polyphony is achieved differently. In some, it may be reduced to one acceptable ("right") perspective, outlawing (and repressing) all alternatives. In others, it may be attained by enforcing a duality (or multiplicity) of perspectives, both (or all) of which are de facto similar in their nature. As a result, possible alternatives are rendered implausible. While active (and at times verbally aggressive) political debates may capture attention on U.S. television screens, the option of changing the political power balance in Washington DC through military intervention is an option that has not surfaced in the political realities of the United States since the Civil War. Yet most of the World has experienced the use of the military in public dialogues of political kinds.

Social Representing in Political Processes

The games of political discourse are played at the level of socially representing complex human and social phenomena in a goal-directed way (Valsiner, 2002). Different idea complexes are means for grounding of the system of thought, allocation of meanings, and instrumental functioning of knowledge. Newly objectified meaning complexes become anchored in others that already exist. For example, the notion of "conspiracy," "democracy," "justice," or "corruption" exist in societies in a generic pivotal form, that is filled in by varied material at different historical periods. When a goal is set to create uncertainty within the existing social order, some unexplainable or negatively valued events become explained by anchoring those within a social representation.

Social representations—idea complexes—are used by agents in socially presenting some aspect of social world in ways that are supposed to maintain or change the existing social order. Hence political action operates mostly at the level of trading social representations—with occasional linking of those with everyday realities. Politicians who rush to tour "disaster areas" are displaying their "compassion" and "leadership" by being shown on television screens doing so. Their visit to that area in itself is of no immediate consequence—in fact it is a kind of act of "tourism." Yet it is "tourism" of a special kind—through their publicly visible "participation" in the lives of the disaster victims they add to their social capital through leaving expected impressions with other consumers (who are far from the disaster areas). Similar functions can be found in politicians' constant concerns about "world problems"—AIDS, poverty, civil wars (in other countries), human rights, and so forth. Political discourse about those themes is often disconnected from—or even contrary to—the actions by the same talking politician.

U.S. PRESIDENTIAL DEBATES:
BUSY SYMBOLIC WORK OF COMPETITIVE PRESENTING

What is a "political debate?" It is a dramatized "show" that is played by strict rules—a game that is played by the debaters where the outcomes are formulated in terms of symbolic actions by the consumers—their opinions, "ratings," commentaries, and—eventually—in their actual voting. Some possible forms of conduct are carefully ruled out from the repertoires of the debaters—for instance, they are not expected to enter into an actual fist-fight (or shoot the other)—the debate is a symbolic, not actual, duel:

> Choreographed and unscripted, contrived and authentic, debates straddle the fault line between artifice and reality—like everything else on TV, only more so. With their clashing co-stars, enormous stakes, and "must-see" status, presidential debates are nothing so much as television writ large. (Schroeder, 2000, p. 10)

In the U.S. political context, debates between presidential candidates are, for the most part, only as recent as the television set. The notion of a debate, for most of American history, chiefly involved debates within the legislative branch of the government where members argued the important concerns of their time. The earliest manifestation of the modern political debate, excluding the atypical and famous Lincoln-Douglass senate debates, was between Thomas E. Dewey and Harold Stassen in the 1948 Republican primary race (Corrado, 1995, p. 50). This hour-long radio debate focused singularly on the issue of outlawing communism in the United States and was vastly different in format than the debates of today.

While a few other examples of pretelevision political debates exist, the 1960 televised debate between Richard Nixon and John Kennedy created the trend of candidates rhetorically sparring for the privilege of the presidency. This debate, and arguably all debates thereafter, had a greater impact on the impression voters formed of the combatants, than it had on an understanding of their respective platforms (Kirkpartrick, 1979, p. 32). Kennedy, youthful and striking on camera, projected a degree of stature that his haggard, pasty opponent, Nixon, failed to match. The lessons of the first televised debate have not gone unlearned by subsequent candidates—and the modern manifestation of the presidential debate is rooted in a format defined by the interests of the candidates to be as sterile as possible.

The debate has the function of encouraging uninformed decisions on the part of the voter as if those were informed. It creates the illusion of power for the audience—they are to decide "who wins." It redirects the focus of attention from the actuality of a politician's policy suggestions as actual action program (e.g., "lower—or raise—taxes") and its actual consequences, into a symbolic duel using these action programs as means to a simple (temporary) end—winning an upcoming election. If politician A claims "I want to lower/raise taxes because this is good for all" and his opposing B claims that any tax increase/decrease is "bad for all," the economic realities of the actual action (tax change) becomes transformed into an affective opinion formation *about* the issue. Elections are won (and lost) on the basis of strategically facilitated sentiments rather than actual policies.

Candidates actively work to foster these affective grounds by employing strategies, often using strategic disclosures about their own selves as vehicles to create fusion between their personae and the political programs. They attempt to display a construction of their own publicly presented selves that can easily be reconstructed by the audience, in a form that is in line with the recipients' system of I-positions. The reality of a debate, therefore, is not a discussion of the issues for the purpose of fostering novel solutions to social problems, nor even of clarifying candidates' purposed solutions to allow the voter to decide which set of solutions he/she deems best. It, instead, exists as a slightly more interactive soap opera where candidates vie for the role of the "handsome doctor" rescuing the audience from their opponent who they cast in the role of the "evil villain." Although U.S. political conduct patterns are built upon the uniqueness of the history of the United States, these patterns presently proliferate into the political systems of other countries, facilitated by the medium of television. Hence our coverage of the U.S. examples can have generality beyond the special case.

The recent 2000 presidential debates were replete with such acting – both displayed candidates[1] worked to cast themselves in a role their audience would relate with easily. The actions of the debaters have been wittily described:

The role, of course, was that of the nice guy, the mildness was all Bing Crosby with a sprinkling of Bob Hope. Clearly they had both been coached <u>not to threaten the audience</u> *with too much passion*, but rather to reassure that <u>if elected they would not disturb any reasonable person's sleep</u>. (Miller, 2001, p. 33, added emphases)

This dialogical opposition between "the comfortable" and "the novel" —or dispassionate↔passionate—that is evident here may underlie the cyclical conservatism of U.S. social system. The United States is a country of contrasts between opposites (see Mead, 1930/2001), among which the belief in technological progress is linked with slowly changing deeply seated ideological values. The dramas of presidential debates are carefully scripted as <u>socially acceptable</u> forms of conflict—sufficiently distanced from reality, yet tied to it through symbolic threads. Our goal here is to analyze the basics of the construction of such dramas. Given the nature of the debates, these can be understood in terms of new forms of game theory.

LOOKING CLOSELY ON "TWO FRIENDS": AL GORE AND GEORGE W. BUSH

One segment of the second 2000 U.S. presidential debate was chosen to examine the process structure of political communication. The segment was chosen for its particular focus on one specific issue. Although it is obvious that the statements are an attempt at commenting on more than just the issue of healthcare (e.g., the character of the opponent), the multiple sections chosen stay close to the topic and provide a good example of the point counterpoint format political debates are known for.

Sections were first delineated by social representations that were supported by surrounding sentences.[2] In some cases however sections were lacking in identifiable social representations, but where still separated because they dealt with a discrete topic. Below a quote from the debate is given. It is separated into two discrete sections, illustrating how distinct sections where identified.

Some of the healthy folks, healthy young <u>kids</u> say, "I never get sick, therefore I'm not going to have—don't need **health** care right now." And for those, what I think we need to do is to develop an investment-type vehicle that would be an incentive for them to invest, like medical savings accounts with rollover capacity. In other words, you say to a youngster, "It would be in your financial interest to start saving for future illness." (Governor Bush at the second 2000 presidential debates)

But for the <u>working folks</u> that do want to have health care that can't afford it, a couple of things we need to do. One, we need more community **health** centers. I've developed—put out money in my budget to expand community health centers all around the country. These are places where *people* can get primary care. Secondly—and they're good. They're very important parts of the safety net of health care. (Governor Bush at the second 2000 presidential debates)

While the second quote is a continuation of the first, the second quote is separated because the social representation is changed from kids to working folks. Social representations identify both the orientation of the message, as in to whom it is directed,[3] and the core idea of the message. For ease of analysis the who is highlighted by an <u>underline</u> and the core idea is in **bold**. By identifying quotes by social representations the intent of the speaker can be identified, because the social representation is the context in which the message is understood.

The political game is an instance of a social situation that greatly benefits from being modeled as a game. The traditions of game theory have gone a long way beyond the most familiar classic "prisoner's dilemma" games (Harsanyi & Selten, 1988; Howard, 1971). The classical game theory was limited in its ability to model real life situations. The natural uncertainty inherent in the political game is accounted for in the hypergame model.

What are Hypergames?

The hypergame theory (Takahashi, Fraser, & Hipel, 1984) is an extension of classical game theory. A game in normal form, as per classical game theory, is a game where two or more players, each with two or more strategies, act towards an outcome based on their preferences. Players are assumed to have full information about all aspects of the game. This traditional game theory approach is limited in its capability to model real situations. Real life "games" are full of uncertainty about players' strategies and preferences that, in turn, effect the real strategies and preferences of the other players.

Hypergames are games where the partners do not possess full information about the possible strategies of the others, nor one's own. They do not have full information about the payoffs of each strategy they know they— or their partner(s)—can use at the given moment. They can only guess— mostly projecting one's own position into the partner—what might happen in the immediate future of the interaction process. Yet such projection is always incomplete—because novelties emerge due to the changing external (context) and internal (goal orientations) circumstances.

Political debates, the particular topic of focus for this paper, are replete with uncertainty about the preferences and strategies of the players involved in the debate. There is a difference between general positions of the partners, and their actual game strategies within the debate.

The <u>general positions</u> can be known by both partners—it is made clear (rhetorically) Let us assume that the set of topics in the debate is limited to three: T = {P, Q, R}, and the debaters know in advance what the opponents' positions are:

T	Debater A	Debater B
P = "taxes"	P + ("raise taxes")	P - ("lower taxes")
Q = "social welfare"	Q + ("improve")	Q - ("get rid of")
R = "family values"	R + ("important")	R + ("important")

So far, the agreements and disagreements are clear—both A and B take a similar rhetorical stand on R, while holding opposite opinions on P and Q. Obviously in the context of the symbolic duel (debate) <u>all</u> aspects of the topics are to be used as means to attack the other. In addition to the obvious disagreements, the rhetoric agreement is likely to be used in a strategic way to attack the opponent—yet in ways that are not clear from the outset.

While entering the debates, the debaters have different expectations about the other's strategies. Each of the topics and known position by the opponent may be used to build up a game strategy. The basic directions of translation of the positions into strategies can be guessed—each of the general positions can be translated in terms of **assertions** (ASS: "I stand for X") **direct attacks** (DIR: "My opponent opposes X which I support") **disagreement by agreement** (DIA: "I agree with my opponent about importance of X, but I stand for it and he opposes it"), and **ridiculing** (RID: "How *can* one be against X!?"). Let us work out the two perspectives (A's and B's) on each other's possible game strategies.

Debater A Expecting B to act Toward A:

Topic	ASS	DIR	DIA	RID
P = "taxes"	yes	yes	no	**yes**
Q = "social welfare"	no	**no**	yes	yes
R = "family values"	yes	**no**	no	yes

B Actually Planning to act Toward A:

Topic	ASS	DIR	DIA	RID
P = "taxes"	yes	yes	no	**no**
Q = "social welfare"	no	**yes**	no	**no**
R = "family values"	yes	**yes**	no	**no**

The boldfaced parts in these two sets are the ones where A's expectations of B's actions upon A, and B's actual action plans, differ. Of course this is known to us—but not to A or B. Obviously, A expects B to openly ridicule him or her in all topics—which, however, B does not plan to do. A does not expect B to attack him directly on issues of "social welfare"—while B plans precisely such attacks. A expects B to attack him (or her) on that issue by the "disagreeing by agreeing" (i.e., attack in a nondirect way), while B actually does not plan that kind of attack (and prefers the "direct attack" instead). Once the actual debate starts, A is up for surprises from B's side—and needs to adjust one's selection of preferred strategies on the spot.

This example shows how strategies may be misperceived between the players, but what constitutes the core of the game—the <u>payoff function</u>? In case of political debates there is no preset "payoff matrix" (as is usual in assumed traditional games)—all of it consists of the politicians' imagery of the relationship between their communicated message (of an attack on one's opponent) and the linkage of that message with some inherent characteristic of the audience. In case of televised debates, such audience is expected to be heterogeneous—the expected payoffs are located in the unknown domains of the selves of persons who watch the debates.

As candidates volley attacks back and forth, in an attempt to "win over" the audience, mapping the dialogical moves via hypergame theory can elucidate the strategies and preferences that the candidates are employing. In terms of the multiplicity of I-positions, the payoff goal for the debaters can be set as maximizing the link between one's constructed image (message) and an individual recipient's I-position, while minimizing the link between one's opponent's constructed image and individual's I-position. It is a triangular situation where each of the debaters try to "capture the recipient":

A: By my set of I-positions {A1, A2, A3} I am close to your—recipient's—set of I-positions {R1, R2, R3}, while my opponent B's I-positions {B1, B2, B3} are far from yours

B: By my set of I-positions {B1, B2, B3} I am close to your—recipient's—set of I-positions {R1, R2, R3}, while my opponent A's I-positions {A1, A2, A3} are far from yours

The values of the payoff matrix are thus not pregiven, but constantly renegotiated in the debate through the opposition of this "double triangular" relation. Hence the political debates can be modeled as a hypergame—the partners do not have full knowledge of each other's strategy preferences (intentions), and the pay-off matrix <u>is not preknown</u> (but becomes created through the debate). In previous applications of the hypergame notion (e.g., Takahashi, Fraser, & Hipel, 1984) that latter condition was not included. We can consider hypergames with not yet existing payoff functions as <u>open-ended</u> hypergames.

In formal sense, the two opposing "message pressures" create a zone of expected payoff. This zone includes a heterogeneous movements of the recipient's I-positions in varied directions—triggered by the actual move in the open-ended hypergame (combination of A's and B's strategic actions in relation to each other). The recipient here is given in a generalized form

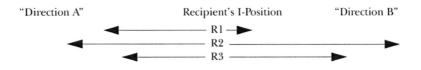

In this graphic example it becomes obvious that the recipient's I-positions R2 and R3 are moved in the direction congenial to B's message, while R1 moved in the opposite direction. In realistic terms, after watching an episode of a debate the hypothetical (generalized) recipient may say "I think A is a better person than I ever thought, but I now strongly agree with B's assertion X and he seems clearer than A on Y"

How does this take on hypergames map upon our selected excerpts from the presidential debate? Beginning with the debate transcript already divided based on the aforementioned criteria; sections were further identified by which strategy category they fell into. The transcript was then analyzed as a whole by looking at the movement between different strategies. The strategy movements by the candidates followed an interesting pattern. At the beginning of the health care discussion, both candidates focused primarily on what they themselves supported (ASS). After a move by Gore on line 11 (at the end of his first statement) from employing an ASS strategy to a RID (ridiculing) strategy both candidates begin to move away from their initial strategic direction. This move is a drastic strategic shift as 100% of Gore's remarks before it employ the ASS strategy while only 1 of Gore's subsequent remarks employ this method. The table below illustrates the strategies employed by the candidates at each of their subsequent opportunities to speak (See Table 11.1)

In fact, as Appendix A shows, the candidates shift their strategies into new form of combining assertion of their own position with ridiculing the opponent's not doing that. Ridiculing is a affect-laden communicative strategy that is put in place as the background for foregrounding the assertive message. Thus, consider the perceivable "power" of two messaged:

Table 11.1.   Strategy Movements by the Candidates

	% ASS	% DIR	% DIA	% RID
Bush 1	100%	0%	0%	0%
Gore 1[a]	80%	0%	0%	40%
Bush 2	40%	20%	20%	20%
Gore 2	0%	33%	0%	66%
Bush 3	66%	0%	33%	0%

[a] Numbers do not add up to 100% because one of the messages could fall into either or both the ASS strategy or the RID strategy—are combined.

Message 1:   I stand for X
Message 2:   I stand for X, and—like you—wonder how can anybody in one's sane mind oppose X

Message 2 ridicules the opponent—yet never directly attacking him or her. Of course Appendix A gives more complex forms of combination of the strategies. This opens to our scrutiny yet another aspect of open-ended hypergame perspective here—the <u>combinations</u> of known strategies themselves belong to the set of strategies. Note that excerpts at each turn in Appendix A are relatively long and include concatenation of materials that are combined categories, as well as repeated ones (especially for repetition of assertion).

The critical moments of the debate—when seen from hypergame viewpoint—are transitions from one to another strategy by one (or both) participants (e.g., line 11 in Appendix A). The hypergame assumed options table (as one shown above) changes as the partners reveal the acceptance or rejection of the other's move. Thus, A may move from asserting to asserting + ridiculing, expecting the other to follow suit. But the other may move into direct attacks (e.g., about ridiculing). And so on.

GENERAL CONCLUSIONS:
GAMES AND SOCIAL CONSTRUCTION

Political debates are complex events. Our study has barely covered a small aspect of the phenomena, and perhaps leading to more open questions than answers. Perhaps the most important side to be taken from the present analysis is that of the indeterminacy of the outcomes of processes that can be modeled by open-ended hypergames. That there is expected to be some payoff is taken for granted—yet what it is precisely is not known before it becomes negotiated. Open-ended hypergames are arenas for negotiation of the payoffs, where only directions of such outcomes are specified. This is yet another way to indicate the similarity of communicative processes with basic developmental processes—those of bounded indeterminacy (Valsiner, 1987).

What does our analysis contribute to the questions of "dialogical self?" A careful look onto political debates of one unique country—U.S.—leads us to conclude that the "dialogical self" is also a "targeted self." Precisely because of the dialogical organization of the various I-positions of a person—be that a consumer or exploiter of the political processes—efforts to reorganize the space of I-positions by somebody in the direction of some goals is taking place. The "voices of the mind" are not just in dialogue— they are directed by the dramatizations of <u>observed</u> kinds (such as watching a TV show—a debate, news discussion, or soap opera). Both the actors (the debating politicians) and the nonactors (recipients of the messages communicated through the debates) are involved in the re-construction of the social world (political power transitions, and social changes), each in their own ways. All such social re-construction takes place through the dialogical selves of the persons—whose sets of I-positions are constantly being relocated in their space through purposeful communicative encounters—direct or vicarious.

ACKNOWLEDGMENTS

This paper is an elaboration of poster presented at the *Second International Conferenceon Dialogical Self: Meaning in Movement*, Ghent, Belgium, October, 20, 2002, the cooperation of Corey Carrier in the planning and executing empirical part of the work covered here. The Harrison Fund of Clark University's Communication and Culture Program provided support for the research project.

NOTES

1. It is interesting to note that despite the presence of a rather large list of candidates in the United States, public presentation becomes limited to two (sometimes three) of them.
2. This step was taken after extensively dissecting the debates trying different systems. Utilizing social representations provided the best tool to stay close to the primary ideas when separating sections of the text.
3. In many case it is even more general than the example above: people or Americans for instance and in other cases the focus is implied.

Appendix A: Breakdown of the Debate Including Strategy Moves

#	Statement	Orientation	Type	Strategy/Comments
		Message		
1.	**J**: Both of you—Governor, both of you have talked much about Medicare and health care for seniors. What about the more than 40 million younger Americans who do not have health insurance right now? What would you do about that?			
2.	**B:** Well, I've got a plan to do something about that, to make health care affordable and available, this way. First, there are some who should be buying health care who choose not to. There are some— **J**: Some of the 40 million			
3.	**B**: Some of the **healthy** folks, **healthy** <u>young kids</u> say, "I never **get sick**, therefore I'm not going to have—don't need **health care** right now." And for those, what I think we need to do is to develop an investment-type vehicle that would be an incentive for them to invest, like medical savings accounts with rollover capacity. In other words, you say to a youngster, "It would be in your financial interest to start saving for future illness."	On Candidate	Ideological	ASS/
4.	But for the <u>working folks</u> that do want to have health care that can't afford it, a couple of things we need to do. One, we need more **community health** centers. I've developed—put out money in my budget to expand **community health** centers all around the <u>country</u>. These are places where <u>people</u> can get primary **care**. Secondly—and they're good. They're very important parts of the **safety net** of **health care**.	On Candidate	Ideological	ASS

5.	Secondly, that you get a $2,000 rebate from the government if you're a <u>family</u> of $30,000 or less—it scales down as it gets higher—that you can use to purchase **health care** in the private markets. It's going to be a huge down payment for a pretty darn good system if you allow›—also allow—convince states to allow— allow states to allow the <u>mother</u> to match some of the <u>children's</u> **health** insurance money with it, to pool purchasing power.	On Candidate	Ideological	ASS
6.	And to make **health** care more affordable, allow business associations, like the National Federation of Independent Business or the Chamber of Commerce or the National Restaurant Association, to write association plans across jurisdictional lines so that small businesses have got the capacity of national pooling to drive the cost of insurance down.	On Candidate	Ideological	ASS
7.	I think that's the very best way to go. It **empowers** <u>people</u>. It trusts <u>people</u>. It makes—it—and it's a practical way to encourage <u>people</u> to purchase **health care** insurance.	On Candidate	Ideological	**ASS**/ Special type of assertion (STA) that brings all substantive points together in the singular message "Helathcare is important"
	J: Vice President Gore?			
8.	**A**: It's one of my top priorities, Jim, to give every single <u>child</u> in the <u>United States</u> affordable **health care** within the next four years. I'd like to see eventually in this <u>country</u> some form of universal **health care,**	On Candidate	Ideological	ASS/ (STA)

9.	but I'm not for a government-run system. In fact, I'm for shrinking the size of government. I want a smaller and smarter government. I have been in charge of this Reinventing Government streamlining project that's reduced the size of government by more than 300,000 people in the last several years. And the budget plan that I've put out, according to the Los Angles Times, again, the way these things are typically measured as a percentage of the GDP, will bring government spending down to the lowest level in 50 years. So I want to proceed carefully to **cover** more people.	On Candidate Ideological	ASS
10.	But I think we should start by greatly expanding the so-called Child **Health** Insurance or CHIP Program, to give **health** insurance to every single child in this country. I think it's intolerable that we have so many millions of children without any **health** insurance. So it's one of my top priorities.	On Candidate Ideological	ASS
11.	Now I know that we have some disagreements on this, and I'm sorry to tell you that, you know, there is a record here, and Texas ranks 49th out of the 50 states in **health care**—in children with **health care**, 49th for women with **health care**, and 50th for families with **health care**.	On Opponent Personal	**RID/** First break by either candidate from solely asserting position; Move to ridicule
12.	So it is a priority for me, I guarantee you. I'm not aware of any program—well, I'll just leave it at that. I think it ought to be a top priority. J: Governor, did the vice president —are the vice president's figures correct about Texas?	On Candidate Ideological	**ASS/RID** Comment has multiple elements; starts out as an STA begins move to ridicule and then moves back to STA

13.	**B**: Well, first of all, let me say, he's not for a government-run **health care** system. I thought that's exactly what he and Mrs. Clinton and them fought for in 1993, was a government-run **health care** system. That was fortunately stopped in its tracks.	On Opponent	Personal	**RID** / Note Bush's move to ridicule from previously relying only on assertions
14.	Secondly, we spend $4.7 billion a year on the uninsured in the state of <u>Texas</u>. Our rate of **uninsured**, the percentage of **uninsured** in <u>Texas</u> has gone down, while the percentage of **uninsured** in <u>America</u> has gone up.	On Candidate	Both	DIA
15.	Our CHIPS program got a late start because our <u>government</u> meets only four months out of every two years, Mr. Vice President. It may come for a shock for somebody who's been in <u>Washington</u> for so long, but actually, **limited government** can work in the <u>second largest state</u> in the union.	On Both	Personal	DIR
16.	And therefore, Congress passes the bill after our session in 1997 ended. We passed the enabling legislation in '99. We've signed up over 110,000 **children** to the CHIPS program. For <u>comparable states</u> our size, we're signing them up fast as any other state.	On Candidate	Personal	**ASS** / Bush returns from attacks to assertions
17.	And I—you can quote all the numbers you want, but I'm telling you, we **care** about our <u>people</u> in Texas. We spend a lot of money to make sure <u>people</u> get **health care** in the state of Texas. And we're doing a better job than they are at the national level for reducing uninsured. **J**: Is he right?	On Both	Personal	**ASS** / STA; notice the return to the Special type of Assertion with "I'm telling you, we care about our people"

18.	**G**: Well, I don't know about all these percentages that he throws out, but I do know that—I speculate that the reason why he **didn't answer your question** directly as to whether my numbers were right, the **facts were right** about Texas ranking dead last in <u>families</u> with **health** insurance and 49th out of 50 for both <u>children</u> and <u>women</u> is because those facts are correct.	On Opponent	Personal	**RID** / Gore continues on ridicule path
19.	And as for why it happened, I'm no expert on the Texas procedures, but what my friends there tell me is that the governor opposed a measure put forward by Democrats in the legislature to expand the number of <u>children</u> that would be **covered**, and instead directed the money toward a tax cut, a significant part of which went to <u>wealthy interests</u>. He declared the need for a new tax cut for the oil companies in Texas an emergency need. And so the money was taken away from the CHIP program.	On Opponent	Ideological	**DIR**/ Considered a direct attack (I support x while my opponenet does not) because Gore's "friends" supported a measure that Bush didn't
20.	There's a—you don't have to take my word for this. There is now a federal judge's opinion about the current management of this program, ordering the state of Texas to do -- and you should read that judge's language about this. There are 1.4—I believe there are 1.4 million <u>children</u> in Texas who do not have **health** insurance; 600,000 of whom—and maybe some of those have since gotten it—but as of a year ago, 600,000 of them were actually eligible for it, but they couldn't sign up for it because of the barriers that they had to surmount. **J**: Let's let the governor respond to that. **B**: I—	On Opponent	Personal	RID

J: Are those numbers correct? Are his charges correct?

21. **B**: If he's trying to allege that I'm a hard-hearted person and I **don't care** about <u>children</u>, he's absolutely wrong. We spend $4.7 billion a year in the state of Texas for **uninsured** <u>people</u> and they get **health care.** Now, that's not the most efficient way to get <u>people</u> **health care**. But I want to remind you, the number of **uninsured** in <u>America</u> during their watch has increased. And so he can make any excuse he wants, but the facts are that we're reducing the number of **uninsured** as a percentage of <u>our population</u>. And as a percentage of the <u>population</u>, it's increasing <u>nationally</u>. But somehow the allegation that we **don't care** and we're going to give money for this interest or that interest and not for <u>children</u> in the state of Texas is totally absurd.

On Both   Personal   DIA

22. And let me just tell you who the jury is—the <u>people of Texas</u>. There's only been one governor ever **elected to back-to-back** four-year terms, and that was me. And I was able to do so with a lot of Democrat votes, nearly 50 percent of the <u>Hispanic</u> vote, about 27 percent of the <u>African-American</u> vote because <u>people</u> know that

On Candidate   Personal   ASS

23. I'm a **conservative** <u>person</u> and a **compassionate** <u>person</u>. So we can throw all kinds of numbers around. I'm just telling you our state comes together to do what's right. <u>We</u> **come together**, both Republicans and Democrats.

On Candidate   Personal   ASS (STA)

REFERENCES

Corrado, A.(1995). *The report of the twentieth century fund task force on presidential debates: Let america decide*. New York: Twentieth Century Press.

Harsanyi, J. C., & Selten, R. (Eds). (1988). *A general theory of equilibrium selection in games*. Cambridge, MA: MIT Press.

Hermans, H. J. (2001). The dialogical self: Toward a theory of personal and cultural positioning. *Culture & Psychology, 7*(3), 243-281.

Hermans, H. J. (Ed). (2002). Special issue on dialogical self. *Theory & Psychology, 12*(2), 147-280.

Howard, N. (1971). *Paradoxes of rationality*. Cambridge: Massachusetts Institute of Technology.

Kirkpartrick, J. (1979). *Presidential candidate "Debates: What can we learn from 1960?: The past and future of presidential debates* (pp. 1-56). Washington, DC: American Enterprise Institute for Public Policy Research.

Mead, G. H. (2001). The philosophies of Royce, James, and Dewey in their American setting. *Culture & Psychology, 7*(1), 49-64. (Original work published 1930)

Miller, A. (2001). On politics and the art of acting. *The Penguin Group, 31*.

Schroeder, A. (2000). *Forty years of high-risk TV, presidential debates*. New York: Columbia University Press.

Takahashi, M. A., Fraser, N. M., & Hipel, K. W. (1984). A procedure for analyzing hypergames. *European Journal of Operational Research, 18*, 111-121.

Valsiner, J. (1984). *The childhood of the Soviet citizen: Socialization for loyalty*. Ottawa, Ontarios, Canada: Carleton University Press.

Valsiner, J. (1987). *Culture and the development of children's action*. Chichester, England: Wiley.

Valsiner, J. (2002, August). *Beyond social representations: A theory of enablement*. Invited lecture at the 6th International Conference On Social Representations, Stirling, Scotland.

White, R. (1949). Hitler, Roosevelt and the nature of war propaganda. *Journal of abnormal & Social Psychology, 44*, 157-174.

INTERVIEW FOR PART IV

QUESTIONS ABOUT THE FUNCTIONS OF OTHERNESS

Subject Endangered
Commentary on Papers in the Section of "Self in Collective Otherness"

Gyuseog Han

The three papers in this section "Self in Collective Otherness" all deal with otherness operating in political sphere but each with very distinctive colors. No coherent theme is penetrating at surface among them. Each paper certainly shows originality of its approach to the phenomenon of the authors' concern.

Rosa, Castro, and Blanco's paper provides a penetrating analysis on four types of different otherness which the Spaniards were confronting at the demise of Spanish Empire circa 1878. It took a renowned regenerationist writing to show how the Spanish collective self was wrestling with four types of different otherness; the historical other, the social other, the intranational other, and the international other. Some of these others need to be subdued, to be preserved, to be negotiated, to be confronted

Otherness in Question: Labyrinths of the Self, 297–301
Copyright © 2007 by Information Age Publishing

for the new collective self. Their analysis shows highly illuminating "case of identity crisis in modernity" which was manifest in one Spanish writing but certainly applicable to other countries at the dawn of modernity. Their analysis examined how Otherness emerges in a particular historical time and how the encounter with otherness becomes critical for self identity and thus culturally relevant issue for collectivity.

Shi-xu, taking a local culturalist perspective, proposed a scheme of cultural analysis of intercultural communication and illustrated the scheme by examining a series of Chinese media texts responding to the American official reports of human rights on global community. Looking at the intercultural communication in terms of dynamic contestation between the cultural Others, Xu argues more attention should be paid to the historically concrete, local, forms of intercultural communication. His theory of the contemporary Chinese public communication with the cultural West can be applicable to the repressed, unvoiced, Third World countries. Repression and domination, and attempt for counterbalancing to restore equilibrium are certainly key features of international communication.

Richer and Valsiner (RV) analyze rhetorics of political debate between two candidates in U.S. presidential race by taking microgenetic approach. RV apply the social representation theory to divide the rhetoric into units of analysis and analyze each arguments made by the candidates in terms of strategy of presentation (assertive, ridiculing, etc.) by employing hyper-game approach. They were able to show that a political debate is not simply win-over the other party but to capture the audience to their side. Each contestant tries to convey his/her set of I-positions are close to the audience while the opponent's set of I-positions are far from the audience. They were able to show the changes of rhetorics but within a boundary, "a bounded indeterminacy" (Valsiner, 1987). A new insight gained from this analysis is that the "dialogical self" is also a "targeted self."

Perhaps, it is useful to note what is common in the three papers and then pose my questions. First, apparently they all deal with politics from a vintage point of psychological analysis. To me, Rosa et al's work draws particular attention. They provide a good model of psychological literary analysis. And also, they showed the different Otherness entangled in any historical time of a collectivity. Second, it seems to me that all the authors espouse a dialogical perspective in broad sense. Dialogical perspective, especially the theory of dialogical self originated from Bakhtin and popularized by Hermans, is a very useful frame undoubtedly for psychology. But, it has limitation of understanding human communication and human affairs in more general term. In this interview, I would like ask questions delving on such limitations to each authors. They are questions about the function of otherness and of dialogue.

Q1. What is the Function of Otherness?

Three papers analyze all in common with different emphasis the otherness for the purpose of shaping up and understanding the self and identity. Here the Otherness gets attention for the sole purpose of shedding light on the self. This is most apparent in Rosa et al's but apparent in Shixu and RV too. In carrying out this kind of analysis, the otherness is juxtaposed as some entities out there to have relevance to self. Otherness is objectified to be disentangled and consequently confronted. My question is "Does Otherness have to be confrontational to have useful function in human existence?" The essence of sociocultural perspective lies in the view that human beings are social inherently. Being social necessitates otherness and self; however, it is not necessary the two entities are antithetical. "We celebrate the other; for without the other there is no existence for us either" (Sampson, 1993). But there are certainly other reasons to celebrate Otherness too. They are the source for humanity. Otherness provides the self reasons for living a worthy life. They are sources of all the emotional life. This function of Otherness is no less important for society.

Q2: "What is Dialogue?
How is it Different From Monologue?"

Broadly speaking, conversation between two parties constitutes a dialogue; debate, talk, or statement can be dialogical as long as those involve other parties to address. When parties engage in a dialogue, exchange of information is certainly important but not all there is. People talk or stop talking not necessarily from the need to talk but from totally different motive of relating. Here relating is not in terms of relationship building, sustaining, or even getting to know further about the other. It is more to do with experiencing the other's mind; how the other is feeling, what the other is experiencing in his/her mind. This dialogue seeks coexperiencing the other's lived through experience. When the parties are able to reach such status, they experience complete understanding of the others, experience the empathic feeling of sameness phenomenologically. Here dialogue has served its function completely. My point of departure here is that dialogue seeks for understanding of other's mind going beyond the information.

Communication is not exchange of utterances or voices. Exchange of understanding seeking behavior constitutes communication and dialogue. Korean word, *ui-mi* for understanding of something (texts, objects, events, mind etc.) takes the object of understanding consisted of meaning (*ui*) and feeling (*mi*). Understanding of meaning is primarily cognitive work but the feeling is primarily affective tone. Here two different body organs are involved for the understanding; the brain for grasping the meaning which is primarily semantic and cognitive and the bodily sense organs for the feeling. Feeling state of understanding is the phenomenological experience about the target. In human interaction it is the complete understanding of the other's mind; it is the otherness felt into one's mind.

True dialogue requires arguing and acquiescing mind. Dialogue becomes monologue when each party is determined to stand on their original position, not to listen what the other is saying or unable to accommodate the other party's argument. Bakhtin emphasizes the key of dialogism is on dialogue. For a dialogue to occur, at least two differing points of view must be engaged. Anything that tries to fuse these different perspectives into one undoes the truth of dialogism. He challenges the idea of empathy as a kind of fusion between self and other, because such fusion offers yet another device for making a monologue out of a potential dialogue. Fusing of dialogue into a monologue can be problematic if one voice becomes the dominant subjugating the other voice. What needs to be feared is not the monologue but the domination-submission relationship. Shi-xu and RV showed this power contest yields no dialogue but a series of dialectical monologues.

Now I want to raise a question here "what the dialogue is for then?" Dialogue completes its mission when the feeling part of understanding is achieved. When the Buddha showed a flower, only one disciple smiled among many. This is the ultimate form of mutual understanding; the experiential state of mind is communicated. Here, words lost its function but the dialogue perfected. If dialogue requires incessant exchange of ideas and feeling, the communication will break down along the way. As Shi-xu points out, in the Oriental philosophical thinking, language and communication are not a form of representing the world, but they are a mode of activitiy for the sake of maintaining a harmonious relationship with social others. The bond of relationship requires exchanges of lived experience. Through this exchange, interactants get assured of their bonding and trust (Choi & Han, 2007).

I fear that the dialogical self theory, relying too much on Bakhtin, places the foremost importance to the dialogue itself and pays not enough attention to their relevance to human life. Self and dialogue has no inherent value for psychology; they are invaluable target of analysis only when we situate them in human experience. In fact, this problematic treatment of the subject matter is widespread in many theories of psychological analysis.

REFERENCES

Choi, S -C., & Han, C. (2007). Embedded trust in the close relationship: A cultural psychology of trust. In I. Marková & A. Gillespie (Eds.), *Trust and culture.* Greenwich, CT: Information Age Publishers.

Sampson, E. E. (1993). *Celebrating the other: A dialogic account of human nature.* Boulder, CO: Westview Press.

Valsiner, J. (1987). *Culture and the development of children's action.* Chichester, England: Wiley

Part V

THE OTHER WITHIN THE SELF: DYNAMICS OF MULTIPLICITY

CHAPTER 12

HONORING SELF-OTHERNESS

Alterity and the Intrapersonal

Mick Cooper and Hubert Hermans

Within the contemporary literature on alterity (e.g., Davis, 1996; Gantt, 2002; Levinas, 1969) the concept of otherness is intimately linked to the existence of an actual, physical other. Otherness—that enigmatic, mysterious "strangeness" beyond synthesis, thematization, and comprehension—is equated with the face of the Other, while the self is ascribed the qualities of sameness and identity (e.g., Williams & Gantt, 2002). Such an association between "I" and identity is particularly explicit in the work of the founding philosopher of alterity, Emmanuel Levinas (1969). In the first part of his magnum opus, *Totality and Infinity,* he writes that, "The alterity, the radical heterogeneity of the other, is possible only if the other is other with respect to a term whose essence is to remain at the point of departure … to be the same not relatively but absolutely" (p. 36): that is, the I. Here, Levinas does not suggest that the I is a being that always remains the same, but he does state that it is "the being whose existing consists in identifying itself, in recovering its identity throughout all that happens to it" (p. 36). In other words, faced with its own alterity, the I "merges with

Otherness in Question: Labyrinths of the Self, 305–315

itself'" (p. 36). It is, states Levinas, "incapable of apostasy with regard to this surprising 'self'" (p. 36).

As with the work of the Jewish philosopher of dialogue, Martin Buber (see Buber's dialogue with Rogers in Anderson & Cissna, 1997), such an association of otherness with an actual, physical other serves an important philosophical function: defending a radically intersubjective standpoint from a collapse back into individualism and intrapsychically-orientated solipsism. The aim of our chapter, however, is to suggest that the notion of otherness *can* be usefully extended from the interpersonal realm to the intrapersonal one in a way that does not compromise an intersubjective position. In other words, what we wish to argue is that otherness—understood as that which is alien, strange, and radically different from the "self"—*can* be experienced within one's own being as well as without, and that a concept of *self-otherness* can serve a valuable psychological and psychotherapeutic function.

THE SELF: IDENTITY AND MULTIPLICITY

Levinas argues that the self is characterized by its capacity to survive change, and that it identifies itself as the same even as it becomes different (Davis, 1996). But is this really the case? At an empirical level, both these claims are open to question. That the self is characterized by its capacity to survive change, for instance, is brought into question by cases of "dissociative fugue," in which knowledge of one's identity and past is lost (Kihlstrom, 1994). Instances of severe psychosis, in which a dissolution of the sense of self comes about (see Laing, 1965), also call into question the assumption that the self is characterized by its capacity to survive change. Equally, that the self is characterized by its capacity to identify itself as "the Same" even as it becomes different is strongly challenged by instances of dissociative identity disorder (formerly known as "multiple personality disorder"), in which "a single individual alternates between two or more identities" (Kihlstrom, 1994, pp. 378-379). Here, the existence of symmetrical or asymmetrical amnesia barriers between the different personality states means that the person, in one state, may entirely dis-identify with experiences, behaviors, or characteristics associated with an alternate personality state.

Furthermore, in recent years, "self-plurality" theorists such as ourselves (see Hermans & Dimaggio, 2004; Rowan, 1990; Rowan & Cooper, 1999, for overviews and summaries) have argued that the existence of multiple identities within one individual is by no means limited to cases in which severe psychological disturbance exists. Coming from a phenomenological perspective, for instance, Cooper (1999) has argued that human beings, when experiencing thoughts or emotions that are highly inconsistent with a preestablished sense of self, may switch in to an alternate concept of who they are. A person who perceives themselves as calm, for instance, on experiencing rage, may "flip" into a sense of self as righteous or aggrieved. This, then, becomes an alternate identity that is incompatible with the previous one. Cooper, drawing on Lecky (1945), suggests such a "flip-flopping" takes place so that the person can maintain some semblance of self-consistency, and in this respect his argument *is* consistent with Levinas's (1969) contention that the self is characterized by a striving for unity. Yet the unity attained here is an entirely synchronic one: an in-the-moment presence-to-oneself. Diachronically, by contrast, the self has fundamentally renounced its own identity, become other to itself: come to a "mode of being" in which its previous identity may be experienced as utterly alien and strange. Taking this further, Hermans (Hermans & Kempen, 1993, p. 215) suggests that this potential for "inner otherness" exists, not only diachronically but also synchronically, and he conceptualizes the self as a "dynamic multiplicity of relatively autonomous *I* positions in an imaginal landscape." Here, a plurality of independent, unmerged voices are seen as having the capacity to enter into dialogical relationships with each other, forging a self that is characterized by a meeting of othernesses within time as well as across it.

Evidence for the existence of self-plurality—preliminary though it is— comes from a variety of sources. With respect to multiple self-perceptions, Lester (1992), drawing on self-report data, has shown that around 84% of students are able to describe several subselves in their mind, with an average of three to four stated selves per student; and Hermans and colleagues (Hermans, Rijks, & Kempen, 1993) have shown that people will describe their lives in very different ways when talking from different I-positions. Numerous clinical case studies have also demonstrated that many clients will spontaneously describe themselves in pluralistic ways. "Dominic," for instance, a client of person-centered therapist Dave Mearns who wanted to overcome alcohol abuse (Mearns & Cooper, 2005), described himself as having two sides: "sober me" and "drunk me." Other evidence for the existence of multiple self-concepts comes from a study by Rosenberg and Gara (1985), which demonstrates that people's self-descriptions (for instance, "psychologist," "historian," "overeater") tend to cluster around a smaller number of higher order identities.

With respect to synchronic plurality, Hilgard (1977) has shown that hypnotized subjects, given the instruction to become deaf to all sounds, do not flinch when wooden blocks are banged close to their heads, and fail to report any sounds once their hearing is restored. When asked, however, to speak from "a part of themselves" that has been listening and processing the information, they can fully recall the sounds. This suggests, then, that the participants could simultaneously process the same event in two radically different ways; and research from the neuropsychological field with "split-brain" patients (i.e., those with a severed corpus callosum where signals can not be transmitted between the different sides of the brain) supports this notion of modular coprocessing (e.g., Gazzaniga, 1985). In one study, for instance, Gazzaniga exposed only the right half of a split-brain patient's brain to a "terrifying" fire safety film. He hypothesized that, because the speech-processing module is in the left half of the brain, the patient would be unable to verbalize the content of the film she has seen, and this was indeed the case. The patient, however, still reported feeling afraid and jumpy after seeing the film, and Gazzaniga suggests that this was due to the activation of an emotional, nonverbal module in the right brain hemisphere—thus supporting Gazzaniga's view of the brain as fundamentally modular and pluralistic in nature.

What such evidence suggests, then, is that the trajectory of the self is not only toward sameness and identity. Alongside it, and, perhaps, instead of it at times, is a movement toward diversity and difference: a creation or acknowledgement of alterity within the same person. And while such an understanding of the self is by no means incontrovertible (see, for instance, Braude, 1991), the degree of dissociation and dis-identification that some people can experience between different "personality states" suggests that, at the very least, an otherness "within" the self is on a continuum with an otherness "outside." Indeed, as Spinelli (1994) points out, the act of dis-identifying with a particular mode of experiencing may actually take the form of attributing it to an Other, and he gives the example of a fundamentalist lay-preacher who, on experiencing sexual arousal in the presence of certain members of his religious commune, attributed these feelings "to a temporary possession by Satan" (p. 345). What is being proposed here, then, is that we can experience elements of our own being as mysterious, enigmatic, and transcendent to our "self" just as we can experience the being of an Other. In this sense, phenomenologically at least, it is legitimate to talk of a "self-otherness," just as we can talk of the otherness of an Other.

Of course, the fact that a pluralistic conception of self opens the door to a notion of self-otherness does not in any way circumscribe the forms that that self-otherness might take. Indeed, as we shall see shortly, the history of psychotherapeutic theory can be seen as a history of attempts to delineate the nature of this self-otherness. Self-otherness, then, may take the form of semiautonomous "voices," but it may also take the form of something far more fragmentary: for example, a passing thought, a burning desire, or a habit. All these aspects of the "self," and many more, have the capacity to be experienced as alien, enigmatic, and unknown; indeed, Levinas (2001), himself, writes of the anonymous, impersonal *"il y a"* ["there is"] that constitutes the "dark background" of existence. Other examples abound: I conceptualize myself, for instance, as someone who is "with-it," but find myself dancing like my father at my children's birthday parties. Physically, too, there is much of me that can be seen as having a quality of alienness about it. The mechanism by which blood is pumped around my body, for instance, is not something that I experience any affinity or identity with. If someone were to reveal my heart on an operating table, it would seem little more "mine" than the heart of another person. Similarly, while I can choose to move my fingers, the mechanism by which my choice gets translated into action is utterly alien to me: beyond my jurisdiction, identity, and control. Even at the level of immediate sensate experiencing, processes such as reading these words here feel penetrated by something enigmatic and unknown: in this case, the mechanism by which these black marks are translated into meaningful phrases. In other words, while I can choose to redirect my attention, I cannot penetrate to any level of depth the mechanism by which these marks *mean* letters, these letters *mean* words, and these words together form a coherent whole. Such processes are incomprehensible, mysterious, and strange: fault-lines through which a familiar and integral sense of self is disrupted. What is being suggested here, then, is that, at the physical level, human existence has something of a "cybernetic" quality to it: that at the core of our being lies mechanistic, electronic processes that are devoid of those characteristics commonly associated with human beings, such as intentionality. More broadly, we would suggest that human beings are riddled throughout by otherness. Indeed, to re-coin a phrase used by Sartre (1958), otherness (as opposed to nothingness) lies coiled in the heart of being—like a worm.

Such a statement is complicated by the fact that, from a contemporary intersubjective standpoint (e.g., Gergen, 2001; Heidegger, 1962; Hermans, 2001), the self, itself, is riddled with the mysterious and alien otherness of Others. That is, other beings exist within our very essence: through the language and tools that we use (Heidegger, 1962; Vygotsky, 1962), through the internalization of cultural and individual voices (Hermans, 2001) through the multiple roles that we adopt (Gergen, 1991) and, from a Levinasian perspective, through our preontological obligation to the Other's call (see Cohen, 2002). To write of "self"-otherness, then, is not to suggest that this alterity exists within a self-contained, isolated monad. Rather, in Hermans' (2003) terms, it is to suggest that this otherness penetrates being from the most explicitly "external" realms to the most seemingly "internal" ones, whether carried in the voices and images of actual others or through the less obviously interpersonal mediums of biological and affective mechanisms. In other words, otherness is everywhere.

Self-Otherness in Psychotherapy

The domain of psychotherapy is one in which these issues of self, alterity and plurality take on real, practical significance. If the self, then, is characterized as plural and penetrated by otherness, this could have fundamental implications for psychotherapeutic practice. Yet if one looks at the history of psychotherapy, one sees that, in many respects, it is *already* a history of attempts to conceptualize, and engage with, those aspects of the "self" that are most enigmatic, alien, and unknown. Like his forerunners in the field of dynamic psychiatry (in particular, Charcot and Janet), Freud took otherness from the realms of myth, superstition, and religion and relocated it firmly in the depths of the human psyche (Ellenberger, 1970). Here, through his concept of the "unconscious," and later of the "id," Freud attempted to say something of the "chaos" and "cauldron of seething excitement" that lay beneath, and bubbled through, the conscious sense of self (Freud, 1923). Post-Freudian psychoanalysts, such as Klein, attempted to do much the same, though their views on the content and the structure of the "unconscious" were very different from Freud's. Humanistic therapists, too, like Carl Rogers (1959), set up their therapeutic approaches around an understanding of that which was alien and incomprehensible to the person's sense of self. Similar moves were made by existential psychotherapists such as Irvin Yalom (1980), who construed the unknown in terms of "ultimate" existential concerns: anxieties about death, freedom, isolation, and meaninglessness.

When viewed as attempts to conceptualize, and engage with, self-otherness, the history of psychotherapeutic thought and practice reveals something of a trend—one which, to some extent, mirrors wider cultural attitudes to the Other-as-foreigner.

In the earliest writings, the stance toward this self-otherness seems primarily to be one of *colonization*. This is encapsulated in the Freudian phrase, "Where id was, there ego shall be." Here, the mysteries of the psyche are to be exposed, uncovered, and revealed for what they are; replaced with a more rationale, ordered, and controlled way of experiencing the world. Freud is not suggesting in any way that we can vanquish the unconscious or Id, but like an African people in imperialist times, it is seen as a chaotic and instinctual force to be dominated and contained.

In the writings of many post-Freudian psychotherapists, however, the attitude toward this self-otherness becomes more benign. In the writings of humanistic and transpersonal psychotherapists such as Rogers (1959) and Assagioli (1965), in particular, this self-otherness is seen as having the potential to enhance and contribute toward the wider self. Hence, the attitude becomes less one of colonization, and more one of *integration*: of bringing the self-otherness into the mainstream of psychological func-

tioning and tapping its resources. Here, we see some parallels to the attitude of integrationism that has existed toward immigrants in postcolonial
times: of bringing them in to the dominant culture and adding their
potential to the melting pot of skills and resources.

More recently, however, many psychotherapeutic theorists—particularly within the self-plurality field—have moved away from an attitude of
integration to an attitude of *dialogue*. Here, there is an increasing acceptance of voices or selves in their own right, such that the desire for assimilation is replaced by a desire to engage and meet with the self-otherness is
a nonpossessing, nonabsorbing way. Drawing on Buber's (1947, 1958)
writings on dialogue and the I-Thou attitude, for instance, Cooper (2003,
2004) outlines a mode of self-relating in which two different aspects of the
person are able to communicate with each other in an open, fluid,
empathic, and compassionate way, maintaining a cooperative and mutually enhancing relationship. He terms this an "I-I" self-relational stance,
and contrasts it with an "I-Me" stance in which, like Buber's "I-It" attitude, the person relates to themselves in an objectifying, de-humanizing
and rigid way. Cooper argues that this I-Me self-relational stance is associated with psychological distress for a number of reasons—high levels of
internal conflict, low levels of self-liking, and the creation of "suppressed
selves" (Hermans & Kempen, 1993) that demand repatriation—and he
argues that a key goal of therapeutic work should be to help clients establish a higher level of I-I self-relating. At the cultural level, such an attitude
of dialogue has parallels with the notion of multiculturalism: a willingness
to engage with others and to learn from them, without attempting to
assimilate the other's culture into the mainstream way of being.

As a foundation for respectful, ethical, and effective relating—whether
to self or others—the concept of dialogue would seem an important step
onwards from that of integration. Yet just as Levinas's (1967, 1969) work
in the interpersonal sphere has extended Buber's thinking toward a
greater appreciation of the Other—reconfiguring the I-Thou attitude to a
"Thou-I" one, in which the Other comes first—so we might draw on Levinas's writings to consider a level of self-otherness relating that exists
beyond the dialogic: what we might call a stance of *honoring*. Here, there
is a respect and openness toward one's own mysteriousness, but in contrast to the dialogical relationship, there is no expectation of engagement
or understanding. Rather, there is a willingness to accept self-otherness is
all its "irreducible strangeness" (Davis, 1996, p. 3), without a demand to
fully see, know and unveil it. In contrast to the more integrationist, holistic perspectives (e.g., Rogers, 1959), a stance of honoring also moves
beyond a "nostalgia for totality" (Levinas, 1982, p. 76), toward an acceptance of the incompleteness of the self, a willingness to live with the
unknowability and uncertainty of who we are. To follow Levinas more lit-

erally, we might even say that, in this honoring stance, there is a prime ethical directive to allow our self-otherness to *be*: a willingness to say "After you, sir!" to different aspects of our being without a desire for reciprocation or symmetry. Here, perhaps, we are particularly referring toward "the poor, the stranger, the widow, and the orphan" (Levinas, 1969, p. 251) "within" ourselves—in self-pluralistic terms, those aspects of the person that are "disowned" (Stone & Winkelman, 1989) or "suppressed" (Hermans & Kempen, 1993) such as the "vulnerable child" or the "shadow." In cultural terms, this stance of honoring self-otherness would seem to parallel a recently emerging attitude toward external Others which holds that they should be respected and valued, *without* being required or expected to reciprocate or engage in dialogue.

Honoring Self-Otherness in Practice

Such move toward an honoring of our own otherness would have subtle, yet significant, implications for the conceptualization and practice of psychotherapy and counseling. In particular, contrary to much of the contemporary emphasis on insight and self-understanding, this shift would lead to a form of practice in which the orientation of the work would be more toward helping clients accept and value their own unknowability and indeterminability. In other words, rather than encouraging clients to understand *why* they think, feel, and act in particular ways; or inviting them to dialogue and encounter suppressed "parts," a therapy at this level of self-otherness-relating might be more concerned with helping clients to simply—yet deeply—honor these unacknowledged voices, *without demanding or expecting engagement or explanation.* And while such an approach is, in many ways, radically new, there are echoes of it in previous psychotherapeutic writings. For instance, in the work of the existentially-informed psychoanalyst Leslie Farber (2000), who equates psychological distress with the desire to control those aspects of our being that cannot be controlled (such as the person with anxiety attacks who panics because he cannot stop his panicking), and he writes of the importance of coming to terms with the limits of our conscious will. There is also the work of psychoanalyst Hans Loewald (1988) who, like Freud, distinguished between primary and secondary processes but, unlike Freud, believed that the primary processes have an essential role to play in life as the source of creativity, fantasy, imagination, and enchantment (see Mitchell, 2000). For Loewald, as Mitchell writes, "an adult reality that has been wholly separated from infantile fantasy is a desiccated, meaningless, passionless world" (2000, p. 24), and here we can see, as in the work of Farber, a deep respect and willingness to honor the enigmatic, uncontrollable, and seemingly alien aspects of our being.

Conclusion: The Otherness of Being

Given that Levinas's writings were primarily concerned with issues of ethics, it is no surprise that he made a clear distinction between the self, characterized by identity, and the Other, whose otherness demands an ethical response. What is more, given that his writings were at the philosophical and ontological, rather than the empirical and psychological level, it is entirely understandable that he did not concern himself with the more ontical evidence and applications discussed in this chapter. Nevertheless, what we have argued is that there is a value in going beyond Levinas's characterization of the self as sameness, toward an understanding of the self as having the potentiality for an internal diversity and alterity. Yet, here, Levinas's writings on the meeting with the otherness of the Other provide an invaluable guide to understanding how people might encounter their own self-otherness and the most psychologically beneficial form that such an encounter might take.

Of course, as highlighted in the introduction, one must be extremely cautious in developing a notion of self-otherness, lest the radically intersubjective foundations of a Levinasian worldview be reduced to the kind of intrapsychic psychologizing that it is most explicitly designed to reject (Cohen, 2002). Yet if the notion of self-otherness is seen as an extension of "Other-otherness" rather than as an alternative to it, it can serve to further intersubjective thinking, not only be showing how the intrapersonal world is an internalization of interpersonal existence (cf. Vygotsky, 1962), but also by demonstrating that even the most "internal" self-experiences are infused with something nonself.

Where does this leave human being? As a fragmentary, dispersed experiencing; "doomed" to be incomplete and unknowable; and with a "self" that walks the narrow ridge between the otherness of others and the otherness inherent to its own being. Is this a problem? Yes, if we hanker after a totality of knowing and being; no, if we can learn to tolerate unknowing and imperfection. Whilst this chapter, then, has argued that the self is fundamentally riven with alterity, it has also argued that there are ways by which we can relate to this otherness in a constructive manner. Through processes such as psychotherapy, we can move away from attempts to dominate or colonize this self-otherness, and toward a place of accepting, honoring, and drawing creatively from it—living constructively and passionately with this otherness within.

REFERENCES

Anderson, R., & Cissna, K. N. (1997). *The Martin-Buber-Carl Rogers dialogue: A new transcript with commentary*. Albany, NY: State University of New York Press.

Assagioli, R. (1965). *Psychosynthesis: A manual of principles and techniques*. London: Aquarian/Thorsons.

Braude, S. E. (1991). *First person plural: Multiple personality and the philosophy of the mind*. London: Routledge.

Buber, M. (1947). *Between man and man* (R. G. Smith, Trans.). London: Fontana.

Buber, M. (1958). *I and thou* (2nd ed.) (R. G. Smith, Trans.). Edinburgh, Scotland: T & T Clark.

Cohen, R. A. (2002). Maternal psyche. In E. E. Gantt & R. N. Williams (Eds.), *Psychology for the other: Levinas, ethics and the practice of psychology* (pp. 32-64). Pittsburgh, PA: Duquesne University Press.

Cooper, M. (1999). If you can't be Jekyll be Hyde: An existential-phenomenological exploration on lived-plurality. In J. Rowan & M. Cooper (Eds.), *The plural self: Multiplicty in everyday life* (pp. 51-70). London: Sage.

Cooper, M. (2003). "I-I" And "I-Me": Transposing Buber's interpersonal attitudes to the intrapersonal plane. *Journal of Constructivist Psychology, 16*(2), 131-153.

Cooper, M. (2004). Encountering self-otherness: "I-I" and "I-Me" modes of self-relating. In H. J. M. Hermans & G. Dimaggio (Eds.), *Dialogical self in psychotherapy* (pp. 60-73). Hove, England: Brunner-Routledge.

Davis, C. (1996). *Levinas: An introduction*. Cambridge, England: Polity Press.

Ellenberger, H. F. (1970). *The discovery of the unconscious*. New York: Basic Books.

Farber, L. H. (2000). *The ways of the will* (Exp. ed.). New York: Basic Books.

Freud, S. (1923). The ego and the id (J. Strachey, Trans.). In *The standard edition of the complete psychological works of Sigmund Freud* (Vol. 19, pp. 12-59). London: Hogarth Press.

Gantt, E. E. (2002). Utopia, psychotherapy and the place of suffering. In E. E. Gantt & R. N. Williams (Eds.), *Psychology for the other: Levinas, ethics and the practice of psychology* (pp. 65-83). Pittsburgh, PA: Duquesne University Press.

Gazzaniga, M. (1985). *The social brain*. New York: Basic Books.

Gergen, K. J. (1991). *The saturated self: Dilemmas of identity in contemporary life*. London: Basic Books.

Gergen, K. J. (2001). *Social construction in context*. London: Sage.

Heidegger, M. (1962). *Being and time* (J. Macquarrie & E. Robinson, Trans.). Oxford, England: Blackwell.

Hermans, H. J. M. (2001). The dialogical self: Towards a theory of personal and cultural positioning. *Culture and Psychology, 7*(3), 243-281.

Hermans, H. J. M. (2003). The construction and reconstruction of a dialogical self. *Journal of Constructivist Psychology, 16*(2), 89-130.

Hermans, H. J. M., & Dimaggio, G. (Eds.). (2004). *Dialogical self in psychotherapy*. Hove, England: Brunner-Routledge.

Hermans, H. J. M., & Kempen, H. J. G. (1993). *The dialogical self: Meaning as movement*. San Diego, CA: Academic Press.

Hermans, H. J. M., Rijks, T. I., & Kempen, H. J. G. (1993). Imaginal dialogues in the self: Theory and method. *Journal of Personality, 61*(2), 207-236.

Hilgard, E. (1977). *Divided consciousness*. London: John Wiley.

Kihlstrom, J. F. (1994). One hundred years of hysteria. In S. J. Lynn & J. W. Rhue (Eds.), *Dissociation: Clinical and theoretical perspectives* (pp. 365-394). New York: Guilford Press.

Laing, R. D. (1965). *The divided self: An existential study in sanity and madness*. Harmondsworth, England: Penguin.

Lecky, P. (1945). *Self-consistency: A theory of personality*. New York: Island Press.

Lester, D. (1992). The disunity of self. *Personality and Individual Differences, 13*(8), 947-948.

Levinas, E. (1967). Martin Buber and the theory of knowledge. In P. A. Schlipp & M. Friedman (Eds.), *The philosophy of Martin Buber* (pp. 133-150). London: Cambridge University Press.

Levinas, E. (1969). *Totality and infinity: An essay on exteriority* (A. Lingis, Trans.). Pittsburgh, PA: Duquesne University Press.

Levinas, E. (1982). *Ethics and infinity: Conversations with Philip Nemo* (R. A. Cohen, Trans.). Pittsburgh, PA: Duquesne University Press.

Levinas, E. (2001). *Existence and existents* (A. Lingis, Trans.). Pittsburgh, PA: Duquesne University Press.

Loewald, H. (1988). *Sublimation*. New Haven, CT: Yale University Press.

Mearns, D., & Cooper, M. (2005). *Working at relational depth in counselling and psychotherapy*. London: Sage.

Mitchell, S. A. (2000). *Relationality: From attachment to intersubjectivity*. Hillsdale, NJ: The Analytic Press.

Rogers, C. R. (1959). A theory of therapy, personality and interpersonal relationships as developed in the client-centered framework. In S. Koch (Ed.), *Psychology: A study of science* (Vol. 3, pp. 184-256). New York: McGraw-Hill.

Rosenberg, S. S., & Gara, M. A. (1985). The multiplicity of personal identity. In P. Shaver (Ed.), *Self, situations and social behaviour: Review of personality and social psychology* (Vol. 6, pp. 87-113). Beverly Hills, CA: Sage.

Rowan, J. (1990). *Subpersonalities: The people inside us*. London: Routledge.

Rowan, J., & Cooper, M. (Eds.). (1999). *The plural self: Multiplicity in everyday life*. London: Sage.

Sartre, J. -P. (1958). *Being and nothingness: An essay on phenomenological ontology* (H. Barnes, Trans.). London: Routledge.

Spinelli, E. (1994). *Demystifying therapy*. London: Constable.

Stone, H., & Winkelman, S. (1989). *Embracing our selves: The voice dialogue manual*. Mill Valley, CA: Nataraj.

Vygotsky, L. S. (1962). *Thought and language*. Cambridge, MA: MIT Press.

Williams, R. N., & Gantt, E. E. (2002). Pursuing psychology as science of the ethical: Contributions of the work of Emmanuel Levinas. In E. E. Gantt & R. N. Williams (Eds.), *Psychology for the other: Levinas, ethics and the practice of psychology* (pp. 1-31). Pittsburgh, PA: Duquesne University Press.

Yalom, I. (1980). *Existential psychotherapy*. New York: Basic Books.

CHAPTER 13

INTERSUBJECTIVITY
AND OTHERNESS

A Stage For Self Strivings

Danilo Silva Guimarães and Lívia Mathias Simão

The human symbolic action is developed in the cultural fabric of the I-Other inextricable relations. In that relational context, the Other can be experienced by the subject as present, absent, real, or imaginary. The domain of I-Other intersubjectivity is marked by negotiations and renegotiations of propositions among the interlocutors that function as organizing constraints of personal experiences (Valsiner, 1998). Taking for granted that human development is an open-ended process, people should do establish in their interactions a temporary basis or a shared domain that allow them to negotiation. It is that shared domain that we are meaning here by "intersubjectivity" (Rommetveit, 1992).

Borrowing from Rommetveit, Valsiner (1998) additionally points that intersubjectivity is only possible through some decentration of the subject's Ego, which happens when the subject tries to "take the role" of the other person. In other words, when the subject assumes not only the interlocutor's point of view, but also when he believes that the interlocutor

Otherness in Question: Labyrinths of the Self, 317–347

is striving for understanding him as well as for being understood. In that sense, both—subject and interlocutor—transcend their own individual worlds toward each others'. Thus, "the intersubjectivity is a metaprocess of reflexivity which constantly leads to creation, maintenance, and changes in the personal 'background' sense of dialogical activity (the foreground)" (Valsiner, 1998, p. 33). As human reasoning works on the basis of lived experience, intersubjectivity is a process that happens not only among persons, but also among the different levels of the semiotic functioning in the individual subject (Valsiner, 1998; Valsiner, 2005). In the latter case, the individual acts according to many different positions emerged from the personal elaboration of his relationships to Others, where he can act "as if he or she were the other" (Hermans, Kempen, & van Loon, 1992).

HUMAN INTERSUBJECTIVITY AND OTHERNESS RELATIONSHIP

Social interactions happen through involved persons' communicative actions which are mutually directed to one another. Communicative actions are the basic analytic category for understanding human mental development in the sociocultural mediational context (Wertsch, 1998).

Bakhtin (1997) proposes the *utterance* as the unit for analyzing communicative processes. These processes always occur from specific points of view of each interlocutor—the speaker's perspective, for instance. Each utterance is characterized by the peculiarity of its content embedded in the speaker's emotional referential when he addresses *that* talk to *that* listener. So, what matters is "who said what for who and when" (Simão, 2003, p. 453; Wertsch, 1991, p. 109).

This means that each speech can produce multiple interpretations, instead of a unique and correct one, because its correctness will depend on the listener's and speaker's ways of questioning for intersubejctivity. In sum, it will depend on coauthoring negotiations through the polyphonic encounter of the various voices involved in the conversational process. The meaning of each speech is, therefore, dialogic (Bakhtin, 1997; Holquist, 1990; Linell, 1995; Wertsch, 1993).

We are also assuming the I-Other relationship as a process in which the particular feature is complementariness and interdependency of the actors, instead of relative independency of one another. Accordingly, in the approach to I-Other and I-World relationships none of its elements can be conceived a priori of the other, because—like figure and ground or the inside and outside of a circle—they come to existence together and have its individual meaning attached, although not reduced, to their relationship. Their meaning is, therefore, contextual to their relationship (Herbst, 1995; Marková, 1997).

This perspective guarantees that we will take the constituent elements of the relation as distinct from one another. The maintenance of the distinctive character of the elements involved, by its turn, allows us to keep their relational position, which is necessary for understanding the nature of the events (Bergson, 1896, 1934). This is also true for the individual development because of its nature of continuous flux of transformation and differentiation toward to *come to be*. As Valsiner has pointed out, to make distinctions is part and parcel of the quest for understanding human development. This principle brought to psychology by Heinz Werner's orthogenetic principle, which emphasizes differentiation and hierarchical genetic integration of structures along the human development. Differentiation means a process of distinction elimination, giving rise for new structures, which will be the basis for new distinctions, and so on. The main aspect of this process of differentiation is the hierarchical integration, which reorganizes the previous lower levels of the living system, allowing the emergency of higher levels of organization (cf. Valsiner, 1998).

One of the main sources of transformation in human development is through the subject's quest for I-Other sharing, that is, for intersubjectivity. Discussing intersubjectivity, Crossley (1996) starts from four central premises: (a) subjectivity is not a matter of the private world, but it is intersubjective in itself; (b) subjectivity is constituted by a prereflexive engagement to the other, instead of reflexively experiencing and objectifying it; (c) human acting in general—and human speaking in particular—are social-institutionalized forms of human action and that is essential for their meaning; (d) a great part of the human experience and action comes from dialogical situations and can not be reduced to the individual subjects.

According to Crossley (1996) it is possible to distinguish two mainly phases of intersubejctivity that are not excluding one another: radical and egological intersubjectivity. As we shall see, they are genetically linked, as radical intersubjectivity is the condition for the emergence of egological intersubjectivity. Emerged, however, they both remain as different possibilities of I-World relationship, alternating in a to-and-fro movement.

Radical intersubjectivity encompasses prereflexivity in the relationship with the other, while egologic intersubjectivity involves reflexivity by the subject. In the first kind, there would be an unconditional openness to the other, similar to the Levinas' view. In the last case, the self would put himself in the place of the other, through the analogical process of thinking, as in Husserlian subject-object relationship.

Radical intersubjectivity requires mutuality and immediate harmonization of the I with the other's self. Addressivity to the other prevails over the self experience as such. This notion refers to an irreducible inter-world of meanings that are shared by the subjects thanks to their pre-reflexive engagement to the other, that is, to their openness to the other's alterity[1] (Crossley, 1996).

Egologic intersubjectivity, by its turn, encompasses an emphatic intentionality in which the I reflectively experiences the other, trough an imaginary transposition of himself to the other's place, by analogy.

Borrowing from Mead, Buber, and Merleau-Ponty, Crossley (1996) states that children are already born with a predisposition to communicate with others. This allows to them to realize that they are perceived by the others, as well as perceive them. However, this happens always from different points of view. Therefore, the egologic intersubjectivity emerges genetically as derived from radical intersubjectivity. Most important, it is trough this twofold intersubjective process that the I, the Me and the Other—in G. Mead's terms—will be constructed in its relational difference.

The desire of power and recognition, in Hegelian[2] terms, is always present in this process. It is a desire of the subject for the I-expansion and growing (Simão, 2006, p. 10). However, he never has the guarantee about the achievement of his desires, which are also changing in the process itself and for which quest he lasts striving for all his life (Boesch, 1991; Crossley, 1996).

The relationship of otherness can be preliminarily understood as the moments in which the difference between I and Other takes the form of radical intersubejctivity as though the figure and egological intersubjectivity the ground. Given this relational configuration, it is a moment when I-Other differences are pre-reflectively and strongly felt by the I, as well as his desire of surpassing himself in the direction of the Other. The Other, however, also in his always other embodiment, constant movement, and changing is never attained by the I in his trials. In this sense, we can see the otherness relationship as moments of I-Other relations when disquieting and rupture prevail over attunement and sharing (Simão, 2003). Or if we prefer, they are moments when the attunement and sharing take the form of experiencing differences. They are challenging and uneasy experiences.

The figure of the Other can also encompass the multiple selves of the I (Bakhtin, 1986; Holquist, 1990; Hermans, 1996).

Inspired on I-Me Jamesian distinction and on polyphonic Bakthinian metaphor, Hermans proposes that the I fluctuates among different voices oppositions in the self that interacts among them as if they were characters. Each of these voices has its own history and interacts with the others in a asking-answering process, sometimes agreeing, and sometimes dis-agreeing. As for the society, the self would be intrinsically involved in many dissonant and consonant voice oppositions, in a dynamic process of intersubjective exchange. These exchanges are also characterized by dom-inance and social power, either at the macrosocial level or at the micro-genetic level of subjectivity. They may cause ruptures and uneasy experi-ences for the self. Reorganizations after ruptures, by its turn, are easier during interactions with significant others (Hermans, 2002, pp. 147-148).

Uneasy experiences require symbolic reorganizations by the self, what means to make a transition from a previous constructed symbolic configu-ration to another. This new emerged configuration includes transforma-tive the former, in a kind of fitness process and thanks to the mediation of symbolic resources. The use of symbolic resources always involves ele-ments that circumscribe its character, in the sense that the I can not use unlimited resources at any time for any purpose. As the symbolic ele-ments are stabilized interactive patterns that turn to be a resource when used for someone, with some specific aim in a particular transition, are forcefully context-circumscribed (Zittoun, Duveen, Gillespie, Ivinsion, & Psaltis, 2003).

The process of using symbolic resources is future oriented and can occur in different levels of reflexivity. It is through the interpersonal inter-actions and from the use of symbolic resources that the objectives for interactions can be constructed. Symbolic resources offer temporally sta-ble definitions for goals, allowing for scheduling possible ways for their attainment. Symbolic resources are a special kind of constraint (Valsiner, 1998) that allows to the subject produce the necessary tension for realiz-ing differences between what is going on and what could be the respect to some future situation (Zittoun, et al., 2003).

Future situations usually involve relationship with others. In our per-spective, symbolic resources constraint the I-Other relationship for moments of radical intersubjectivity as figure, when ruptures and disqui-eting are experienced, as well as for moments when egological intersub-jectivity as figure allows for transitions and transformation in a new reflexive pattern of interaction.

Following we will present a more detailed discussion of these aspects with the aid of an empirical material, drawn from role-playing game ses-sions (RPG sessions).

SELF AND OTHERNESS ON THE ROLE-PLAYING GAME STAGE

We considered RPG sessions an interesting material to this kind of analy-sis because, on the one hand, the RPG is an inherent part of the players group's ordinary life, being then submitted to the same guiding principles of their lives. On other hand, RPG is a ludic space where players simulate some life contexts. Therefore, the I-other relationships are realized by the subjects in both levels, the other and the I as sometimes real and sometimes imaginary entities. These simultaneous and peculiar aspects of RPG led us to the supposition that its analysis could bring evidences about the constraints that take part on the establishment of otherness relations in contexts of I-other group relations. It could also give some hints about the implications of its unfolding to the continuity of those relationships. Additionally, it could also put in evidence some possibilities and limits of the game as symbolic device for the player's psychological development, as for instance in the direction in study by Chmielnicka-Kuter (2004).

Nevertheless, to go further in our discussion, it is necessary to present now some details of the interactive context from where we have draw our empirical material.

About Role-Playing Games

Dave Arneson and Gary Gygax published the first version of modern role-playing games in 1974. It was an adaptation of the war-games—very popular at those times—in order to play with fantastic singular characters. The first edition, by TSR Ltd., was labeled *Dungeons and Dragons* (D&D). It contained some elements of the strategy games as checkerboard, miniatures, and cards. The fantasy and myths described in D&D were based on J. R. R. Tolkien books *The Hobbit* and *The Lord of the Rings*, among others.

Role-playing games are like child pretend games, in which each child takes the role of a character, which is different from him, acting according to the plot as if they were those characters. In the first D&D edition, for example, it was pointed that imagining oneself as other person is the essence of RPG. Adults role-playing games, for instance, have explicit rules aiming to "solve discussions and make the game funny," as it is explicit in the folder of the first Brazilian edition of D&D (1991). D&D proposes to its players to imagine themselves as heroes of another time and another world "on a land of swords and castles," sorcery, treasures, and daily confrontation between "good and evil forces." Since its origins, many RPG supplements were written, trying to develop and multiply rules and game settings. Many systems of RPG (composed by a consistent group of rules) were developed with the intention of regarding a multiplicity of fiction universes (the campaign setting).

We selected a small excerpt of a dialogue from the second edition of *Advanced Dungeons and Dragons* (Gygax & others 1994, p. 10), which may well illustrate the game play:

DM: [Dungeon Master] You've been following this tunnel for about 120 yards. The water on the floor is ankle deep and very cold. Now and then you feel something brush against your foot. The smell of decay is getting stronger. The tunnel is gradually filling with a cold mist.

Fighter 1: I don't like this at all. Can we see anything up ahead that looks like a doorway, or a branch in the tunnel?

DM: Witching the range of your torchlight, the tunnel is more or less straight. You don't see any branches or doorways.

Cleric: The *wererat* we hit had to come this way. There's nowhere else to go.

Fighter 1: Unless we missed a hidden door along the way. I hate this place, it gives me the creeps.

Fighter 2: OK. We keep moving down the tunnel. But keep your eyes open for anything that might be a door.

DM: Another 30 or 35 yards down the tunnel, you find a stone block on the floor

Fighter 1: A block? I take a closer look.

DM: It's a cut block, about 12 by 16 inches, and 18 inches so high it looks like a different kind of rock than the rest of the tunnel.

Fighter 2: Where is it? Is it in the center of the tunnel or off to the side?

DM: It's right up against the side.

Fighter 1: Can I move it?

DM: (Checking the character Strength score). Yeah, you can push it around without too much trouble.

Fighter 1: Hmmm. This is obviously a marker of some sort. I want to check this area for secret doors. Spread out and examine walls.

DM: (rolls several dice behind his rule book, where players can't see the results). Nobody finds anything unusual along the walls. (Continue)....

As we can gather from this illustration, each game player takes the role of a character who should act in an imaginary adventure (Jackson, 1994). Among them, the one who has a differentiated actuation is called the Game Master (GM). The GM is like an arbitrator and narrator. He describes the scenes to the others players, telling them what they can perceive, see and listen to, etc., as characters. To that description, it is then added some object or person that could be perceived as 'a problem' by the players. The players, by their turn, describe what their characters will do, trying to solve the challenge emerged in the dialogue. Following, the GM describes the results reached with those character's actions, and so on.

The RPG system is composed by a set of rules detailed in a guidebook. There it is specified the main constitutive rules of the game. Besides the system, it is necessary also a scenery elaboration for playing the game. The scenery corresponds to an imaginary environment description, providing the character's actions context. When it is connected to a more extensive virtual world, is called campaign setting. The campaign is understood as a continuity of adventures, played by the same group of characters, related with a central theme and in the same virtual environment.

The Game Master is the group member responsible for guaranteeing the rules observance and the elaboration/expression of the scenery elements. Typologically, each character's action is based on a guiding file card, which is constructed taking into account interrelations between the system and the campaign setting. Each character's guiding file card has some quantitative values, which is established by the rolling of dices, or by some other random way of values stipulation. These obtained values are free distributed by the players in their guiding file cards, in addition to a predetermined set of attributes.[3] That is, in short, how each player elaborates his character's ID-sheet.

The Game Master elaborates the script of each adventure from a joint criterion: his assessment of the peculiarities of the players group and of their interests. It is so established a perceptive field for each character in the campaign setting.

At a certain point of the adventure, from the suggestions offered by the master, as well as from their own "motivations," the players can establish some objectives, clear enough for allowing to the character's behaviors.

In such a manner, the players group composes a relational system in which, at least, two different elements are mutually related: a Game Master and a player. The players' actions are then constantly differentiating and reorganizing the system, and part of this reorganization is registered in the character's guide-file card. Therefore, the guide-file cards are modified many times during the development of a campaign.

According to Steve Jackson (1994), "part of the objectives of a role-playing game is to make that the player faces the situation as his (or her) character would do" (p. 8). Thankful to its particularities and of being a kind of interpretive game, RPG makes possible life simulations between a Game Master and a player, as well as among players. In the set of the game virtual reality, the Game Master represents a virtual environment and each player is like a subject in front of the other characters. If we consider the systemic and co-constructed nature of human everyday reality, we can see the game set as a model near that, as we already have pointed.

The distancing of the actor from his own action is also present in RPG, as it can be frequently observed players' reflections about his/her characters' actions. In addition, they are used to having pauses during the game in order the players could plan the future actions of their characters. That reflexivity allows to the already referred distancing and to the construction of the characters as types.

Dialogues among RPG players put in evidence the human functioning directed to objectives which are, according to Ford and Lerner (1992, in Valsiner, 1998), oriented to the future and, in such a way, anticipatory of desired results. Steve Jackson (1994) emphasizes the active feature of that functioning. For him, RPGs are different from other leisure activities because of its participant vivid creative process: The Game Master tells the story but it is the players who are responsible for the creation of the characters that integrate the scene and change the course of the story during the adventure. So, players not only can, but are constrained to act according to their fantasies and desires rose by the imaginary situation.

Accordingly, RPG players are semiotic operators like, providing a generic orientation of their characters to the future. Each player creates an expectative on what he aims for his character at the macrolevel of the campaign formerly proposed by the Game Master, or at the microlevel of a specific adventure. In both cases, the player should select some current aspects for reaching some co-constructed objective. Furthermore, as we have just noted, the game itself imposes constraints to the player's possibilities for construction. These constraints are dynamic and temporary regulators of development. They are the result of negotiations and agreements among the group members and are part of the temporary and tacit group culture. They are also established by the rules of the system and campaign setting and by the Game Master's composition of the adventures as well.

Another important feature of RPG is its dependence on the cooperation among the players and among the characters, in order they can reach their aims (cf. Jackson, 1994). Thus, each player's interest should be coordinated to those of his group partners. In such a way, the actor is simultaneously collective and individually oriented. That happens as the personality system that composes a character gives the organization of its motivational predispositions, leading to the selection of actions aims. For each action could happen in cooperation, each subject should be involved in a process of differentiation, specialization, communication, and mutual exploration. Each group player explores the differential skills of his/her characters, resulting in integration among various systems. This integration makes the group capable of properly surpassing a great variety of problems emerged in the game.

Considering the aspects we have just highlighted, we can see that RPG can only be constituted as such in the intersubjective dialogue among its players. As typically for the dialogue situations, also here "each actor … actively transforms the communicative messages received from the other, trying to integrate them in his/her affective-cognitive basis which, by its turn, can also be subjected to transformations during that process" (Simão, 2006, p. 3). Those transformations take place thanks to the tension present in the dialogue, which in fact imposes itself as the proper condition for changes. As the tension is generated in the dialogue, it leads to affective-cognitive reconstructions in the actors, which can continue to dialogue or not, in one or another direction, producing these or those tensions, and so on (Simão, 2003, p. 6).

From that perspective, when tension is present in the dialogues among players, it can lead to the reconstruction of the group action proposals in some direction or, in other cases, to action proposals leading to the group fragmentation. For the purpose of coordination of those multiple courses of message reconstructions by the participants, in patterns of an efficient group action, the participants should establish a good communicative channel among them. That implies a relationship with the other as alterity, and demands a disposal for dialoguing or a dialogical attitude (Tunes & Bartholo, 2004).

In the RPG, character's choices are made in the context of the irreversibility of time. It is usual that, as the adventure develops, the Game Master makes some notes about the character's actions, which could be useful for supporting forthcoming adventures. At times some pauses in the game are consensually allowed, when the Game Master can reorganize the adventure and the players can reorganize their characters as well. The pauses indicate the striving of the participants for keeping some coherent line of the story development in the ever changing context of the game. As Jackson (1994) points, "in the end, the Game Master and the Players have created [and lived] a story … the story of engagements, disengagements, and challenges surpassed (or not) by they characters" (p. 8). The character's reorganization implies the establishment of some autonomy from the semiotic organized context which already present in the adventure. It also implies some change and restructuring of the Zone of Freedom Movements in the Game, promoting differentiated spaces for privileged actions, which are created by the canalization in the dialogue itself (Valsiner, 1998).

Origins and Production of Research Data

The whole set of our data has about ten hours of video recorded interactions, including game sessions, interviews between the researcher and the Game Master and interviews with the players.

During the sessions, while Game Master and players interact, the researcher proceeded the video recording. The sessions took place in 4 different days in which the group had spontaneously met to play, always in the same place where the group was using to meet. They did not meet for playing in between the sessions. The interviews to the Game Master and to the players were made in the same days of the sessions, with 5 minutes of duration each one.

The participants were university-educated or were finishing they bachelor in biology, at the University of São Paulo, Brazil. Some of the students were attending to the graduate program in biology, at the same university. The researcher was friend of them and had already played sometimes with them, before starting the research.

All the participants knew the objectives of the research and granted to give interviews and be recorded during playing the game.

At the beginning, the introduction of a camera on the game field and the interviews starting the game session produced some discomfort in some players. We could realize that by their constant look at the camera and by some expressions of excitement. Afterwards, however, they became at ease, as we observed by unbend dialogues and the progressive unconcern with the camera.

As the group aim in their meeting was to play RPG, we were worried about the disturbing character of being long interviewed for some of them. So we decided to invite player A, who had more free time, to be interviewed. These interviews were aimed to catch the player's perspective about the moment just filmed, as well as about its relation to the whole campaign. In addition, we also consulted the books on system and scenery they were using and the campaign design done by the Game Master as well.

We have chosen to focus on the game moments in which we could catch ruptures in the dialogue. This decision was settled on the presumption of the otherness relation as embedded in disquieting experiences that emerge in the I-Other relationships, for everything that disquiets and counteracts to the subject's expectations will affect something co-constructed in his relationship with others (Simão, 2003). Sharing, then, would imply intense intersubjectivity. Ruptures, on the other hand, could lead the subjectivities to the contact with the other's alterity.

We proceeded to the microgenetic analysis of the filmed episodes, trying to identify those moments in which alterity were in evidence. This analysis was done according to three main steps.

In the first step we have transcribed and systematized the verbal interactions among the players, as well as among the researcher and the players. The aim of this step was mainly to map the main symbolic resources that were constraining player's actions (Zittoun et al., 2003). For the achievement of this aim, we have also count to the additional help of the game book and the player's interviews.

In the second step we have proceeded to the interview analysis, trying to organize them according to the player's semantic referential. The semantic referential so identified were topics, spheres and themes present in the focus of their own expressions (Wertsch, 1993).

The third step was constituted by the identification of ruptures and transitions in the dialogues, whether among the characters or the players, which seemed to signalize the end of conversational turns (Zittoun et al., 2003).

These three steps have worked for generating data that allowed us to identify moments of symbolic rupture and stabilization in the dialogues, as well as its unfolding in the continuity of the playing.

This option should be understood in the frame of our option to practice research as a constructive activity, in which the researcher actively selects and proposes a way of viewing the nature of reality. It touches, therefore, to the possible forms of apprehending (or not) in the empiric event the manifestations suggested by the theoretical approach. It touches also to the possibilities of renewing the theoretical domain through the interpretation of the events (Branco & Valsiner, 1997; Bettoi & Simão, 2002; Simão, Bettoi, Canto, & Guimarães, 2005). In the last resort, they are related to the consistency and plausibility of theoretical-empirical bidirectional relationships, engendered in the interactive activities of the researcher. This activity, by its side, poses scientific and ethics questions to the psychological research. It is worth remembering that the multiple "social others" of the researcher concur for this process, being among them the main figure of the "research subject" who, according to our view, is in reality the main "co-constructor participant" (Simão, 1988).

Movements in I-Other Relationships in the RPG World: Ruptures, Transitions and Commuting Of Positions

In general, the data analysis have showed moments of tension and disquieting in the dialogues, which are typical of alterity relationships (Simão, 2003). These moments were alternated to those in which the dialogical tissue pointed to the convergence, sharing, and consensus whether on the conversational topic or on the relative interlocutors' positions.

The process of reorganization through symbolic resources was achieved basically through: (1) reversal role dominance between subjects, allowing shifts in the players' or characters' perspectives (Hermans, 1996, 2002); (2) distancing and reapproximation of their multiple selves, allowed by situated actions involving the imaginary selves and the other's (Hermans, Kempen, & van Loon 1992); (3) constraints and active selection of the symbolic resources by the players, establishing both a shared action field and particular scene versions in the course of interaction (Valsiner, 2001).

Ruptures, Transitions, and Dominance Inversions

In the set of RPG, the dominant figure is usually the Game Master. The first fragment we will present illustrates a moment marked by an inversion in this dominance. It is a moment that the Game Master gets surprised by the skillful of one of the players in the use of symbolic resources to attain his goals.

As we have pointed to earlier, the Game Master should be simultaneously the judge and the narrator in the game set. Additionally, he has to plan the script and try to guess of the following characters' actions. Last, he should sometimes interpret a nonplayer character, when that character was not chosen by any of the players and need to be interpreted in behalf of the script cohesion.

In the first of the following fragments, the campaign hold by the group for around a year (2003/2004) had as scenery a region called the *Moon Sea*,[4] placed in the *Forgotten Realms*. The *Moon Sea* is a deep and small lake, with independent state-cities around it, controlled by "evil groups of power." The central city is *Phlan*, which is presented partially impoverished (Greenwood & Grubb, 1995).

As reported by player A in his interview, initially the characters group went after an advertisement to adventurers' work, which could make a ransom. Getting the job, they started by investigating the old town of *Phlan*. While doing the job, they discovered that *Phlan* government has been corrupted by the *Barbarian Forces*. They changed then their initial objective—established by the ad—to that of investigating corruption. In the new investigation, they entered in contact with *Evil Forces* that were impregnated by some magic devices, like the *Gothmanis Armor Pieces*. The *Armor Pieces* have the power to allow to their users to invoke the *Daemons*, as well as to open the *Hell Portals*. The players' characters so decided to find out where the *Armor Pieces* were and destroy them. For that, they should to fight against *Fuzoul Chembryl's Army*. *Fuzoul Chembryl* was the preferred priest of the *God Bane*, elected to be the most important leader of *Bane's Church* in the future.

The first instrumental objective was then to take back the *Temple of the God Tyr*, used for the *Bane Cult*. Doing that, they hope both to weaken *Fuzoul Chembryl* and fortify some groups already opposing him.

The excerpt that will be presented next is a transition in face of a rupture provoked by the *Phlan War Warning*. It is not the direct fight yet, but an previous objective to be attained: to conquer the local leaders patronage for the union against the enemy.

In the focalized moment *Indigus* had left *Oromé*, in front of the *Phlan City Hall*. Next, he flied with his *Pegasus* to the old town, which needed his protection.

At this point the players discussed about a topic that was previously accorded, that is, if the *Tyr Knights* were inside or outside the city rampart. The Game Master turned then to the second Player saying:

M[1]:   Ok ... the Mayor is there. [Game Master talking as Game Master].

S: Mayor, I need to know what the actual situation is and consult you about the possibilities of joining our armies, because there are some other forces outside the city; they are already in combat with the Orcs. I want to know another thing.... [Player talking as his character].

M: Which are those forces? [Game Master, now, acting as a character, the Mayor]

We can see here a change in the self positions, when the Game Master assumed the character of the Mayor of Phlan and the Player S the character of Oromé. Exchanging positions have required the players to distance from themselves as players to experience the scene. Openness to a shared way of interaction by both players, at the same time keeping and distancing from their personal focus, was also implied in this fragment. On the other hand, the last talk of the Game Master in the fragment can be understood as trying to keep his dominant role, although through the voice of a character— the Mayor, a dominant character, by the way.

In some moments, the tone of the players' talks has changed, inaugurating a more prereflexive and unconditional interaction, as illustrated in the next fragment, which happened just after the previous one:

S: ... yours ... our team forces those are attacking these evils Orcs, which are invading.

M: But why they didn't attack yet, those ... those Orcs came without ... without guardian warnings.

S: They are just in combat, now I want to know if your reinforcement from Fuzoul Chembryl will come or not? Will arrive or not?

M: Wait, which reinforcement? [Game Master, as Phlan Mayor, serious tone]

F: Be cool, S. [Comment of a player, which character was not in the scene].

In this fragment we can note that Game Master's question changed the course of Player S's speech for few moments. After his fast answer, the Player did a symbolic rupture through a new question, shifting the semantic reference from the actual situation to a future possibility. At this moment, Player F, whose character was not in the scene, has noted the rupture provoked by Oromé's trick and discouraged Player S of going ahead in that approach to the Master's character (i.e., the Mayor). F's speech indicated that Oromé's intimidation strategy had been pretentious, in contrast with a considerable asymmetry in his relation with the Mayor. She (the Mayor) reacted seriously to Oromé's questioning, signalizing it as a misunderstanding of Oromé's talking. His question provoked a rupture in Mayor's expectation that Oromé did not know anything about her actual government and the city situation.

S: How? You didn't have a partnership with him?

M: No, no....

S: No?

M: I have a, the partnership that I just told you, the partnership....

S: But isn't a city allied to yours? (M bends his face, M and S eye one another and smile, A claps).

S: Did you like? [A comment as player, noncharacter]

M: Yes I did. Put about a two hundred points of experience there [in the S's guide-file card]. [Comment as Game Master, noncharacter]

A: S is a son of a bitch! He didn't say that anything would happen here! [Player's comment, which character was not in scene]

At this moment, S have had actively selected a gap in Mayor's discourse and utilized it in favor of reaching his group objectives. We have indications that this selection was planned even before the adventure starting. In his previous interview, S has expressed his desire that his character could have a dialogue to the Mayor. When asked about his expectations for the next session, S said: "I ... I think that we have to succeed in trying to talk.... Take back the temple, and, I wait that we succeed in taking back the temple. And I also want solve some quarrels with the Mayor, you know. I think that we have much more issues to solve after that."

S did not complete his sentence at the beginning of the above talk probably because the Game Master was present. Master's previous knowledge about the plans could prevent the surprising aspect at the moment of the game itself. The Mayor's talk, by its turn, gave evidences of a gap in justifying the fact of not have been taken into account the help of an ally in the war. This talk produced a rupture in the Master's dominance in that moment, who was caught in a surprising situation, smiling and rewarding S with the game resource of displaying experience points.[6]

This situation of alternating in player's positions and dominances points to the dialogue among voices in diverse worlds dialogically structured by the self. These voices are related to a context of fantasy and to the face-to-face perceptive reality (Hermans, Kempen, & van Loon, 1992).

The other players that were following the scene celebrated the new dialogic situation, as it would increase their power over the game scenery. The celebrating reactions were clearly pre-reflexive and affective, as for instance their applauses and exalted comments.

M   Ok, what you.... Ok, I wouldn't count with Fuzoul Chembryl.

S: No, I have other people outside and the Tyr Knights those are here to; ... those are here and are just protecting your city from the Orcs.

M: Unite the guardians and go support the archers at ... at ... at towers, our guardians ... our local guardians will ... so they will react....

S: Yes, we need to protect the old part, I have listened callings from that direction.

M: Yes..., yes, no just ... just, I just know about these attacks. We have to protect all fronts, in all ... in ... in, in all combat fronts ... here!

S: I want your permission to command the ... our armies inside the town.

M: Don't disappoint me! (The group reacts euphorically).

In the above fragment, the Game Master and the players were back to their character positions in the dialogue. The Mayor perceives herself as more fragile than before, because it became explicit that she couldn't count to Fuzoul Chembryl. Her fragility is clearly expressed in her prereflexive truncated speech. On the contrary—and simultaneously—it also became explicit that Oromé had indeed the resources to collaborate to a goal shared by both, that is, the salvation of the town.

The asymmetric positioning in the dialogue is recovered, but now with reversal dominance: Oromé has reinforced his dominant position, pointing to the fact that he knew the most pressing problems of the town at that moment. The reversal shifting has culminated with the Mayor's agreement to Oromé's request. Indeed, the Mayor could not deny that request any more, because her own perspective was channeled by the players' action. Now she was seeing the option proposed by Oromé as the unique for solving the war conflict.

It is interesting to note at this point that a residue of the transition from the rupture caused by Oromé's action has constituted in a new field for the characters' action, the possibility of controlling the army. Oromé reached his goal because he could actively select a gap in the Mayor's discourse related to the problem of saving the town from the war.

The euphoric reactions of the Players can be seen as a moment in which radical intersubjectivity is figure and egological intersubectivity, as well as reflexive thinking, are ground.

S: (Answering the mayor) don't care about that.

M: So, go and…. [As the mayor] "Unleash hell above them" [talking in English] [players smile]. Unleash hell above them [now translating it in Portuguese]. Go! [clapping] Ok, you have, now, the control of all … all city guardians [talking as Game Master]

F: Carte blanche.

M: Carte blanche for beating. You have your unity there, already prepared, later we will give the … the statistic data … F (backing to F), when you have left….

S: I am going to the rampart, there…

M: Ok, cool … anh … when you have arrived….

In this fragment we can note in Master's speech an alternating of positions from the Phlan Mayor to the Game-Player. The latter position seems not be exactly the Game-Master position, but one of the players in a group rooting, supporting the group. Next, by confirming F's desire, authorizing him to act as the Army Leader, the Master has defined a new scene configuration.

The main focus of tension in the scene was overcome when the players have reached their objective of conquering support for the war. This point was considered as the main condition for the campaign continuity, for pursuing broader objectives.

After the mentioned transition, it was possible to go ahead with the game under a new semantic referential constituted by the relationship between Player F and his character, Indigus.

Ruptures, Transitions, and Continuities in Interactions

Considering that RPG relations happens, as some social interactions, through communicative actions mutually directed among involved persons, now we will analyze how those communicative actions takes place on ruptures, transitions and continuities relations during the game.

In fact, the interaction among players on RPG session is through scenery and characters verbal descriptions. Observing game sessions we noted that its dialogues are permeated by discussions about rules, questions about scenery composition and constant reflexive work, discussions and evaluation of characters actions and players attitudes. The communicative process propitiated on RPG is complex thankful the multiplicity of voices and themes that compose its interactions.

RPG stage permitted us to observe, recurrently, many types of polarities emergences. For example, from our selected session excerpt, we could establish dialogical oppositions, and multivoicedness supplementary convergences, between: *Game Master and players*, negotiating a scenery symbolic resource (Phlan army); *Player and character*, with Game Master representing Phlan mayor and player S representing his character Oromé; *system and campaign setting*, with Game Master experience points distribution to player because of his good character representation, or when he talks about statistic subsequently necessary to army analyzes; *fantasy and reality* on the voices exchange among their characters to a third person analysis of the lived scene, when player S asked the Game Master if he liked his representation; *player and player*, noted at the first S representation disapproval, with players F and A comments and gestures and his insistence on represented strategy.

We think that, dialogues are essential element in RPG. As we could see, it facilitates the subjects' experimentation of what is diverse from their perspective, either on speaking content or selves in relation positions. Dialoging with others can open the subject to a possibilities field related to experiment something that did not might be, but however, appears be. Heterogeneity gives ruptures on expectancies and uneasiness to subjects (Simão, 2003).

This open-way of experiencing diversity creates a new meaning field and facilitates the externalization of changes on relations with others.

In fact, the studied sessions, permitted us to observe novelties emergencies in relation to each symbolic resource methodically analyzed. The excerpt used to illustrate evinced some of that emergences. Referring to the RPG System, the mass combat, arisen from playing with illustrated conquered armies, would be subsequently practiced with a players group invented rule. On the campaign setting level, players conquered the possibility of using symbolic elements, as the inner Phlan armies, which were before of the exclusive use of the Game Master. On characters dimension, the accumulation of experience points, either earned on that scene, after permitted a level crossing to S character and the player could select new resources—skills, abilities, life points and so forth—to him. On the campaign sphere, the possibility of use those armies allows players realize some of theirs campaign goals and the construction of new objectives.

In this way, either those moments, as a dialogical implication (Wertsch, 1991, p. 13), the subjects can approach multiples realities representations. Facing ruptures on expected interaction with other, each subject can recognize their own identity while linked to his historicity, as well as legitimate other's identity as different from him. In sum, each subject can tacitly recognize that the other is also a subject acting through mediational means, with his representations of "reality." The key-point is that those representations are usually "foreign representations" if compared to the subject's own representations, which opens to him the possibility of entering in otherness relationship. In this case, the subject apprehend the other as a comparable subjectivity even that empirically different of him/herself (Simão, 2006).

This process depends on the permeability, or porosity, of a subject, allowing exchanges on current dominance context. In the dialogue with the mayor, for example, her availability to listen Oromé, through a conducted process of dominance reduction allows the rupture and a transition to a new situation in the context of the sitied Phlan.

Uneasy experiences (Zittoun et al., 2003) are fundamental on RPG adventures involved processes. Following the *Game Master Advanced Dungeons & Dragons Guidebook*, "the encounters [that happen on adventures] are motors which puts the game in movement," and more "the presence of an active external force [which can be comprised as a Game Master controlled element] and the possibility of changes based on Player decision, are factors that makes the genuine RPG encounter." On "genuine" encounter, despite apparently an external observer cannot see many things happening, Players need to make significant decisions and are faced with something unknown, which they have to take the chance of discover what is (Gygax, 1995a). Players are faced, following this, with uneasiness experiences that require symbolic reorganizations to continue playing, either on the same direction, either in a new way.

We could observe the use of symbolic resources, for example, when a character expressed the possibility of use a magic to help his/her group partners (other characters) transforming them physically stronger face to an unexpected superior enemy during a recorded RPG session.

The notion of use corresponds, in this case, to employment of objects as a device to act upon or from physical and social world and the psych reality. Symbolic resources reorganizes chaos and uncertainties of present situation, as it appears to each actor, suggesting possibilities of act and inevitably producing new problems (new symbolic elements). In this process of transformation, are the symbolic devices that sustain the reorganization. It is internalized, modifying experience understandings, and making available readjustments from new experiences (Zittoun et al., 2003, pp. 418-419).

From the selected excerpt used on this work, we could observe that player S used his knowledges about the war at Phlan as a symbolic resource that organized his action face to the mayor. Among some used symbolic resources was certainly war eminence, Fuzoul Chembryl treason, his character group army allies and the mayor fragility supposition. This fragility, attached to the mayor was a central reference to Oromé action. Face to her, the character had to use these symbolic resources linking to himself non-her power threatened identity elements. Otherwise, he has to arrange effective conditions to help her on city liberation. As previously detached, player S was, indeed, able to make it in his role-playing interaction.

Intersubjectivity Ways and Self-Constructions on RPG

Until here, we were talking about dialogic oppositions at semantic references, from a RPG session. Now, we will emphasize the context of personality systems (the human subjective self), which produces presented utterance dynamics.

Microgenetics ruptures and transitions analysis on dialogic interactions among RPG players permitted some reflections about intersubjective relations on game and other fields. As we could observe, some rupture moments was marked by uneasiness experiences. In other words, those experiences were out of expectance and leads the subjects to think and act affective-cognitively reorganizing their lived interactions (Simão, 2003). Those uneasy experiences were brought from other's actions, which make evident different perspectives to the subject. In this way, reorganizing the field of experience meanings, making transitions implicates, to each subject, try some interaction ways with the others, and so, try changes their own intersubjective actuation.

In some cases, symbolic resources, semiotically regulating, and canalizing actions, had unawareness and unintentional use. Despite this, as Zittoun et al. (2003, pp. 419-420) says, the use always happen in interaction contexts upon other look presence.

We noted radical intersubjectivity (Crossley, 1996) many times, during RPG sessions. Indication of this interaction way, we could detach: from euphoric players reactions reaching a goal, for example, when they reached support and Phlan army control; from dialogue rhythm accent transformations when interpreting characters; and, fundamentally, from players availability and openness to scene representation.

In our studies, the egological subjectivities (Crossley, 1996) perception way, for example, permitted Player S plan a scene. He actuated to reach his character and characters group objective according to his interview declared intention. Besides, in an other dimension, according to his personal and friends group objective. Following this, we can differentiate the recognition dimension in two self systems, supposed to a player: since Oromé intended recognition of Phlan Mayor, player S intended the Game Master recognition.

Besides, we can note that imagination is a intersubjective phenomenon, at least because the imaginary activities are normally collectives, being shared in narratives or in subjects constructed images. A RPG character composition, while a personal and creative construction, is ruled and Campaign Setting possibilities are constrained. The experience of an imaginary other of I, player lived from RPG sessions, during character interpretation and according to the cited imaginative process, brings some elements of personal players culture. On the studied session, players characters constitution was an intersubjective work, which all players actively engaged, suggesting (canalizing) possibilities and constraining others, in a way that is coherent with some group shared objective.

RPGs can be considered a team game, because the character is an adventurers group member that needs to work together. Nevertheless, part of game reflection is made on a player voice demanding cooperation, inclusive, with the player which used assume the opponent position, the Game Master. This condition is because the group enjoying demands constitution of a identified relationship with this frequently power posited element. The identification, however, is made in common narrative construction context that can follow unexpected ways, as just discussed.

Self-Positions and Selectivity on RPG

We came discussing dialogic relations since their multiple system oppositions, RPG manifested. These relations were marked by ruptures, dominance, and relevance inversions on power positions, related to otherness emergence aspects. Besides this, we made an approach to intersubjective relations, focusing on self system and its ways of intersubjective interaction. Now, we will contemplate the self polyphony on intersubjective and intrasubjective conditions that its enable, since a RPG sessions study.

Following Merleau-Ponty, Hermans, Kempen, and van Loon (1992) situate the body as the element that enables the perception. The body is in the world and is composed of its same materiality. Body provides a specific position, which permits the occurrence of subject-world relation. Following this, the perception does not is a private thing, it occurs between the other and the I. It is not the experience of objects, but a dialectic process on organisms' interaction with their environment (Crossley, 1996).

From RPG narratives, the scenery is the perceptive element, since the characters point of view. During the game, the scenery demonstrated to be result of dialogical interaction between Game Master and players. The scenery elements description is made from symbolic resources, initially elaborated by the Game Master, among a multiple possibilities of constructions. The campaign, in its way, occurs in a world previously described and imagined by RPG authors (Greenwood & Grubb, 1995a, 1995b). The Game Master presentation has to maintain a strength coherence inspired on these material content. Its presentation has, besides, to be coherent with characters positions on the scenery. Players, in their turn, will select some aspects from GM presentation, related with their character future actions, reconstructing their particular perspective.

Sometimes, the Game Master dominance on description is emphatically questioned and he is obliged to re-elaborate its description, including the other's perspective. This process leads to dominance exchanges at some of these narrative elements constitution. In general, this exchange is linked to comprehension divergences of what happened at story. Its causes a rupture with transition demands to a more organized context, with less tension. In other way, the characterized GM perception of imaginary world can be player canalized in new ways, through questioning and characters actions.

On RPG, we can observe this phenomenon in some analyzed oppositions. For example, the player historicity is different of his/her character; and the RPG System has a construction relatively different from the campaign setting.

The construction of a new rule, in a campaign studied moment, is an important element to think the interaction system-campaign setting (including in this pole, narrative fantastic aspects). Face to an imminent combat between the armies, was necessary to players the use of rules to play with many characters in the same time. The system used, nevertheless, had a gap in relation to this function rule, nondescribed on its manual. They needed to create a rule. The mass combat situation, observed on the first section, indicated the player's gap recognition between their necessities and the symbolic resources guide handbook contented. Their invention extended game field actuation possibilities. The new created symbolic resources could be structured as new constraints that passed to be part of the "intersubjective culture" of that group and, occasionally, can transform the "game culture," in a possible interaction of their proposition with others RPG groups.

Embedded in rules and power relations marked social context, which constraints subjective interaction possibilities, intersubjective relations are asymmetric. On dialogical interactions, asymmetry is always present, at least because who speak/acts has the initiative privilege to show his/her point of view. This privilege, however, is not a permanent propriety of a subject, and power positions exchange in interaction turns. This relation, nevertheless, can follow rigid patterns (with little submission to novelty emergence). It coexists with more creative patterns, characterized by co-actives improvisations, with more extended self-discovering possibilities (Hermans, 2002, pp. 150-153). Besides, the dominance is present, neither just at actual subject interactions, but either at imaginary interactions. Imaginary dialogues can also be extremely asymmetric (Hermans, 1996, pp. 9-10).

On the illustrative excerpt selected, as we said, we could clearly observe a dominance inversion between Oromé and Phlan mayor: an inversion that occurred linked to expectation broken surprise context. Player S elaborated a rupture that destabilized the mayor dominance upon the character, reaching from her confidence and resources to actuate as his shared goal of city salvation.

Game Master and players porosity to otherness messages needs to permeate some moments of all RPG campaign curse. Is interesting to note that, is just from this, afterwards some adventures, that the game can be organized around a central theme, with an explicit group shared objective. In other words, something becomes part of all players desire field. Face to this central objective, situated as a future realization possibility in comparison to the actual context, players are involved with sub goals, considered necessary and in the same way to a major realization.

An evidence of this process is the studied campaign title, Game Master created, that we obtained from the first played adventure script: "Tales of Unknown" (originally in English). This title indicates, immediately, non-definition of a central campaign theme. Otherwise, it points that the group will leads with something strange and possibly uneasiness. Saying in other way, the theme is a "non-theme" in relation such as usual thematic definitions. According to an excerpt obtained from campaign introduction, the Game Master points that "the principal game theme is offer some missions apparently isolated to the players, but in really, it is part of a bigger objective ... part of this objective is discover it." Despite the Game Master indicates a "bigger objective" existence, he does not make it explicit and, either, he indicates its discovery as sub-objective. At the first interview realized with Game Master, he said "all the story was about it, the armor that would be joined and arouses many disasters. So is ... characters mission avoid that these disasters arrive to the city." This affirmation points to Game Master supraplayer role on campaign conduction. He appears to be possessor of a privileged knowledge since the beginning.

In fact, the possibility that the Game Master, since the beginning of his campaign plan, just had established a final objective could not be discarded. At the final campaign moment he appeared be experimented a process in coherence with his intentions.

In this process, collective social voices are not just internalized by the subjects, but also actively reconstructed in a personal way. It happens because of the dynamic process that occurs in the dialogue among collective voices and those just organized on the personal systemic spectrum. The self works as a system that regulates and controls changes in function of stability and flexibility, not just in respect to immediate experience, but constructing abstracts meanings that constraint the process as a whole. This construction also creates a semiotic hierarchy of affective meanings (Valsiner, 2001), more or less defined, generalizing some contents of experience in a flexible way and avoiding similar generalizations in others.

As we pointed, the Game Master appears to recognize the coauthor level of campaign. It implicates availability to emergence of something not yet present as a symbolic resource, but at some moment become to be a voice on the representational group system. Since the moment that it happens, the new objective becomes a strength characters actions constraint element. So, the desire sphere emerged, expressed by objectives and goals to be reached, and attained to the game narrative. In other words, emerges the relation between the desirable and the possible, which the adjustment or socket is obtained with intersubjective negotiations between Game Master and players. With this, players perceive themselves also as campaign coauthors. From imaginary characters corporeality, they live the campaign setting inherent opacity unveil and the game objective negotiation as discovery. This idea is recurrent at some moments of realized interview:

Researcher: What each of you think that will happen on today's session?
Player F: ... what have is go upon the guys and discover what is happening ...
Player D: ... so we will start to know what will happen on the continuity ... ahn ... on the adventure continuity ...
Researcher: What you want that happen?
Player F: What is behind is a story, ok? And we are participating of a story ... my part has to do and see what will happen ... have to accomplish and play and see what happen.

Player A narrative, presented on contextual detached scene to this work, shows a campaign objectives establishment process. This process was desire oriented from an intersubjective relation with the initial Game Master proposition. In those moments, they saw their characters inside a nebulous and opaque context that caused tension. The Game Master did not make clearly explicit what had been done. Otherwise, through façades that hides possible previous planned elements to the situation, he attracted and conducted characters and players to unknown ways.

Gygax (1995b) orienting the Game Master demands from him a planning and awareness of his objectives about a storytelling adventure. He orients too, a presentation to players, in an indirect way, using hints:

Each game session has to has an objective (or objectives). Some are constants and is applicable to any AD&D game. Other depends on the campaign, the woof, characters levels and specific adventure. All objectives have to be clear, comprehensible to the players look or decipher them from found hints during the game. (Gygax, 1995b, p. 66)

The created tension in the group, by its turn, demands some dialogues during the game sessions. It over-changes the objective. Sometimes the Game Master can be surprised with the symbolic resources that players use in their symbolic elaborations, as we just showed.

According to Hermans (1996), imaginary others, which permeates our life in private dialogues, are clearly perceived as outside from ourselves. They are result of a derivation from "objective" reality others (pp. 6-8). Complementarily, Crossley (1996) points from this dialogues that the Me, usually present in autobiographical narratives, helps the subject to identify him/herself for the I and the others. It constructs and holds the continuity sense during time (Crossley, pp. 59-60).

The studied session semantic reference analysis facilitate us identify that dialogues which establishes greater tension focus make significant transformations on scenery field, either on characters characteristics, on game system elements, either on campaign continuity definition. Besides, this analysis presented symbolic elements on transition process after ruptures, beyond that described in RPG guidebooks on campaign settings. Among these elements, we detached particular strategies from different groups and persons involved in the game: own skills creation (definition) to a character; resources negotiation strategy; peculiar players' imagination with a specific fantasy world creation.

In relation to game field emerged themes, we saw that RPG session continuity depends on transition conclusions from emerged ruptures. During the game, nevertheless, many themes emerge and compete among themselves, to be focused in the game process. It remits to player's selectivity in relation to many problems solution. This selectivity, as symbolic resources use, can occur in different reflexivity levels of interactive subjectivities. Opting to a problem solution, players have their symbolic elements affected, exchanging theme dominances, creating new dialogue focus. We could observe that RPG transition processes did not occur in a linear way, with the solution of just a problem later the other.

Otherwise, many ruptures can emerge after a elaborated resolution of another, before emerged. The problem option selection depends on players' desire negotiation, producing definitive alterations on possibilities actuation game field. This construction process can be exemplified with the RPG "encounter" situations. As we tried to show, in these moments the player is obliged to think a choice involving significant character changes in his/her contact with a thing, which relation will produce some unpredictable things. On the studied situation, the "encounter" between Oromé and Phlan mayor produced significant changes to all characters and to the adventure in general way. That encounter happened as narrative in time parallel with Indigus scene (F player character), which went defend the "old city" ramparts. Despite the simultaneity of events in a narrative comprehension, the Game Master and players corporeality did not allowed this parallel scene experimentation at the session stage.

The most important group considered problem was experimented in priority. The player's success on this occasion, in its turn, decreased the importance of others problems, previously emerged, as Tyr Knights, the general Phlan situation, the old city part and so forth. From that scene, the adventure was rapidly directed to mass combat. In this sense, a new theme could be chased since its importance to the campaign and its relation with the group player's objectives.

Some aspects of relation dynamics face to ruptures and observed ways of doing transitions, involving the actors' multiples selves, lead us to some suppositions about the desire role on the tension RPG field. Next, we will summarize, as final considerations, ours principal suppositions about this.

Final Considerations

The just presented analysis put in evidence the orientation to the future by the players. However, if we consider that they were not obliged to play—in the strict sense of the word—an important aspect of futurity comes to evidence. It is the desire for playing, which put the dynamic of the game and specially the Master direction as key-points to the maintenance of playing. Additionally, to consider the dimension of desire can also be important for understanding player's openness to alterity.

The Game Master's actions are one of the most important sources of rupture during the sessions, creating semiotic gaps to be fulfilled by player's symbolic actions.

However, as for the "opacity" in the meanings of players' actions for the Master, the formers also create symbolic ruptures in the meaning tissue of the game.

In this dialogic interplay, the Master tries to picture the desires and intentions of the players more clearly, asking them about they characters' actions. As far as the Master obtains some explicitness, the situation comes to reorganization—in the hierarchical terms already referred—giving raise for new meanings, "opacities" and meaning ruptures.

As the Game Master needs to describe what happened after each characters action, he needs to make transitions and reorganizing the preexistent construction about the scene at each moment of rupture. This reorganization is made at each game turn, according to two possible ways: (1) the Game Master can change his script, causing a rupture in relation to his previous intentions and suppositions; (2) thankful to his role attributions, he can resignifying the characters' verbalized actions, in order to coherently fitting their actions to the initial script. In the first case, players' dominance on the game narrative course takes place; in the second case, the Game Master's desires, expectancies, and intentions have dominance over the Players'.

In both cases, however, as far as the players observe the effects of their actions, they try to re-elaborate their knowledge about strategies for organizing the symbolic resources present in the story. They can also use that re-elaborated knowledge for continuing to select and create new sub-goals, in order to attain their main goals (Boesch, 1991).

Besides, as the Master privileges both the group diversion and his own, he is constantly interested in acting on the players' field of desires. For that he allows them to conquer some of their goals step by step.

However, if players' dominance persists for a long time in that co-constructed affective-cognitive field of meanings, in the opposite direction of Master's desires, he will try to redirect the happening flux again to his former goals. He can create, for instance, a new scene by handling symbolic resources, in order to constraint the characters' actions to directions more compatible to his desires.

At these moments of the process the group dynamic can even reach a temporary state of reduced tension related to the Master-Players oppositions, thanks to the reorganization of the desires of both parts in a new and more convergent one. This new negotiated organization of the desires usually takes a form of a Game goal, added to the formers in a way of fitting to the previous co-constructed narrative.

In the frame of intersubjective relationships, the character interpretation allows to each of the players to experience him in other place, yielding a confrontation with other voices present in his subjectivity. Borrowing from Mead, Crossley (1996) points to the fact that this kind of experience is in the basis of the I's imaginary projections to the future, allowing to an internal dialogue which leads to the desire acknowledgement.

According to our analysis, the players could identify and differentiate their desires as players, in the frame of the diversion, as well as their characters' desires in the frame of the fictional world. While conducting the game, the Master narrated and supervised the game, and also rewarded the players granting them points for experience, devices, information and social recognition of characters in the game scene.

Playing RPG implies, therefore, the development of investigative methods of I-Other and I-I relations, where the other's desires are always supposed, questioned, and confronted to the I's desires. It seems that many questions involved in RPG relations lead to a tacit hermeneutic investigation of other's action meanings. This reminds us some psychological professional practices, like in the comprehensive clinical approaches, where to unveil desires plays a central role in the intersubjective client-therapist relations. The same for some research practices in Psychology, as in the contemporary idiographic approaches. In all cases, each actor (player, character, client, psychotherapist, researcher, research participant) creates the narrative of his unique story, as a clipped re-elaboration of the group story, needing for that taking into account that the others are making the similar as well as different processes.

If we go to Boesch's ideas, we can find a frame that allows us to summarize and at the same time enlarge the relationship between goals and desires. According to him (Boesch, 1991), decisions about goals are mainly of subjective-affective order. The goal appeal is fundamental in this process, because it constrains the establishment of consistent (or not) I-world relationships.

This is so because the objectives are one of the ways through which the subject is related to the unknown and unpredictable world he feels outside him. Through the establishment of goals, the subject pictures a more predictable and stable future, although momentary.

The dynamic of this process functions in terms of the relationship among *should-values*, *is-values* and *action potential* (Boesch, 1991).

Should-value and *is-value* are concepts based on the Pierre Janet's distinction between the *anticipation of action*, on the one hand, and *realizing the result of the real action*, on the other hand. In real life situations, the effective result of an action never corresponds exactly to its anticipation by the subject-actor. This means that there never is a perfect correspondence between *should-value* and *is-value*. At each step the actor subjectively realizes differences or deviants between what is desired and expected and what really happened, trying to minimize that difference. The *action potential*

> might be defined as the extent to which one feels confident of meeting one's personal standards in any kind of situation' (Boesch, 1991, p. 108). It is defined by the 'capacity that an individual attributes to him/herself of doing actions with a positive valence and of avoiding those with a negative one', where the valences 'refer to attractions, hopes and beliefs according to which we try to guide our actions', with the action potential based mainly on anticipations and prospectives, although also depending on previous experiences. (Boesch, 1979, p. 24)

From this perspective, we can say that through interactions like those in the RPG set, I and Other quest for mutual influence, aiming to make symbolic transitions in face of ruptures in their fictional and "real" world visions, to attain their goals. Attaining goals are, most of all, reaching some possibility of actualizing their desires and increasing their action potential. That means feeling himself nearer to his beliefs, hopes, and desires. For a slight moment, it is true, but it can reverberate.

ACKNOWLEDGMENTS

The data here analyzed and discussed are part of a research conducted by first author, under the advisement of second author, and supported by The State of São Paulo Research Foundation, Brazil-FAPESP (Proc. no. 03/12190-7).

NOTES

1. We are taking here the notion of otherness as discussed by Simão (2006).
2. Hegelian meaning of Other's power addresses to the subject's desire of being desired by the Other and being recognized by the Other as a legitim consciousness.
3. The possible character attributes are stipulated according to the system/campaign setting or through the negotiations among Game Master and Players.
4. We will use italics for signalizing the names of imaginary places and characters.
5. The used letters A, C, D, F, and S make reference to players and the letter M represents the Game Master.
6. The group, in this case, normally uses the third D&D edition rules but players agreed about use some AD&D rules, besides.

REFERENCES

Bakhtin, M. M. (1986). *Speech genres and other late essays* (C. Emerson & M. Holquist, Eds.). Austin: University of Texas Press.

Bakhtin, M. M. (1997). *Estética da criação verbal* [The esthetic of verbal creation]. São Paulo, Brazil: Martins Fontes.

Bergson, H. (1896). Matière et mémoire: Essai sur la relation du corps avec l'esprit [Matter and memory: Essay on the relationship between body and spirit]. In A. Robinet (Ed.), *Oeuvres* [Collected works] (pp. 159-379). Paris: Presses Unversitaires de France.

Bergson, H. (1934). La pensée et le mouvement: Essais et conférences. In: *Ouvres*, pp. 1248-1482.

Bettoi, W., & Simão, L. M. (2002). Entrevistas com profissionais como atividade de ensino-aprendizagem desejável na formação do psicólogo [Interviewing professionals as a desirable teaching-learning activity for the psychological formation]. *Psicologia: Reflexão e Crítica, 15*(3), 613-624.

Boesch, E. E. (1979) Action et Object - deux sources de l'identité du moi. [Action and object: Two sources of the me identity] In P. Tap (Ed.), *Identité Individuelle et Personalization* (pp. 23-37). Privat.

Boesch, E. E. (1991). *Symbolic action theory and cultural psychology.* Berlin-Heidelberg: Springer-Verlag.

Branco, A. U., & Valsiner, J. (1997). Changing methodologies: A co-constructivist study of goal orientations in social interactions. *Psychology and Developing Societies, 9*(1), 35-64.

Chmielnicka-Kuter, E. (2004, August). *Role-playing game heroes as partners of internal dialogues.* Paper presented at the 3rd international conference on The Dialogical Self, Warsaw, Poland.

Crossley, N. (1996). *Intersubjectivity: The fabric of social becoming.* London: Sage.

Gygax, G., & others (1994). *Advanced dungeons & dragons: Player's handbook* (2nd ed.). Cambridge, England: TSR.

Gygax, G. (1995a). *Advanced dungeons & dragons: Livro do jogador* (2nd ed.) São Paulo, Brazil: Abril Jovem

Gygax, G. (1995b). *Advanced dungeons & dragons: Livro do Mestre (*2nd ed). São Paulo, Brazil: Abril Jovem

Greenwood, E., & Grubb, J. (1995a). *Conquistando os reinos* [Conquering the realms]. São Paulo, Brazil: Abril Jovem.

Greenwood, E., & Grubb, J. (1995b). *Uma viagem aos reinos.* São Paulo, Brazil: Abril Jovem.

Herbst, D. P. (1995). What happens when we made a distinction: an elementary introduction to co-genetic logic. In T. Kindermann & J. Valsiner, J. (Eds.), *Development of person-context relations* (pp. 67-79). Hillsdale, NJ: Erlbaum.

Hermans, H. J. M. (1996). Opposites in a dialogical self: Constructs as characters, *Journal of Constructivist Psychology, 9*(1), 1-26

Hermans, H. J .M. (2002). The dialogical self as a society of mind: Introduction. *Theory & Psychology, 12*(2), 147-160.

Hermans, H. J. M., Kempen, H. J. G., & van Loon, R. J. P (1992). The dialogical self: Beyond individualism and rationalism. *American Psychologist, 47*(1), 23-33.

Holquist, M. (1990). *Dialogism: Bakhtin and his world.* New York: Routledge.

Jackson, S. (1994). *GURPS* [Generic Universal Role Playing System]*: Módulo Básico.* São Paulo, Brazil: Devir Livraria Ltda.

Linell, P. (1995). Troubles with mutualities: Towards a dialogical theory of misunderstanding and miscommunication. In I. Marková, C. Graumann, & K. Foppa (Eds.), *Mutualities in dialogues* (pp. 175-213). Cambridge, MA: Cambridge University Press.

Marková, I. (1997). On two concepts of interaction. In M. Grossen & B. Py (Ed.), *Pratiques Sociales et Mediations Symboliques* (pp. 23-44). Berlin, Germany: Peter Lang.

Rommetveit, R. (1992). Outlines of a dialogically based socio-cognitive approach to human cognition and communication. In A. H. Wold (Ed.), *The dialogical alternative: Towards a theory of language and mind* (pp. 19-44). Oslo: Scandinavian University Press.

Simão, L. M. (1988). *Interação verbal e construção de conhecimento* [Verbal interaction and knowledge construction]. Unpublished doctoral dissertation, Institute of Psychology of the University of São Paulo, Brazil.

Simão, L. M. (2003). Beside rupture—disquiet: Beyond the other—alterity. *Culture & Psychology, 9*(4), 449-459.

Simão, L. M. (2006). Why "otherness" in the research domain of semiotic-cultural constructivism? In L. M. Simão & J. Valsiner (Eds.), *Otherness in question: Labyrinths of the self*. Greenwich, CT: Information Age Publishing.

Simão, L. M., Bettoi, W., Canto, C. R. E., & Gumarães, D. S. (2005, May). *A Pesquisa de Processos de Construção de Conhecimento durante Interações Sociais: questões teórico-metodológicas revisitadas* [The research on processes of knowledge construction during social interactions: Theoretical-methodological questions revisited]. Paper presented at the 4th. North-Northeast Congress of Psychology, Salvador, Bahia, Brazil.

Tunes, E., & Bartholo Jr., R. (2003). Da constituição da consciência a uma Psicologia ética: alteridade e zona de desenvolvimento proximal. In A. Mitjáns Martinez & L. M. Simão (Eds.), *O outro no desenvolvimento humano: Diálogos para a pesquisa e prática profissional em psicologia* (pp. 41-60). São Paulo, Brazil: Pioneira Thomson-Learning.

Valsiner, J. (1998). *The guided mind: A sociogenetic approach to personality*. Cambridge, MA: Harvard University Press.

Valsiner, J. (2001). Comparative Study of Human Development. Madrid: Fundación Infancia y Aprendizaje.

Valsiner, J. (2005, May). *Duality in self-other relation: Elaboration of George Hebert Mead's scheme*. Paper presented at the 4th North-Northeast Congress of Psychology Salvador, Bahia, Brazil.

Wertsch, J. V. (1998). *Mind as action*. New York: Oxford University Press.

Zittoun, T., Duveen, G., Gillespie, A., Ivinson, G., & Psaltis, C. (2003). The use of developmental resources in developmental transition. *Culture & Psychology, 9*(4), 415-448.

CHAPTER 14

HUMAN DEVELOPMENT AS MIGRATION

Striving Toward the Unknown

Jaan Valsiner

We are all migrants. Our living is in movement—not in any stationary "snapshot" of that movement (Abbey, 2006). Therefore any theoretical account that attempts to make sense of human development is necessarily an account of processes (rather that of their outcomes—Valsiner, 1997). Furthermore—the movement as the core of human living sets up the notion of otherness (alterity) as the center of theoretical inquiry. The person simultaneously **IS** and **IS-NOT-YET**—in every act of being is a process of potential becoming (Valsiner & van der Veer, 1993). The person is constantly on one's way that entails some form of ambivalence between *Heimweh* and *Fernweh* (Boesch, 1997, pp. 79-128)—our movement is oriented toward exploring the unknown while holding on to the known. We may experience that tension at any moment—yet it is one of those existential themes that cannot easily be put into words.

Otherness in Question: Labyrinths of the Self, 349–378

COMMON LANGUAGE AND
THEORETICAL LANGUAGES IN PSYCHOLOGY

We are conceptually movement-blind. At the same time as we are involved in our perpetual movement, we fail to see it. Our human common sense—mediated by language use—guides people away from the focus on the processes that maintain our being and becoming. Common sense operates with essentialist statements, projecting static causal entities onto the processes of *dureé* (Bergson, 1889, 1896/1988, 1907/1945).

Psychology as science often borrows not only its phenomena but also its terminological bases from the common language. While keeping close to the former is a crucial imperative to maintain the scientific nature of the discipline (Cairns, 1986; Branco & Valsiner, 1997), it is the use of the latter that creates theoretical pitfalls for psychology. There is a curious paradox in the reliance upon common language in creating psychological theories—while closeness of the language use to everyday richness of psychological phenomena allows for rich description of those phenomena, it also reduces the explanatory capability of theoretical thought. On the other side—if the theoretical explanations are created in terminology far removed from the everyday discourse, their value can be doubted precisely because of such distance from the richness of everyday language uses.

Research on affective phenomena is a good example where the common sense and language use direct the set of research questions asked. It largely depends upon the "secondary agenda" of the particular researcher in what ways affect is treated—ranging from interest in physiological functioning of the organism to the semantic universals of the language, and to issues of aesthetics. William James's example of encountering a bear in the forest still sets into motion academic discussions of how emotions function—100 years and two World Wars later.

Broadly speaking, theoretical accounts of affective phenomena can be viewed as organized into three classes of approaches. First, there is the biological mechanism orientation within which the bases for emotion expression and phenomena of feelings are located in the functioning of the nervous system. Second, there is the phenomenological orientation that focuses on the subjective, lived-through experiencing of affective phenomena. Much of the work done by psychoanalysts belongs to this category. Finally there is the ever-active contemporary tradition of social constructionism that opposes itself to the biological mechanisms seeking traditions—as if the personal living-through of affect can occur only on the basis of human speech and without the body that enables that experience. Still, all these three directions have presented affective states—feelings and emotions—as if these were entities—emotion categories or feeling states.

Continuous Experience Contra Discrete Referencing

The subjective world of a human being is constantly in the state of a complex whole of the immediate experience which is dynamically changing (dureé). The dureé is the subjective reality of the "here-and-now" personal being. Yet as such it is not open to be made into a target of communication by the person—with oneself, or with others. For that purpose, the fullness of the flowing subjectivity needs to be violated—by turning parts of it into relatively stable reflexive entities. That discretization is accomplished by the invention and use of signs—semiotic mediation.

All semiotic processes that the person brings into one's life are oriented toward regulating and directing that flow into some selected future direction (Valsiner, 2001, 2004). In experimental psychology of mental phenomena, processes of such realization of affective processes within body were investigated by way of precise introspective methodology by researchers of the "Würzburg tradition" (e.g., Bühler, 1907, 1908a, 1908b; Külpe, 1892, 1903, 1912-1913; Ogden, 1951; Selz, 1924/1982; and others). They demonstrated the relevance of the affective processes within the microgenesis of ideas in their thinking process elicitation tasks.

Constraints of Time

Irreversibility of time sets up duality of human psychological functions—our actions and reflections upon those are necessarily focused on the processes in between of ourselves and our environment, as well as between present and the impending future that flows upon us in all of its uncertainty. In order to handle that uncertainty, persons act *as if* they were different from what they are like (in present) as they anticipate their future (as they might be in the future). Likewise, they act as if they were another person— a rap-singer (Abbey & Davis, 2003) or as-if they were "in love" (Smythe, 2005, p. 292). In reality they remain themselves—albeit the simulating being the other or in another state is part of the movement toward *some other* state.

Human living is a process that entails a number of forms of AS-IF relations between the past and the future. In a general scheme, these can include a number of parallel future-oriented apperceptive stes (Figure 14. 1)

This example illustrates a special case of the duality As-IS <> As-IF that references the unknowable future by way of different active cognitive operators indicated by COULD, SHOULD, MAY NOT orientations toward the future. The affective anticipation of the future sets up the ways in which the new present—the AS-Will-BE (actually) becomes created.

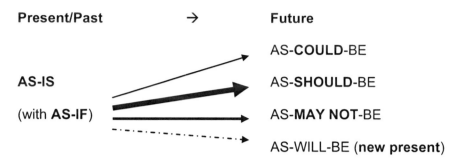

Figure 14.1.   Apperceptive extensions of a given AS-IS state.

The example above is one of "moralistic" future constructors (where SHOULD is dominant over others). An "adventurous" constructor would emphasize the COULD operator, while a "moralistic fearful" one would prioritize the MAY NOT. In all versions, however, the basic duality that guides human development is that of constant process of construction of the contrast between the present state ("as-is") and the desired state ("as-if") that is anticipating the future (Boesch, 1997; Hermans, 2001; Ferreira, Salgado, & Cunha, 2006).

This contrast **AS-IS < > AS-IF** is the constant process of making of the future. At the boundary of the infinitely small time moment between the past and the future that contrast is the birthplace of novelty. Ontogenetically, this boundary is conceptualized by other terms that are more widely known for developmental psychologists—such as Zone of Proximal Development (Valsiner & van der Veer, 1993), "the orthogenetic principle" of the Goethe-Werner line of theorizing (Valsiner, 2005a), or of the construction of the developmental web (Fischer, Yan, & Stewart, 2003). This boundary of ever on-moving irreversible present is the construction site for both continuity and qualitative change—ruptures in the developing system (see Zittoun, 2006, and in this volume).

The making of the future entails inherent and inevitable duality. This is captured in Figure 14.2 that represents the basic notion of alterity that G. H. Mead formulated in early twentieth century (Mead, 1912, 1913). It is based on the inevitable nature of getting feedback from one's own actions while those are taking place. A person says something to another and in the process of doing so hears oneself doing it before the other responds. So—the first response to the self's efforts to express oneself is by the self (the IMMEDIATE FEEDBACK LOOP in Figure 14.2), and it is only after that that the other may respond.

It becomes evident from Figure 14.2 that *two* primary alterity relations—I < > ME and OUTWARD PROJECTION < > IMMEDIATE

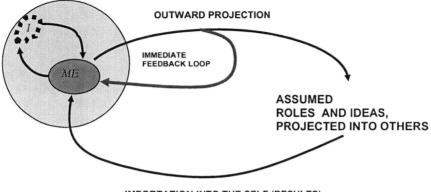

OUTWARD PROJECTION

IMMEDIATE
FEEDBACK LOOP

ASSUMED
ROLES AND IDEAS,
PROJECTED INTO OTHERS

IMPORTATION INTO THE SELF (RESULTS)

Figure 14.2.   Microgenesis of the future: Two feedback loops (after G. H. Mead).

FEEDBACK—constitute the domains where the person's Self <> Other relations are being worked out in the course of everyday living. In some sense, the self contains one's own "other"—a point made axiomatically by dialogical self theorists (see Salgado, this volume). Thus, the person is social through treating one's own self as "the other," in addition to the obvious importation of the social input from other human beings, in the communicative act. If we add to this one's own assuming social roles and its feed-forward onto the I <> ME system we can see the redundancy of communication and action in Mead's scheme.

The other important feature in Mead's scheme is its open-endedness in both internal (I <> ME relations) and external (person <> "other") loops. The latter of course guarantees uncertainty of living, yet the former is the key for innovation in case the external loop becomes "fixed" or stable. Hence the self-system is inherently novelty-constructive on both sides.

MAKING SENSE OF AFFECTIVE PROCESSES

The difficulty of using language to denote something felt (but not immediately language-encoded) has been a problem for psychology ever since the disputes about William James' ideas about feelings (Dewey, 1896; James, 1890). James emphasized the need to consider feelings within a framework of making sense of human mental functions:

> the bodily changes follow directly the perception of the exciting fact, and
> that our feeling of the same changes as they occur IS the emotion. <u>Common</u>

sense says, we lose our fortune, are sorry and weep; we meet a bear, are frightened and run; we are insulted by a rival, are angry and strike. The hypothesis here to be defended says that this order of sequence in incorrect, that the one mental state is not immediately induced by the other, that the bodily manifestations must first be interposed between, and that the more rational statement is that we feel sorry because we cry, angry because we strike, afraid because we tremble... Without the bodily states following on the perception, the latter would be purely cognitive in form, pale, colourless, destitute of emotional warmth. We might then see the bear, and judge it best to run, receive the insult and deem it right to strike, but we could not actually feel afraid or angry. (James, 1884, pp. 189-190, added emphases)

What James emphasized is the interposing of bodily manifestations in the process of perception; it is clear from the above quote that his example is used to emphasize the "purely rational" (or cognitive) action as contrasted with felt-through ones. In the latter case, the bodily manifestations of the feeling-through provide the emotional character to the event. The tension between the chain-like nature of the emotional reaction processes, and their view in terms of unity (interposing) of visceral and subjective experiences in the process of perceiving is already visible here.

The Feeling Tone

Affective phenomena are dynamically complex, often defying even elaborate description. One of the pioneers in the study of affective phenomena, the founder the "Second Leipzig School"—Felix Krueger, emphasized the distinction of these phenomena:

the experience of a normal individual (and also all social experience) consists in its main bulk of indistinctly bounded, diffused, slightly or not at all organized complexes in whose genesis all organs and functional systems take part. It is significant and not at all obvious that, at least in adult human beings and higher animals, the total state of their experience often unfolds into a multitude of relatively closed part-complexes. But even in the highest stages of development, this is not always the case, e.g., in states of the highest, permanent excitement, great fatigue, most complete self-subservience. Even when we observe experience in relief, its organization, as a rule, does not correspond at all and may never correspond exactly to the limitations of objects created by intellect, or to objective "situations".... Never are the differentiable parts or sides of real experience as isolated from one another as the parts of physical substance, i.e., its molecules and atoms. (Krueger, 1928, p. 67)

Krueger's viewpoint would certainly be rejected by our post-modern ("modular") thinkers who reduce the complexity of human psychological worlds into separated complexes of settings where the persons act. Yet even in these settings a general affective tone (*Gefühlston* in Krueger's terminology) that the person generates would have a role to play in development. For instance, the feeling tone of "dangerousness" of an empty street at night, as well as "safety" of the same street crowded by people in daytime, are subjective generalized feeling tones that guide the person's actions.

Appraisal of Cognitive Approaches

Revolutions are dangerous. The success of the "cognitive revolution" in psychology is a remarkable testimony to the historical myopia of the discipline, as well as its overlook of basic problems if human sciences. Richard Lazarus' (1991) and Lazarus and Folkman's (1984) appraisal theory of emotion solved the problem by turning the affective domain into an add-on to basic cognitive processes.

The appraisal theory of emotions is a bastard—a historically illegitimate offspring of the rationalist model of human mental functions and the necessity to accept the irrationality of the human affective sphere. This rational irrationality resulted in the superimposition of the optimal evaluation strategies onto the affective phenomena.

Appraisal is

an evaluation of what one's relationship to the environment implies for personal well-being. Each positive emotion is said to be produced by a particular kind of appraised benefit, and each negative emotion by a particular kind of appraised harm. The emotional response is hypothesized to prepare and mobilise the person to cope with the particular appraised harm or benefit in an adaptive manner, that is, to avoid, minimize or alleviate the appraised harm, or to seek, maximize, or maintain an appraised benefit. (Smith & Lazarus, 1993, p. 234)

Contemporary cultural psychology includes some renewed efforts to look at affect in its empirical investigation (Briggs, 1975, 1979, 1991; Menon & Shweder, 1994). Norman Denzin (1985) has proposed a theoretical orientation to affect that unites the personological-phenomenological and symbolic interactionist viewpoints. For him, emotions are

temporally embodied self-feelings which arise from emotional social acts persons direct to self or have directed toward them by others. Emotions are lodged in social acts and self-interactions. (Denzin, 1983, p. 404)

Denzin recognizes the biological basis for all affective phenomena—yet the actual nature of such phenomena becomes defined through person's relating one's self with the social world. The biological basis merely makes affect possible—while the agency of the experiencing person turns it into an actual feeling and emotional expression.

The actualization of feelings is a phenomenon of human subjective personal worlds—albeit based on the physiology of the body and the social rules of a society the person lives in. The appropriate level of analysis for such phenomena is that of human subjective worlds—available to study through the externalization of the personal culture. Human subjective experience is an objectively existing phenomenon—given in the objectivity of subjectivities. That objectivity is granted through the possibilities of communication across persons—between the researcher and the research participant, at the least. Human subjectivities are mediated by cultural means—signs created for communication with the self and others.

HIERARCHICAL SEMIOTIC REGULATION OF AFFECTIVE FIELDS

Human affective processes are of the kind of complexity that has been a problem for straightforward efforts to describe and explain those. Cultural mediating devices—meanings—are closely intertwined with that complexity. They emerge from amidst of that complexity. Human experiencing of every here-and-now setting is embedded within a field of self-generated affect.

Scientific Terminologies: Point Versus Field Depictions

There are two directions in which scientific depictions can be takes—toward creating an idealized categorical set of entities that become seen as "causal" (point depiction); or toward use of field notions to capture the embeddedness of the phenomena (Valsiner & Diriwächter, 2005).

A *field* is a mental construct through which properties of the object of interest can be thought of as mutually related within a space and time. Instead of being entities ("things"), the objects of investigation are turned into *events* which have structure both in time and space (Smith & Smith, 1996). Field conception allows researchers to solve the problem of actions at distance—by the use of terms like forces operating in the field:

> It needed a great scientific imagination to realize that it was not the charges nor the particles but the field in the space between the charges and particles which is essential for the description of the physical phenomena. (Einstein & Infeld, 1938, p. 259, cited via Deutsch, 1954, p. 182)

As a scientific tool, the concept of field has been developing in the physical sciences over the last two centuries. Concepts like gravitational field and electromagnetic field have been productive tools in physicists' thinking. Descriptively the notion of field has been used since the beginning of psychology (e.g., the notions of visual field, tactile field).

Field-theoretic depictions have been used in psychology at times—especially during the first half of the twentieth century. Yet that direction of thought has become underestimated by the reduction of the formal models in psychology to statistical ones (Gigerenzer, 1993; Valsiner, 1997). The notion of field was utilized by holistically oriented German psychologists of the turn of the twentieth century (Felix Krueger—see Krueger, 1913, 1926, 1928a, 1928b), and especially Kurt Lewin. Lewin's impressions about the change in the meanings of everyday objects when the general life situation changes from wartime to peacetime (or vice versa—Lewin, 1917) led him to attempts to develop a general psychological theory based on the mathematical system of topology (Lewin, 1936) on the one hand, and on the observation of complex phenomena, on the other.

Field-theoretic thinking allows the researcher to move from assuming essences and thinking in terms of *entities* (graphically depicted as points) to that of conceptual capturing of the processes behind the entities (circumscribed areas or).

Generalization and Hypergeneralization

In the processes of human mental reflection (cognition) the central issue for thinking is that of *abstraction*. Abstraction entails mental operation with mental tools that are distanced from the specific referents they represent. Abstraction leads the way to *generalization*—the abstracted general features of the representation become applicable to new specifics via extension of the abstracted features to phenomena that were previously not considered as the basis for abstraction. Finally, generalization can lead to a state of hypergeneralization

How does generalization of meanings (and their hypergeneralization) work? Any concept used in our social lives is already a result of generalization—it rises above the here-and-now situation by way of abstraction. Any concept entails the construction of mental "sameness" on the basis of various kinds of similarities in experiencing over time (Sovran, 1992).

Yet generalization can proceed further toward loss of clearly definable features of the abstracted concepts. Our most general meanings go through such process—meanings of JUSTICE, or LOVE in English, or AMAE in Japanese (Morsbach & Tyler, 1986), or PREM in Hindu meaning system (Derne, 1994)—may begin from specific lived-through experiences, lead to abstraction and generalization of those, and reach at a state where these overgeneralized notions become basic personal or human values. Such values then permeate human conduct at all levels—from immediate reactions to new situations to processes of long soul-searching and life-philosophical contemplation.

The valuation involved in feelings—viewing the immediate world as value-imbued-- can be viewed in terms of opposites of feeling orientation ("good" feeling ←→ "bad" feeling—cf. Kahneman, 1998). These opposites are united in a system of a functioning whole.[1] The person in every new moment is faced with the uncertainty of relating with the immediate ambience. The feeling orientation serves as a priming device that enables (or blocks) the "on-line" action. As human experience is constantly directed toward the future—in preadaptation to the uncertainty of that future—the evaluation in the feeling is diffuse, yet directed. Feelings play their role in human adaptation precisely because of their "fuzzy" character—their "aboutness"[2] rather than certainty. This "fuzzyness" of hypergeneralized meanings—which proliferate the field of personal experiencing—is itself a result of semiotic mediation (Valsiner, 2001b, 2004).

Semiotic Mediation—Signs as Fields

It is the human invention—creating and using signs—that makes such transfer of generalized experiences possible. The role of cultural psychology is to enrich psychological theorizing and empirical work by keeping that process—of semiotic mediation—in the central focus of investigators. Phenomena of human affectivity are organized at different levels, from those closest to immediate physiological processes, to abstracted and hypergeneralized higher level total feelings (see Figure 14.3).

The hierarchy of levels of semiotic mediation of affective processes that is depicted in Figure 14.3 sets up within the same scheme emotions and feelings of different generality.

The Undifferentiated Fields

Level 0 is the universal physiological anticipation—or orientation-- about the immediate next future event. Based on that level, the organisms can develop generalized, nonmediated "feeling tone" (or anticipatory affective state, kind of undifferentiated awareness of something—positive, negative, or ambivalent—that is about to happen). These Level 1 phenomena do not require semiotic mediation—they are preverbal generalizations. In terms of Frijda (1986, 1988) these are nonreflexive

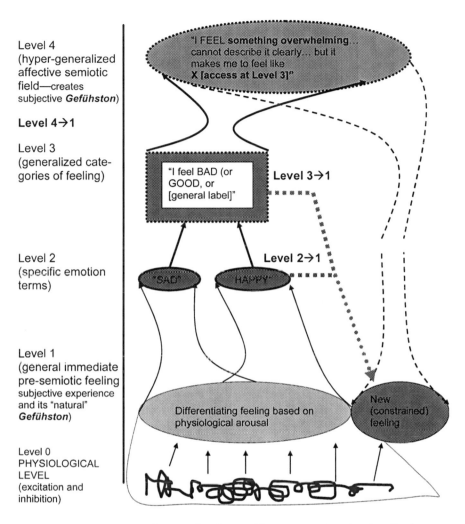

Figure 14.3.   Processes of generalization and hypergeneralization in affective regulation of the flow of experience.

experiences—perceptions of the situation (here-and-now, or imagined). These are akin to affordances (in the sense of J. J. Gibson) with added projection of personal subjectivity:

> The properties [of objects] are out there. These properties contain the relationship to the subject: Emotional experience is perception of horrible objects, insupportable people, oppressive events. They contain the relation-

ship implicitly: the "to me" or "for me" <u>dissolves into the property.</u> (Frijda, 1986, p. 188, added emphasis)

At Level 0 we can observe the immediate "feeling in" by the person into the situation. Pre-verbal generalization allows for the organism to maintain previous experiences for further use, but does not require their encoding through signs.

Emergence of Cultural Organization

Semiotically mediated (i.e., cultural) organization of the affective field begins at the move from Level 0 to Level 1. The person's primary affective field is already oriented by the person's previous experience—yet it remains undifferentiated. The affective field becomes articulated at Level 2—where specific naming of emotions present. The undifferentiated field of a particular directional quality (e.g., positive, negative, or ambivalent) becomes reflected upon through assigning the present state of the field a specifying name for the emotion felt. So, the person can say "I am sad," "I am disgusted," "I am happy" or talk about emotions like HAPPINESS, SADNESS, ANGER, SURPRISE, and so forth, **as if** those were **permanent** properties of human affective life. Yet there is nothing permanent in the flowing experience of the person. Naming an emotion one feels is a way to temporarily "arrest" the dynamic process at the level of reflection.

Sign mediation creates the psychological distance of the thinker/talker from the differentiating affective field—discussing issues of human happiness does not mean that the discussing person oneself is happy. All the cognitive activity of persons that concentrates upon the decontextualizing emotions—in terms of their specific categories or general prototypes—takes place at Level 2. That is the level of maximum **articulation** of the semiotic encoding of the affective field (in terms of the Werner-Kaplan "orthogenetic principle"—Werner & Kaplan, 1956).

The articulated meaning of an emotion constrain the flow of experience by its role as **presentation** (*Vorstellung*). Each presentation has simultaneously three functions—it **re**-presents something, **co**-presents that something in the here-and-now situation, and **pre-**presents something else to come in the immediate future. Hence it is through presentations that human beings link the past, present and expected future (Cole, 1992, 1995). Knowing one's emotion has been shown to feed forward into the further conduct of the person (Laird, 1974; Laird & Bressler, 1992).

Higher Level of Organization: Two Kinds of Hierarchical Integration

The "orthogenetic principle" of Werner and Kaplan (1956) posited that the state of hierarchical integration is the highest level of developmental organization. Yet they failed to specify what kinds of hierarchical integration can exist. Of course our occidental thinking—supported by basics of classical logic—entails the image of transitive hierarchy as *the* model for hierarchical organization. Yet that is a poor choice for any open-ended (developing) systems, as a transitive hierarchy fixates the order and idealizes the fixed subordination of parts (e.g., A>B>C with A subordinating B and C, B subordinating C). Developmental (open-systemic) phenomena are better characterized by intransitive (or cyclical) hierarchies (Poddiakov & Valsiner, 2006). The state of hierarchical integration looks very different from a static subordination picture in the case of latter model of hierarchy.

Werner and Kaplan failed to clarify the nature of hierarchical integration, leaving that concept itself undifferentiated. DeRivera has explained the reasons for this oversight:

> While developmental theory ... draws a sharp distinction between <u>integration</u> (of differentiated parts) and <u>merger</u> (or diffuseness), it seems constantly to confuse the idea of <u>unification</u> and merger. This confusion arises because in both states there is a breakdown of differentiation, a "primitivization". However, in merger—a state of lesser development—there is either a failure to differentiate (the egocentricity a child manifests when it believes its mind is transparent to others) or a confusion of identity (The psychotic hallucinating a voice).... In unification this egocentricity or confusion and lack of identity is not always present. The person who experiences anger, love, or some other emotion is not necessarily being egocentric or confusing identities. (DeRivera, 1977, pp. 29-30)

Thus, the highest level of hierarchical integration (within the framework of intransitive hierarchy model) can entail a state of de-differentiation of the field by the irradiation of a hypergeneralized feeling from the self to the other (nonself). William James' (1890, p. 295) example of the self of a medical doctor supports DeRivera's critique of the traditional differentiation theory. A doctor, while hearing about a cholera epidemic in a nearby town, would move *toward* it to help to cure people—while all "rational" people escape in the opposite direction. It would be slightly absurd to consider the doctor confused in one's identity, or primitivized in his actions. Something else is the case—an extension of the hypergeneralized affective field (identity as doctor—duty to help others).

Emergence of Higher Level of De-Differentiation

The mediational processes of Level 2 can become further generalized in ways that lead to higher-level (in terms of abstraction) de-differentiation of the affective field. Level 3 in Figure 14.3 depicts a situation where a person—after excessive use of emotion categories in one's internal self-dialogue—arrives at a new generalized—yet ill-defined—self-reflection.

Thus, a statement "I feel bad" can result from generalization higher in abstractness than specification of emotion categories (sad, disgusted).

Finally, the generalization of the sign-mediated field of feelings can reach the highest level of hypergeneralization—that of a semiotically mediated state which is at the same time de-differentiated (Level 4). The person "just feels" something—but cannot put that feeling into words. Examples of aesthetic feelings—catharsis experienced during a theater performance, reading deeply moving poems or prose, or in an interpersonal situation of extreme beauty indicate that human affective field can become undifferentiated as a result of extensive abstraction of the emotions involved, and their overgeneralization to the person's general feelings about oneself or about the world. Theoretically, that process entails internalization and abbreviation (Lyra, 1999). Psychological functions that develop in interaction with the social world—and are hence visible during their development ontogenetically—disappear into the interior of the person's subjective world and lose their duration—become established, undoubted base for acting and knowing.

Hypergeneralization of Affect Leads to a Semiotically Mediated new De-Differentiated State

It becomes important to emphasize that the highest levels of hierarchical integration do not entail increased articulation of the parts of the affective system, but just to the contrary—the highest level of hierarchical integration is that of an hypergeneralized ("nebulous") semiotically mediated feeling ("higher feeling") subordinating all rational (Level 2) discourse about emotions to its ever-present (inarticulate) guidance. The example of the difficulty that psychology has had with the treatment of some higher-order affective phenomena—such as values—is indicative of this process. Even as values can be posited—and traced—to be present in human conduct, bringing them out into the domain of explicit reflection by the carriers of values has been difficult. Values are so basic—ontogenetically internalized—that they are no longer easily accessible through verbally mediated processes.

Higher Feeling Fields as Semiotic Mediators of Future Affect

In human life, affective fields of higher kind—as depicted in Figure 14.3—regulate experience in its totality. Affective fields can be overgeneralized meanings that have left their original context of emergence and flavor new experiences. Phenomenologically, the picture is rather ordinary, A flow of a general feeling just takes over the intrapersonal world of the person, begins to control one's concrete actions.

Redundant Feed-Forward Regulation:
Emergence and Escalation of a Panic Attack

It is precisely the hypergeneralized—and de-differentiated—nature of higher-level integration of the affective field that allows for **redundant** feed-forward guidance of the person's further experiencing. Each of the other three levels of semiotic mediation becomes canalized by Level 4. The overgeneralized unarticulated feeling—in the form of a general value, religious, or ideological conviction, or pathological overconcern—guides the ways in which the person is expecting to make the first step in the direction of semiotic mediation of the affective field (Level 1). At the same time, it guides the ways in which emotions can (are to) be discussed explicitly—at the maximum state of articulation (Level 2). Finally, it is involved in a "self-study" of its own nature—in guiding the self-reflection of Level 3.

The hypergeneralized nature of signs that results in fields of feeling (Level 4) guides the movement from perception to primary feelings through generation of personally senseful imagery—episodes created in the mind, or in the person's interpretation of a concrete situation. An example of the emergence of the first panic attack during a holiday at wartime can illustrate the tension emerging in the field of feeling and the imagery generated:

> On the morning of the fifth day I went for a haircut and shampoo, arranging to meet my wife later by the big clock near the pier. I had to wait some forty minutes before my turn came to occupy the chair, and I began to feel uneasy. For the first twenty minutes I felt no more than a pleasant languor, a not uncomfortable and unnatural feeling for someone on holiday. This sensation slowly dispersed to be replaced by a growing rigidity I couldn't understand. I began to long for the procedure to be over, I longed to get outside again. I felt I'd be all right once I got out into the sparking sunlight. (Law, 1975—cited via Baker, 1989, p. 72, added emphases)

The emergence of the vague feeling—described as "growing rigidity"—of the current situation felt as confining evoked the positive imagery of getting into "sparkling sunlight." The tension led to active efforts to stop the growing anxiety by way of overgeneralized signs—"X seems absurd":

> Yet to get up and leave would have seemed absurd, especially after waiting so long. The haircut itself went off all right, the barber chatting away blithely. I bent over the bowl for the shampoo, and the tension began to

build up again. <u>With tremendous relief</u> I sat back and waited for my hair to be dried. Usually, of course, an electric hair-blower was used for this purpose, but this establishment didn't seem to boast such modern luxuries. The man picked up a towel and rubbed away vigorously. ... sensations stronger and stronger than I had previously known charged through my body. My throat seemed on fire; it screamed for water gasping, my heart thundering away, <u>I thought my hour had come</u>. I jumped up, threw money toward the barber, and stumbled into the street. (Law, 1975—cited via Baker, 1989, p. 72, added emphases)

Here the generalized notion of "the absurd" failed to regulate the flow of experiences. Enhanced by the other overgeneralized feeling ("my hour had come") the panic exploded. The imagery contrast (in/outside: here/there) made it possible for the panic to escalate (cf. Baker, 1989, p. 73 for dramatic extension and conclusion of the episode).

Hypergeneralized feelings can become an accepted personal platform for life satisfaction—"personal identity" state of a kind. Thus, a female patient told the therapist that she "always wanted to feel like an oppressed person. That makes me feel alive." Another remarked "When I feel angry, I feel stronger. I can fight you better" (Bonime, 1983, p. 252). In both cases we can detect the personal setting of an overgeneralized feeling tone that allows the persons to function. That feeling tone becomes the "normal general state" of the person, and efforts to change such states may be resisted as a way to preserve one's established *status quo* of "identity."

How the Hypergeneralized Affective Fields Function: Some Examples

Examples of the first kind of feed-forward relations can be found of varied kinds. Some of them are of episodic nature, others become relatively fixed and recognizable as "personality characteristics" or even become labeled within systems of pathology. Yet all of them share the same feature—a sign (as a field) reorganizes the intrapsychological and interpsychological conduct of the person involved.

Example 1: Semiotically Mediated Physiological Reactions

On many occasions where the person who had done something ordinary—or so it was assumed—and then finds out that some of the aspects of the action were culturally ruled out—can resort in purely physiological reaction. For instance, a person has eaten a piece of meat—perhaps with pleasure—and is informed of that the meat just eaten is of a culturally unacceptable category. Thus, as long as the visiting person may initially believe that the meat was that of a rabbit, he or she may feel positive about the experience. If later it comes out that the meat was that of a cat, vomiting can occur. It is only the mentioning of the culturally hypergeneralized value (cats are not eaten and pets are special humanized animals) that—as evoking a Level 4 meaningful framing of the immediate past event—can lead to such result.

Less dramatic examples about similar issues can occur on a daily basis—a person has internalized the value of specific kinds of foods can feel disgust when having to face foods of nonkosher kind (or of kosher foods contaminated by "impure" actions—see Nemeroff & Rozin, 1992). In a more general vein—any aspect of body-related actions (intake of substances, excretion of substances, marking of the body by substances, public display of different body parts, etc.) can be governed by such overgeneralized Level 4 semiotic. Similarly, the overgeneralized meaning of different graphic symbols operate through feed-forward from Level 4 to Level 1 of the semiotic mediation of feelings.

Example 2: Life-Philosophies and Depression

In a series of events of mistreatment over childhood, a person may arrive at the generalized feeling that "life is unfair." Once overgeneralized, that affective tone begins to color many—sometimes each and every—new experience. The person can look at the rising (or setting) sun and consider this to carry the flavor of "unfairness of life."

Collective-cultural canalization (Valsiner, 1997) of the construction of personal-cultural higher levels of feeling fields can provide an alternative valuation of such generalizations. What in Western mental health talk becomes labeled as the core of depression—feeling of hopelessness of one's life—looks very different in the framework of the Buddhist world view:

> The Buddhist would take one further step in generalization: it is not simply the general hopelessness of one's own lot; that hopelessness lies in the nature of the world, and salvation lies in understanding and overcoming that hopelessness. Thus the problem raised here: How is the Western diagnostic term "depression" expressed in a society whose predominant ideology of Buddhism states that life is suffering and sorrow, that the cause of sorrow is attachment or desire or craving, that there is a way (generally through meditation) of understanding and overcoming suffering and achieving the final goal of cessation of suffering or nirvana? (Obeyesekere, 1985, p. 134)

The general feeling field of suffering (Level 4 phenomenon in terms of Figures 14.3 and 14.4) is thus regulated through even further generalized life-philosophical field. That field integrates the generalization of suffering into a scheme of its overcoming by the person—while in case of Western mental health talk the field becomes attributed to a label (Level 2) "depression" that leads to efforts to block or suppress it—rather than overcome.

Example 3: Alexithymia

A person's depressive feelings can give coloring to each and every encounter with the world, even if it is impossible for her or him to describe those verbally. Even more dramatically—overgeneralized feelings (Level 4 phenomena that are not open to verbal depiction) can pre-emptively block the capacity of human beings to feel anything, and to reflect upon the world in affective terms (e.g., as in cases of *alexithymia*—Sifenos, 1974; Taylor, Bagby, & Parker, 1997). Alexithymic persons are generally unable to put their emotions into words, and often are not aware of their immediate affective phenomena in new situations—yet they can emit the appropriate physiological responses (e.g., crying). Two kinds of alexithymia can be posited to exist—one would constitute the developmental arrest of reflexivity (no emergence of Level 2 in ontogeny), another—blocking of the transition Level 1—> Level 2 by higher affective field (Level 4) that has overtaken the control over verbalizability of feelings. The Level 4 overgeneralized field here blocks the formation of Level 1 (from Level 0—in Figure 14.3), and, obviously, that of the transition into Level 2. Blocking the capacity to talk about one's feelings can be expected to limit further affective development, as well as verbally-oriented therapeutic efforts (Carpenter & Addis, 2000).

Example 4: The Feeling Field of a Setting

The relations between Level 3 and Level 4 in Figure 14.4 are bidirectional. On the one hand, the generalizing semiotically encoded feeling keeps open the general direction of feeling. On the other hand, that feeling becomes constructed as a de-differentiated field, and thus "vanishes" from the direct and crisp linguistic depiction, and becomes a "feeling-at-large." Consider the following depiction of the "Christmas spirit":

A major festival like Christmas among English-speaking North Americans is accompanied by a stereotypical set of emotions. Certainly, we do not all actually feel these emotions: for many, Christmas is primarily lived, according to self-reports and actions, in a mode of disgust at overindulgence or in a heightened sense of loneliness. But this does not mean that Christmas evokes feelings at random ... [factors evoking feeling] depend ... on personal elements that to a large degree are common to those who share common experiences and a common exposure to stories, songs, images, and ritual practices—all features that reinforce a message of comfort and joy, homeyness, and familial good cheer. For most English-speaking North Americans ... such evocation of "Christmas cheer" or "Christmas spirit" extends beyond the words or images used to provoke it to involve in what we commonly call feelings. The exact nature of one's feelings will depend on background and circumstances but include a range of positive and negative emotions that are themselves reactions to the central stereotypical emotion of familal and universal love and coziness. (Leavitt, 1996, p. 527, added emphases)

The "Christmas spirit" is an overgeneralized field which—being labeled as such (Level 3)—entails feelings which guide lower levels of dealing with bodily experiences and categories of emotion. Any encounter by a person with an environment filled with Christmas paraphernalia (e.g., pervasive Christmas songs) can lead to primary feelings (Level 1) that become framed by the highest (Level 4) affective field. The person may feel in the bliss of "Christmas spirit"—or in the middle of unspeakable alienation (dependent upon the semiotic organization of the Level 4 field). Both of these extreme ways of structuring the feelings can be accomplished without direct verbal mediation—the persons need not talk about their feelings in the setting, neither to one another, nor within themselves.

The Importance of Nothingness

In the history of Oriental societies, the highest level of semiotic regulation of the affective fields is that of being "beyond the ordinary" life experiences—as oriental ascetics create their highest goals in living. In the Buddhist world, the suffering is to be eliminated by distancing:

"Elimination of suffering" in Buddhist thought means no more than to unmask, by means of spontaneously obtained knowledge, the chimera of objects existing independently of us. This means locating the void of "nothing"—in the sense that things no longer resist us—at exactly the point where the things previously appeared in their separate existence with all their prominence, freshness, and splendor. As seen with complete knowledge, the world and nothing, nirvana, are strictly parallel correlates. For Buddha, knowledge is not "participation," "image," "order," or "form," but an emptying of the contents of the world from our apprehension by severing the chain of desire that binds us to these contents and makes their existence possible. Knowledge is thus a stopping of the conflict as to whether our worlds contents exist or do not exist in our immediate present; in this respect, knowledge is primarily an abolishing of all affirmations or denials of existence. (Scheler, 1992, p. 105)

An alternative treatment of suffering in human cultural history is its elimination by persons' active work of psychological distancing of the generalized feeling from the rest of experiences. In terms of the contents of Figure 3, that entails turning the two-sided relation Level 3←→Level 4 into a single-direction relation (Level 4→Level 3). As a result, the over-generalized feeling becomes unmentionable in terms of verbal encoding (or it becomes "empty"—see the Taoist notion of **mu**—in Ohnuki-Tierney, 1994). Yet it remains functional in coordinating the other parts of the affective life—how one talks about one's feelings, how one acts in line with (or opposite to) the verbalized self.

Generalized personal life philosophy guides the persons toward acting (either in suffering-in-the field, or in distancing in-relation-with the field), and through such acting—to the acceptance of the given life philosophy. That philosophy becomes personal—through internalization/ externalization (see Valsiner, 1997). Individuals need not become followers of the given religion—in fact they may be active opponents of the organizer religions—yet their life philosophies are framed by the orientation toward suffering within which they develop.

Also the past experiences can be those of other generations—internalized through one's personal experiences with collective-cultural objects. The basic form of any sign is iconic—the indexical and symbolic transformations of that form are parallel fortification of the semiotic presentations (Nöth, 1998, 2001). Cultural objects that embrace human beings as their constructed environments are iconic, indexical, and symbolic at the same time. The architect of a medieval cathedral can encode into the building the feelings of "hardness" of the warfare of the knights and "softness" of love songs (Vygotsky, 1925/1971, pp. 237-238; Vygotsky, 1987, pp. 227-228). The contemporary recipient of such architectural message can affectively relate with it if s/he has experienced the history of the medieval times through the formal or informal education (Wertsch, 1998), as well as through the establishment of Level 4 hypergeneralized affective sign fields in the personal culture.

HOW THE SEMIOTIC HIERARCHY WORKS: SIGNS REGULATING THEMSELVES

Processes of semiotic self-regulation operate through temporary hierarchies of signs (Valsiner, 2001). Generalized and overgeneralized feelings, as well as differentiated emotions—all encoded as signs—operate as parts of such hierarchy. Signs operate upon signs, and become regulators in respect to one another. The multifunctional nature of signs guarantees the emergence of flexible hierarchical systems of semiotic regulation. The move of a sign into a regulator's role creates the minimal case of a hierarchical dynamic system of semiotic regulators—a superior sign regulates its underlying process. Thus, the person's self-awareness "I am angry" leads to constraining of the primary feeling field.

The hierarchy of semiotic regulation is dynamic— a constructed regulator can immediately be superceded by another level of hierarchical semiotic regulation. Thus, the person who has just entered the regulation of the primary field through the labeling of anger, can generate yet another sign of higher generality that regulates the use of that emotion label—"it is UNFAIR for me to be ANGRY." The regulation by signs includes—recursively—constraining (enabling) the generation of a super-ordinate organizer from the field of possible signs. We may encounter potentially ever-increasing and ever-generalizing growth of the semiotic regulatory hierarchy.

From the instant of the recognition "I am angry," the feeling realm becomes redirected. The previous feeling becomes now as part of the system of anger, and widens to include other feeling phenomena through the sign of "anger". This widening guides re-defining the range of senses at the sign level. It can lead to the emergence of <u>unfairness,</u> so the person creates a sign hierarchy:

I feel
< something disturbing>
(Level 4)→
    →It is **unfair** (Level 3)→
        →that I am **angry** (Level 2)
            →**feeling** <this all> (Level 1)

The levels of hierarchy entail hypergeneralization on the top. It is a case of meanings-filled de-differentiation of the sign into an all-encompassing field that is not open for discursive inquiry unless it is brought down the hierarchy to the "domain of speakability" (Levels 3 and 2). It is not always the case that such translation downwards takes place—many human experiences remain processed speechlerssly, within the field of hypergeneralized affect. Thus, aesthetic experiences that results in catharsis involve the general law (suggested by Vygotsky) in the opposition of two feelings, which

> while developing in opposite directions, reaching the final point, as if in case of short circuit, find their extinction (Vygotsky, 1987, p. 204)

That extinction is the birthplace of a new feeling that emerges as an example of synthesis. A painting or poem may leave us speechless (Level

4 in Figure 14.3)—yet that speechlessness is the basis for further meaning construction about further experiences (Abbey & Valsiner, 2006).

Semiotic Terminators

A hypergeneralized affective field can terminate further construction of the sign hierarchy, and demolish the hierarchy itself. The terminators are metalevel commands to interrupt the work of a subroutine (cf. Simon, 1967, p. 34). The situation here is more complicated than in the case of cognitive processes since the hypergeneralization of affect leads to the construction of semiotic terminators.

Semiotic terminators are special relations within the systemic fields of dual signs (A <> non-A—Josephs, Valsiner, & Surgan, 1999). They can be constructed at levels 2, 3, and 4 (of Figure 14.3). Consider an example from Level 2 semiotic terminator:

I feel SAD and DISGUSTED but I MUST NOT feel SAD and DISGUSTED

has the underlying structure

[A <dominates>> non-A]   [non-A<dominates>> A]
                    IMPERATIVE→
[B <dominates>> non-B]   [non-B <dominates>>B]

The semiotic terminator here is an evaluative imperative operator ("I MUST NOT") that binds to the emerged sign and extinguishes it. It can be described as **PRESCRIPTIVE NEGATION** of the sign. Such operators can occur similarly at other levels (3 and 4)—albeit depending upon the nature of the signs at these levels (e.g., Level 3—"I feel BAD but I must not feel bad"; Level 4—"I just FEEL but I must not feel"). These entail signs' self-termination (by way of tension of the A & non-A complex).

The second kind of semiotic terminator is the **DISPLACEMENT OF SIGN**. Here the emerged sign becomes replaced by way of another (same-level) sign. In the cognitive therapy of panic disorders, the focus on *reappraisal* of ideations makes use of this terminator:

> The patient's specific thoughts, meanings, interpretations, and images are elicited retrospectively (recollections of previous attacks) and prospectively. Fortified by the knowledge that their ideation about the pathological nature of their experience is erroneous, the patients can reappraise their specific interpretations and images. If the patient experiences tightness in the chest, for example, and ascribes this to a coronary attack or to imminent cessation

of breathing, <u>he can tell him/herself that this simply is a tightness of the muscles in the rib cage</u> (if he can indeed demonstrate that this is the case) and not a sign of serious abnormality. (Beck, 1988, p. 103, emphasis added)

Finally, we can consider **AFFECTIVE FLOODING** as a terminator. Here a created affective superordinate field stops the functioning of the subordinate sign. Explicit referencing (Level 2) becomes blocked without explicit explanation – yet under the influence of the general feeling of "speechlessness" about the particular theme. The person's subjective world is literally "flooded" by the superordinate affective field that dilutes the particular signs of lower level in the field, binding them so that their use is no longer possible.

Semiotic Enhancers

Semiotic enhancers are signs that reorganize the quality of experience in a catastrophic (cascadic) way. These are generalized and hypergeneralized signs that change the feeling tone of the given setting cardinally, so that the person may act and think in ways. Real-life examples entail the growth of panic attack (see above), manic phenomena, falling in love—or into jealousy or rage, and following one's ideological "calling" of professional, religious, or political kind—often with detriment to one's own well-being. Devotion is a commitment that is often unspeakable—yet proves to be strong in the history of human lives.

There are ways to create control over the controlling fields of feeling. This pertains to the **intentional enhancement** of the affective fields Imagery can play a crucial role in that. An example from the person whose panic attacks were described above illustrates how he managed to regulate one's feelings to stop further attacks:

I learned to gradually create or quickly diminish the most intense feelings of peace or terror. I would, for example, concentrate on a particularly tranquil scene, concentrate on it intently for about ten minutes. A deep feeling of rest would result, a feeling of infinite relaxation of the soul and mind. Deliberately I would attain and then disturb this condition, introducing into the <u>field of tranquility</u> a rampaging bull. With picture after picture I would tear the beatitude to shreds, gradually bringing on tremors and the usual physical and mental distress. I would then deliberately <u>wipe away</u> the disturbing visions, replacing them with the original scenes of <u>serenity</u>. (Law, 1975, cited via Baker, 1989, p. 78, added emphasis)

Here mental imagery operates as a domain for creating signs to reorganize the Level 4 fields of feeling (tranquility into distress). In their turn, the field of feeling tranquil sets the stage of constraining experience to move within that—rather than return to the distressful plane.

GENERAL CONCLUSIONS: AMBIVALENCE IN MOTION

The migrating self is powered by the mechanisms of dialogical negotiation of ambivalences (Abbey, 2006, and in this volume; Ferreira, Salgado, & Cunha, 2006; Salgado, this volume). These are partly visible in action—yet the meanings of such actions remain hidden in the dialogical complexity of the personal cultures. A young man, arriving in a foreign country, buys a pistol for self defence—against all kinds of large beasts (for whom the pistol would not work), or small ones (for whom it is not needed). Yet the feeling of security that object—or knowing that it exists—provides is a symbolic regulator of the ambivalence of the encounter with a foreign environment (Boesch, 1997, p. 111). Or a woman acquires a chest for dirty clothes and the mundane process of doing laundry becomes imbued by the hypergeneralized feeling field of "freedom" (Lang, 1993). We migrate psychologically even in the middle of most mundane everyday activities, like preparing a lunch-box for one's child going to school, or making sure the clothes and hair of the child "looks nice."

The power of the culturally structured mundane activities is substantial—precisely because these activities are necessary, and so ordinary that they are not even noted as of any consequence. Thus, the most ordinary event of children's mealtimes is redundantly and abundantly filled with meanings (Valsiner, 1997). Furthermore—some of the meanings created within such mundane environments can give rise to impetus to temporarily exit from such environments—through pilgrimage, travels, and tourism (see Gillespie, this volume).

Pilgrimage (and its contemporary secular version—tourism) is an example of semiotic construction out of the extended process of moving:

> A pilgrim is an initiand, entering into a new, deeper level of existence than he has known in his accustomed milieu. Homologous with the ordeals of tribal initiation are the trials, tribulations, and even temptations of the pilgrim's way. And at the end the pilgrim, like the novice, is exposed to powerful religious sacra (shrines, images, liturgies, curative waters, ritual circumambulations of holy objects, and so on), the beneficial effect of which depends upon the zeal and pertinacity of his quest.... In pilgrimages of the historical religions the moral unit is the individual, and his goal is salvation or release from the sins and evils of the structural world in preparation for participation in an afterlife of pure bliss. In tribal initiation the moral unit is

the social group or category, and the goal is the attainment of a new socio-cultural status and state. (Turner & Turner, 1978, pp. 8-9)

In terms of the semiotic hierarchy of self-mediation processes, the experiences of the pilgrimage are conducive of developing the Level 4— hypergeneralized feeling field kinds of signs for one's personal culture. In a way, pilgrimage is a planned rupture. The notion of rupture (and its repair) can lead to various implementations in different areas of developmental science—yet retaining one crucial feature—that of the autocatalytic nature of the system that innovates itself (Zittoun, this volume).

The theoretical system outlined here brings the notion of affect—in the form of semiotically mediated presentational fields—into the center of theory construction efforts. The crucial feature of the system is recognition of limited access to parts of the system both at the "low" (immediate feeling) and "high" (semiotically mediated overgeneralized affective fields) levels. The centrality of the use of language in its narrow meaning—verbal representation—is here transcended by indicating where in the system that kind of language functions, and under which circumstances can it be used to study the basic phenomena of human conduct. Surely the centrality of language is not diminished by this representation—what we do in our lives by its use remains as important as ever. Yet its importance is put into a helical structure of dynamics of development—in the affective life of human beings, the domains of language use are interspersed (and overcome) by unverbalizable higher-order semiotic means which in their turn regulate the very beginnings of feeling as it emerges in experience, and the way that feeling becomes available through referencing by way of language use. The eternal merry-go-round of human psychological development is that of trying to say something about the unspeakable, and not to speak about some of the speakables. Coordination of affective fields makes such complex dynamic possible.

We also experiment with scientific language of psychology, by making the notion of point-like concepts (categories) inclusive in field-like concepts, and by emphasizing the notion of infinity in case of hypergeneralization of the fields. The openness of meaning systems in science has been a tool for the development of new perspectives (Löwy, 1992). Psychology has usually hung on to the common language as its last resort for remaining close to human lives. It seems an unproductive strategy for a science—one that maintains the pseudoconceptual state of the theoretical enterprise and disallows formal generalization.

By moving to a hierarchical field theoretic model of affective self we expand our understanding of the role of language in human psychology beyond the usual view that gives language-mediated psychological materials dominant privileges over the ones that cannot described by words.

Human ordinary language is an intermediate level semiotic device for catering for many—but not all—of human psychological self-regulation needs. It is how all these symbolic means are used together in the process of negotiating one's relations with "the other"—within oneself and beyond—that is the main question.

ACKNOWLEDGMENTS

This chapter is a result of work prepared for different conferences. The bulk of it was a part of an invited lecture at the 15. Tagung der Fachgruppe Entwicklungspsychologie der Deutschen Gesellschaft für Psychologie, Potsdam, September, 5, 2001. A different rendering of the ideas expressed there has appeared in German (Valsiner, 2005b). The support of the Alexander von Humboldt-Stiftung for participating in the Tagung is gratefully appreciated. The original work was supplemented by ideas developed in conjunction with presentations at the IV Congresso Norte Nordeste de Psicologia, Salvador, Bahia, May, 28, 2005.

NOTES

1. For example, the God and the Devil—opposites as they may be—are mutually related opposites whose relation creates psychological tensions leading to violence (Rakhimov, 2001, p. 412). Likewise, the Kali myth-story speaks of the mutuality of opposites and their transformation into each other (Menon & Shweder, 1994).

2. Consider examples such as "the night feels dangerous"—there is no specifiable reason for the person who experiences the feeling to be cautious—yet the feeling provides the "this is about danger" kind of flavor to the setting.

REFERENCES

Abbey, E. A. (2006). Triadic frames for ambivalent experience. *Estudios de Psicologia, 27*(1), 33-40.

Abbey, E., & Davis, P. (2003). Constructing one's identity through autodialogue: A cultural psychological approach. In I. Josephs (Ed.), *Dialogicality in development* (pp. 69-86). Stamford, CT: Greenwood.

Abby, E., & Valsiner, J. (2005). Poetiken des Selbst: Zwischen Ambevalenz, Bedeutung, Formolösigkeit und Wandel. *Psychologie & Gesellschaftskritik, 29*(3/4) (whole No 115/116), 133-149.

Baker, R. (1989). *Panic disorder: Theory, research and therapy*. Chichester, England: Wiley.

Beck, A. T. (1988). Cognitive approaches to panic disorder: Theory and therapy. In S. Rachman & J. D. Maser (Eds.), *Panic: Psychological perspectives* (pp. 91-109). Hilldale, NJ: Erlbaum.

Bergson, H. (1889). *Essai sur les données immédiates de la conscience*. Paris: PUF.

Bergson, H (1945). *L'Evolution créatrice*. Genève, Switzerland: Éditions Albert Skira. (Original work published 1907)

Bergson, H. (1988). *Matière et mémoire*. Paris: PUF. [English translation 1988 by Urzone/Zed Books] (Original work published 1896)

Boesch, E. E. (1997). *Von der Sehnsucht*. Saarbrücken: Privater vor-abdrück.

Bonime, W. (1983). Anger as a basis for a sense of self. In M. B. Cantor & M. L. Glucksman (Eds.), *Affect: Psychoanalytic theory and practice* (pp. 249-254). New York: Wiley.

Branco, A. U., & Valsiner, J. (1997). Changing methodologies: A co-constructivist study of goal orientations in social interactions. *Psychology and Developing Societies, 9*(1), 35-64.

Briggs, J. L. (1975). The origins of nonviolence: aggression in two Canadian Eskimo groups. *The Psychoanalytic Study of the Child, 6*, 134-203.

Briggs, J. L. (1979). The creation of value in Canadian Inuit Society. *International Social Science Journal, 31*(3), 393-403.

Briggs, J. L. (1991). Expecting the unexpected: Canadian Inuit training for an experimental lifestyle. *Ethos, 19*(3), 259-287.

Bühler, K. (1907). Tatsachen und Probleme zu eine Psychologie der Denkvorgänge. I. *Archiv für die gesamte Psychologie, 9*, 297-365.

Bühler, K. (1908a). Tatsachen und Probleme zu eine Psychologie der Denkvorgänge. II, III *Archiv für die gesamte Psychologie, 12*, 1-92.

Bühler, K. (1908b). Antwort auf die von W. Wundt erhobenen Einwände gegen die Methode der Selbstbeobachtung an experimentell erzeugten Erlebnissen. *Archiv für die gesamte Psychologie, 12*, 93-122.

Cairns, R. B. (1986). Phenomena lost. In J. Valsiner (Ed.), *The individual subject and scientific psychology* (pp. 97-111). New York: Plenum.

Carpenter, K. M., & Addis, M. (2000). Alexithymia, gender, and responses to depressive symptoms. *Sex Roles, 43*(9-10), 363-378.

Cole, M. (1992). Context, modularity and the cultural constitution of development. In L. T. Winegar & J. Valsiner (Eds.), *Children's development within social context: Research and methodology* (Vol 2, pp. 5-31). Hillsdale, NJ: Erlbaum.

Cole, M. (1995). Culture and cognitive development: From cross-cultural research to creating systems of cultural mediation. *Culture & Psychology, 1*(1), 25-54.

Denzin, N. (1983). A note on emotionality, self, and interaction. *American Journal of Sociology, 89*(2), 402-409.

Denzin, N. (1985). Emotion as lived experience. *Symbolic Interaction, 8*(2), 223-240.

DeRivera, J. (1977). *A structural theory of emotions*. New York: International Universities Press.

Derne, S. (1994). Structural realities, persistent dilemmas, and the construction of emotional paradigms: love in three countries. In W. Wentworth & J. Ryad (Eds.), *Social perspectives on emotion* (Vol. 2, pp. 281-308). Greenwich, CT: JAI Press.

Deutsch, M. (1954). Field theory in social psychology. In G. Lindzey (Ed.), *Handbook of social psychology* (pp. 181-222). Cambridge, MA: Addison-Wesley.

Dewey, J. (1896). The reflex arc concept in psychology. *Psychological Review, 3*(3), 357-370.

Ferreira, T., Salgado, J., & Cunha, C. (2006). Dialogical self and ambiguity. *Estudios de Psicologia*.

Fischer, K. W., Yan, Z., & Stewart, J. (2003). Adult cognitive development: Dynamics in the developmental web. In J. Valsiner & K. J. Connolly (Eds.), *Handbook of developmental psychology* (pp. 491-516). Ondon: Sage.

Frijda, N. (1986). *The emotions*. Cambridge, MA: Cambridge University Press.

Frijda, N. H. (1988). The laws of emotion. *American Psychologist, 43*(5), 349-358.

Gigerenzer, G. (1993). The Superego, the Ego, and the Id in statistical reasoning. In G. Keren & C. Lewis (Eds.), *A handbook for data analysis in the behavioral sciences: Methodological issues* (pp. 311-339). Hillsdale, NJ: Erlbaum.

Hermans, H. J. M. (2001). The Dialogical Self: Toward a theory of personal and cultural positioning. *Culture & Psychology, 7*(3), 243-281.

James, W. (1884). What is an emotion? *Mind, 9*, 188-205.

James, W. (1890). *The principles of psychology* (Vol. 1). New York: Holt.

Josephs, I. E., Valsiner, J., & Surgan, S. E. (1999). The process of meaning construction. In J. Brandtstätdter & R. M. Lerner (Eds.), *Action & self development* (pp. 257-282). Thousand Oaks, CA: Sage.

Kahneman, D. (1998). Objective happiness. In D. Kahneman, E. Diener, & N Schwarz (Eds.), *Well-being: The foundations of hedonic psychology* (pp. 3-25). New York: Russell Sage Foundation.

Krueger, F. (1913). Magical factors in the first development of human labor. *American Journal of Psychology, 24*, 256-261.

Krueger, F. (1926). Über psychische Ganzheit. *Neue Psychologische Studien, 1*(1)-121.

Krueger, F. (1928a). Das Wesen der Gefühle. *Archiv für die gesamte Psychologie, 65*, 91-128.

Krueger, F. (1928b). The essence of feeling. In M. L. Reymert (Ed.), *Feelings and emotions: The Wittenberg symposium* (pp. 58-86). Worcester, MA: Clark University Press.

Külpe, O. (1892). Das Ich und die Aussenwelt. *Philosophische Studien, 7*, 394-413.

Külpe, O. (1903). The problem of attention. *The Monist, 13*, 38-68.

Külpe, O. (1912-1923). *Die Realisierung: Ein Beiträg zur grundlegung der Realwissenschaften*. Vol. 1(1912), Vol. 2 (1920), Vol. 3 (1923). Leipzig: S. Hirzel.

Laird, J. D. (1974). Self-attribution of emotion: the effects of expressive behavior on the quality of emotional experience. *Journal of Personality & Social Psychology, 33*, 475-486.

Laird, J. D., & Bressler, C. (1992). The process of emotional experience: A self-perception theory. In M. S. Clark (Ed.), *Emotion* (pp. 213-234). Newbury Park, CA: Sage.

Lang, A. (1993). Non-Cartesian artefacts in dwelling activities: Steps towards a semiotic ecology. *Schweizerische Zeitschrift für Psychologie, 52*(2), 138-147.

Lazarus, R. (1991). *Emotion and adaptation*. New York: Oxford University Press

Lazarus, R., & Folkman, S. (1984). *Stress, appraisal, and coping*. New York: Springer.

Leavitt, J. (1996). Meaning and feeling in the anthropology of emotions. *American Ethnologist, 23*(3), 514-539.

Lewin, K. (1917). Kriegeslandschaft. *Zeitschrift für angewandte Psychologie, 12*, 440-447.

Lewin, K. (1936). *Principles of topological psychology.* New York: McGraw-Hill.

Löwy, I. (1992). The strength of loose concepts—boundary concepts, federative experimental strategies and disciplinary growth: The case study of immunology. *History of Science, 30*(90), Part 4, 376-396.

Lyra, M. C. D. P. (1999). An excursion into the dynamics of dialogue. *Culture & Psychology, 5*(4), 477-489.

Mead, G. H. (1912). The mechanism of social consciousness. *Journal of Philosophy, 9*, 401-406.

Mead, G. H. (1913). The social self. *Journal of Philosophy, 10*, 374-380.

Menon, U., & Shweder, R. A. (1994). Kali's tongue: cultural psychology and the power of "shame" in Orissa. In S. Kitayama & H. Markus (Eds.), *Emotion and culture* (pp. 237-280). Washington, DC: American Psychological Association.

Morsbach, H., & Tyler, W., J. (1986). A Japanese emotion: Amae. In R. Harre (Ed.), *The social construction of emotion* (pp. 289-307). Oxford, England: Blackwell.

Nemeroff, C., & Rozin, P. (1992). Sympathetic magical beliefs and kosher dietary practice: The interaction of rules and feelings. *Ethos, 20*(1), 96-115.

Nöth, W. (1998). Ecosemiotics. *Töid margisüsteemide alalt/Sign System Studies, 26*, 332-434.

Nöth, W. (2001). Semiotic foundations of iconicity in language and literature. In O. Fischer & M. Nänny (Eds.), *The motivated sign* (pp. 17-28). Amsterdam: John Benjamins.

Obeyesekere, G. (1985). Depression, Buddhism, and the work of culture in Sri Lanka. In A. Kleinman & B. Good (Eds.), *Culture and depression* (pp. 134-152). Berkeley: University of California Press.

Ogden, R. M. (1951). Oswald Külpe and the Würzburg school. *American Journal of Psychology, 64*(1), 4-19.

Ohnuki-Tierney, E. (1994). The power of absence: Zero signifiers and their transgressions. *L'Homme, 34*(2) (Whole No. 130), 59-76.

Poddiakov, A. N., & & Valsiner, J. (in press). Intransitivity cycles and their transformations: How dynamically adapting systems function? *Theory & Psychology.*

Rakhimov, R. R. (2001). Nasilie v kul'ture Tadzhikov [Violence in Tajik culture]. In V. V. Bocharov & V. A. Tishkov (Eds.), *Antropologia nasilia* [Anthropology of violence] (pp. 382-475). Sakt-Peterburg: Nauka.

Rosenberg, M. (1990). Reflexivity and emotions. *Social Psychology Quarterly, 53*(1), 3-12.

Scheler, M. (1992). *On feeling, knowing, and valuing.* Chicago: University of Chicago Press.

Selz, O. (1982). Die Gesetze der produktiven und reproduktiven Geistestätigkeit: Kurzgefasste Darstellung. In N. H. Frijda & A. D. DeGroot (Eds.), *Otto Selz: His contribution to psychology* (pp. 20-75). The Hague, Netherlands: Mouton. (Original work published 1924)

Sifenos, P. E. (1974). Reconsideration of psychodynamic mechanisms in psychosomatic symptom formation in view of recent clinical observations. *Psychotherapy & Psychosomatics, 25*, 151.

Simon, H. A. (1967). Motivational and emotional controls of cognition. *Psychological Review, 74*(1), 29-39.

Smith, C. A., & Lazarus, R. S. (1993). Appraisal components, core relational themes, and the emotions. *Cognition and Emotion, 7*(3-4), 233-269.

Smith, N. W., & Smith, L. L. (1996). Field theory in science: its role as a necessary and sufficient condition in psychology. *Psychological Record, 46*, 3-19.

Smythe, W. E. (2005). On the psychology of "as if." *Theory & Psychology, 15*(3), 283-303.

Sovran, T. (1992). Between similarity and sameness. *Journal of Pragmatics, 18*(4), 329-344.

Taylor, J., Bagby, M., & Parker, J. (1997). *Disorders of affect regulation.* New York: Cambridge University Press.

Turner, V., & Turner, E. (1978). *Image and pilgrimage in Christian culture.* New York: Columbia University Press.

Valsiner, J. (1997). *Culture and the development of children's action* (2nd ed). New York: Wiley.

Valsiner, J. (2001). Process structure of semiotic mediation in human development. *Human Development, 44*, 84-97.

Valsiner, J. (2002). Forms of dialogical relations and semiotic autoregulation of the self. *Theory & Psychology, 12*(2), 251-265.

Valsiner, J. (Ed.). (2005a). *Heinz Werner and developmental science.* New York: Kluwer Scientific/Plenum.

Valsiner, J. (2005b). Affektive Entwicklung im kulturellen Kontext. In J. Asendorpf (Ed.), *Enzyklopädie der psychologie: Soziale, emotionale und Persönlichkeitsentwicklung* (Vol. 3). Göttingen: Hogrefe.

Valsiner, J., & Diriwächter, R. (2005). Qualitative Forschungsmethoden in historischen und epistemologischen Kontexten In G. Mey (Ed.), *Qualitative Forschung in der Entwicklungspsychologie* (pp. 35-55). Köln: Kölner Studien Verlag.

Valsiner, J., & Van der Veer, R. (1993). The encoding of distance: The concept of the zone of proximal development and its interpretations. In R. R. Cocking & K. A. Renninger (Eds.), *The development and meaning of psychological distance* (pp. 35-62). Hillsdale, NJ: Erlbaum.

Vygotsky, L. S. (1971). *Psychology of art.* Cambridge, MA: MIT Press. (Original work published 1925)

Vygotsky, L. S. (1987). *Psikhologia iskusstva.* Moscow: Pedagogika.

Werner, H., & Kaplan, B. (1956). The developmental approach to cognition. *American Anthropologist, 58*, 866-880.

Wertsch, J. V. (1998). *Mind as action.* New York: Oxford University Press.

Zittoun, T. (2006). *Transitions: Development through symbolic resources.* Greenwich, CT: Information Age.

INTERSUBJECTIVITY AND THE EXPERIENCE OF OTHERNESS

A Reflection Upon Relational Accounts of Subjectivity

Carla Cunha

Otherness is a dynamic ingredient of human living. However, this commentary pretends to show, how this phenomenon's conceptualization reflects its multiple dimensions and ontologies. The present commentary has different goals it aims to achieve. I will initially try to highlight some of the working definitions of otherness attributed by the different authors in this part of the book and the different ontologies of intersubjectivity that underlie them (Marková, 2003a). Since I feel that the different and complementary looks on otherness are intimately linked to our understanding of intersubjectivity, this issue will also be further explored, in a personal reflection regarding some of the works referenced by these authors. I conclude this commentary with an integrative synthesis of the explored theoretical approaches and some practical implications to psychological intervention.[1]

Otherness in Question: Labyrinths of the Self, 379–391

INTERSUBJECTIVITY AND OTHERNESS

When initially reading these chapters, my first thoughts were that the notions of *otherness* or alterity developed by each author were built out of some kind of conception of intersubjectivity, either regarding the external relationship between I and *Other* or the internal relationship between I and myself (as an *Other*). I sensed that each author presented different ontological commitments toward their notions of *otherness*, perhaps steaming from different perspectives upon intersubjectivity.

Regarding these matters, Ivana Marková (2003a) describes two generic approaches to intersubjectivity: a first approach conceives the relationship between I and *Other* (or *Ego* and *Alter*) as an irreducible dyad of interdependent and bounded elements. As she states elsewhere (Marková, 2003b), this corresponds to a dialogical—Bakhtinian conception, since every act of meaning is based on the communicational relationship between *Ego* and *Alter*. Therefore, within this perspective, I and *Other* simultaneously work as different but mutually bounded elements. Primacy is given to the relationship (between I and *Other*), instead of the autonomous substance of each of these elements (Ferreira, Salgado, & Cunha, 2006). This first kind of ontology emphasizes the dynamic features of relationships treating them as an irreducible unit of analysis that is brought to the foreground. This strategy is not exclusive of dialogism, since there is a long tradition of thought within Psychology that shares the same ontological principles—for example, the works of James Baldwin, George Herbert Mead and Lev Vygotsky (Marková, 2003a). An essential common feature to these traditions is "the idea that the mechanism of knowing oneself and the mechanism for knowing others are one and the same" (Marková, 2003a, p. 250).

The second generic ontological approach described by Marková (2003a) assumes I and *Other* "as existentially separated from one another. This means that their point of departure is either "I" or "Other" and that they pose the question as to how the gap between I and Others can be reduced" (p. 250). In the first ontology, I and Other are taken as separated, but bounded together. Here, the separation takes the form of an exclusive separation (Valsiner, 1998). Therefore, this second kind of ontology focuses greatly on separateness and permanence of the elements. When we draw attention to this gap between I and Other as an unattainable separateness we are emphasizing exclusion between these elements. Usually, focusing and elaborating on one of the elements leads to devaluing the other and its role on the relationship. Consequently, this leads to giving priority to one element or to the other and not to the relationship in which they are involved. Furthermore, losing the focus on the relationship is losing track of the process of transformation and its dynamism. Losing dynamism leads to substantiation. In this sense, I and *Other* may relate because they are beings, instead of assuming that "to be is to communicate" (Bakhtin, 1929/1984, p. 187).

This has lead to very different theoretical and ethical ideas, varying in the kind of primacy given to I or *Other* in human existence (Marková, 2003a). On the one hand, we have the self-centred, egological traditions (like Descartes and Husserl), that emphasize the *Ego*, and, on the other, we have some phenomenologically oriented thinkers that give primacy to the *Alter* (the *Other*) such as Levinas.

With these ontological frameworks in mind, each of the authors was asked to explain how they would position themselves in regards to the described distinction, since I assumed that this clarification would allow a better understanding of the notions of *otherness* and alterity explored in their chapters. The following presentation will reflect my reading about their specific positioning, departing from a more interpersonal to a more intrapersonal point of view regarding intersubjectivity, and in a movement from the second kind of ontology of intersubjectivity to the first kind, as described by Marková (2003a).

The interpersonal domain of intersubjectivity sets the tone of work developed by Danilo Guimarães and Lívia Simão (this volume). Even if they conceptualize the possibility of internal intersubjectivity (as in their reading of Hermans' dialogical self theory), they choose to focus on the interpersonal domain of intersubjectivity (taken as a shared domain between I and *Other*), and on the consequent notion of *otherness* (as the acknowledgment of differences between I and *Other*) (Guimarães & Simão, this volume). For them, following Rommetveit (1992), this communion between I and *Other* is always illusory and presupposed. Accordingly, intersubjectivity is always a situated event, specific in time and relationship, that implies the decentration of the subject in assuming his interlocutor's perspective or at least that his interlocutor will try to act as if he also assumes the same (Guimarães & Simão, this volume). Following this, experiencing alterity is being confronted with the illusory aspect of this supposition. Alterity is "a kind of I-Other relationship encompassing the openness to being touched by the Other's diversity" (Guimarães & Simão, personal communication, December 9, 2005) and "although misunderstandings are part and parcel of the dialogue, ... the main issue for the relation of alterity is the availability of being touched by contextually situated misunderstandings" (Guimarães & Simão, personal communication, December 9, 2005).

Hence, regarding the two alternative types of ontologies described by Marková (2003a), Guimarães and Simão (personal communication, December 9, 2005) subscribe to the second kind of ontology of intersubjectivity. However, "I and Other, in their existence, tacitly try to fit their 'phenomenology as beings' to the first ontology, although always accomplishing to fit into the second one" (Guimarães & Simão, personal communication, December 9, 2005), since they never diminish the gap between I and *Other* and always fall into the realization that their sharedness is illusory. "If we consider the permanent quest of the I for relating to the *Other* and—more important—its permanent relationship and never accomplished longing for coinciding with the Other, we could say that I and Other do not form an irreducible unit, but that the irreducible fact is precisely the permanent relationship searching for that coincidence" (Guimarães & Simão, personal communication, December 9, 2005). We could then say, that they present a sceptical view of intersubjectivity as they seem to highlight the radical and unattainable distance between I and *Other*, while the possibility of attunement and mutuality (even tentative) within this relationship is undervalued. The separateness between I-Other precedes and proceeds the attempt to establish and accomplish a relationship between them. "It is in this pursue for accomplishment that the I faces itself with the alterity of the Other" (Guimarães & Simão, personal communication, December 9, 2005). They further define the distance between I and *Other*, taking the issue of corporeality into account as brought to discussion by phenomenologists like Merleau-Ponty. "I and Other are existentially separated in their corporeality: before my existence, the Other is already there. This event establishes the I-Other asymmetry even at those moments they feel meeting one another" (Guimarães & Simão, personal communication, December 9, 2005). As we can see, this phenomenological Merleaupontian influence clearly places them in the second kind of ontology when assuming the existential, corporeal and phenomenological separateness between I and *Other*.

In turn, Mick Cooper and Hubert Hermans choose not to commit to one of the alternative ontologies described by Marková (2003), preferring "to regard human beings both as interdependent and as existentially separate – albeit at different levels of being" (personal communication, Cooper & Hermans, November 17, 2005). However, they assume that their chapter is "based on certain intersubjective principles, inspired in the works of Vygotsky, particularly the assumption that our mode of self-relating is an internalised form of relationships with others" (Cooper & Hermans, personal communication, November 17, 2005), but prefer to focus on intrapersonal processes and to explore the mode of self-relating (with inner-*otherness*). In this sense, if Marková's (2003a) reading of Vygotsky's work and his dynamic intertwining of "inter- and intra-psychological processes" (p. 250) were to be taken into account through her classification of ontologies of intersubjectivity, we would place Cooper and Hermans' work in the first kind of ontology described.

Nevertheless, another quite important aspect that Cooper and Hermans (personal communication, November 17, 2005) highlight, and that is perhaps at the basis of their refusal to make a definite ontological commitment regarding these issues, is the clarification that one of the contemporary challenges to the several theoretical attempts of describing human beings as relational beings is "how to find a way of advocating an intersubjective position while still retaining some space for notions of agency and independence" (Cooper & Hermans, personal communication, November 17, 2005).

In my view, Cooper and Hermans' concerns relate to the insufficient theoretical approaches linked to the notions of *otherness* and intersubjectivity. In this sense, they acknowledge that: (1) the contemporary literature on *otherness* generally dismisses the discussion of this concept from an intrapersonal point of view (Cooper & Hermans, this volume), and (2) the notion of intersubjectivity is generally associated to the relationship with an (external) *Other* and is also treated and studied with a wide range of meanings, resulting in difficulties in communication between researchers or theorists (Beebe, Knoblauch, Rustin, & Sorter, 2005). Following this, and while the theoretical answers still are not enough; they think it is more useful to explore the coexistence of an intersubjective and independent human existence, rather than assuming these characteristics as opposed (Cooper & Hermans, personal communication, November 17, 2005).

In their personal view on *otherness*, Cooper and Hermans (this volume) try to take the contemporary theoretical approaches on these issues to the next level of being—the intrapersonal domain. Doing this, they argue that *otherness* can be experienced within one's own being as self-*otherness*, but not as a constitutive quality of the self (and this argument separates them from Valsiner's work that we will discuss next). Inner-*otherness* is in a continuum with the *otherness* experience of an external *Other*, and is linked to the phenomenological experience of the self with that mysterious and enigmatic quality of the *Other*'s being (Cooper & Hermans, this volume). Assuming that the movement of the self toward sameness and identity can be intertwined with its diversity, difference, and alterity, the question that seems relevant to ask is what is the genetic process of these strange or alien I-positions. Concerning this, Cooper and Hermans state that their chapter

is very much phenomenological in its ontology, and in this respect, 'the self' is not conceptualized as a fixed generative force or entity but a concept that is held within the person's phenomenological field. In this respect, therefore one might argue that alien positions are generated through the interaction of the organism with their environment and with others.... It's when we shift to a phenomenological understanding of the self that *otherness* can have meaning. (personal communication, November 17, 2005)

As we can see, to these authors, inner-*otherness* is an important experience of the self which "lies coiled in the heart of being—like a worm" (Cooper & Hermans, this volume) and consists in, the self confronting its own alterity. This experience can be met with a refusal or a difficulty to accept inner multiplicity and engage in dialogue with these more obscure and strange parts of being. This represents a very important and pragmatic psychotherapeutic challenge, so I will try to return to this question later on.

Following G. H. Mead, Jaan Valsiner's theoretical work (this volume), like Cooper and Hermans (this volume), also tries to surpass some of these difficulties in bringing intersubjectivity (or relation) into the inner dynamics of the self. Following G. H. Mead, he presents an integration of the interpersonal with the intrapersonal domain of human development. As G. H. Mead points out, any communicational act or *project* is not only individual but also social, because it depends on an *Other* that completes and validates it—mutual recognition of each of the interlocutors is an imperative in order to attain a shared intelligibility (Linnel, 1998). However, in the precise process of carrying out that communicational project of saying something to another, an immediate feedback loop is established, and the first response is from the self itself (Valsiner, this volume). His conception of human living as the movement of potential becoming, always put in motion by the passing of time, sets the notion of *otherness* (treated with the same meaning as alterity) at the centre of theoretical enquiry (Valsiner, this volume). This *otherness* is not only interpersonal but also intrapersonal since it is implied in all relationships, external and internal, as the irreversibility of time also implies the necessity of relating to me (I and Me—as an *Other*). In this sense, it came as no surprise to me the fact that he clearly subscribed the first ontological framework of intersubjectivity (Valsiner, personal communication, November 23, 2005). He further elaborates this commitment, claiming that only this kind of ontology—a dynamic abstraction—would take into account the irreversibility of time that he brings into the core of human living (personal communication, November 23, 2005).

In synthesis, the working understandings entailed in the notion of *otherness* developed in each of the chapters are particular to its authors and seem to be important and complementary parts of this phenomenon. Guimarães and Simão focus on the notion of *otherness* in the interpersonal domain, highlighting that the difference between I and *Other* is an ever-present phenomena, even if we sometimes engage in everyday relationships acting as if we could surpass it or deny it. Cooper and Hermans (as well as Valsiner) discuss this notion at an intrapersonal domain, and stress its importance in the relationship with ourselves. To Cooper and Hermans, even if *otherness* is a common experience in our everyday lives, the experience of the self confronting its own alterity may be a challenging one and is particularly important for psychotherapeutic purposes. In turn Valsiner, assumes an ontological commitment with the notion of movement in human living and construction of identity, bringing the question of *otherness* at an ontological level of being. Assuming *otherness* and alterity as constitutive parts of the self, his concerns are toward our ignorance of it, and how human beings construct their sameness and identity in the midst of a migrating existence.

Exploring Intersubjectivity

Given this reflection so far, intersubjectivity theories seem to me an important resource to understand the notion of *otherness* (and complementary versions of it). Since all the authors mentioned some interesting works in this field, it seems pertinent to me to present some reflections upon this field of study and its contributions to an understanding of human existence (in the interpersonal and intrapersonal domains).

Some interesting work about intersubjectivity is found in the reflections of Beatrice Beebe and colleagues. Since this observation is both shared by me, Cooper and Hermans (personal communication, November 17, 2005), I will take this opportunity to point out some of the most interesting remarks I found in her work. Beebe, Knoblauch, Rustin, and Sorter (2005) start acknowledging that in spite of the importance that the concept of intersubjectivity has to the understanding of infant intersubjectivity and adult treatment, the multiple uses and working understandings of this notion create obstacles to the integration of knowledge. In light of this conceptual *heteroglossia* (Bakhtin, 1981), the authors claim it preferable to use the notion *forms of intersubjectivity* (Beebe, Knoblauch, et al., 2005).

In a critical review of three leading theorists and researchers in the field of infant intersubjectivity (Meltzoff, Trevarthen, & Stern), Beebe, Rustin, Sorter, and Knoblauch (2005) emphasize that a complete account of intersubjectivity needs to intertwine issues of matching, difference, and complementarity, in a more complex view that integrates the contextual meanings (of the specific interactions and responses of each of the communicational agents) and the interpersonal history of the dyad in action (cf. Lyra, in press, for a specific effort of developing this issue in infant research). To me, this seems to be an acknowledgement that the field of intersubjectivity studies needs to incorporate the complementary notions

of connectedness and asymmetry in the conceptualization of human relationships. Overall, the most eminent theories of intersubjectivity tend to
depart from the face-to-face paradigm in the interactional context
between infant—caregiver (or infant—experimenter) and elaborate their
findings upon the "similarity" form of matching (focusing on imitation,
behavioral similarities or mutual sensing the other interlocutor). This
view of intersubjectivity is rather narrow, since it only emphasizes *sharedness* between two minds. However important these findings are to the
development of a more accurate and complete view of a theory of mind,
they disregard the role of difference, mismatching, and complementarity,
also important factors to a better understanding of human interaction
processes in a broader sense. As such, it is at the heart of difference and
complementarity that *otherness* and alterity come to being. According to
Marková, "the key to intersubjectivity was not only mutuality and reciprocity, but, above all, the dialogical asymmetry and tension" (2003a, p.
256).

Beebe, Knoblauch et al. (2005) realize that theoretically this issue is
not being sufficiently taken into account, and add that "it is the process
of moving back and forth between similarity and difference that constructs and fine-tunes the alignment" (p. 73). Following this line of reasoning, they prefer to define intersubjectivity as what is going on
between two minds, instead of committing only to a specific feature of
sharedness. This acknowledgment creates space not only for the already
accepted knowledge about correspondence and similarity but also for
the theoretical and empirical exploration of difference and complementarity.

Although this previously presented synthesis based on the extensive
critical work of Beebe, Knoblauch, Rustin, and Sorter (2005) represents
an important recognition of the empirical and theoretical paths regarding
intersubjectivity in infancy and adult psychotherapy still waiting to be
developed, I still notice a strong emphasis on the interpersonal realm that
is felt throughout the several approaches in this field. The theoretical
attempts to conceptualize intrapersonal intersubjective processes are still
very scarce and this contributes to the general assumption that intersubjectivity is only related to the interpersonal domain. This specific concern
has already been highlighted by Cooper and Hermans (personal communication, November 17, 2005) and touches an issue also elaborated by
Guimarães and Simão (this volume).

More specifically, Guimarães and Simão (this volume) present an interesting theoretical contribution to the discussion of intersubjectivity in the
intrapersonal domain which complements the present reflections. They
relate to Nick Crossley's work (1996) in distinguishing two different types
of intersubjectivity in human development. This author (Crossley, 1996),

coming from a phenomenological background, argues "that self and other are necessarily relational terms and that neither can be conceived as pre-existing the other" (p. 15) and assumes that infants bring "a pre-reflective opening out onto an engagement with alterity" (p. 24). He assumes that this innate openness to the *Other* (radical intersubjectivity) is prior to the egological sense of the *Other*. Therefore, radical intersubjectivity implies this mutuality and immediate harmonization of the I with the *Other* (Guimarães & Simão, this volume), that precedes and facilitates the creation of "our sense of self and the possibility of our adopting a reflective attitude" (Crossley, 1996 p. 47) necessary to the egologic intersubjectivity. The notion of egologic intersubjectivity accounts for reflection and selfhood. The experience of the *Other*, in this intersubjective mode, is not as immediate, since it is allowed by imagination (Crossley, 1996). Egological intersubjectivity "is precisely mediated by way of our anticipations, our 'taking the attitude of the other' and staging" (Crossley, 1996, p. 68).

Personally, I think Crossley's approach is an interesting attempt to solve some of the ontological problems presented to the phenomenological movement, creating a more relational account of human beings and human experience. However, the task of conceptualizing consciousness as relational when coming from a phenomenological tradition does not seem to be an easy one. Crossley attempts to achieve it conceptualizing that the sense of selfhood and the construction of a personal identity is relational in its nature. In his view, this happens because radical intersubjectivity—the complete openness to the *Other*'s alterity—is an innate feature of human development, prior to the sense of ones' Ego. From my personal point of view, it is here that I find some unresolved issues. About his notion of radical intersubjectivity, I ask: how is it possible for the conjugation of minds to happen without a simultaneous however rudimentary sense of differentiation with the Other? I personally share the assumption that human beings are born with innate capabilities for establishing relationships (Trevarthen & Aitkin, 2001) but I also believe that they must also bring a rudimentary sense of being separate and different, therefore experiencing the world (and the *Other*) from a specific event of being (Holquist, 1990). Some infancy intersubjectivity researchers like Fogel, de Koeyer, Bellagamba, and Bell (2002) argue that

> self-awareness can be directly perceived from the first days of life and perhaps during the late fetal period. The neurophysiology of perception requires that individuals must perceive themselves, their spatial and temporal location, in order to be able to locate and identify an object. (p. 194)

In my view, this means that we cannot expect that an egological sense of being is not there from that very beginning of human life—we must assume that it is there simultaneously with the ability to connect with the Other.

Concerning the discussion of egological intersubjectivity Crossley (1996) repeatedly relies upon a notion of human imagination that allows us to sense the Other, and states that "relations to the other, in this mode, I have argued, are based upon an imaginary transposition of one's thoughts and feelings to the other" (p. 68). Being aware of the intimate association, in common understanding, between imagination and private images and representations, he questions himself: "Does this mean that imagination is the constituent of subjectivity which finally individualises us, breaking the intersubjectivity fabric?" (p. 68). He denies this later on, advocating a definition of imagination as relationally constituted because even if it uses the common private images and representations or discourse, it has all been the result of a process of an individual incorporation of social *praxis*. This seems an important remark, but it feels incomplete, because he does not address the possibility of establishing a relationship with ourselves prior to the ability of representing something through imagination. From a phenomenological point of view, what happens when I am communicating with myself? Is this a relational experience only because I am using a representational/imaginative mind? Are infants unable to communicate (and relate) to themselves until they are imbued with a representational mind? Crossley's account on reflectivity seems an important step forward, but leaves a prereflective level of being still resting ambiguously unproblematized.

A human beings primary tool for *relating* is affectivity (Valsiner, this volume)—and this is especially true for infants. In this sense, I believe that a more complete description of human beings as relational beings must allow for a relational account of affects. Even if it explains how affective experience, then, becomes socially mediated by culture and society. To me, this seems to be the attempt made by Valsiner throughout his work. The development of generalization and hypergeneralization processes in affective experience that is initiated in the first moments of life, lead to the construction of rhythms, behavioral patterns, and expectancies that constitute a "sameness" in the sense of self, motivate the individual orientation (toward the future and toward others) and lead to the construction of identity and stability. This way, agency and independence are explained by these recursive (implicit and explicit) patterns in affective experience, motivated orientation and meaning-making. In this sense, becoming a person is an affective process, socially and semiotically mediated.

Some Theoretical Conclusions and Practical Implications

Independently from the way we conceptualize it, otherness is a constant phenomenon of human existence. The different chapters in this part of the book explored different versions of this issue. Guimarães and Simão focused on the otherness that is present in our interpersonal relationships, as a pervasive remembrance of the illusive possibility of complete sharedness and synchrony with an Other that is not I, and in this sense, is very different from me. Cooper and Hermans explored inner-otherness as our confrontation with strange and unfamiliar constituents of ourselves that challenge our ability to accept them as part of our being. Valsiner brought otherness to an ontological level of human existence, as an inevitable by-product of our constant moving in a process of potential becoming.

If we assume, as Valsiner says, otherness at an ontological level, our task as human beings is to ignore it constructing our unity, our sameness, our identity. In this sense, human beings are constantly trying to make (usual) sense of the novelty imposed by our moving experience. But what happens when we are confronted with difficulties in achieving this task? As Cooper and Hermans explore, our being is sometimes confronted with the impossibility of ignoring our inner-multiplicity, experiencing it as a difficulty in engaging in dialogue with it, sometimes alienating it and disowning it when that happens. Other times, our troubles with otherness come from our difficulties of engaging in dialogue with other human beings, while we are too concentrated in the differences between us and incapable of presupposing the possibility of communion and complementarity in order to achieve it.

I believe these difficulties place important challenges to psychological intervention—whether we talk about interpersonal relationships with different others or about our intrapersonal relationships. Following Cooper and Hermans (this volume), at the macrolevel of society and culture, difficulties in accepting otherness create multicultural and social conflicts and alienation; at the microlevel of human beings, we may conceptualize several (if not all) individual motives for engaging in psychotherapy as difficulties in relating to inner-otherness or other-otherness. Psychotherapy should provide a context of facilitation of the dialogue with an otherness that is alienated. Honoring this Other is, in my opinion, a bit different from what Cooper and Hermans (this volume) defend. We have no alibi to (an addressed and addressing) existence (Bakhtin, 1993). Hence, to dialogue with otherness is engaging in an interaction that expects this reciprocal movement and accepts the consequent "surplus of seeing" (Holquist, 1990), this complementary version of the world that is created. Facilitating this dialogue in a psychotherapy context may imply the facilitation of communication between the self and the alienated parts that are being avoided socially and cast away from (a dialogical) existence.

NOTE

1. This commentary was structured departing from interviews to the authors in this part of the book, concerning some of the ideas explored in their chapters. Some of their reflections are cited throughout this commentary, under the reference of personal communication. Although I tried to remain faithful to their answers, I must assume full responsibility for selecting some extracts of the whole interviews.

REFERENCES

Bakhtin, M. M. (1981). *The dialogic imagination: Four essays by M. M. Bakhtin* (C. Emerson & M. Holquist, Trans.). Austin: University of Texas Press.

Bakhtin, M. M. (1984). *Problems of Dostoevky's poetics* (C. Emerson, Trans.). Minneapolis: University of Minnesota Press. (Original work published in 1929, revised in 1963)

Bakhtin, M. M. (1993). Toward a philosophy of the act (V. Liapunov, Trans.) Austin: University of Texas Press.

Beebe, B., Knoblauch, S., Rustin, J., & Sorter, D. (Eds.). (2005). *Forms of intersubjectivity in infancy and adult treatment.* New York: Other Press.

Beebe, B., Rustin, J., Sorter, D., & Knoblauch, S. (2005). An expanded view of forms of intersubjectivity in infancy and their application to psychoanalysis. In B. Beebe, S. Knoblauch, J. Rustin, & D. Sorter (Eds.), *Forms of intersubjectivity in infant research and adult treatment* (pp. 55-88). New York: Other Press.

Crossley, N. (1996). *Intersubjectivity: The fabric of social becoming.* London: Sage.

Ferreira, T., Salgado, J., & Cunha, C. (2006). Ambiguity and the dialogical self: In search for a dialogical psychology. *Estudios de Psicologia, 27,* 19-32.

Fogel, A., de Koeyer, I., Bellagamba, F., & Bell, H. (2002). The dialogical self in the first two years of life: Embarking on a journey of discovery. *Theory and Psychology, 12,* 191-205.

Holquist, M. (1990). *Dialogism: Bakhtin and his world.* New York: Routledge.

Linnel, P. (1998). *Approaching dialogue: Talk, interaction and context in dialogical perspectives.* Amsterdam: John Benjamins.

Lyra, M. C. D. P. (2006). Mother-infant communication development and the emergence of self: The constributions of dynamic systems and dialogism. In C. Lightfoot, M. C. D. P. Lyra, & J. Valsiner (Eds.), *Challenges and strategies for studying human development in cultural contexts.* Greenwich, CT: Information Age.

Marková, I. (2003a). Constitution of the self: Intersubjectivity and dialogicality. *Culture & Psychology, 9,* 249-259.

Marková, I. (2003b). *Dialogicality and social representations*. Cambridge, England: Cambridge University Press.

Rommetveit, R. (1992). Outlines of a dialogically based social-cognitive approach to human cognition and communication. In A. H. Wold (Ed.), *The dialogical alternative: Towards a theory of language and mind* (pp. 19-44). Oslo: Scandinavian Press.

Trevarthen, C., & Aitken, K. J. (2001). Infant intersubjectivity: Research, theory, and clinical applications. *Journal of Child Psychology & Psychiatry, 42,* 3-48.

Valsiner, J. (1998). *The guided mind: A sociogenetic approach*. Cambridge, MA: Harvard University Press.

GENERAL CONCLUSIONS (EDITORS)

Multiple Faces of OTHERNESS Within the Infinite Labyrinths of the Self

Lívia Mathias Simão and Jaan Valsiner

The main purpose of this book was to stimulate reflections on the issue of otherness in the research domain of self and cultural psychology. Otherness necessarily entails duality with a center point (Figure 1).

The issues of "otherness" in the social sciences concentrate on the issues of that "other" relates back with the myriad of phenomena we designate as "the self." Thus, the discourse of SELF <> OTHER RELATIONS is what we are involved in while trying to unveil the secrets of the labyrinths of the human *psyche*.

As could be expected the various contributions here presented have made it possible for us to arrive at plural perspectives about the focused issue. Talking about them only in terms of their complementarities or nonexclusiveness seems not to do justice to their richness. As human

Otherness in Question: Labyrinths of the Self, 393–405

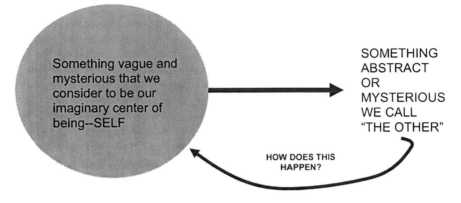

Figure 1.   Duality entailed in I-Other relationships.

selves are dialogically heterogeneous, so are the perspectives of research-ers who try to make sense of those.

THE UNITY IN DISUNITY:
THE MOSAIC OF THE OTHER IN THE SELF

There are two mutually opposed—yet related—tendencies of thought present in this book. First, we can see convergence among the contribu-tors' proposals referring to I-Other relationships under the label of *alter-ity*—there is always some dimension of change that happens to the I thanks to the *tensions-filled relationship* with the *different, alien, strange, or disquieting* character of the other. The "other" is not just different—but also strange, foreign, alien—yet by being that—challenging, appealing, and motivating. In sum, the I creates the "other" and is then *affected* by that "other."

However, on the other side—a multiplicity of "faces of otherness" emerges from the contributions in this volume, each of them corre-sponding to different models about the process by which the I is affected. They form a mosaic of theoretical-methodological and ethical approaches to the issue of alterity in the contemporary domain of cul-tural psychology of the self. If taken from the perspective of research-ers' quest for constructing new approaches to realities—or constructing new realities—the polyphonic character of this book can be fruitful for our research domain (Poddiakov, Interview Part III, this volume). But there is still a long road from the potential usefulness to actual theoretical advances.

In these final conclusions we want to highlight some additional aspects of this mosaic, specially trying to point to other features that can also be part of the whole mosaic. The proposals here presented by the contributors seem to emerge from, as well as are constructed by, a theoretical field that makes them more similar than different one another respect to the various psychologies they belong. However, behind that apparent similarity, there are different ontologies concerning intersubjectivity in I-Other relationships (Marková, 2003a, 2003b) that guide each of them (see for instance Cunha, Interview Part V, this volume). The issue of otherness brings in to discussion different forms of I-Other relationships present in each of the different ontologies that govern the field of knowledge construction in psychology.

Open Nature of "Otherness"

The issue of otherness usually sets up a dichotomous discussion about the subject-other inseparability (fusion) versus the isolation of the subject (solipsism). As far as the core of the notion of otherness is the subject's openness to somebody else, both inseparability and isolation seem to be out of the field of alterity. Inseparability is a theoretical claim of inherent unity of the phenomenon with its environment, while isolation is its oppo-

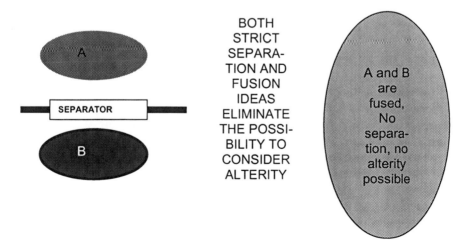

Figure 2. Forms of I-Other relationship that eliminate alterity.

site tendency to exclusively separate the two. Both of them would prevent the essential openness. Isolation and inseparability are both forms of non-openness to the alterity (Figure 1). If A and B are strictly separated, there is no relationship between them enabled. Hence no alterity is possible. If the two are fused and there is no boundary between them—again no relationship is possible—hence no alterity.

At the metaphorical level, isolation and inseparability of subject-other are analogous to dogmatic and eclectic epistemological and ethical positions, where differences are denied and become flattened. According to Figueiredo (1992), the difficulty for understanding a situation usually brings anxiety to the subject. Dogmatic and eclectic positions are both defense against such anxiety that block the subject's contact with the source of anxiety. The dogmatic attitude prevents the subject from the contact with the different by disqualifying it as not reasonable or admissible because it does not fit to his previous frame of knowledge, values, and beliefs. The eclectic attitude also prevents the subject from the contact with the different, now by disqualifying the difference itself: in the last resort, everything can be fitted (reduced) to his previous frame of knowledge, values and beliefs (pp. 17-18).

Thus, the issue of otherness challenges us with the idea that keeping in relation cannot mean fusion or isolation. Both of these concepts miss the possibility of charting out the processes between the One and the Other. In other words, a dialogical understanding of otherness requires taking into account that being separate does not mean being in isolation—but rather—through such separation an integrated relation develops. Within the frame of the philosophy of alterity, this perspective appears for instance in Lévinas' (1998) statements about the difference between to be *with* the Other and to be *in face of* the Other.

Lévinas on Intersubjectivity

Lévinas rejected the idea of sociability as necessarily being *with* the other—an idyllic collective fusion in the communality of others, where people tend to identify one another around a communion. According to him, the I-Other interpersonal relation is not a reciprocal relation between two interchangeable terms, because the I and the Other are not interchangeable. The Other is whom the I is not—yet to whom the I relates knowing one is not. In this specific sense, Lévinas says that the Other is not an *alter ego*, because the intersubjective space is constitutively asymmetrical. In this asymmetrical space, the subject's exteriority is not due to its physic-spatial separateness of the Other as it is in relations between things. The subject's exteriority is a social exteriority

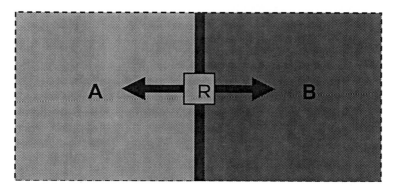

A and B are separated—yet remain parts of the same whole so that their RELATIONSHIP – R – can be investigated

Figure 3.   A and B are separated—yet remain parts of the same whole so that their RELATIONSHIP—R—can be investigated.

thanks to the *living tension* (the *Eros*) that keeps the subject simultaneously near and far from the Other, *facing* him, but not fusing with him. Only in such an extent they can really be in relationship (Lévinas, 1998, pp. 112-114).

In the frame of semiotic-cultural constructivism this perspective is present, for instance, in the notions of I-Other *inclusive separation* (Valsiner, 1989)—they are in a systemic relationship forming a temporarily organized whole (Figure 3).

In terms of the I-Other dialogical relationship the use of inclusive separation entails intersubjectivity without Ego-Alter fusion (Marková, 2003b, pp. 103-104). Both Ego and Alter not only keep their separate-but-united structural status but also "are enriched in and trough their interdependence," while "seeking visibility and recognition by one another" (Marková, 2006, p. 127).

From this perspective, to be separated from the other does not mean to become isolated from that other—but merely to set up conditions for their relationships to develop. It is an advantageous developmental life-situation where it is allowed to the I to be touched by the strangeness of the Other; where it is allowed to the I to transform himself in the struggle for overcoming the Other's strangeness, while both are trying to assert themselves as a discrete agents, although dependent on the relationship (Marková, 2003b).

SHARING AND BEING

The focus on otherness sets up the stage for a new look at the notion that social philosophers seem to like at times—sharing. Therefore, the above-mentioned advantageous developmental life-situation depends—almost paradoxically—on the possibility of not *always* nor *completely* sharing the world with the other.[1] In such an extent, the assumed dichotomy between subject-other inseparability (fusion) or isolation (solipsism) gives place to the issue of microgenetic nuances and simultaneously different forms of the process of I-Other dialogicality. In order to be in dialogue the partners need to (simultaneously) share and nonshare. In this sharing-nonsharing their worlds in the constitution of their particular subjectivities. Being able to live within the *sharing <> nonsharing* meaning system, as well as the tacit recognition of otherness, are essential for sociocultural human development, at both filogenetic and ontogenetic levels (Chaudhary, Interview Part II, this volume). Structurally this may be set up by a scheme (Figure 4).

Here we see the process of SHARING <> NONSHARING regulating the SELF <> OTHER relation. The latter is therefore always rendered ambivalent in its nature. The question of alterity becomes thus a question of negotiating the unknown (OTHER) through a prism of ambivalent open/closed lens. In some situations the result can be a blockage of action.

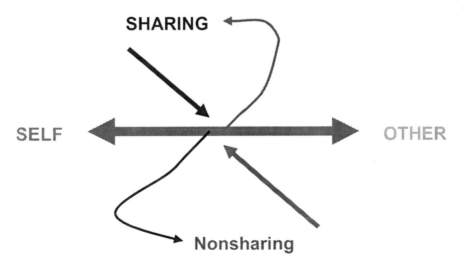

Figure 4.   The dialogical process of sharing-nonsharing in the regulation of I-Other relationships.

Realities of Tensions

The dialogical self can be seen as self-regulating of the ongoing action process while creating general personal sense of the kind of "what is it that is going on." If the orientating to the OTHER overtakes the psychological system we get various kinds of anomalies of feeling and acting—ranging from complete appropriation of the other's conduct to blocking of one's own conduct.

The Fear of Action

Pierre Janet reported a case of a 49-year-old man who blocks each of his action by a semiotic mediation device that he invents. The man is self-reflective of his inability to act. He describes it:

> I cannot ... perform a single new activity without representing it to myself that it is going to entail diabolical consequences. If I buy new shirts it seems as if I were preparing for the assassination of my two children. If I rent an apartment it is only in order that I may place under the big entrance door the coffin of my wife where it will rest very nicely.; I have selected this apartment (it would seem) only because of the convenience which the entrance way presents for the coffin of my wife. If I open this book it is with the idea that I am preparing a cataclysm which will involve the whole city of Paris. All this frightens me so that I take back my recent purchase of shirts with the excuse that they do not fit: I give up the apartment, and I close the book. (Janet, 1921, pp, 153-154)

For our present analysis this psychopathological example consider the following scheme (Figure 5).

Eating up the Other in One's Self

The process of disorganization of the semiotic self-regulatory system is further exemplified by a young anorexic woman (Isabella). She explained,

> I assure you ... I am not at all possessed with the idea of not eating; it seems to me even that I should like to eat; but at the moment of beginning, the thought of it chokes me, disgusts me, and I cannot. Why? I don't know; I assure you it is not that I wish to die; I begin even to be afraid that I may; but despite all my efforts to eat there is something that prevents me. (Janet, 1901, pp. 288-289, added emphases)

In Isabella's dream material as well as in her delirium states, the interpersonal symbolic regulators become clarified:

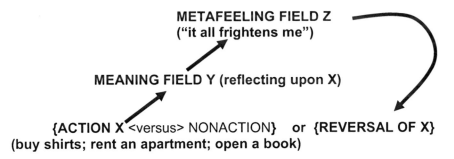

METAFEELING FIELD Z
("it all frightens me")

MEANING FIELD Y (reflecting upon X)

{ACTION X <versus> NONACTION}   or {REVERSAL OF X}
(buy shirts; rent an apartment; open a book)

Figure 5.   Hierarchical levels of action-meaning-feeling intrapersonal organization.

> Her mother, who is dead, appears to her during the attacks, blames her for some fault she has committed, tells her that she is not worthy to live and that she ought to join her in heaven, and bids her for this reason not to eat. (Janet, 1901, p. 289)

The proof that this semiotic organizer is indeed the major metalevel regulator of Isabella's relating to herself via eating comes from hypnotic suggestion to her that undoes the mother's image. When waking up, Isabella finds herself eating with ease—until the next episode of delirium occurs.

SHARING THE NONSHARING IN THIS BOOK

This I-Other dialogue in that sharing-non-sharing symbolic field assumes different faces that we can metaphorically call "the faces of otherness." They are extensive present in this book. At the metapsychological level of our "being in the world," the face of otherness in I-Other relationship appears in the meaning and quest for *belongingness*. The fundamental questions as tacitly posed by persons in their humanity—"In what kind of universe am I living?" (Boesch, Interview Part I, in this volume), "Who am I? Why am I here?" (Chaudhary, Interview Part II, in this volume)—are emblematic here.

The belongingness/nonbelongingness also addresses us as to the face of the otherness at the historical, social, intranational and international level of the I-Other relations. At this level self-positions are sheltered or denied by the subjects while constructing I-Other historically meaningful versions of their relationships (Rosa, Castro, & Blanco, chapter 9, in this volume). This latter aspect, by its turn, leads us to its dialogical kin, the feeling of nonbelongingness. The issue of belonginess/nonbelongingness also challenges for a culturalist account of intercultural psychological phenomena in the frame of its historically, concrete, local, forms of communication (Shi-xu, chapter 10, in this volume).

Still from the dimension of historicity we are addressed to the *self-narrative* level, where the face of the otherness is a dialogically constructed instance where the subject can present itself as *other selves* (in self descriptions), as *present others* (in conversational episodes) or as *referred others* (the third persons mentioned in conversational episodes) (Japur, Guanes, & Rasera, chapter 6, in this volume). The narrative level accomplishes—among other—the figure-ground relational context where the Other can be experienced by the subject as *real or imaginary* in the subject's *search for feeling nearer to his beliefs, hopes and desires* (Guimarães & Simão, chapter 13, in this volume).

Dialogically, the openness for "feeling his own feelings" allows to the subject *to be touched by the otherness*, usually meaning *to be involved in ambivalent existential situations* (Abbey, chapter 4, in this volume, in this volume). This happens *as if* in a hypergame of I-Other relationships, in which each partner's action is responsible for the uncertainty present in the relationship scene (Richer & Valsiner, chapter 11, in this volume).

Uncertainty and ambivalence are sources of *ruptures* in I-Other or I-I relational meanings, demanding *transitions* and *reorientations* toward the self construction and self-belongingness (Zittoun, chapter 8, in this volume). Aiming to accomplish that, the I also strives in the internal dialogue among its I-positions (Gillespie, 2007, and chapter 7, in this volume). The simultaneity of *openness to the other* and *impossibility of completely sharing worlds* allows to the subject to relate to the other as alter, *as someone who surpasses him*, who *requires a response from him* (see Coelho, chapter 5, in this volume).

This process is possible only thanks to the *dialogicality inherent* to the constitution of the self, in which to be is *being addressed to* someone else (Salgado, chapter 3, in this volume) that *can be experienced intra as well as intersubjecitvely* (Cooper & Hermans, chapter 12, in this volume). In this way, *to be* means *to be able to constantly construct oneself* in the field of the *uncertainty* of the relationship with the *enigmatic Other* (Boesch, chapter 1, in this volume), that is, in an *hermeneutic task addressed to the uncertainty of the future* (Simão, chapter 2, in this volume). This task implies the subject's openness for *feeling otherness into his mind* (Han, Interview Part IV, in this volume). This is a kind of openness for a constant *migration movement* of the self from its actual being in direction to a *not yet* being, a movement always in the boundaries of becoming other (Valsiner, chapter 14, in this volume).

THE CENTRALITY OF TENSION-IN-RELATIONS

All the heterogeneity of discussions in this book seems to lead us to a major unresolved problem—the nature of the relation in the Self <> Other link. Having established the "doubleness" of the relation (dialogicality), a theoretical next step is needed to make it clear what is the process nature of the phenomenon we easily label "relationship" and stop ourselves from, studying further.

Relations as Composed of Vectors

Let us elaborate—the nature of the relationship is crucial for our theoretical models. Perhaps we can start from the dialogical opposition for encompassing the *tensional relationship* with the *different, alien, strange, or disquieting* character of the other we have mentioned at the very beginning of this chapter. Focusing on:

OPPOSITIONAL <> NONOPPOSITIONAL

or its more general version

Non-HARMONIOUS <> HARMONIOUS

can be fruitful for approaching the notion of the relationship. When viewed within the 2-valent logical schemes, these oppositions stop being mutually interdependent processes and are treated as exclusive opposites. Thus, it can be said that not all nonharmonious relations are oppositional, and neither are all harmonious oppositions nonoppositional. We end up, this way, in the domain of infinite cross-classification of static properties, rather than dynamic processes.

To live up to the dynamic focus that prevails in the area of self <> other relations study, we need to view these opposites not as static states, but as processes that mutually generate[2] each other (Josephs, Valsiner, & Surgan, 1999). We can now begin to look at the relation between A and non-A (the Other—B—as it is created from the non-A). IF A is the subject's auto-centered positioning, knowledge and feeling about himself in the relationship, the other, both, whatever...), based on what he was already experienced and constructed as self; and this construction encompasses nebulosity, gap, uncertainty (as highlighted by the contributors in this book), then A's self-centered position will tend to change, that is, will be oriented to futurity aiming to diminishes that

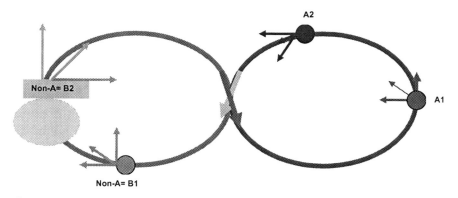

Figure 6.   Vectorial representation of the I-Other relational field.

gap. Changing means becoming in other direction, that of being Other than A, the non-A, the B. It is A's movement based on desires, expectations about being different from what he realizes he presently is, meaning a selective de-centration.

Relations as Vector Patterns Within Fields

Second, all relationships are of field kind (see also Diriwächter & Valsiner, 2006). Vectors have direction and magnitude—so we can imagine the dynamic movement of the opposite parts of the same system to be characterized by mutually nonconvergent families of vectors forming the field of relationships (Figure 6).

Here A and non-A (Other = B) are continually in development, moving and changing, depending on the "economy" of the vector forces of their symbolic actions (Boesch, 1991) addressed to one another or to other actors but them. It is worth remembering that A, B, and others but them can all be part of the internal dialogue of A, B.... (see, for instance, Marková, 2006).

The relationship between vectors of different orientation can be viewed through the notion of tension. There is no tension if two vectors have similar (X) or parallel (Y) orientation (Figure 7).

Figure 7.   Vectorial representation of nondisquietness in I-Other relationships.

In this kind of situation, the symbolic actions (Boesch, 1991) one another addressed are not disquieting (Simão, 2003); they do not challenge any expectation, that is, they do not challenge the causality that is tacitly presupposed to unit present and future on the basis of interpreted previous experience and desires. As the symbolic actions are not in tension, they do not create a field of forces from where dialogicality can emerge. However this disquiet would emerge if the vector directions do not coincide. Dialogicality emerge from the tension between change in the direction of the vectors—in other terms, otherness is a vector at a different angle in relation to the self. Such dialogicality creates a field where actions have different meanings, opposite or supplementary. It is in this later case of supplementation that A's self-centered position is defied by the strangeness of the Other's (Non-A, B) symbolic action, displacing it in the quest for a new congruency, and so on, and so closing the otherness meaningful cycle. The labyrinth of the self is in eternal movement—through the creation and use of the Other.

NOTES

1. This is related to Bakhtin's distinction between pure emphasizing and active emphasizing to the other (see Marková, 2003b, p. 103).
2. Sometimes much is made out of claims that A and B "mutually constitute" each other. This way of referencing still maintains static quality of the relation—what constituting-as-process entails is not clear.

REFERENCES

Boesch, E. E. (1991). *Symbolic action theory and cultural psychology.* Berlin, Germany: Springer.

Diriwächter, R., & Valsiner, J. (2006). Qualitative Developmental Research Methods in their Historical and Epistemological Contexts [53 paragraphs]. *Forum Qualitative Sozialforschung/Forum: Qualitative Social Research, 7*(1), 8. [Online Journal] http://www.qualitative-research.net/fqs-texte/1-06/06-1-8-e.htm

Figueiredo, L. C. (1992). Convergências e Divergências: A questão das correntes de pensamento em Psicologia [Convergences and Divergences: The question of thinking strands in Psychology]. *Trans-in-formação, 4*(1, 2, 3), 15-26.

Gillespie, A. (2007). *Becoming other: From social interaction to self-reflection.* Greenwich, CT: Information Age.

Janet, P. (1901). *The mental state of hystericals.* New York: Georgew Putnam's Sons.

Janet, P. (1921). The fear of action. *Journal of Abnormal and Social Psychology, 16*(1), 150-160.

Josephs, I. E., Valsiner, J., & Surgan, S. E. (1999). The process of meaning construction. In J. Brandtstätdter & R. M. Lerner (Eds.), *Action and self development* (pp. 257-282). Thousand Oaks, CA: Sage.

Lévinas, E. (1998). *Da existência ao existente* [From the existence to the existent]. Campinas: Papirus (Translation of De l'existence à l'existent].

Marková, I. (2003a) Constitution of the self: Intersubjectivity and dialogicality. *Culture & Psychology, 9*(3), 249-259.

Marková, I. (2003b). *Dialogicality and social representations: The dynamics of mind.* Cambridge, MA: Cambridge Universit. Press.

Marková, I. (2006, Spring) On "the inner alter" in dialogue. *International Journal for Dialogical Science, 1*(1), 125-147.

Simão, L. M. (2003). Beside rupture—disquiet; Beyond the other—alterity. *Culture & Psychology, 9*(4), 449-459.

Valsiner, J. (1989). *Human development and culture: The social nature of personality and its study.* Lexington, MA: D. C. Heath

ABOUT THE AUTHORS

Alberto Rosa, PhD, is professor of psychology at the Autonomous University of Madrid (Spain). Editor of the *Journal Estudios de Psicología*. He teaches courses on history of psychology and cultural psychology. Besides these fields, he has done extensive research on the cognitive development of the blind and the cerebral palsied. His current research interests focus on the psychological use of cultural materials, particularly the relationship between historical knowledge, collective memory, and national identity. He authored several books on these matters and over 100 book chapters and scientific articles.

Alex Gillespie is a lecturer in social psychology at the University of Stirling. His main theoretical interest concerns the formation of intersubjectivity, the self, and self-reflection in social interaction. This line of enquiry follows the work of James, Mead, Vygotsky, and Bakhtin. The empirical site for pursuing this line of research has been a study of tourists visiting a remote region in northern India. He has recently published a book on this theoretical and empirical work titled *Becoming Other: From Social Interaction to Self-Reflection*, which appears in Valsiner's *Advances in Cultural Psychology* series, published by Information Age Publishing.

Alexander Poddiakov is a professor of the State University—Higher School of Economics, Moscow, Russia. He received his doctorates from Moscow University, and from the Psychological Institute of the Russian Academy of Education. Areas of scientific interests are development of exploratory behavior, thinking, creativity, and strategies of social interactions. Books: *Exploratory Behavior: Cognitive Strategies, Help, Counteraction,* *and Conflict* (2006, Moscow: Erebus) (Russian); *Psychology of Competition in Teaching/Learning* (2006, Moscow: VShE) (Russian). Articles: "Ambivalence and Cognitive Heuristics for Dealing With Ambiguity in Complex Social Worlds." *Estudios de Psicología, 2006, 27*(1), 101-116; "Trojan Horse" Teaching in Economic Behavior, 2004, at: http://ssrn.com/abstract=627432; commentaries in *Culture & Psychology* and *Narrative inquiry.* The Award "For Academic Achievements and Contribution Into Scientific Reputation of the State University—Higher School of Economics" (2005). Address: Sadovnicheskaya St. 27-30, 115035 Moscow, Russia. E-mail: alpod@gol.ru.

Álvaro P. Duran, PhD, is a psychologist who presently acts as a private constructivist psychotherapist in São Paulo, Brazil. He was also a professor in various universities of the country, being the last one at the State University of Campinas. He has been consultant of the main Brazilian agencies of research funding and also of scientific journals. Besides the practice issues of psychotherapy, he is particularly interested in theoretical issues of cognitive/affective self-organization and epistemological reflections on constructivism in psychotherapy. His most recent publications are on this last subject. E-mail: apduran@uol.com.br

Carla Guanaes, PhD, is a psychologist and professor of public health at the Medicine Faculty at the Centro Universitário Barão de Mauá (Ribeirão Preto/Brazil). She is interested in group work and psychotherapeutic processes based on a social constructionist approach. She is author of the book *A Construção da Mudança em Terapia de Grupo: Enfoque Construcionista Social* [The Construction of Change in Group Psychotherapy: A Social Constructionist Approach].

Carla Cunha is a postgraduate student at the University of Minho (Portugal), an assistant in the Department of Psychology of ISMAI (Instituto Superior da Maia, Portugal) and a researcher at GEDI (Group of Studies in Dialogicality and Identity), Unidep, at ISMAI. Her contributions can be found in the following journals or books: *Psychologica* (Portugal), *Studios de Psicologia* (Spain), *The Dialogical Self: Theory and Research* (Poland). Mailing address: Instituto Superior da Maia, Av. Carlos Oliveira Campos, 4475-695, Avioso S. Pedro, Portugal; E-mail: ccunha@ismai.pt

Danilo Silva Guimarães is presently a MA student of the University of São Paulo, Brazil, sponsored by the state of São Paulo Research Foundation (FAPESP). He was also a sponsored student by the same Foundation during his undergraduate program of scientific initiation at the University of São Paulo. His current research interests are mainly related to the understanding of imagination and creativity involved in dialogical pro-cesses from the Levinasian perspective of alterity and desire. E-mail: dansgui@gmail.com

Emerson F. Rasera, PhD, is psychologist, professor of group theory and supervisor of group practice in the Institute of Psychology at Univer-sidade Federal de Uberlândia/Brazil. He is interested in studying social constructionist contributions to psychological practices, especially in the health context.

Emily Abbey is generally curious about the perpetual transformation of phenomena in irreversible time. Working from an explicitly present-to-future developmental orientation and a cultural perspective, she is inter-ested in meaning-making and the ambivalence of the person's present and future relations to the environment. Recently, she has published in the journals *Culture & Psychology, Estudios de Psicologia, FQS: Forum Qualita-tive Sozialforschung* and is coeditor of a forthcoming volume on microge-netic approaches titled, *Microgenesis: Relations of Phenomena, Theory and Method in Psychology* (with Rainer Diriwächter, InfoAge). She teaches classes in the areas of developmental and cultural psychology at the Col-lege of the Holy Cross. Address: Emily Abbey, Clark University, 950 Main Street, Worcester, MA, 01610, USA. [e-mail: eabbey@clarku.edu]

Ernst E. Boesch born December 1916 in St-Gall, Switzerland. Studies in Geneva (Psychology, Philosophy, Education). School-Psychologist of the Canton of St-Gall, 1943-1951. 1951-1982 Professor of Psychology, University of the Saar in Saarbruecken. 1955-1958 on leave to direct the "International Institute for Child Study" (UNESCO) in Bangkok. From 1962-1987 director of the "Socio-Psychological Research Centre on Social Development" at the Saar University with main research emphasis in Thailand and Africa on psychological problems of social change. Over 120 publications. Calls to universities in Mannheim, Bochum, Geneva and Basel, but all declined. Honorary doctorates by universities in Bangkok and Berne, honorary membership in several learned societies.

Florentino Blanco is professor of psychology at the Universidad Autónoma de Madrid. He teaches epistemology of psychology and psy-chology of care for health workers. He has published extensively on his-tory of psychology in Spain, the rhetorical form of psychological texts, aesthetic experience and psychology of art. His book *The Culture of Mind: a Theoretical-Critical Essay About Psychological Culture* is a theoretical reflec-tion on how psychological ideas are a result of sociocultural change, but also shape the way psychology become culturally relevant. Among his current research interests are the study of the role of technical aids and symbols for directing and shaping action.

Gyuseog Han is currently a professor of psychology of Chonnam National University in Gwangju, South Korea. His primary research area is sociocultural psychology. Particularly, he is interested in the characteristics of mind psychology manifest in Korean society. He believes mind goes beyond cognition and plays significant role in human relationship everywhere. He is also keen to working of social hierarchy and mechanisms of hierarchy in a given society. His previous publication covers social values, indigenous psychology, history of psychology in Korea, and working of self-esteem. E-mail contact is ghan@jnu.ac.kr

Hubert Hermans is emeritus-professor of psychology at the University of Nijmegen, the Netherlands. He developed a valuation theory and a self-confrontation method. In his later work he developed a dialogical self theory, originally published in the *American Psychologist* (1992) and in *Psychological Bulletin* (1996) He is "First International Associate" of the *Society for Personology*, president of the *International Society for Dialogical Science* (ISDS) and chief editor of the *International Journal for Dialogical Science* (IJDS). He was guest editor of special issues on the dialogical self: in *Culture & Psychology* (2001), *Theory & Psychology* (2002), *Journal of Constructivist Psychology* (2003) and *Identity* (2004), and *Counselling Psychology Quarterly* (2006). Address: Hubert J.M. Hermans, Bosweg 18, 6571 CD Berg en Dal, the Netherlands. E-mail: HHermans@psych.kun.nl. Homepage: www.dialogicalself.info

Jaan Valsiner is a cultural psychologist with a consistently developmental axiomatic base that is brought to analyses of any psychological or social phenomena. He is the founding editor (1995) of the Sage journal, *Culture & Psychology*. He is currently professor of psychology at the Department of Psychology, Clark University, USA, where he also edits a journal in history of psychology—*From Past to Future: Clark Papers in the History of Psychology*. He has published many books, the most recent of which are *The Guided Mind* (1998, Cambridge, MA: Harvard University Press), *Culture and Human Development* (2000, London: Sage) and *Comparative Study of Human Cultural Development* (2001, Madrid: Fundacion Infancia y Aprendizaje). He has edited (with Kevin Connolly) the *Handbook of Developmental Psychology* (2003, London: Sage). He has established the new journal on individual case analyses—*International Journal of Idiographic Science* (2005—www.valsiner.com).

João Salgado, PhD, is the director of the program in psychology at ISMAI, Portugal. He is also a psychotherapist and the director of the counseling service of his university. His main research interests are associated with the theoretical and methodological developments of a dialogical perspective within psychology, and with the applications of this framework to the field of psychotherapy and clinical psychology. He published several articles on different journals, such as *Culture & Psychology, International Journal for Dialogical Science, E-Journal of Applied Psychology* or *European Journal of School Psychology*. He has also contributed with some chapters to different books (e.g., *Cambridge Handbook of Socio-Historial Psychology*, in press) and wrote a book in Portuguese under the title of *Narrative, Psychology and Self-Identity: A study on Self-deception* [Psicologia Narrativa e Identidade: Um Estudo Sobre Auto-engano]. Address: Prof. João Salgado, Instituto Superior da Maia, Avenida Carlos Oliveira Campos, Castelo da Maia, 4475—690 S. Pedro Avioso, Portugal. [e-mail: jsalgado@ismai.pt]

Jorge Castro received his PhD in psychology at the Universidad Autónoma de Madrid (Spain), and teaches at the Universidad Nacional de Educación a Distancia. He has taken part in several research projects on history of Spanish psychology, and on construction of collective identities. Following on both research lines, he has published papers and coauthored books about the professional identity of psychologists, and Spanish and Argentinean psychology development, its main authors and institutions. His PhD thesis (2004) has analyzed the sociopsychological construction of Spanish identity during the 1898 crisis. His latest works have been oriented towards the study of the relationship between psychology and aesthetics, and the analysis of psychological theory from a sociohistorical and cultural point of view. At present, he takes part in the research project titled "A Historical-Genealogical Approach to the Problem of Agency in Psychology."

Lívia Mathias Simão, PhD, is assistant professor at the University of São Paulo, Brazil, where she coordinates the Laboratory of Verbal Interaction and Knowledge Construction at the Institute of Psychology. She is a also sponsored researcher of the Brazilian National Council for Scientific and Technologic Development, as well as consultant of research foundations and scientific journals. Her main research interest concerns with issues embracing the ontological construction of human subjectivity in I–world, I–other and I–self relationships from the perspective of the semiotic-cultural constructivism in psychology and from the broader perspective of the philosophy of psychology. She has authored and coauthored articles, chapters and books. Among her recent publications are *Simão, de Sousa* *and Coelho, Jr.* (2002) *Noção de Objeto, Concepção de Sujeito: Freud, Piaget e Boesch* [Object Notion, Subject Conception: Freud, Piaget, and Boesch]. *São Paulo: Casa do Psicólogo,* and articles published in *Culture & Psychology, Theory and Psychology* and *Psicologia: Reflexão e Crítica* [Psychology: Reflexion & Critics]. E-mail: limsimao@usp.br

Marisa Japur, PhD, is psychologist and professor at the University of São Paulo (Brazil). She is involved in the training of group coordinators (undergraduate and graduate level). She is the leader of the research group "Group Practice and Social Constructionism." Her publications include 29 articles, 9 book chapters, and many papers presented in national and international congresses. She was the advisor of 20 students. She was consultant of different Brazilian agencies of research funding (CNPq, Capes, and Fapesp). She was effective member of the National Commission for the Evaluation of Psychology Graduate Programs and advisory member of the National Commission of Specialists in Psychology Training, of the Brazilian Ministry of Education.

Mick Cooper is a professor of counseling at the University of Strathclyde and a UKCP-registered psychotherapist, whose work is informed by person-centred, existential, interpersonal, and postmodern ideas. Mick has coauthored, with Dave Mearns, *Working at Relational Depth in Counselling and Psychotherapy* (2005, Sage), is author of *Existential Therapies* (2003, Sage) and has written several papers and chapters on person-centred, existential and self-pluralistic approaches to therapy. Mick lives in Glasgow with his partner and three daughters

Nandita Chaudhary, PhD, is a reader at the Department of Child Development, Lady Irwin College, University of Delhi. Over the last 2 decades, she has been involved with research, teaching, and administration in child and family studies in India. She is particularly interested in issues linked with communication, education, family relationships, parenting, self and identity as culturally constructed. She has presented her perspectives of community and family life and childhood in India in several conferences and publications. A synthesis of her views is presented in *Listening to Culture* published by Sage, New Delhi, India.

Nelson Ernesto Coelho Jr., PhD is a psychoanalyst and a lecturer and researcher at the Institute of Psychology, University of São Paulo (Brazil). He is currently directing research in the history and philosophy of psychology and psychoanalysis. His most recent books are *Ética e Técnica em Psicanálise* (2000) [Ethics and Technique in Psychoanalysis], with Luis Claudio Figueiredo; and *Noção de Objeto, Concepção de Sujeito: Freud, Piaget* *e Boesch* (2002) [Notion of Object, Conception of Subject: Freud, Piaget and Boesch], with Livia Simão and Maria Thereza Souza. E-mail: ncoelho@usp.br

Shi-xu (Ê©Ðñ, b. 1960, PhD University of Amsterdam) has been a Research Fellow at the University of Amsterdam, Lecturer at the National University of Singapore and Reader at the University of Ulster, United Kingdom. His books in English include *Cultural Representations, A Cultural Approach to Discourse, Read the Cultural Other* (lead-editor) and *Discourse as Cultural Struggle* (editor). He is the founding editor-in-chief of *Journal of Multicultural Discourses* (Multilingual-Matters Ltd, England) and series lead-editor of *Multicultural Discourses* and serves on the international editorial boards of *Discourse & Society, Culture & Psychology, Journal of Language,* and *Social Psychology.* He is a recipient of the New-Century Outstanding Researcher Fund from the Ministry of Education, China (2005-2007). Currently he is Qiushi distinguished professor and director of the Institute of Discourse and Cultural Studies, Zhejiang University, Hangzhou. His central academic position is that language/communication/discourse, in both everyday and scientific domains, is a site of cultural contest, cooperation, and transforamtion, and that this neglected dimension needs urgent attention.

Tania Zittoun is junior associate professor at the University of Lausanne, Switzerland. She is the author of the books *Transitions: Development through symbolic resources* (2006), *"Insertions: A Quinze ans, Entre Échec et Apprentissage"* (2006) [Being Fifteen, Between Failure and Apprenticeship], *Donner la vie, Choisir un Nom. Engendrements Symboliques* (2005) [Giving Life, Choosing a Name. Symbolic Begetting], and coeditor of *Joining Society: Social Interaction and Learning in Adolescence and Youth* (2004) with A. -N. Perret-Clermont, C. Pontecorvo, L. Resnick, and B. Burge.

Printed in the United States
90445LV00001B/302/A